D1519560

THE MYTH OF NAZARETH

THE MYTH OF NAZARETH

The Invented Town of Jesus

Scholar's Edition

René Salm

2008
American Atheist Press
Cranford, New Jersey

American Atheist Press
P. O. Box 5733
Parsippany, NJ 07054-6733

www.atheists.org

ISBN-10: 1-57884-003-1
ISBN-13: 978-1-57884-003-8

Published February, 2008
Printed in the United States of America

Library of Congress Cataloging-in-Publication Data

Salm, René.
  The myth of Nazareth : the invented town of Jesus / René Salm. -- Scholar's ed.
    p. cm.
  ISBN 978-1-57884-003-8
  1. Nazareth (Israel)--History. 2. Excavations (Archaeology)--Israel--Galilee.
  3. Galilee (Israel)--Antiquities. 4. Jews--History--168 B.C.-135 A.D.
  5. Jews--History--70-638. I. Title.

DS110.N3S35 2008
933--dc22
                              2008004416

Contents

vii

*Seek not to worship
but to understand.*

Introduction

> *This need is prevalent, in what must be construed as an irrational manner, ...that the archaeologists prove that all the events described in the Bible did indeed occur and that all the figures mentioned and the episodes described are entirely consistent with reality. There is in this demand a violation of archaeological integrity and an attempt to impose upon archaeology unattainable objectives—that is, the proof of faith.*
>
> *...It is therefore not a coincidence that a considerable proportion of the archaeologists active in the Land of Israel over the past one hundred years have come from the religious establishment. Many of them received a large part of their education at various theological seminaries, while their archaeological training was often deficient. This is particularly evident among American archaeologists...*
>
> *This state of affairs has given biblical archaeology a reputation for amateurism in some archaeological circles. Modern scientific excavation is so complex that those who have not received adequate training (which is the case with most of those educated at theological seminaries) cannot conduct one properly.*
>
> —Amnon Ben-Tor, *The Archaeology of Ancient Israel* (1992, p.9).

The archaeology of Nazareth fully corroborates Ben-Tor's words. The early history of that hallowed ground is as unknown today as when digging first began, one hundred and fifteen years ago. Despite excavations conducted over many generations, mystery covers Nazareth like a blanket protecting a precious baby. In some circles, questions regarding the history of the village are unwelcome, as if the baby might be disturbed by too much probing. So, a venerable hush has settled over the place, a quiet acceptance in catholic circles that the *mysterium verbi*, and all associated with it, is beyond man's understanding.[1]

No one really knows what happened at Nazareth two thousand years ago. Some scholars, uncomfortable with a posture of pure veneration, have attempted to peel back the blanket, at least slightly, only to confront a thick wall of tradition. "Go no further!" is the stern message conveyed to him who asks too many questions. Yet the questions multiply. Already in the nineteenth century some liberal scholars wondered why the town was not mentioned in the Jewish scriptures, nor in the Talmud, nor even once in the prolix writings of the first-century Galilean general, Josephus. The latter had, after all, lived in Japhia, a town less than two miles from Nazareth. Why, they asked, did the first Christian generations either completely ignore the place, or appear to not know where it was? The first writer to mention Nazareth (Julius Africanus,

---

[1] In this series I follow the convention whereby *catholic* (small "c") denotes "universal" Christian belief shared by Roman Catholic, Protestant, and Greek Orthodox persuasions, while *Catholic* refers only to Roman Catholicism.

THE MYTH OF NAZARETH

c. 200 CE) locates it in Judea.[2] Again, why in the *Acts of the Apostles* (24:5), is Paul called a "ringleader of the sect of the Nazoreans"? Certainly he was not the leader of onetime inhabitants of Nazareth! "Nazorean," these questioners opined, must once have referred to something other than a place. If so, then what *was* a "Nazorean" (Ναζωραῖος)? That term seems to be first used by Matthew, for Mark does not know it—the latter exclusively uses Ναζαρηνέ. In any case, English translations invariably read "Jesus of Nazareth" for both Ἰησοῦ Ναζαρηνέ and Ἰησοῦς ὁ Ναζωραῖος. But was this the original meaning? Finally—for these questions are without end—why in his birth story does the evangelist Matthew introduce Nazareth with a perfectly unknown saying?

> And he went and dwelt in a city called Nazaret, that what was spoken by the prophets might be fulfilled, "He shall be called a Nazorean [Ναζωραῖος]." (Mt 2:23)

No such text, "He shall be called a Nazorean," exists in Hebrew scripture. Often called the most Jewish of the evangelists, Matthew was surely the least likely to make such an error.

From the Enlightenment until today scholars have questioned the historical foundations of the Christian religion. Some have even had the impertinence to deny that Jesus ever existed at all, at least as a flesh-and-blood human being (a few opine that Jesus was a spirit).[3] Yet, mere opinion is weak, like a little water thrown against a wall. It will not bring down two thousand years of tradition. But, with demonstrable facts on its side and backed by science, a position rises above mere opinion. Though facts are fundamental, however, one should not suppose that they alone decide the issue, for everyone claims to have them. After all, in the realm of imperfect human discourse a "fact" is only that which is provable.

This is what gives the Nazareth issue such great potency. Unlike aspects of the gospel story that are quite beyond verification—the miracles of Jesus, his bodily resurrection, his virgin birth, or even his human nature—the existence of Nazareth two thousand years ago can be proved or disproved by digging in the ground. Because the archaeology of a site is empirically demonstrable, "Nazareth" is in a category apart. To this day, it preserves the explosive potential to either prove or disprove the gospel accounts.

Upon that determination depends a great deal, perhaps even the entire edifice of Christendom. For more is involved here than the mere imputation of error to holy writ, grave as that may appear in conservative circles (though hardly new). Motive must also be considered. If Nazareth did not exist in the time of Jesus, then questions quickly arise: Why did the evangelists place him

---

[2] *Epistle to Aristides* 5; also cited in Euseb. *Eccl. Hst.* I.7.14.

[3] For older scepticism see A. Schweizer's *The Quest of the Historical Jesus*, Chp. 22.

there? Was there something regarding his *real* provenance that they found objectionable? What *was* that provenance? If Nazareth was a persistent and recurrent invention in the gospels, then we leave the realm of error and enter the realm of elaborate fiction. This recognition would require a fundamental reappraisal of the Jesus story, and a paradigm shift in Christianity.

Most scholars summarily dismiss the "invention" of Nazareth on the grounds that the town is frequently mentioned in the Christian gospels. Unwittingly, archaeology is thus held hostage to literary considerations. The textual case for Nazareth in the gospels is much weaker, however, than is generally supposed. The settlement is named only once in the Gospel of Mark, at 1:9 (other instances in the Greek text read Ἰησοῦ Ναζαρηνέ). The passage as it stands demonstrably conflicts with the remainder of the gospel, which locates Jesus' home in Capernaum. Thus, it can be shown that the Gospel of Mark contains the later interpolation of a single word, "Nazaret" at 1:9. Furthermore, the literary genesis of Nazareth occurs in one of the most problematic passages of Christian scripture, Mt 2:23 (cited above). For its part, the Gospel of Luke is equally problematic. It demonstrates a strident anti-Capernaum stance and the enigmatic scene in the Nazareth synagogue (Lk 4:16–30) has been shown to be an elaborate reworking of prior materials.

A textual examination of "Nazareth" and its cognates in the New Testament must be left for another work,[4] but it can at least be recognized that if Nazareth did not exist in the time of Jesus then many of the problems mentioned above come closer to resolution: why it was not mentioned in the Jewish scriptures, the Talmud, or Josephus; why the first Christian generations ignored the place and appeared not to know where it was; and why the Greek gospels so often wrote "Jesus the Nazarene" instead of "Jesus of Nazareth."

Though this study focuses on the archaeology of Nazareth and on the material aspects associated with the site, I have presented those facts in the broader context of geography and history. The context is critical, for it alone will validate the radically different history of the site which is presented here. These six parts show that in each era the existence or non-existence of a settlement in the Nazareth basin is consistent with what we know of surrounding settlements in Lower Galilee. Multiple surveys of the area have been conducted, and many sites in the region have now been excavated. Whatever we may say of the history of Nazareth, it was certainly compatible with broader considerations.

About twenty primary reports form the backbone of this study. These reports are "primary" because firstly, they include published information on specific finds and loci (itemizations, *etc.*), and secondly, they were authored by the excavators themselves or, if not by them, then by experts in subspecialties (*e.g.* oil lamps) who have reviewed specific finds from Nazareth. Specificity is essential, for the Nazareth literature is laden with

---

[4] This is taken up in a second volume, *A New Account of Christian Origins.*

unsubstantiated conclusions, over-generalizations, and not a little vagueness. Typically, the primary reports represent the first time new evidence appeared in print. Many were written by priests under the auspices of the Custodia di Terra Santa, for the Franciscan Order owns the area of the venerated sites in Nazareth, the only area in the basin to have been extensively excavated.

It is important to note at the outset that the Christian excavators at Nazareth have not all been expert in assessing the nature of the finds they themselves report. This was especially the case with the earlier excavators, who were digging before archaeology became a modern science. The principal archaeologists at Nazareth have been three: Brother Vlaminck in the late nineteenth century, Father Viaud, and Father Bagatti. The first two did not receive any scientific training. Père Viaud was by his own admission an "improvised archaeologist... with no serious acquaintance of archaeology." His book *Nazareth et Ses Deux Eglises* (1910) was the primary source for the archaeology of the site until the 1960s. It was then superceded by Father Bellarmino Bagatti's two-volume work, *Excavations in Nazareth*. The principal archaeologist at Nazareth, Bagatti (1905–1990) fits Ben-Tor's description of the seminary-trained archaeologist. He received his training at the Pontifical Institute of Christian Archaeology in Rome, where in 1934 he was awarded the degree of Doctor of Christian Archaeology. Beginning in 1935 he held a chair at the Studium Biblicum Franciscanum in Jerusalem teaching Christian Archaeology.

The books of Viaud and Bagatti have traditionally been the main sources for information on Nazareth. Through the years, Bagatti also authored a number of dictionary articles and smaller studies on Nazareth. There is, however, a major flaw in all this Catholic literature: it is unabashedly apologetic. Its interpretations and conclusions have been largely shaped by the exigencies of doctrine and scripture, not by science.

This study attempts to arrive at an objective assessment of the site independent of doctrinal exigencies. To do so, it is necessary to carefully separate the wealth of evidence conveyed in Catholic publications from the conclusions contained therein. The critical distinction between evidence and conclusion is not made in the mass of secondary literature, which has accepted both the data from Nazareth and conclusions of "conformist" archaeologists, conclusions that are often completely unrelated to the evidence. The secondary literature consists of dictionary and encyclopedia articles, as well as many sections on Nazareth in scholarly monographs. Unfortunately, the vast majority of scholars and laypeople consult the secondary literature when reaching an opinion about Nazareth. Thus, the average person is two steps removed from a correct appreciation of the site: he must deal with the problems of conformism in both the secondary and the primary literature. This has allowed a very erroneous view of the site to hold the field and remain fundamentally unchallenged.

Introduction

Fortunately, in recent decades the Catholic reports have been supplemented by a number of studies written principally by Israeli specialists. They deal with tombs outside the Franciscan property, and also have redated many of the artefacts first published by Bagatti. Until *The Myth of Nazareth*, these independent studies have not been incorporated into the overall assessment of the site. This series brings together all the primary reports for the first time, and allows an independent and objective opinion to be formed regarding the site's history. Some of the ancillary reports are quite obscure and have never been translated into English. At least one was at the time of this writing unavailable in the U.S.A. In all, the sources span half a dozen modern languages. It is of course possible that one or two brief reports may have eluded my gaze, and I am mindful that excavations and discoveries continue in Nazareth. Yet I am confident that new results will support the conclusions of this study. The score of primary reports used in *The Myth of Nazareth*, encompassing both traditional and non-traditional sources, represent the essential results of excavations that span over a century. Their combined verdict will not be overturned by an overlooked shard.

The argument of *The Myth of Nazareth* presumably qualifies as "real knowledge... of an objective, external world that can be perceived by the human senses," in the words of one prominent American archaeologist.[5] Yet, those who seek to demonstrate the hand of God in human affairs and in holy writ will be sorely disappointed in these pages, whose facts accord neither with tradition nor with scripture. The anchor of biblical inerrantism must be hoisted, that the ship of free inquiry may finally sail unfettered. For some this is too much freedom, tantamount to being cut adrift in a sea of godless relativism. They prefer to view tradition as the natural repository of all that is worthy of serious consideration. And tradition maintains that man's history is ordained and guided from on high, and a divine plan infuses the cosmos. The sun rises every morning and sets every evening, *and God is in his heaven*, taking an interest in us, benevolently watching and sustaining the universe. We are not alone. These are the sentiments of the traditionalist who fears change and who will fashion an anchor—any anchor—against the engulfing chaos of life. If that anchor is imagined, so be it. To the traditional believer it is real, and that makes it efficacious.

The real battle, however, is not empirical, nor even about how we view the evidence of Nazareth or of any other site in biblical archaeology. The battle is not between postmodernists and conservatives, minimalists and maximalists, nihilists and positivists. It has nothing to do with facts but has to do with human needs, *for if need be, man will invent*. He desires comfort, not facts. The two thousand years of Christian tradition have nothing to do with the facts of history. They never did. They have to do with human desires and needs.

---

[5] W. Dever, "Save us from postmodern malarkey," *Biblical Archaeology Review,* Mr/Ap 2000, p. 30.

THE MYTH OF NAZARETH

The incipience of "Nazareth" in the gospels, textual and literary considerations, the motives behind its invention, and some consequences of that invention, will be taken up in a second volume, *A New Account of Christian Origins*. Together, these publications reflect recent scholarly scepticism concerning traditional views of Jesus, the gospels, and early Christianity. Based on a non-doctrinal view of the primary sources, *A New Account* considers the disparate views of so-called "heretical" writings on a par with those in the New Testament canon. It uses the scientific tools developed by modern theological research to arrive at a wholistic and historically accurate portrait of early Christianity.

A battle has raged over the Nazareth evidence from ancient times, ever since problematic claims were made about the town. That which is problematic must be doubly defended, and it is not coincidence that the myth of Nazareth has needed hiding under a thick blanket of tradition. Remoteness confers safety, which is one reason Christian scripture was elevated to unquestioned status and placed out of the reach of ordinary inquiry. Yet, the questions raised by objective inquiry must be answered if one is to understand the complex beginnings of Christianity. *The Myth of Nazareth* is one element of that inquiry. The repercussions of the resulting reassessment of the gospel record upon the traditional interpretation of Christian origins can hardly be exaggerated.

In this new millennium, the historical basis of Christian belief is being investigated in ways unimagined only a few generations ago. Abject veneration is finally yielding to free inquiry, allowing us to approach and see what tradition has solicitously protected for two thousand years. Let us peel back the blanket and look. Perhaps nothing is there at all.

Chapter One

The Stone, Bronze, and Iron Ages

The Stone, Bronze, and Iron Ages

The Nazareth basin

Nazareth lies in the hills of Lower Galilee, approximately equidistant from the Mediterranean Sea and the Sea of Galilee. The Nazareth Range, in which it lies, is the southernmost of several parallel east-west ranges that characterize the elevated tableau of Lower Galilee.[1] Both the wide and fertile Jezreel Valley to the south, as well as the Tir'an valley to the north were major conduits for trade in antiquity, linking the two major north-south routes that traversed the Holy Land: the *Via Maris*, or "Way of the Sea,"[2] and the more inland Ridge Route (*Illus 1.1*). The more southerly route ran from Megiddo to Beth Shan, while the route through the Tir'an Valley (the Trunk Road or Caravan Route)[3] connected Akko on the coast with the Sea of Galilee in the east.

Yet, though trade routes passed within a few kilometers of the site, ancient Nazareth was separated from them by hills. It sat in a small basin, valley, or plateau (all these words are used to describe it) about two kilometers long and scarcely one kilometer wide (*Illus. 1.2*). The basin is oriented north-south. Its floor is 320 meters above sea level, and the area below the 350 m contour line is about 400 acres (162 hectares).[4] This expansive area furnished many possible sites for habitation.

The backbone of the Nazareth Range, known as the Nazareth Ridge, runs east-west and forms the steep northern side of the basin. It divides the watershed of the Tir'an Valley from that of the Jezreel Valley, rising to several modest summits at the Nazareth basin. These heights are collectively called the Jebel Nebi Sa'in.[5] Its peak of 495 meters (1,624 ft.) interposes itself on a line between the basin and the onetime settlement of Sepphoris, six kilometers to the north. To the west and east of this summit the Nebi Sa'in reaches somewhat lesser peaks of 471 and 482 meters respectively.[6]

Though not particularly high, the Nazareth Ridge forms a physical divide. Lying to the south of this ridge, the Nazareth basin is naturally oriented towards

---

[1] In order from south to north, these ranges (ridges) are the Nazareth, Tir'an, Yodfat, Shezor, and Mount Haluz. The valleys between them are the Tir'an, Bet Netofa, Saknin, and Bet Ha-Kerem.

[2] Heb. *Derech HaYam*, Isa 9:1 (Heb. 8:23); Mt 4:15 (Vulgate). Today it is the International Coastal Highway.

[3] *Darb el-Hawwarnah* in Arabic. In Roman times this route passed by the hilltop town of Sepphoris.

[4] In comparison, the surface area of Megiddo encompassed 12 hectares (*c.* 120 dunams). One hectare is a square with 100 m per side = 10,000 sqare meters = 2.47 acres (about 10,000 square feet). A dunam is 1,000 square meters.

[5] Also known as the Jebel es Likh.

[6] The highest point in the area is the Jebel En Namsawi (presently Nazrat Illit). It is located about 1.5 km east of Mary's Spring and rises to slightly over 500 m.

THE MYTH OF NAZARETH

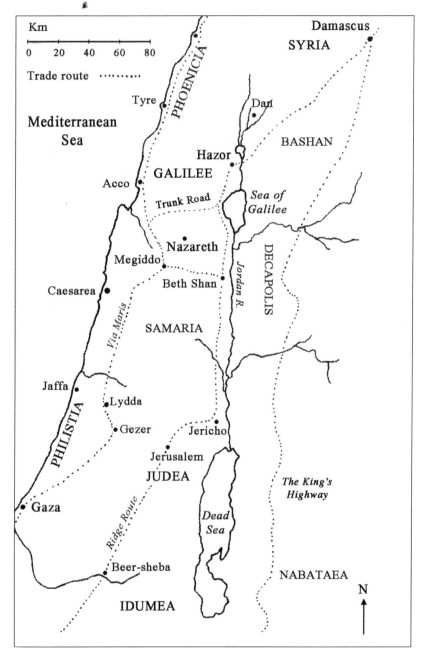

Illus. 1.1. Palestine and its principal trade routes

The Stone, Bronze, and Iron Ages

the Jezreel Valley to its south, and not to the north. This fact must be taken into account when considering the history of the basin in successive epochs. Jezreel Valley, a scant 2 km from the southern edge of the Nazareth basin. Just 17 km to the southwest was the fortress of Megiddo, the most important town in the Jezreel Valley in Bronze and Iron Age times. Megiddo was located on the Via Maris at the mouth of the Wadi 'Ara, the narrow pass traversing the Carmel Range. Thus, it commanded both the Via Maris and the Jezreel Valley. Auspiciously situated, hilltop Megiddo (Har-Megiddo, from whose name we derive Armageddon) was the focus of continual military designs, alternately ruled by Egypt, Syria, and Mesopotamia. It was splendidly defensible and fortuitously watered by several springs. For millennia, from about 3100 BCE to the seventh century BCE, Megiddo fed a number of satellite villages in the broad Jezreel Valley, over which it held sway like a queen over her courtiers. The city has been well studied,[7] and offers an excellent compass by which to orient proximate finds in the Nazareth basin which fell within its zone of influence.[8]

The Nazareth Range is approximately 15 km long and 5 km at it widest point. It is primarily an Eocene limestone, whose softness is conducive to pitting and to being worked by human hands. More than sixty underground hollows have been identified in the vicinity of the Church of the Annunciation, the area generally referred to as the "venerated sites" or "venerated area." The Church of the Annunciation (CA) has been the principal focus of pilgrimage and also of excavations carried out in Nazareth. The venerated area is quite modest in size, encompassing approximately 100 m by 60 m. The modern Church of the Annunciation is at the southern end and the Church of St. Joseph at the northern end. In the roughly 100 meters between the two churches lies the Franciscan convent (see *Illus.* 1.3.)[9] The venerated area has been owned by the Franciscans since 1620.[10]

There is one year-round spring in the Nazareth valley, known as Mary's Spring (Ain Maryam). It is located at the northeastern tip of the basin.[11] Today, the spring is under the Greek Orthodox Church of St. Gabriel, and its waters are piped a few hundred feet downhill to Mary's Well, readily

---

[7] Continuing excavations began in 1992 sponsored by Tel Aviv University and Pennsylvania State University. See Silberman *et al.*, 1999.

[8] The archaeological history of Megiddo is summarized in Appendix 3, "The Stratigraphy of Megiddo."

[9] The venerated area is treated more fully in Chapter 2.

[10] The Custodia di Terra Santa is the arm of the Franciscan order which manages five sites in the Nazareth area: the Church of the Annunciation, the Church of St. Joseph, the Mensa Christi, the Chapel of Fright of Mary, and the Precipice.

[11] A second spring which dries up in summer is located near the present Mensa Christi church (RPTK 678). It is called *'En ed-Jedide* (New Well). See Dalman 65.

accessible to the townspeople. Nazareth lies in the territory traditionally allotted to the tribe of Zebulun.[12] No settlement of Nazareth is mentioned in Jewish scripture, though Japhia occurs once (at Josh. 19:12).[13]

In contrast to the drier southern and eastern parts of Palestine, Lower Galilee receives abundant rainfall, sufficient for good crops and pasture.[14] The Nazareth basin's removed location was conducive to a peaceful life, and its temperate climate and physical attributes accommodated an economy of agriculture and pasturing.

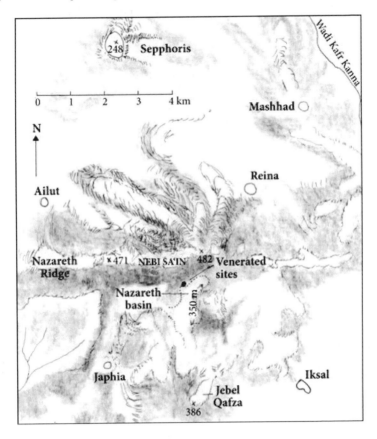

Illus. 1.2: The Nazareth Range.

---

[12] Josh 19:10–16.

[13] See pp. 53–55..

[14] In ancient times the annual rainfall in Lower Galilee was about 63 cm (25 in.). For the geology of Lower Galilee see Orni and Efrat 61 *ff.*

The Stone, Bronze, and Iron Ages

The Stone Age
(*c.* 600,000 – *c.* 4,500 BCE)

The Cave of the Leap

In 1933 René Neuville, the French Vice-consul to Palestine, learned of an interesting cave at the northern edge of the Jezreel Valley, on the side of the mountain called the Jebel Qafza two kilometers south of the Nazareth basin. The following year Neuville, an archaeologist himself, excavated the cave together with a colleague from the Hebrew University of Jerusalem. They uncovered two skulls dating 40,000 years BP, corresponding to the Fourth (Würm) Glacial Period. Astonished, the archaeologists dug deeper and unearthed numerous Paleolithic tools. These were of the Mousterian culture, typically associated with Neanderthal Man (*fl.* 85,000–35,000 BP). Continuing to dig, they discovered the most prized finds of all—four hominid skulls, each far older than Neanderthal Man. Artefacts from this deep layer had Levallois flaking techniques (100,000+ BP).[15] In sum, this cave contains

---

[15] Köppel 1935. The Levallois technique involved the flaking off of large chips from a stone core shaped like an inverted tortoise shell. These chips were rarely trimmed

23

the earliest evidence of habitation in the Nazareth area, and represents one of the oldest caves in Palestine used by humans.

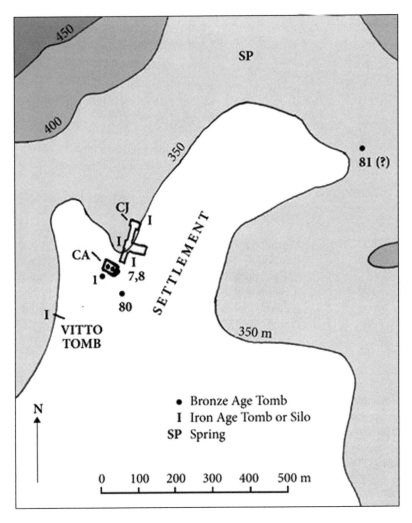

Illus. 1.3: The Nazareth basin with Bronze and Iron Age loci.
The venerated sites are included for reference.
(CA = Church of the Annunciation. CJ = Church of St. Joseph.)

---

further. They were flat on only one side and had sharp cutting edges used for skinning. The Levallois technique contrasts with the earlier Acheulian, in which both sides of the chip were worked to produce a smooth tool with a sharp, straight edge.

The Stone, Bronze, and Iron Ages

Between 1965 and 1979 a second series of excavations was carried out at the Qafza Cave.[16] Remains of hominids, known as Proto-Cro-Magnon man, were found dating 120,000 to 80,000 BP. A twenty-year old male, with a child buried at his feet, is the only known example of a double-burial from that long-forgotten era. It became evident that the entrance had served as a burial ground for a very long time. More than a dozen skeletons, as well as numerous Stone Age artefacts, have been unearthed in the Qafza Cave. Thus, the hill is called Har Qedumim ("Mount of the Ancients"). It rises to a height of 386 m and overlooks the Jezreel Valley.

Christian tradition, however, names the hill Jebel Qafza, "Mount of the Leap," so called because from this hill—according to the Gospel of Luke—the angry Nazarenes attempted to cast Jesus to his death: *And they rose up and put him out of the city, and led him to the brow of the hill on which their city was built, that they might throw him down headlong* (Lk 4:29).[17]

The most recent evidence from the Qafza Cave dates to 40,000 BP. After that time, no evidence of human presence in the Nazareth area is attested until the beginning of the Bronze Age (*c.* 3,200 BCE). During this long time span Neanderthal man and the giant woolly mammoth became extinct, the glaciers of the most recent ice age receded, and *Homo sapiens* began to organize socially in ways that eventually led to settlement and civilization. He and she learned the rudiments of agriculture, began to domesticate animals, started to use skins for clothing, and learned how to construct dwellings. Humans mastered the use of tools and weapons, including thread and needle, hafted stone and bone implements (that is, affixed to a handle), and bow and arrow. They also became artists, as witnessed by beautiful cave paintings, carved Venus statuettes, and decorated finds. In the late Stone Age we discern the first evidence of religion, with ceremonies, the use of masks, dancing, music, and sacrifice. In short, man and woman became worthy of the appellation *sapiens*. Collective hunting, social stratification, and perhaps even private property came into existence. In this remote past the basis for civilization was laid.

In purely scientific terms, the Cave of the Leap must be reckoned the most important archaeological site in the Nazareth area.[18] The hominid bones,

---

[16] These excavations were conducted by B. Vandermeersch, joined by O. Bar-Yosef in 1978. The former authored *Les Hommes Fossiles de Qafzeh* (Israel, *Cahiers de Paléontologie*, Paris 1981). This monograph is the principle publication regarding the Qafza cave. In addition, both excavators authored an informative article, "Qafzeh Cave," in *NEAEHL* 1196–97 (1993). The article contains an extensive bibliography.

[17] See Chapter 4, pp. 202-203.

[18] One report (Mansur 1923) describes a cave-tomb next to the Church of the Annunciation. It may date to Mousterian times, the same epoch as the most recent stratum of habitation at the Cave of the Leap. The author writes: "Two flint

tools, and worked objects found there (some over 100,000 years old) are of great scientific value, and of immense intrinsic worth when compared with the fairly ordinary pottery, tombs, and associated artefacts that will be discussed in the following chapters of this series. Nevertheless, the more recent finds assume an importance quite in excess of their intrinsic value—to Christians at any rate—in view of the fact that they decide the central issue of this work: whether the village of Nazareth did or did not exist in the time of Jesus.

Photograph of the modern town of Nazareth as viewed from the southeast. The Roman Catholic Church of the Annunciation is marked by the conical dome just to the right of center.

---

instruments were found by one of the natives, which he described as a kind of axe, and a smaller instrument, but these he unfortunately threw away in the debris. It is still hoped that they may be found again... It is most likely that the cave dates back to the flint period" (p.91).

The Bronze Age
(To 1200 BCE)

Bronze Age Chronology

		Amiran's Chronology[a]
3800–3100	Chalcolithic ("Copper-Stone Age")[b]	4th mill. BCE
3100–2200	Early Bronze (EB)	3100–2250/2200
2200–2000	Intermediate Period (IP)[c]	——
2000–1550	Middle Bronze (MB)	2250/2200–1550
1550–1200	Late Bronze (LB)	

[a] *APHL* 12.

[b] The beginning and end of the Chalcolithic Period in Palestine are disputed. *Cf. Arch.* 42, Lance 97. Some date EB I to *c.* 3500–3100.

[c] The Intermediate Period or Intermediate Bronze Age is considered part of the Middle Bronze I by Amiran. It refers to a culturally-depressed era between two flourishing urban civilizations (*Arch.* 128).

A warming trend began in the ninth millennium and continued into the eighth. The massive round tower and earliest wall of Jericho, possibly the first urban settlement in the world, date to the eighth millennium. Such precocious urbanization, however, was exceptional. For another five thousand years (*c.* 8000– *c.* 3000) man was a semi-nomad, making use of temporary lodgings for a season, a year, or (more rarely) longer periods of time. Two tendencies co-existed in the Middle East during these millennia between the Stone and Bronze Ages—the peripatetic hunter-gatherer culture, and the sessile farmer-hunter culture. The former predominated, and man was primarily hunter and herder, to a lesser extent farmer and potter.

Slowly, however, humans ceased to wander. The fourth millennium, in particular, witnessed the transition to a settled mode of life. This was the Chalcolithic (literally "copper-stone") Age, in which humans first mastered metalworking. They continued to move their domiciles for special reasons: to follow the hunt, when the soil was exhausted, or when a site became encumbered with refuse. Yet, they also began to stay in one place the year around, fashioning pottery, farming in season, or sometimes moving on with their flocks and relatives in the winter. Many important cities, including Jerusalem in Judea and Ur in Sumeria, were settled during the Chalcolithic Age.

THE MYTH OF NAZARETH

Though some continued to make use of caves and temporary dwellings, by the end of the fourth millennium many people in the Levant had firmly renounced the peripatetic life known since time immemorial. With that momentous decision came a liberating openness to things new. Change of place gave way to something much more powerful: change in quality of life.

New factors encouraged a sedentary existence, especially domestication of the olive and of the grape. These were the basis for the new Mediterranean diet. Tending of olive trees and vine bushes required, at the minimum, annual return to a place. There is evidence that for a time such annual return was practiced. But it was impractical, given the fickleness of nature and the threat of squatters. Presence on site was required, and with it came ownership and the notion of landed property. Sheep and goats continued to be husbanded, now in the same place that fruit trees were tended. Urbanization was not far behind.

Villagers buried their dead in the ground, sometimes under houses. In Chalcolithic times pits or 'silos' were already being used for grain storage. Pottery began already in the sixth millennium, and with the establishment of villages and farming we reach the dawn of history.

Chalcolithic man discovered copper and used it with a sophistication not seen again for thousands of years. In 1961 several hundred metal objects were found at Nahal Mishmar in the Judean desert. This hoard from the fourth millennium contains a panoply of simple and ornate objects—including crowns, scepters, maces, and standards. The objects were made by the lost wax (*cire perdue*) method, "a technique far more sophisticated and complex than simple casting," writes Rivka Gonen. "The end of the Chalcolithic period signaled the end of a golden age of metallurgy."[19]

The Early Bronze Age

When did settlement in the Nazareth valley begin? We can answer this question by examining the evidence from the basin and also by looking at settlement patterns in the area. We shall consider the general region first. In 1990–91 the University of Haifa conducted an archaeological survey of the Nazareth-Afula area and identified fifteen sites inhabited in the Early Bronze Age.[20] Afula is a village ten kilometers south of Nazareth, and like several other settlements in the Jezreel Valley it was already inhabited by the middle of the third millennium. In that era, urbanization was wedded to the new Mediterranean economy of pasturing, agriculture, oil production, and viniculture. In the Early Bronze Age the art of producing olive oil developed, and Egyptian records dating as far back as 2500 BCE refer to the use of grapes for making wine.

---

[19] Gonen in *Arch.*, p. 60.
[20] *ESI* vol. 12 (1994) pp. 19–21.

The welfare of the rural areas was intimately linked with that of the major towns. "The rise of Megiddo," writes Israel Finkelstein, "was coupled with prosperity in the entire Jezreel Valley: the important [neighboring] sites of Taanach, Yokneam, Affula, Jezreel and Beth-shan were founded, or grew in importance, in the EB III" (2650–2350 BCE).[21] Every valley in Palestine had its dominant city (or cities). Each urban center provided a market for the goods produced in the surrounding area, a central depot for trade, specialists and craftspeople, defensive walls, and organized protection in times of attack. Finkelstein divides Palestine into eleven major regions in the EB, each dominated by a major town in symbiotic relationship with many subsidiary villages. Urban, semi-urban, and non-urban populations cooperated for the first time, and specialization emerged. The improved quality of pottery, with thinner walls and higher firing temperatures, suggests the development of a dedicated class of artisans and workshops which served an entire region. The success of the Mediterranean economy also led to a dramatic increase in the need to transport oil and wine. The introduction of the potter's wheel in the mid-third millennium met this need and vastly increased the number of vessels produced. As the millennium progressed, the proportion of wheel-made vessels increased steadily, along with affluence and population growth.

Communication and trade were long-range and probably more extensive than we suspect. For example, an impressive hoard of metal objects was found at Kfar Monash along the coastal trade route. It dates to the third millennium and contains raw material from the Sinai, Syria, Anatolia, and Armenia, attesting to contemporary contact with those remote places. Amnon Ben-Tor notes that Beth Yerah ware, a ceramic style dating to the middle of the third millennium, had its roots as far away as South Russia.[22] Palestine exported oil, wine, and date honey in large jars, while cosmetics (scented oils), resins (for sealing and embalming), bitumen (for caulking rafts, baskets, and monuments), and higher-quality substances were transported in smaller jugs. Interestingly, trade went overland because, as opposed to Syria, until the second millennium Palestine had no coastal ports.

With the rise of permanent settlements in the Early Bronze Age came many new challenges. Settlements needed to be organized, governed and defended. This demanded a degree of planning, specialization, and cooperation not known before. For defensive reasons, villages were generally established on promontories or high places. Many towns without walls in the first part of the Early Bronze Age had acquired impressive fortifications by the middle of the millennium. The wall of Megiddo was over eight meters (26 ft.) thick. Such massive walls were evidently not built to counter battering rams, which were

---

[21] Finkelstein 1995:62.
[22] *Arch.* 111, 123.

not yet invented, but to hinder sapping. Their great width also allowed many men to be stationed atop, aiding in defense and preventing scaling.

As mentioned above, Megiddo was arguably the most important town in Northern Palestine in pre-Exilic times. It has been the object of several archaeological expeditions and has been well studied. Because this city dominated the region in which Nazareth is located—economically, militarily, and culturally—it furnishes an important reference point in our discussion of Nazareth archaeology. Twenty strata have been excavated (*cf. Appendix 3*). Father Bagatti, the principal archaeologist of Nazareth, makes frequent typological comparisons between the pottery of Nazareth and that of Megiddo (*Appendices 1* and *2*). In the latter were numerous workshops which supplied the surrounding area with wares:

> The most extensive pottery workshop area yet found in Palestine is on the east slope of the Megiddo mound. As at Lachish, the Megiddo ceramicists set up their shops in the various caves that dot the hillside. This was a cemetery area in antiquity—a common place to find pottery workshops... At least 12 kilns were found... Although it is difficult to date the period of use of the various potters' caves with certainty, the associated pottery indicates that they were in use in the Late Bronze and Iron Ages. [Wood/41]

Pottery was mass-produced in urban centers even before the Late Bronze Age.[23] Ceramic usage and production in satellite villages such as Nazareth generally followed the form, style, and manner of production of the dominant city.

It should be noted that concentrations of people and commercial production activities required large and reliable quantities of water. In urban settlements without perennial water resources cisterns and/or communal reservoirs were cut into the limestone for the collection of rainwater. Some cities also had a planned drainage system and a sewer.

Cities also had a temple. In the Early Bronze Age, Megiddo had several temples within a complex sacred area, with a gigantic circular cult platform upon which animal sacrifices were performed. The need for cooperative building projects such as temples, walls, large cisterns, and for cohesion in times of attack, empowered urban settlements and fostered an allegiance second only to that of family. The earliest urban settlements were, in fact, among kinfolk and an extension of tribal power. The settlement enhanced the identity of the clan, created wealth, and increased prestige. It was greater than the sum total of its individuals. The city was new, marvelous and powerful.

---

[23]   Wood 1990:16, 39.

The Stone, Bronze, and Iron Ages

The demise of cities

Before the third millennium ended every city in Palestine either lay in ruins or had been abandoned. We are not sure what caused the vast and auspicious urban experiment to fail, but the failure was complete. Israel Finkelstein speaks of the collapse of fragile "peer-polity systems," social, political, and commercial webs made up of urban centers, nearby villages, and interrelated rural elements. "The rise of peer-polity systems," he writes, "creates new perils and instabilities, such as competition for limited resources and attempts at territorial expansion... Due to the interdependence of the entities, such political tensions, or environmental dangers, can bring about the breakdown of the entire system in a short period of time..."[24] It is as if mankind, having discovered this marvelous, complex new mode of social organization and source of power, was still too immature to control it. Cities require an enormous investment of energy in subtle, long-range, and unseen elements such as governing, organization, mediation, decision-making, allocation, and planning. For an urban environment to endure, the level of cooperation required of its residents is considerable and unceasing. It may be that the mental apparatus for successful city life had not yet evolved in what was still an essentially tribal society.

Some scholars have suggested that foreign military expeditions destroyed the first cities. We do know that a general deterioration in relations between Egypt and Palestine occurred by mid-millennium and ended trade between these two regions. Thereafter, the towns that continued to prosper in Palestine traded not with Egypt but with Syria.[25] A testament from the tomb of the Egyptian general Weni (*c.* 2300 BCE) boasts of his sack and destruction of strongholds in "the land of the sand-dwellers," which could refer to Palestine. The town of Ai was indeed sacked and burned about 2350, and it remained empty for over a thousand years. On the other hand, the destruction could have come from a very different direction. About this time King Sargon (2340–2284) and/or his grandson Naram-Sin of Akkad invaded Syria, and the cities of Ebla, Ugarit, and Byblos were destroyed. Whether the Akkadians also entered Palestine we do not know.

Another theory is that the cities destroyed one another. "In all sites a number of phases or strata of the period were observed, often separated by conflagration layers testifying to destruction, probably the result of wars."[26] The walls of Jericho were rebuilt or extensively repaired no fewer than sixteen times. All this strife suggests not occasional and distant foes, but perpetual enemies near at hand.

---

[24] Finkelstein 1995:48.

[25] *Arch.* 119-120.

[26] *Arch.* 97.

THE MYTH OF NAZARETH

Whatever the reason(s), urban society in the third millennium vanishes before the archaeologist's eyes. The process was not sudden but gradual. Some sites were abandoned or destroyed early in the millennium (Mezer), never to be rebuilt. Others were forsaken in the middle of the millennium (Gezer, Arad, Tell el-Farah North). Many were abandoned toward the end of the millennium (Beth Shean, Megiddo, Beth Yerah). By 2200 BCE no urban settlements were left in Palestine.[27]

The Intermediate Period

For two centuries, known as the Intermediate Bronze Age or Intermediate Period (2200–2000),[28] the reduced population of Palestine either reverted to nomadism or made use of transient, unfortified settlements. The people were once again hunters, herders, and agriculturalists. Broad areas west of the Jordan River lay uninhabited. Caves resumed an importance held in much earlier times. The short-lived sites from the Intermediate Period that have been identified are small and located in the hill country. Sometimes cemeteries are found, but without traces of habitation—as if people returned regularly to a certain special place to bury their dead. Kathleen Kenyon has shown that bodies were often entombed in a disarticulated state, that is, the bones already jumbled up.[29] This is possible if death occurred a considerable time before burial. This in turn suggests that the person died elsewhere and his or her relations carried the remains to the communal burial ground, probably on an annual trip. In the Intermediate Period, the majority of burials at Jericho are of this type, as are those at Megiddo and Tell Ajjul.

Pottery continued to be made, but it is notably poor in quality and pale in color. The ceramics of the Intermediate Period are handmade and often marred by finger marks, dents, and a general lack of polish. Use of the wheel, common in the Early Bronze Age, almost completely ceased. "Apparently the Land of Israel as a whole," writes Ram Gophna, "became the most backward part of the Levant, a land inhabited only by poor settlements of farmers and herders."[30]

Yet the backwardness of Palestine was not unique. Towards the end of the third millennium a series of convulsions seized the entire Near East, accompanied by a period of confusion and universal poverty. In Egypt, the Old Kingdom collapsed about 2130 BCE. This was followed by two centuries

---

[27] *Arch.* 128.

[28] These two centuries are variously termed the Early Bronze IV B-C (Dever), the Middle Bronze I (Amiran), or the Intermediate Period (Gophna). This book follows the latter terminology. *Cf. Arch.* 128; *APHL* 12.

[29] Kenyon 1966:15–26. The disorganized bones are not evidence of secondary burial (re-burial after the body had decomposed). Secondary burial in ossuaries was practiced for a fairly short time at the turn of the era.

[30] *Arch.* 157.

The Stone, Bronze, and Iron Ages

of famine, decentralization, and almost continual violence. The state of anarchy continued from the ninth to the eleventh dynasties until Mentuhotep reunited Egypt at the beginning of the new millennium. In Mesopotamia the Akkadian empire also came to an end, as did the short hegemony of the Gudean dynasty. Finally, the old civilization of Sumer collapsed. The entire Levant experienced two centuries of crisis.

Some scholars, such as Kenyon, consider that a major cause of this wide-ranging dislocation was the incursion of a people known as the Amorites. This nomadic and aggressive tribal people came from the north, captured some cities, and installed itself on the desert fringes of the areas it could not control. For centuries the Amorites were a thorn in the side of even great empires from Egypt to Sumer. They were despised by the "high" civilizations of the urban centers, partly because they lacked cities of their own. Yet the Amorites may not merit such low repute. This resourceful people possessed a creative dynamism that influenced the entire Levant. They were certainly a power to be reckoned with, and may have destroyed many more cities in the Near East than we can prove today. Eventually, Amorites became rulers in Aleppo, Mari, Babylon and Qatna—all centers of great power and civilization.[31] As for Palestine, after the utter destruction of the Early Bronze Age there was apparently little left worth ruling. The Amorites on both sides of the Jordan River blended in with the indigenous peoples of the hill country. Invaders in the third millennium, they now constituted a permanent and significant entity. I would suggest that from among their progeny arose the Israelites one thousand years later.

Thus, a conquest of the Holy Land apparently occurred in the third millennium BCE. Is it possible that the "conquest" by the Israelites portrayed in the Bible is approximately one millennium too late? It is becoming increasingly clear that there is little archaeological evidence for such a conquest in the Early Iron Age. If this Amorite-Israelite model is correct, then the Bible preserves dim memories of this early conquest, memories that were long preserved by the victors and that became enshrined in tradition.

The earliest Nazareth evidence

A comprehensive review of the ceramic finds from the Nazareth valley shows that no artefact dates with certainty before 2200 BCE. Bagatti writes: "The oldest appear to be two broken vases (fig, 211:18–19) and one entire (fig. 210:15)."[32] These vessels, diagrammed in *Illus.1.4,* have close similarities with those of the Megiddo family from 2200–2000 BCE. Regarding one jar (top right), Amiran noted:

---

[31] *CAH* II/1 p. 19.

[32] *Exc.* 267. Bagatti also examined shards of similar vessels (no total specified), so that more than three objects date to the Intermediate Period (Exc. 263).

Observation of the vessels by an expert eye reveals an interesting combination technique: the body of the vessel is made by hand, while the neck and rim seem to be wheel made... When both parts of the vessel were 'leather-hard,' the potter joined them and smoothed over the join... Incisions of various kinds are generally used in MB I. These are made either with a point or with a three-to-five pronged comb or fork... The decoration is always placed at the base of the neck, and may have been intended to cover the join between the separately made body and neck.[33]

Following these early artefacts, the Nazareth evidence multiplies rapidly and continues through the second millennium. A summary schema of the Bronze and Iron Age evidence (*Illus.1.5*) corroborates Bagatti's overall estimation: "As a general rule, the material found in the three tombs [*i.e.,* Tombs 1, 7, 80] and off and on out of place, brings us to the Middle and Late Bronze, practically from 2000 to 1200, sometimes with some over the limits."[34]

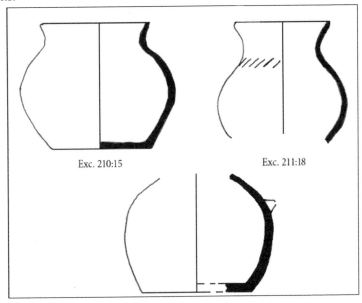

Exc. 210:15   Exc. 211:18

Illus.1.4: The earliest pottery from the Nazareth basin.
(Intermediate Period, 2200–2000 BCE).

---

[33] APHL 80. *Cf.* Engberg Fig. 14:P 4122; Pl. 23:11; Ben-Tor 1992:145, APHL Fig. 5:12. Regarding *Exc.* Fig. 211:19 see Meyerhof Pl. 7/4:10 & 4:17; Engberg, Fig. 4:12P. Regarding *Exc.* Fig. 210:15, for its form see Meyerhof plates 12/3:25; 13/3:47; 17/23:49; 20/33:14, all with spouts or handles.

[34] *Exc* 267.

The Middle and Late Bronze Ages

The second millennium opened with fresh vibrancy and renewed vigor. It is as if the peoples of the Levant had absorbed the foreign energy of the Amorites, and the resultant fusion led to a marvelous renaissance, something wholly new. Cities were reborn. The pottery of the Middle Bronze Age is assured and graceful, exhibiting remarkable inventiveness in form, even playfulness. This is not the work of tense, fearful and impoverished potters, such as we find in the Intermediate Period. MB pottery is relaxed and inspired. After the difficulties of the previous era, one senses that people finally allowed themselves to enjoy life again.

	IP	MB II			LB			Iron		
		A	B	C	I	IIA	IIB	I	II	III
T. 81		6+								
T. 80			3							
		1	2	1						
T. 8		All								
T. 7	2	2+	2							
T. 1						3				
			4			3				
			1	1	9^a	1				
	1	11		3	2	1				
Silos 22 & 57								2		
									22	
									1	3
Church of St. Joseph									4	7
										2
Vitto tomb								7^b		
Loffreda material								12^{bc}	4	
BCE	2200	2000	1730	1630	1550	1400	1300	1200	1000	800 / 587

a. Includes one lamp of unknown provenance (*Exc.* Fig. 235:1).
b. Vitto dates these artefacts to XI BCE (Iron IB).
c. Loffreda dates 6 artefacts to Iron I, and 6 more generally to Iron I-II.

Illus. 1.5: Chronology of the Bronze and Iron Age
Artefacts from Nazareth

The general evidence

The Bronze Age finds at Nazareth come from five tombs and date to the Middle and Late Bronze Ages (2200–1200 BCE).[35] Why, we may wonder, was this ancient pottery found only in tombs? The reason is that no excavations from the Nazareth basin have unearthed habitations dating before Byzantine times.[36] Nowhere in the basin do we find evidence of pre-Byzantine dwellings, wall foundations, hearths, streets, and the like. The astonishing lack of many kinds of evidence may be partly due to the fact that little of the Nazareth basin has actually been excavated. The principal focus of archaeological attention has been in the venerated compound around the Church of the Annunciation. Comparatively little has been excavated outside this modest area—some scattered tombs dating to various periods, and a few non-funerary sites such as Mary's Spring (now the Church of St. Gabriel).

A second reason why no early habitations have been found may be that construction activity has removed many traces of earlier structures. Nazareth has been inhabited since the second century of our era. In the last eighteen centuries much Bronze, Iron , and Roman evidence has no doubt either been destroyed or covered over.

A third reason for the lack of pre-Byzantine structural remains is a startling fact revealed for the first time in this book—for many centuries after the Iron Age the Nazareth valley was uninhabited. These eras, which I refer to as the Great Hiatus, lasted from the Late Iron Age until Middle Roman times, an interval of approximately eight hundred years.[37]

We are not in a position to examine dwellings or the contents of dwellings (wall foundations, domestic pottery *in situ*, hearths, ovens, *etc.*) until post-Roman times. The only structural remains that survive from the Bronze Age are tombs.[38] The artefacts found in them date to many different centuries, and show that there was habitation in the basin both in the Middle and Late Bronze Ages.

A chronology based on the movable finds from the Bronze and Iron Age tombs is presented in *Illus.1.5*. As the MB progresses the number of artefacts noticeably decreases, and four of the five Bronze Age tombs entirely cease to be used after the middle of the millennium. This could mean that there was a break

---

[35] Bagatti devotes ten pages of his *Excavations* to the Bronze Age (*Exc* 258-68. *Cf.* also pp. 74–75).

[36] *Exc* 236.

[37] See Chapters Two, Three, and Four.

[38] In *Illus. 1.5* it will be seen that two pottery vessels found in Silos 22 or 57 may date to the Late Bronze. However, they may in fact be Iron Age vessels. In any case, these objects do not materially affect the argument that all our evidence from the Bronze Age at Nazareth comes from tombs.

The Stone, Bronze, and Iron Ages

in settlement at mid-millennium (see below). We cannot be sure, for Tomb 1 continues in use. *Illus. 1.3* shows that Bronze and Iron Age loci are concentrated in the same general vicinity, on the western side of the basin.[39] This may simply be because that is the only area where major excavations have been conducted. In any case, the material record tells us that there was settlement throughout the millennium, and in the same general vicinity. That settlement may have been continuous or may have suffered a dislocation at mid-millennium.

After about 800 years of use, Tomb 1 was finally abandoned. Iron Age material appears at new locations entirely unmixed with older Bronze Age artefacts, and it is different in character. These facts suggest that a new group of inhabitants entered the basin about 1200 BCE. Again, we cannot be sure. It may be that the inhabitants simply adopted new production techniques and wares as they entered the Iron Age.

Bagatti has published the preponderance of datings for the Bronze and Iron Age material from Nazareth, and many of his estimates are broad, as is evident from the long time spans in *Illus. 1.5*. A thorough redating of these artefacts by specialists is a desideratum. Father S. Loffreda dated sixteen Iron Age objects, and Fanny Vitto then reviewed many of Loffreda's datings and assigned them more precisely to the eleventh century. It should be noted that *Illus. 1.5* represents only a portion of the finds. Many vessels are too fragmentary or damaged to date typologically, that is, by comparison with pottery from other places.

Despite the paucity of material and the imprecise dating of many of the objects, a general picture of Nazareth in the Bronze Age emerges. It is clear that the basin was occupied throughout the MB and LB, with the possibility of a break in settlement at mid-millennium.[40]

The Bronze Age tombs at Nazareth

Bagatti designates these as Tombs 1, 7, 8, 80, and 81. Three are within a few meters of one another on Roman Catholic property, under and next to the present Church of the Annunciation (*Illus. 1.3*). Tomb 80 is about 60 m. south of the others, in an area that until recently was the Greek (Melchite) cemetery. It has since become a commercial district. Evidently, these four tombs were part of a Bronze Age necropolis. As for Tomb 81, it is separate from the others and located on the northeastern side of the Nazareth basin, in the modern suburb of Nazrat Illit (Upper Nazareth). It was excavated by the Israel Department of Antiquities in 1963.[41]

---

[39] Tomb 81 on the east side of the valley appears to be an anomaly. I have not been able to ascertain its exact location.

[40] It may be objected that without actual evidence of Bronze Age habitations in the valley, it is possible that a peripatetic clan used the Nazareth basin only for burial. However, it is hardly conceivable that people returned to the basin annually for a whole millennium without ever settling there.

[41] On this tomb see Yeivin 145; *'Atiqot* IV (1965) Suppl., p. 14; *RB* 70 (1963) p 563;

THE MYTH OF NAZARETH

Two short and practically identical notices regarding Tomb 81 are given in the *Revue Biblique* of 1963 and 1965. The former reads:

> During some construction activity in Upper Nazareth, a burial grotto was discovered dating to the Middle Bronze I. Access to this grotto was by a shaft leading to a central chamber, from which three other chambers branched. The preponderance of pottery was found in the main room; the other chambers contained mostly bones. The pottery consists of "teapots" characteristic of the Middle Bronze I, two small jars with ring handles, and one large jar.[42]

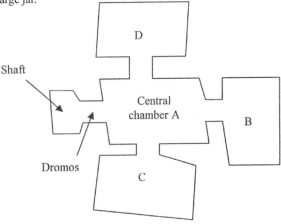

Illus.1.6: Plan of a typical Bronze Age shaft tomb at Megiddo. (Redrawn from Kenyon)

The description of this tomb corresponds to the typical Bronze Age shaft tomb diagrammed above (*Illus.1.6*). Four or more of the tombs at Nazareth are of the shaft type,[43] which was the most common type of burial in Palestine from the second half of the fourth millennium until well into the Iron Age.[44] It was "almost rigidly stereotyped" (Kenyon).[45] The standard four-room plan of this type of tomb consisted of a descending entry shaft, a short entryway (dromos), and a central chamber from which three burial caves radiated, one on each side except the entrance. The small entryway was sealed with a stone, and the shaft subsequently filled in with earth or rubble.

RB 72 (1965) p. 547; *Exc.* 246.

[42] *RB* 70 (1963), p. 563.

[43] The plan of Tomb 80 is unpublished.

[44] Intramural burial (under house floors) was also practiced in the Bronze-Iron ages (*Arch.* 191).

[45] Kenyon describes a typical example from Megiddo (Kenyon 24-28; Guy 136; also Meyerhof, Tomb 3).

The overall plan resembles a cross. The form is exemplified by Tomb 8 at Nazareth, discovered in 1955 by the Franciscans when digging the foundations for the new Church of the Annunciation.[46] Tomb 8 contained numerous Byzantine shards and a few of the Bronze period, which Bagatti dates generally to 2100–1850 BCE,[47] that is, to the same period as Tomb 81 (*Illus. 1.5* and Appendix 1).[48]

The other four Bronze Age tombs which yielded artefacts are reported by Bagatti in his *Excavations*, though the archaeologist itemizes pottery and other movable objects from only three of them (Tombs 1, 7, and 80).

The reuse of tombs was customary in the Bronze Age, with multiple burials over several or many generations, as is evident from the long time spans in which the Nazareth tombs were used. Bodies were usually placed on the tomb floor, on their side and with limbs bent. Once decomposed, bones were moved to the back and sides of the chamber to make room for new bodies. Thus over time bones accumulated along the inner walls of the various chambers.

Of great interest to the archaeologist are the artefacts that were often placed in tombs along with the body, such as pottery, weapons, or glass objects. These items served several purposes. Some were associated with the deceased person while alive, and thus had sentimental value in the minds of the relatives. Some artefacts were associated with belief in an afterlife, such as bowls or jars with foodstuffs placed next to the body for nourishment of the deceased, or weapons for protection in the next world (or in the ongoing spiritual journey). On the other hand, artefacts might have inadvertently been left behind in the tomb, such as practical items belonging to relatives or workmen (*e.g.* oil lamps or tools). Like the bones of the corpses, these also eventually accumulated to the back and sides of the burial chambers. R. Hachlili has summarized typical funerary artefacts of the Middle Bronze Period:

> The most common burial provisions were bowls and platters for foodstuffs, jugs for liquids, and juglets for oil and perfume... These provisions demonstrate that the deceased were thought to need nourishment and the protection afforded both by weapons and symbolically by colored and metal jewelry.[49]

When a Bronze Age tomb is discovered that has not been robbed (a comparative rarity), a good deal of material can thus be found. This was the case with Tomb 1 at Nazareth.

---

[46] Discussion and plan at *Exc.* 37–38. On the shaft tomb see also Finegan 181–82.

[47] Late IP and early MB IIA in this study's terminology.

[48] *Exc.* 37 n.2.

[49] *ABD*, "Burial," vol.1:785. *Cf.* also Kenyon, *Digging Up Jericho,* and *Excavations at Jericho*; P. Guy, *Megiddo Tombs* (Chicago, 1938).

THE MYTH OF NAZARETH

Historical considerations

Do we have enough information to make further historical inferences regarding the Bronze Age at Nazareth? From the fact that five tombs all appear about the same time we can surmise that, in all likelihood, an extended family or group of families related by blood (Heb. *mishpacha,* "clan") entered the Nazareth basin from the Jezreel Valley in the twenty-second century. The use of tombs reflects blood relations, for the tomb was a family affair. Certainly, only an extended family (*beit 'av*) afforded the manpower required to dig a shaft tomb. Blood ties, of course, have always been paramount in the Middle East, especially among groups on the move. The fact that five tombs in the Nazareth basin already exist by the end of the Intermediate Period shows that this quiet and fertile location enticed a substantial group of people to cease their wanderings and settle down.

Towards the beginning of the second millennium there is a great increase in the number of artefacts from these tombs (*Illus. 1.5*). This increase corresponds to the renaissance of settlement and culture that took place across Palestine in the MB IIA. The coast, the valleys, and the major urban centers (including Megiddo) were first resettled, followed by settlement in the hilly interior. By about 1750 the entire country had been settled,[50] and a flourishing settlement existed in the Nazareth basin.

There is considerable MB IIA pottery from Nazareth, and some of it probably came from Megiddo. "The most extensive pottery workshop area yet found in Palestine is on the east slope of the Megiddo mound," writes B. Wood.[51] At least twelve kilns were found there. Elsewhere (p. 36) Wood notes that caves furnish excellent work areas for pottery production. This reminds us of Nazareth, for many caves dot the excavated area under and around the Church of the Annunciation. To my knowledge no kilns or potter's wheels have been found at Nazareth.[52] Thus we cannot affirm that any of the pottery found there was produced on site. Given the limited area of excavations, however, this possibility cannot be ruled out.

After the MB IIA, which witnessed a peak in activity at Nazareth, the number of artefacts and also the number of tombs decreased). Tombs 8 and 81 were no longer used after about 1730 BCE, while Tomb 1 is represented by fewer finds. This diminution in the evidence corresponds with what we know from the rest of Canaan at the time. The lifespan of many MB IIA sites was short and limited to that period, and there was a noticeable abandonment and decline of settlements in the land at the end of the period. Kempinski suggests that much of the rural population was absorbed into cities and fortified

---

[50] *Arch* 166, 193.

[51] Wood 40.

[52] Bagatti signals an "oven" under the CA, which he dates to Byzantine times (*Exc.* 62).

40

settlements.[53] This may partly have been a reaction to Hyksos encroachment. The Hyksos ("rulers of foreign lands") were Canaanites who gained control of Egypt from about 1680 to 1560 (Dynasty XV). They ruled Canaan as far north as the Jezreel valley.[54] Recollections of this period of foreign Canaanite ascendancy may underlie the accounts of Joseph's authority in Egypt (Gen. 41:39*ff*). Indeed, the archaeological connection between Egypt and Canaan is particularly strong during this period (MB II B–C), and we find a wealth of Egyptian imports in Palestine (scarabs, faïence, alabaster vessels, bone-inlaid boxes). In the Nazareth valley, a scarab from Tomb 1 dates to the Hyksos period. Two alabaster jars from Tomb 80 from this time are also probably of Egyptian manufacture.[55]

The Hyksos were expelled from Egypt by the Pharaoh Ahmose in the sixteenth century, and Egyptian control was then reasserted over the length and breadth of Canaan. At that time there was a disruption of settlement patterns on a large scale. Beginning about 1650, migration southwards seems to have been a reason for the increasing impoverishment of northern Canaan. The termination in use of four tombs at Nazareth about this time fits the broad historical context. There may have been a dislocation or great attrition in the settlement at the end of MB IIC. "The end of [the MB]," writes William Dever, "saw virtually every site in Palestine violently destroyed, probably in connection with the expulsion of the Hyksos in Egypt under the renascent Dynasty 18 kings, *ca.* 1540–1480 B.C."[56] Pharoah Thutmose I (reigned 1525–1512) extended the Egyptian sphere into Northern Syria and even crossed the River Euphrates. Megiddo and other Canaanite cities rebelled and supported the Mitanni to the north. As a result Pharaoh Thutmoses III (1504–1450) invaded Palestine and decisively smashed a coalition of 119 Canaanite and Syrian towns at the Battle of Megiddo about 1472. A description of that battle is proudly inscribed in hieroglyphic detail on the walls of the temple of Amun at Karnak, and in more abbreviated versions on stelae in Upper Egypt.

Our word *Armageddon* may contains echoes of that prolonged and decisive conflict. The Egyptian army was so large that it took a full seven hours to defile onto the Plain of Jezreel at the foot of Megiddo. The initial engagement entirely favored the Egyptians, and the Canaanites broke ranks and bolted towards the city gate. But instead of pursuing their advantage the Egyptians fell to looting and allowed the Canaanites to reënter the city. A seven-month siege ensued. Thutmose, recognizing that within the city walls were kings of all the northern principalities, reminded his troops that in

---

[53] *Arch.* 193.

[54] *Arch.*160–61, 179.

[55] For the scarab see *Exc.* fig. 211:14; the alabaster jars fig. 213:1–2.

[56] *ABD*, "Palestine, Archaeology of," p. 111. Dever terms MB IIC "MB III."

conquering Megiddo they conquered a thousand cities. During the long siege the Egyptians extensively looted the area and conducted secondary military campaigns in several directions.[57] It is entirely possible—indeed likely—that the small Nazareth valley, so close to the plain of battle, was also despoiled.

We shall see (below, p. 36) that the settlement we have been calling "Nazareth" was, in all likelihood, the substantial Bronze-Iron Age town of Japhia. If this was the case, there is hardly any doubt that it was also devastated at this time, and that it was one of the 119 Caananite and Syrian towns that opposed Egypt, with its leader besieged in Megiddo.

Indeed, the evidence from the Nazareth basin suggests that after the mid-millennium the population did not recover to the level of former times. Only Tomb 1 continues into the Late Bronze Age, and with the passing centuries the number of its artefacts also diminishes. This corresponds with the results of wider archaeological surveys of Palestine: "Where some 270 Middle Bronze sites were counted, only about 100 Late Bronze Age sites were found, a decrease of more than 60 percent."[58] After the Egyptian reconquest, the hill country of Galilee was virtually empty.

We are thus able to arrive at three general conclusions regarding the Bronze Age in the Nazareth basin: (1) tomb use, and hence human presence in the vicinity, begins in the Intermediate Period; (2) the high point in settlement is reached in the early second millennium; and (3) human habitation continues through the Late Bronze Age, but on a reduced scale.[59]

---

[57] *CAH* II.1.451.

[58] R. Gonen in *Arch.* 217.

[59] The results of this section reveal the impossibility of earlier theories held by the Church. Father C. Kopp postulated that settlement began at Nazareth *c.* 3000 BCE: "Given the parallels with neighboring Megiddo, it is safe to assume that the beginnings of historical civilization [*geschichtlichen Civilisation*] were laid about 3,000 BCE" (Kopp 1938:188). The same writer held that Nazareth moved from the hillside to the valley floor a millennium later: "It seems, accordingly, that as early as about 2000 BCE the inhabitants sought out a place for themselves on the valley floor, one which better met their increased needs" (*ibid.* p. 189). Of course, both theories are untenable as the settlement was only beginning in the late third millennium.

The Iron Age
(1200–587 BCE)

Iron Age Chronology [a]

1200-1000	Iron IA-B	Judges
1000-900	Iron II A	United monarchy (David, Solomon)
900-800[b]	Iron IIB	Divided monarchy
800-587[c]	Iron III	Early prophets; Assyrian conquest; rise of Babylonia

[a] Follows M. Avi-Yonah and M. Stern, *EAEHL* (1976). Alternate chronologies are found in *OEANE*, "Palestine," vol. 3, p. 218.

[b] Bagatti conformed to Amiran's datings after the latter's book (*APHL*) appeared in 1969 (see *Scavo*:18–19). Finegan (p. xix), writing in 1969, uses the dates "900–539 BCE" for Iron II.

[c] Sometimes called Iron IIC (*APHL* 12; 191). Based purely on material considerations, the Iron Age in Palestine extends to the late sixth century (*Arch.* 305).

Towards the close of the thirteenth century Egyptian power waned, and during the early Iron Age Egypt withdrew from Canaan. New peoples entered Palestine, including the Philistines, one of several Sea Peoples who had been marauding along the coasts of the Eastern Mediterranean. The Philistines were probably of Grecian origin and settled the coastal area of southern Palestine (now Gaza) already in the Late Bronze Age. They made attempts to subdue the interior, but were successfully challenged by another group of recent arrivals who ostensibly entered Canaan from the east—the Israelites. There is, in fact, no archaeological evidence that the Israelites were outsiders, despite the well-known literary accounts and traditions to this effect in the Bible. Today, the provenance and genesis of the Israelites are hotly debated issues. A. Mazar suggests that they evolved from indigenous tribal, seminomadic and pastoral elements (see below).[60]

At the beginning of the Iron Age Megiddo was probably the most important Egyptian administrative center in northern Canaan. However, by the close of the twelfth century (Stratum VI B) Megiddo's stature had declined along with waning Egyptian influence in the land. By the year 1000 Palestine moved from being an Egyptian province to an independent Israelite

---

[60] *Arch.* 296.

43

THE MYTH OF NAZARETH

state.[61] Precisely how this transition occurred is debated. Several models have been proposed, of which I will note three: (1) the older "conquest" model (W. F. Albright); (2) the "peaceful infiltration" model (Alt, Noth); and (3) the "peasants' revolt" model (Mendenhall, Gottwald).

If the process was violent, then we can speak of a 'takeover' of the country by the Israelites. If peaceful, then we can conceive of the land "becoming" Israelite. Certainly, a takeover by landless tribes would have been facilitated by the many political divisions in the land and the constant feuding between city states. Already during the Amarna period (fourteenth century) Lower Galilee was disputed between the kings of Megiddo and Shechem, while Upper Galilee was disputed between the kings of Tyre and Hazor. The countryside was occupied principally by a people known as the Habiru. This resourceful and opportunistic people was apparently under the control of no city and seems to have played the role of spoiler, using interurban rivalries to engineer its own success.[62] R. Gonen writes:

> The El-Amarna tablets also mention a group termed 'Apiru, or Habiru, which existed on the periphery of Canaanite society. The 'Apiru lack a clear ethnic identity. They were a motley crowd of social outcasts who coalesced, perhaps in several small, unrelated groups. According to the sources, the 'Apiru had no permanent settlements, social privileges, or property. They played an important role in the rivalries between the city-states, transferring their allegiance from one side to another, according to their own interests.[63]

A "motley crowd of social outcasts" is an admittedly irreverent view of the people that later coalesced into the Israelite tribes during the period of the Judges. However, as early as the thirteenth century the Habiru had gained sufficient power to overthrow many towns, including Hazor, whose violent destruction is credited by the excavators to the Israelites (Joshua 11). They were a power to be reckoned with, and for the first time "Israel" is mentioned in foreign records—it occurs in the Merneptah stele (c. 1210 BCE), commemorating the defeat of several of the pharaoh's enemies.

Between 1974 and 1984 Zvi Gal directed a survey of Southern Galilee and identified fifteen settlements dating to the Iron I period. "In the Iron Age," he writes, "the Galilee was settled by a network of rural villages, many of which have been found in the surveys."[64] Nazareth is among those sites.[65]

---

[61] Singer 282, 293f.
[62] Gal 1988:83; Finkelstein 1995:62.
[63] *Arch.* 214.
[64] "Galilee," in *OEANE*, p. 451.
[65] Gal 1994:43. Japhia, Horvat Maltah, and Horvat Deborah are nearby Iron I sites. None is situated in the Nazareth basin itself.

44

Most of these settlements lasted for only a short time and were located near springs. Gal suggests that "the concentration of Iron I sites in southern Lower Galilee represents the nuclear territory of Zebulun." We have seen in *Illus. 5* that little evidence survives at Nazareth from the end of the Bronze Age (LB IIB). If some Israelites from the tribe of Zebulun indeed moved into the basin, they probably would have found it deserted or almost deserted.

At the end of Stratum VIIA at Megiddo (*c.* 1130 BCE) there was a total destruction of that city, which could have been at the hands of the Israelites. The next stratum (VIB) is quite unlike the preceding. Y. Yadin maintains that a "new and different group of people occupied the site."[66] At Nazareth, too, we note a major change in the evidence. Use of the Bronze Age tombs comes to an end, while novel Iron Age material appears, and at different loci. The considerable number of Iron Age finds suggests that an influx of people moved into the valley after 1200 BCE. This is consistent with a major cultural break throughout the whole region.

However, the evidence does not permit certainty. The model of a major cultural break *c.* 1200 BCE with Israelites entering the basin must be balanced against another model suggesting continuity in settlement. Much depends on how we define "Israelite." J. Dessel writes: "it has not been satisfactorily shown that there are any good archaeological data that support the appearance of a completely new ethnicity or people such as the Israelites in the late thirteenth century BCE." He adds: "the Lower Galilee was an area marked by overall sociocultural continuity from the Late Bronze Age into the Iron Age."[67] This continuity agrees with Mazar's view, stated above, that the Israelite people evolved from indigenous tribal, seminomadic and pastoral elements, and with Gal's view that extra-urban tribes in the vicinity finally took over the urban centers.

Yet another view is that it was Canaanites who entered the Nazareth basin *c.* 1200, and in the course of time they adopted the God Yahweh and aligned themselves culturally, militarily, and ethnically (through intermarriage) with the Israelites, thus becoming Israelites. In this case, what appears in hindsight as radical displacement may be akin to an assimilation.

Nevertheless, a modest Israelite (re-)settlement in the Nazareth valley in the early Iron Age coheres well with what we know of settlement patterns in the Lower Galilee. According to Gal, a number of small villages and hamlets were founded in the Nazareth hills in the Iron I period.[68] Some nearby sites

---

[66] *NEAEHL*, "Megiddo," p. 1013.
[67] Dessel 29, 31.
[68] Gal 1992:82.

of this era have been explored in recent years.[69] Y. Alexandre excavated one burial cave 4.2 km NE of the Church of the Annunciation. It dates to the late eleventh/early tenth century. The excavator concludes that in all probability the tomb "should be associated with Israelite tribal settlement."[70] Farther to the south, "Surveys in the hill country of Ephraim…" writes A. Mazar, "have identified more than one hundred sites of the Iron Age I, indicating a wave of Israelite settlement. Most of the sites, situated in remote hilly areas, are small, ranging from isolated structures to villages of 5–6 dunams."[71]

Whether Israelites of the tribe of Zebulun entered the Nazareth basin, or an indigenous Canaanite/Amorite group 'became' Israelite—the early Iron Age in the Nazareth basin has bequeathed us a greatly expanded number of artefacts and a change in their character. Vitto has been able to pinpoint the dates of nineteen pieces, including Loffreda's material, to the eleventh century.[72] It was in the first part of that century that the Canaanites-Philistines suffered a major defeat at the hands of the Israelite general Barak (Judg 4:14; 5:19) in the nearby Battle of Mt. Tabor. Regarding this event, I. Singer writes: "As far as we know, this was the last serious attempt on the part of the Canaanites to gather their forces in order to block the spread of the Israelite tribes into the northern valleys."[73] It would be natural if, after this victory, Israelites spread out over the Jezreel Valley and surrounding regions. In this case, the indigenous populations either withdrew or converted.

In the second half of the eleventh century the Philistines mounted counter-campaigns into the interior farther to the south, and realized several victories. They captured the Ark of the Covenant at Eben-Ezer, destroyed the temple at Shiloh (the capital) and routed the Israelites at the Battle of Mount Gilboa, in which Saul and his sons lost their lives (1Sam 31). However, after the turn of the millennium King David was successful in removing the Philistines from the hill country of Palestine and set about systematically abolishing all remaining Canaanite enclaves.[74] We can surmise that by the end of the united monarchy (928 BCE) those who lived in the Nazareth basin identified themselves as Israelites. It is probable that only they would have chosen to remain.

---

[69] 'Afula (Dothan); Har Yona (Alexandre); Migdal Ha-'Emeq (Covello-Paran); Ta'anach (Rast); Tel Gath Hefer (Alexandre, Covello-Paran and Gal); Tell Qiri (Ben-Tor and Portugali).

[70] Alexandre 188. Lying outside the Nazareth basin, the data from this tomb are not included in the Primary Reports of this book, nor incorporated into *Illus. 1.5* (above).

[71] *Arch.* 286. A dunam is 1,000 square meters (about 31.6 m per side), equivalent to a quarter acre. Ten dunams make one hectare (100 m per side).

[72] Vitto 167.

[73] Singer 322.

[74] Barnavi 14.

The Stone, Bronze, and Iron Ages

The twelfth and eleventh centuries in Palestine were a period of transition from a sheep and cattle raising economy to the sedentary occupations of vine and olive growing, with a proliferation of small settlements.[75] For the first time we can date structures besides tombs at Nazareth. Two silos used for grain storage contained Iron Age material, and these are our first firm evidence of on-site habitation in the basin.[76]

A brief historical survey of the Iron II and III Ages shows that in the tenth century Megiddo was partially rebuilt (by Solomon?) and the land of Palestine enjoyed an interlude of relative peace. At Solomon's death the empire broke into two inimical parts—Judah to the south, and Israel (Ephraim) to the north. The ninth century witnessed frequent wars between the two kingdoms. Israel was far less stable than its southern neighbor, not surprising in view of the fact that the northern kingdom consisted of a multitude of tribes vying for leadership, producing no less than nine dynasties between the tenth and the eighth centuries. On the other hand Judah knew only one dynasty – the House of David.

About 923 BCE the Egyptian pharoah Shishak invaded Palestine and sacked a number of cities, including Jerusalem and Megiddo. Megiddo was transformed into a garrison city for cavalry.

The ninth century witnessed the rise of Assyrian power, culminating in the conquest of the Northern Kingdom in 722 BCE. The deportation of a great many Israelites and an enforced population exchange followed, with many foreigners settling in Galilee and Samaria, thus laying the ethnic and cultural basis for the future Samaritan schism. We need not here discuss the illustrious and long line of literary and political prophets from Amos to Zechariah, prophets from the eighth to the sixth centuries who play such an important role in both the Jewish and Christian religions.

The end of settlement in the basin

The evidence from Nazareth comes to a definite end with Iron III. After that time no evidence is forthcoming from the basin for many centuries.[77] Iron III is a long period, lasting from 800 to 587 BCE, and many scholars consider that the period continued in the material (rather than historic) domain through the late sixth century. Within these three centuries, is it possible to pinpoint more precisely the end of habitation in the Nazareth basin?

Illus. 1.5 is of little use in this regard, for it tells us only that roughly ten artefacts date to Iron III. These are Bagatti's very general results, incorporated into Appendix 2, *Itemization of the Iron Age artefacts*. There is no published dating of the Iron III material from Nazareth that offers greater precision, but

---

[75] Barnavi 11.
[76] *Exc.* 44 and 73.
[77] See Chapters 2 and 3.

our view of habitation at Nazareth during the eighth to sixth centuries is aided by what we learn from settlement patterns in the surrounding area.

Zvi Gal has done the most work in this field. "It seems," he writes, "that the entire Galilee was abandoned after the Assyrian campaign of Tiglath-pileser III in 733–732 BCE."[78] This is consistent with the Biblical record that "he carried the people captive to Assyria" (2 Kgs 15:29). Gal pointedly notes: "We did not find any evidence of 7th century BCE pottery in any of the Lower Galilee sites which we surveyed... We conclude, then, that the Lower Galilee was almost totally deserted during the 7th century BCE"[79] This important assessment certainly includes the area around Nazareth.

Mordechai Aviam also reviews what is known of Galilee during the Late Iron Age:

> After the conquest of the Galilee by the Assyrians in the eighth century BCE, the population of the Galilee declined. Some scholars have tried to prove extensive continuity in Jewish settlement in the Galilee during the entire period between 732 BCE and 103 BCE.[80]
>
> The archaeological evidence, however, indicates massive destruction and abandonment of almost all excavated sites... Archaeological surveys in the Galilee have not demonstrated almost any continuation of settlements between the eighth and fifth centuries BCE.
>
> The written sources present a clear picture of heavy destruction and extensive deportation of residents from the Galilee without any resettlement of new inhabitants...
>
> In summarizing the data from the Bible, the non-biblical sources and the archaeological finds, it is obvious that the Galilee almost completely lost its Israelite population.[81]

The older theory that there was "extensive continuity in Jewish settlement in the Galilee" from the Iron Age until Hasmonean times has now been discredited. One scholar comments:

> The findings of Zvi Gal's survey of Iron Age III sites (*i.e.*, seventh-sixth centuries BCE) challenge Albrecht Alt's contention, argued from the literary sources for the most part, that the Israelite population in the Galilee was relatively undisturbed throughout centuries, thus providing the framework for the incorporation of the region into the *ethnos ton Ioudaion* by the Hasmoneans in the second century BCE (Gal, 1992; Alt, 1953). Alt believed that Galilee had fared better in the first Assyrian onslaught in 732 BCE than Samaria did in 721, when the native population was replaced by people of

---

[78] "Galilee," in *OEANE*, p. 451.

[79] Gal 1988:62.

[80] Aviam cites: S. Klein, *Sepher HaYishuv*. Jerusalem, 1977 (Hebrew); Horsley 1996.

[81] Aviam 2004:41. *Cf.* also Freyne, "Archaeology," p. 133.

non-Israelite stock (2 Kgs. 14:29; 17:6,24). The absence from eighty-three surveyed sites in lower Galilee of four different pottery types, dated to that particular period on the basis of stratified digs at Hazor and Samaria, has convinced Gal that there was a major depopulation of the area in the century after the fall of Samaria.[82]

In light of the "massive destruction" attending the Assyrian conquest and the subsequent "extensive deportation of residents," one would expect that the Nazareth site was abandoned in late VIII BCE along with the other settlements in Lower Galilee.[83] In fact, this model is entirely consistent with the evidentiary profile from Nazareth that we shall now review.

The Iron Age evidence

This comes from several locations: (1) Two silos under the present Church of the Annunciation; (2) "Subterranean areas" under the nearby Church of St. Joseph; (3) A tomb 300 m southwest of the latter church. This tomb was studied by Ms. F. Vitto and will be referred to as the "Vitto" tomb; (4) A tomb (T. 75), about one-half kilometer from the Church of the Annunciation, which yielded no artefacts.

It should be mentioned that Tomb 1 may preserve a few items dating, at the very latest, to the Iron I period. This tomb is next to the modern Church of the Annunciation, a few meters from the southern edge of the old Byzantine wall.[84] Tomb 1 continued in use at least into XIII BCE. Yet, the three items from this tomb that may date to the Iron Age could have been produced as early as LB IIA (fourteenth century). The objects in question are three similar bowls with a carination just below the rim.[85] Amiran states: "This type of Late Bronze bowl has been found up to the present only in excavations in the south of the country. In the Iron I, at least as far as form is concerned, the type also appears to have spread to the north of the country."[86] These bowls require closer examination to more precisely establish their dating.

(1) *Silos 22 & 57.* Silos are frequently found dating to Iron I in Palestine, but were rare both before and after that period. Finkelstein writes that "A proliferation of silos generally characterizes groups in the process of

---

[82] S. Freyne, "Galilee" in *OEANE* p. 371. The depopulation of Galilee continues to be questioned by some scholars. See Chancey 32–34; Horsley 1995:26–27.

[83] Aviam is of the opinion that "Jewish survivors gradually concentrated in the western part of Lower Galilee" (Aviam 2004:42).

[84] *Exc.* endplate.

[85] See *Exc.* fig. 210:23, 25, 26.

[86] *APHL* 129. Amiran's Plate 39:14 depicts a bowl of similar design, with a ring base (*cf. Exc.* 210:23).

sedentarization of societies organized in local rural frameworks."[87] The former of these possibilities supports the model of a new group entering the Nazareth basin in Iron I.

The purpose of silos was agricultural, to store grain (either wheat or barley). When plastered for the storage of liquids they are called cisterns. In ancient times such underground cavities were rarely located under dwellings, but often at the edge of a village or between houses. Thus they were primarily communal (perhaps shared by several households) rather than private.

The two silos 22 and 57[88] contained pottery from the Iron period. Silo 22 is under the Church of the Annunciation, while Silo 57 is a few meters to its north. These two pits were sealed by dirt at the end of the Iron Age, thus establishing their use in that era.

(2) *Under the Church of St. Joseph.* 28 shards from the Iron Age were recovered on the site of the present Church of St. Joseph. Material from Roman, Byzantine, and Medieval times was also discovered there. These finds are diagrammed and discussed by Bagatti in his article, "Scavo presso la Chiesa di S. Giuseppe a Nazaret."[89] For the dating of the Iron Age material, the archaeologist relies on typological comparisons with examples from Amiran's *Ancient Pottery of the Holy Land.* The Iron Age finds from the Church of St. Joseph date mainly to Iron IIB-C (900–587 BCE), with a few that may possibly belong to Iron IIA.[90]

(3) *The Vitto Tomb.* In 1973 a shaft tomb was discovered during the construction of a house, located approximately 300 m southwest of the Church of the Annunciation.[91] It is one of two tombs dating to the Iron Age which have been discovered in the Nazareth basin. A study of this tomb and its finds was published by Fanny Vitto in 2001.[92] Unlike Tomb 75 (discussed below), this one was not robbed in antiquity. However, perhaps owing to considerable damage by a bulldozer at the time of discovery, the finds were relatively scarce. All seven dated pottery artefacts from the tomb were attributed by

---

[87] Finkelstein 1988:266.

[88] This series follows the numbering system of Bagatti's 1969 *Excavations in Nazareth.*

[89] Bagatti 1971a.:18–19.

[90] In a "Communication" in the *Revue Biblique* of 1971 (Bagatti 1971b) the archaeologist reviews finds from the CJ. He mentions the excavation of "subterranean [cavities] of the Iron *and Bronze Ages*" (emphasis added). The *Scavo* article, however, lacks discussion of any Bronze Age findings.

[91] Map ref. 178040/233975. Bagatti refers to this tomb as the one "built in the style of the Israelite period" (*i.e.*, Iron Age, *NEAEHL*, p. 1104).

[92] *'Atiqot* 2001, pp.160–169

the archaeologist to XI BCE (Iron IB). Other artefacts found include a scarab, beads, and bracelets. The scarab likewise dates to Iron IB.

The Loffreda assemblage. Father S. Loffreda studied sixteen Iron Age artefacts whose provenance was unknown to him. However, it can be concluded that these finds come from the Vitto tomb for several reasons: (a) They are from an Iron Age tomb discovered in the early 1970s during the construction of a house (as was the Vitto tomb). (b) The Vitto tomb "had been disturbed prior to the excavation." One locus was bereft of finds, yet "the cave did not seem to have been robbed in antiquity."[93] (c) Loffreda's material was redated by Vitto to XI BCE, the same century as the Vitto finds. These suggest that the artefacts in the Loffreda assemblage had been removed from the Vitto tomb at or shortly after the time of discovery.

The Loffreda material is now in Jerusalem. Father Loffreda published his results in an article which begins as follows:

> The Museum of the *Studium Biblicum Franciscanum della Flagellazione* in Jerusalem (Old City) received, some years ago, a collection of ceramics of the Iron Age. We know for sure only that the vessels came from Nazareth and that they were found during the construction of a new house, in a chamber tomb excavated in the rock. We also know that other objects were a part of this collection, but unfortunately no one at present can know the complete inventory…
>
> The collection received by the Museum is composed of sixteen clay vessels, one bone handle, and three metal bracelets. At the time of acquisition almost all the pottery had considerable incrustation owing to the humidity of the site. The breaks are almost all recent, and this suggests that the tomb was never robbed in antiquity…[94]

Loffreda dates the collection generally to Iron I which, according to his chronology, ranges from 1200–900 BCE.[95] Vitto reviewed the assemblage and redated it more precisely to XI BCE.[96]

(4) Tomb 75.[97] This bench tomb is located *ca.* 500 m northwest of the Franciscan convent at an elevation of almost 450 m, that is, about a five-minute walk from the crest of the hill. This is a large tomb with side chambers, benches, and a special repository for bones in the NW corner. Kopp, who visited the

---

[93] Vitto 159.

[94] *Liber Annuus* 1977:135-144. The citation is on pp. 135-36 (translation RS).

95 For Loffreda's dating conventions, see his p. 135. He writes: "Also the dating of these two vessels is the same as that of the other vessels from this tomb: the Iron I period" (Loffreda 141).

[96] Vitto 167.

[97] This tomb is Kopp's No. 11. Discussion: *Exc.* 244; Kopp 1938:200. Map: *Exc.* fig. 3, quadrant A3. Plan: *Exc.* fig. 182, top right, and Kopp 1938:200.

tomb, observed no less than six benches for bodies.[98] The tomb was damaged and yielded no artefacts, but its plan conforms to Bloch-Smith's Type 3 and Loffreda's Type RR (rectangular chamber with subsidiary chambers). The type "appeared in the tenth century BCE at sites occupied by Israelites."[99] Hachlili and Killebrew note that this type of rock-cut tomb usually served a large number of people.[100]

Summary of the Iron Age evidence

The tabulation of artefacts shown in *Illus. 1.5* demonstrates continuity of habitation in the Nazareth basin through the Iron Period, sometimes referred to as "Biblical times." Our discussion has shown that the twelfth century is poorly represented by finds at Nazareth, while the eleventh century is well-represented. Because no artefacts from Nazareth definitely date to the twelfth century BCE, we must consider the possibility that the basin was uninhabited at that time. The Iron Age material examined by Vitto, Loffreda, and Bagatti clearly points to the existence of a settlement in the eleventh century. Those people living in the basin after that time probably identified themselves as Israelites, and perhaps with the tribe of Zebulun. For the next three hundred years we also have evidence of habitation and/or of burial in the valley.

It is evident that the Iron Age settlement was of considerable size, even though we only know one tomb (T. 75) from this era. Yet that multi-chambered tomb served many people, and certainly more tombs were in the basin. Eighty-three datable Iron Age artefacts have been found and are itemized in *Appendix 2*. This is a considerable number, and it is likely that a good deal more material, together with structures, lies buried in the basin under the present houses of Nazareth. From the extant evidence we can conclude that the western slope of the basin, including the Franciscan property, was used as a necropolis through both the Bronze and Iron Ages. In the latter period the venerated sites were also used for agricultural purposes, witnessed by Silos 22 and 57.

Due to the sloping and rocky nature of the terrain it is unlikely that there were Iron Age dwellings in the area of the Franciscan property and that evidence of them has long since disappeared. More likely, however, is that the inhabitants lived on the valley floor and used the slope for funerary and agricultural use.[101]

---

[98] Kopp 1938:200.

[99] Bloch-Smith 44. See her Fig. 10 and discussion pp. 41–53.

[100] Hachlili and Killebrew 1983:126. The bench-type tomb continued for many centuries, yielding an "Intermediate" type in the Persian period. *Cf.* Stern in *CHJ* I:93; Finegan 184.

[101] This question is considered in detail in Chapter. 5.

Combining historical data, the evidence from the ground, together with that from surveys of Southern Galilee, it is probable that a new group of people entered the Nazareth basin about 1100 BCE, and that they continued to live there for about four centuries. Habitation in the basin ended within a generation or two of the Assyrian conquest. This model of Nazareth chronology is consistent with the evidentiary profile, and with the assessment of Gal and Aviam, noted above, that Lower Galilee was almost totally deserted during the seventh century BCE.

Excursus: *The Bronze Age location of Japhia*

It was noted above that the most ready access to the Nazareth basin is from the southwest, where the village of Japhia (Yafa, Yaphia) was located in the time of Jesus. This site has been variously measured from one to two miles from Nazareth (1.6 to 3.3 km), depending on the point in Nazareth from which one measures. Modern Nazareth is so much larger than in antiquity that it is now contiguous with the village of Japhia.

The first-century historian and general Josephus wrote that Japhia was the "largest village in Galilee." He strengthened its walls in 66 CE and himself resided there for a time. When the Roman general Trajan besieged the town during the first Jewish War (in the summer of 67), Japhia had a double wall and put up stiff resistance. According to Josephus (admittedly known to exaggerate) 15,000 inhabitants were slain and 2,130 sold as slaves.[102]

Roman Japhia has been located with certainty, and the principal excavations there have uncovered a synagogue of III-IV CE.[103] There was also, however, a much older town known in Jewish scripture as 'Iaphia'(יָפִיעַ Josh 19:12). This is apparently the 'Iapu' mentioned in the Egyptian Amarna letters (XIV BCE). If this literary association is correct, then the settlement had some international significance in the Late Bronze Age, which in turn indicates that it was a town of significant size.

The location of the Biblical town of Iaphia/Yapu is unknown. It was certainly not at the site of Roman Japhia, for no Bronze-Iron age structures or artefacts have been found in the excavations there. Towns sometimes drifted, however, moving one or even more kilometers over time. This typically occurred in three cases: (a) the center of population gradually moved over a period of generations or centuries; (b) after a sudden dislocation (as after destruction by man or earthquake) the town was rebuilt nearby; or (c) after a dislocation or destruction the settlement was left vacant for a period of time, and only later (perhaps centuries later) rebuilt in the general vicinity.

---

[102] Josephus, *Vita* 45, 52; *Wars* 2.20.6; 3.7.31.
[103] Map reference 1763.2326. See D. Barag, "Japhia" in *NEAEHL*.

Some settlements are known to have moved over time. For example, modern Jericho is at some remove from the site of Kenyon's excavations, and present-day Cana in Galilee is almost a mile from the site of the putative ancient town. Settlements often enough changed position from century to century, as inhabitants came and left, as orchards were planted, as the environment changed, and for other reasons.

At least one scholar has argued that the Bronze-Iron Age town of Japhia was 6 km northeast of Nazareth, at the site now known as Mashhad (Mishad, el-Mecheh—see *Illus. 1.2*).[104] According to this theory, Japhia moved to the Roman location (3 km SW of Nazareth) over the course of a millennium. This is improbable, however, not only because of the great distance involved (9 km), but also because Mashhad and Roman Japhia are on different sides of the Nazareth divide, the East-West crest of hills that is quite pronounced in this area.

From the results of this chapter, a new possibility can now be considered. Closer to Roman Japhia, in fact only three kilometers away and on the same side of the ridge, are the Bronze-Iron Age remains of the settlement we have been calling "Nazareth." Though only a small area of the basin has been excavated, it is enough to show that a substantial settlement was there in Bronze-Iron Age times. Five Bronze Age tombs (not an insignificant number) yielding approximately a hundred itemized artefacts have come to light. The four tombs close to one another on the Franciscan property constituted a Bronze Age necropolis, and must have served a town of considerable size. Approximately three-quarters of a kilometer away is Tomb 81 (*Illus. 1.3*). This dispersion suggests that at least during the MB IIA (when Tomb 81 was in use) the settlement was of substantial size.

Such dispersion is equally evident in the Iron Age. Two extant tombs from that period (the Vitto tomb and Tomb 75) are separated by 700 m.[105] Tomb 75 had an elaborate plan and was a type that served many people. Thus, both the type of structural finds and their locations suggest a sizable settlement in the Bronze and Iron Ages, not merely a hamlet of a few people. That settlement might well have been biblical Japhia. The town was important enough to be mentioned in the Bible and Amarna letters, and sufficiently populous to supply a corvee of labor to the Pharaoh. If our suggestion is correct, then much

---

[104] Robert Boling, *Joshua*. Doubleday: Garden City, N.Y., 1982, p. 445.

[105] Under the CJ is probably also a single-chambered Iron Age tomb (Bagatti 1971: "a" in figs. 3–4). We cannot include a distant Iron Age tomb excavated by Y. Alexandre in 1998 (Alexandre 2003) in our calculus. This tomb is 4.3 km NE from the Church of the Annunciation (as the crow flies), well over the crest of the hill and in the area of Har Yona. It certainly was outside the ambit of the Nazareth settlement. Two later tombs from the Roman period, 2.3 and 2.6 km from the Franciscan property, are also doubtful in this regard. They will be considered in Chapter Five.

Bronze and Iron Age evidence of ancient Japhia, probably including more tombs, once existed in the Nazareth basin. Due to the presence of modern buildings much of the basin has, in fact, never been excavated. Unfortunately, again due to those same buildings, much of the ancient evidence has probably been permanently destroyed.

Thus, it is possible that the Bronze and Iron Age evidence discussed in Bagatti's *Excavations* and in other scholarly literature in fact describes biblical Japhia. This possibility is magnified when we consider (in Chapters Two and Three) that there was no habitation in the Nazareth basin between the Iron Age and Middle Roman times. After the dislocations brought on by the Assyrian invasions in the late eighth century, the settlement of Japhia may have moved three kilometers to the southwest, from the higher valley (the Nazareth basin) to the lower. By late antiquity, Japhia was located where its known Roman ruins have been excavated. Those ruins mark the town that the Jewish general Josephus fortified and defended in I CE.

Chapter Two

The Myth of Continuous Habitation

The Great Hiatus: Part I
(732–332 BCE)

The Myth of Continuous Habitation

The Assyrian, Babylonian, and Persian Periods

Chronology 732–332 BCE

732–612 Assyrian period

732   Megiddo is destroyed in the first campaign of Assyrian King Tiglath-Pileser III

722–21 Shalmaneser and then Sargon II of Assyria conquer the Northern Kingdom of Israel and deport its leading citizens; foreigners are settled in Samaria

701   Assyria invades Judah, which resumes paying tribute

689   Assyria utterly destroys the city of Babylon

621   "Book of the Law" found in the Jerusalem Temple; King Josiah institutes religious reforms

612–539 Babylonian period
(Babylonian captivity; Zoroaster; Pythagoras; Lao Tzu; Confucius; Buddha)

612   Assyria is defeated by the Babylonians and Medes

597   Jerusalem conquered by Babylonia; 10,000 led into exile

587   Jerusalem rebels, is besieged and destroyed by the Babylonians; mass deportations; end of 1st Temple Period

587–39 Babylonian captivity

539–332 Persian Period

539–38 Persia conquers Babylonia; Edict of Cyrus allows the Jews to return and rebuild the Temple

515   Second Jerusalem Temple is inaugurated (Ezra 3:10–13)

5th cent. Ezra and Nehemiah arrive from Babylon; last prophetic books; "canonization" of the Hebrew Bible; ongoing confrontation between Persia and Greece

c. 480 Destruction of many towns in Palestine (reason unclear) 4th cent. Building of rival Samaritan Temple on Mt. Gerizim

c. 380 Destruction of many settlements along coast and in Negeb

332   Conquest of Palestine by Alexander the Great

The end of habitation in the Nazareth basin

The armies of Tiglath-Pileser III swept through the Galilee about the year 732, and many inhabitants of the Northern Kingdom were taken into exile and replaced with people from other conquered lands (2 Kg 15:29). Some years later Shalmaneser V invaded Samaria, and finally Sargon II completed the

Assyrian conquest of the Northern Kingdom. By his own records he deported 27,290 inhabitants (2 Kg 16:6). Initially, Aramaeans from the conquered town of Hamath were settled in their place, then inhabitants from defeated Cutha and from Babylon. The contemporary prophet Isaiah lamented: "He has humbled the land of Zebulon and the land of Naphtali," and the region earned the epithet "Galilee of the Gentiles" (Isa 9:1). We recall the words of Zvi Gal quoted at the end of Chapter One: "It seems that the entire Galilee was abandoned after the Assyrian campaign of Tiglath-Pileser III in 733–732 BCE,"[1] and "Lower Galilee was practically deserted by the end of the eighth century."[2] M. Chancey offers the following particulars regarding the general destruction in Galilee associated with the Assyrian conquests:

> Excavations have corroborated the surface surveys. Tel Mador yields evidence of occupation from the tenth and ninth centuries BCE and from the Persian period but only one sherd from the eighth century BCE. Excavations at Tel Qarnei Hittin have demonstrated that a sizable city was destroyed in the late eighth century BCE, with no subsequent occupation. The settlement at Hurbat Rosh Zayit, probably a Phoenician community, was likewise destroyed in the mid-eighth century BCE, with no resettlement afterwards. Excavations at Hurrat H. Malta, Tel Gath-Hepher, Hazor, Kinneret and Tel Harashim have revealed dramatic decreases in population after the eighth century BCE. The implication is that not only did the indigenous population leave Galilee, but the Assyrians did not repopulate it.[3]

The physical record in the Nazareth basin also comes to an end in the Late Iron Age (800–587 BCE).[4] Unfortunately, the published archaeological record alone does not permit a more precise dating. We can affirm, in any case, that no evidence at Nazareth has been dated *with certainty* to the years following the Assyrian conquest of 732.[5] The ten artefacts that have been clearly dated to Iron III may well come from the generations before the Assyrian conquest.[6] The archaeological record of the region, as seen in the above citation and in the conclusions of Zvi Gal, makes it unlikely that the settlement continued into the seventh century. Thus, 732 BCE is a *terminus a quo* for the beginning of a long hiatus in the Nazareth basin. I call it the Great Hiatus (or simply the hiatus), a multi-century gap in evidence of human habitation.

The Babylonian and Persian periods are entirely unattested by evidence in the Nazareth basin. Even the Church itself nowhere claims finds from the

---

[1] "Galilee," OEANE, p. 451; Chp. 1:31.

[2] Gal 1998:52.

[3] Chancey:33.

[4] See Chp. 1:35.

[5] See Chp. 1:*Illus.5*. For the Iron Age evidence see *Exc.* 211:24-25; 214:2; *Scavo* 1–6, 17, 21; Chp. 1:26–38 and Appendix 2.

[6] See Chp. 1:*Illus.5*.

sixth, fifth, and fourth centuries. We shall see that this is odd in view of the fact that the Church maintains the doctrine of continuous habitation, that is, that there has been continuous human habitation in the basin since the Iron Age (see below). Despite this overarching claim, the years 600–300 BCE are "empty centuries," quite ignored in the literature. For example, in his 325-page *Excavations in Nazareth*, Bagatti jumps directly from the Iron to the Hellenistic Period (p. 272), simply skipping the intervening centuries without further ado. He is not the only one to do so. In vain do we scour the literature for any mention of Babylonian and Persian evidence at all. Not a single artefact, much less construction (tomb or wall foundation) dates to those eras. At Nazareth, the years 612–332 BCE are entirely mute.

I have suggested the identification of the Bronze-Iron settlement of "Nazareth" with biblical Japhia.[7] The historical and archaeological data reinforce this identification, for it is altogether probable that Japhia—being a significant town in northern Palestine—was destroyed by the Assyrians, along with Megiddo, in Tiglath-Pileser's campaign of 732 BCE. Perhaps the town survived another decade before meeting destruction in the second wave of conquest under Shalmaneser and Sargon. When eventually rebuilt, Japhia was no longer located in the Nazareth basin but three kilometers to the southwest. We cannot be certain when that rebuilding took place, for to my knowledge no excavations at Japhia have established this fact. This is not surprising, for little evidence from the Galilee survives from the seventh–sixth centuries:

> We have no solid archaeological evidence for events in the abandoned territories of the Galilee. Many sites have been dated to the fifth and fourth centuries BCE, but none could be clearly dated to the seventh and sixth centuries BCE.[8]

The Great Hiatus extended at least until the end of the Persian period, that is, a minimum of four hundred years (732–332 BCE). How much longer it continued will be determined in subsequent chapters..

The Babylonian period

In 612 a Medean-Babylonian coalition, taking advantage of a fortuitous civil war in Assyria, invaded the land and destroyed Kalakh (Nimrud), Nineveh, and other places. They exacted a terrible revenge on the hated Assyrians, and partitioned the land. The Babylonian Nebuchadnezzar, carefully trained by his father for kingship, proved a redoubtable general. Though he ultimately failed in attempts to conquer Egypt, he crushed the Egyptian armies on more than one occasion and was continually campaigning in the Levant.

---

[7] Chp. 1:36–38.

[8] Aviam 2004:42.

THE MYTH OF NAZARETH

The Babylonian period in Palestine was relatively brief but traumatic. On one of his many campaigns Nebuchadnezzar took Jerusalem (in 597) and deported 3,000 of its leading citizens, installing Zedckiah as puppet king. According to the biblical account, Judah rebelled in 589. Nebuchadnezzar returned, laid Jerusalem to an 18-month siege, and then completely destroyed the city. A second, and larger, contingent of Jews was exiled, and Palestine was made a province of the Babylonian empire. A third deportation occurred in 582.

Nebuchadnezzar levied heavy taxes, and Babylon (which had been impoverished under the Assyrians) became the largest city in the known world and fabulously wealthy. Hundreds of thousands of laborers graced it with a moat, multiple city walls (one 30 m high) and terraced gardens. Temples were also built, one being the Tower of Babel. The latter's base measured 91 m (about 300 ft.) per side, the Tower reaching exactly the same height – double the height of other temples.

Nabonidus, from Haran and a devotee of the moon-god Sin, ruled Babylon from 555–539. The powerful Babylonian priests of Marduk, newly delegitimized, looked to Cyrus the Persian for aid, and promised the latter the surrender of the city in return for their ancient privileges. In 539 Cyrus attacked northern Babylonia with a large army, defeated Nabonidus, and entered the city of Babylon without a battle.

Of Achaemenid lineage, Cyrus immediately issued his famous edict allowing the Jews to return to their homeland. Many chose not to, and with that decision began an enduring Jewish presence in the Land of the Two Rivers. Judaism would be bi-polar for many centuries, culminating in the compilation of the two great Talmuds, Palestinian and Babylonian, in Roman-Byzantine times.

The Persian period

The Persian era in Palestine witnessed several waves of destruction, beginning with the initial conquest (539-38) by Cyrus, whose destruction was evidently limited to the Judean hills. The son of Cyrus, Cambyses II, succeeded where his father had failed and conquered Egypt in 525. The Pharaoh was carried off in captivity to Susa and Cambyses proclaimed himself Pharaoh. Darius I (r. 522–486) extended Persian dominions from India to Carthage.

In general, the Persians tolerated religious expression and managed the conquered territories with a light hand. In 516 construction of the Second Jerusalem temple was completed, and sacrifice reinstituted. Incidentally, the Persians employed Jewish mercenaries to garrison Elephantine, on the remote southern border of Egypt. The Hebrews there built their own temple, celebrated Passover and also offered sacrifice, a practice distasteful to the Egyptians and not sanctioned by Jerusalem. In 410 the priests of the local god Khnum incited a riot and the Elephantine temple was destroyed (Judea refused aid). It was rebuilt a few years later with the proviso that animal sacrifice would be discontinued. (Schiffman:42).

A wave of destruction occurred about 480 BCE when many sites in Palestine were leveled due to some unknown cause, perhaps local warfare. A wave of destruction also occurred one hundred years later, and was connected with the Egyptian struggle for independence. "Palestine," writes Ephraim Stern, "was a battleground throughout the fourth century."[9]

Egypt revolted in 405, and to all intents and purposes was independent from that time forward. Persia had become increasingly embroiled in warfare with Greece, and was experiencing a slow decline at home. Opulence, corruption, court intrigues, and regicide were the order of the day, and the Persian hold on the provinces weakened. The fact that 10,000 Greek mercenaries, hired in an unsuccessful revolt, could escape from Mesopotamia in 401 (the famous march recorded by Xenophon in his *Anabasis*) illustrates the essential internal weakness of the Achaemenid Empire.

In the Persian period the Samaritan schism widened, and in the waning years of that period a temple was built on Mt. Gerizim. Samaria was governed by the powerful Sanballats who, together with the Tobiads (rulers of the province of Ammon on the eastern side of the Jordan), constituted a formidable league opposing Jerusalem hegemony.

The material culture of Palestine in Persian times was divided sharply between a coastal Greek-oriented culture and an inland, Eastern-oriented culture. Galilee, of course, belonged to the latter. The period was one of invention, expansion, and building activity. Cement was used for the first time, and new advances were made in cistern and pool construction.[10] Pottery, metal objects, alabaster, faïence, arrowheads, coins (common from the end of the fifth century), statuettes and figurines, seals and seal impressions – all these are attested in Palestinian settlements of the Persian era. None, however, have been found in the Nazareth basin, though numerous settlements of the Persian Period have been discovered in Northern Palestine. As of 1992, Stern counted thirty-one settlements in Galilee and the coastal plain, and additional contemporaneous settlements have since come to light. In the Nazareth region, the closest Persian evidence appears to be a tomb 3.8 km northwest of the CA, near Ailut (Elut) and quite outside the basin.[11] It was excavated in 2005 by Yardenna Alexandre, who writes: "No other caves or settlements from this period have yet been discovered in the immediate vicinity."[12]

---

[9]   Stern 1982:91 and Stern in ABD v. 5:116.

[10]   Stern 1982:91, 93, 110.

[11]   Alexandre 2005. For Ailut, see Chp. 1:*Illus 2*. The tomb is located at map ref. NIG 2247/7356; OIG 1747/2356.

[12]   A cist tomb possibly dating to the Persian period was excavated in Horvat Devora (Dabburiya), 7.2 km east of the CA. See *Hadashot Arkheologiyot* 117 (report date

THE MYTH OF NAZARETH

The Question of Continuous Habitation

The early archaeologists

As late as the 1930s, few people were aware of pre-Christian evidence from the Nazareth basin. Excavating between 1892 and 1909, Fathers Vlaminck and Viaud either did not know that some of the Nazareth material dates to the Bronze and Iron Ages, or they failed to write about it. In his book *Nazareth et Ses Deux Églises* (1910) Père Viaud does not mention pre-Christian times. In fact, he does not discuss pottery or movable finds at all, but contents himself with a discussion of the structural remains of the various Christian edifices, and with pilgrims' accounts. Incidentally, Viaud did not ascertain any masonry evidence before the fourth century CE – a verdict that still obtains today.

In 1935 Henri Leclercq penned a 17-page article on Nazareth which hardly goes beyond Viaud's book and similarly makes no mention of the Bronze or Iron Ages.[13] The older school of Nazareth archaeology, represented by Vlaminck, Viaud, and Leclercq, was exclusively focused on the common era. The pre-Christian history of the site was incidental, if mentioned at all. But Leclercq notes with emergent awareness the unsatisfactoriness of the data: "il semble difficile d'accorder un assentiment sans réserve," he writes in one place. He also chides the imprecise and arbitrary conclusions that were being proffered at the time, most especially regarding the early Christian history of the site, noting "une sorte de vague tradition," and "Nous hésitons, pour notre part, à croire possible une méthode tellement arbitraire et qui consiste à appliquer à Nazareth l'argumentation qui précède."

Already in the 1920s observations were beginning to circulate regarding the existence of Bronze-Iron Age tombs and pottery at Nazareth. This brought a changed focus to the place. The first reaction was to suppose that Nazareth was a very ancient settlement indeed, one with a long and continuous history. However, this view immediately confronted what had been known for a long time: Nazareth is not mentioned in Jewish scripture, nor in the writings of the first century Jewish general Josephus, nor in the Talmud of later times. How, then, was it possible for the town to exist and yet to evade mention for so many centuries?

The convenient riposte, and one which is still prevalent today, is that Nazareth was small and unimportant – too small to be mentioned in the Bible and in later writings. In this connection, the settlement's removed location also comes into play, as mentioned by Leclercq at the beginning of his 1935 article:

6/11/2005, signed by D. Syon).

[13] *DACL* cols. 1021–1054.

64

The Myth of Continuous Habitation

Nazareth is located at some distance from the great roads, though one can reach it easily, and this situation explains the absence of all mention of this hamlet in the Old Testament, as well as in the historical writings of Flavius Josephus.[14]

This opinion assumes that Nazareth existed in biblical times, for otherwise Leclercq would not need to explain why it is not mentioned in the "Old Testament."

Father Clemens Kopp and the new evidence

In 1930, the Franciscan cloister between the Church of the Annunciation and that of St. Joseph was torn down and a new one was constructed. The opportunity was taken to conduct excavations in the area separating the two churches, about 100 m in length and 50 m in breadth. The following year, R. Tonneau wrote an article in which he registered an amazing fact: no evidence of either Greek or Roman settlement had been found in the excavations.[15]

Together with the emerging Bronze-Iron Age evidence, this disturbing new information required reconciliation with tradition, as well as explanation. Between 1938 and 1948 a Jesuit priest, Fr. Clemens Kopp, published a series of articles on the history and archaeology of Nazareth. These appeared in four issues of the *Journal of the Palestine Oriental Society*, all under the title *Beiträge zur Geschichte Nazareths* ("Contributions to the History of Nazareth").[16] In these articles, which total over one hundred pages of text, the author comprehensively reviews the Nazareth evidence known up to his time and attempts to place it in a light acceptable to the Catholic Church.

Fr. Kopp had a keen interest in Palestine archaeology and an engaging literary style, though he himself was not a trained archaeologist but had studied medieval philosophy.[17] Besides a number of scholarly articles, he eventually authored a book that attained wide circulation, *The Holy Places of the Gospels* (1963).[18]

In the first article of his *Beiträge* (1938), Kopp immediately deals with the two novel issues mentioned above: (a) the existence of Bronze-Iron Age artefacts; and (b) the lack of evidence for a settlement in the time of Jesus. He writes:

The observations of R. Tonneau, who also visited the excavations, are very important but unfortunately too short and made in passing. He sees in the

---

[14] *DACL* cols. 1021-22.

[15] *Revue Biblique* XL (1931), p. 556.

[16] See the Bibliography for volume and page numbers.

[17] Kopp's doctoral dissertation is entitled "Die 'Fallaciae ad modum Oxoniae': Ein Fehlschlusstraktat aus dem 13. Jahrhundert" (publ. 1985).

[18] German edition: *Die heiligen Stätten der Evangelien* (1959).

THE MYTH OF NAZARETH

Franciscan zone "the location of the original settlement. The hill is thoroughly honeycombed with artificially worked caves, the remains of a meager hamlet of peasants. It revealed no trace of a Greek or Roman settlement, no remnant of this pagan civilization."[19] It seems, accordingly, that as early as about 2000 BCE the inhabitants sought out a place for themselves on the valley floor, one which better met their increased needs. This wish was awakened in them when they took up house building. In this period they evidently converted a part of the old cave-dwellings into storage for grain (silos). I have been told that during construction the foundations of the cloister began to sag because no less than 68 silos were counted and filled with cement.[20]

This citation contains a series of conclusions which are hardly compatible with the evidence in the ground. Kopp proposes that the village began about 3000 BCE and was characterized by cave-dwelling.[21] As we have seen in Chapter One, he is a thousand years too early. In addition, the inhabitants could not have lived in caves. This is possibly the first mention of a recurring myth in the Nazareth literature, that the early residents were troglodytes.[22] The caves of Galilee "are wet or damp from December to May, and can only be used during the summer and autumn," writes M. Aviam.[23] No humans inhabited the Nazareth caves, at least on any significant scale during historical times. The plethora of "artificially worked caves" and silos in the venerated area that Kopp so heartily acknowledges were for agricultural use, not domestic. Again, they date to Middle Roman times, not Middle Bronze times. Finally, the village could not have "moved" c. 2000 BCE, for it was only then beginning. These errors are hardly slight, and they continue to be postulated even to the present day. The basic fault—if we can extract one common denominator from the above assortment of errors—is a characteristic looseness with chronology. Only a cavalier approach to dates and a spurning of precision would permit Kopp's scenario, which is a veritable chronological mish-mash.[24] The village begins too early by a millennium, moves when it is only beginning, Middle Roman evidence becomes Middle Bronze evidence, people live in caves, agricultural evidence becomes domestic evidence—all these elements produce a confused tale with little foundation in fact. It is a transparent attempt to deal with the new Bronze-Iron evidence in a way fully compatible with Church doctrine. This *modus operandi*, unfortunately, is not unusual in the scholarly Nazareth literature. It exemplifies the scientific difficulties into which the tradition can fall when ruled purely by doctrinal considerations.

---

[19] Kopp quotes from the *Revue Biblique* (see n. 15 above).

[20] Kopp 1938:188–89.

[21] Kopp 1938:189.

[22] See, e.g., Crossan and Reed 2002:34–35.

[23] Aviam 2004:90.

[24] See below p. 77f for similar confusion in B. Bagatti's chronology and discussion.

The Myth of Continuous Habitation

An ominous shadow lurks in the backround, one which I can best describe as an absolute rejection of accountability. It is as if Kopp knows that he can write anything he wishes, with complete disregard for the empirical facts in the ground—as long as he conforms to Church dogma. For anyone who deals with empirical fact, this is a chilling attitude. It is unscientific, and antiscientific. The result, in this particular case, is a complete muddling of data—the village begins too early by a millennium; it moves when it is in fact only beginning; Middle Roman evidence becomes Middle Bronze evidence; people live in caves; agricultural evidence becomes domestic evidence... Thus, the Church produces a confused tale with hardly any foundation in fact. It is a transparent attempt to deal with the new Bronze-Iron evidence in a way fully compatible with dogma. Unfortunately, this state of affairs is not unusual in the scholarly Nazareth literature. It exemplifies the scientific difficulties into which the tradition falls when ruled purely by doctrinal considerations.

Kopp was especially aware of the disturbing implications of point (b) mentioned earlier, namely, the lack of evidence at the venerated sites dating to the eras immediately before and during the time of Christ. The priest rejected the most obvious explanation—that no habitations existed at Nazareth during those centuries. He preferred a complex scheme by which the settlement moved not merely once, but twice (see below). Like subsequent Catholic archaeologists, Kopp insists upon interpreting the hollows in the venerated area as domestic simply because that is where Joseph and Mary were supposed to have lived. Similarly, he calls the Nazarenes "troglodytes," because he saw that the venerated area is characterized by caves and by all sorts of hollows in and under the ground.

It is important that we understand the dynamics of Kopp's argument, for they repeat over and over in the Nazareth literature. The typical scenario is wide of the mark not primarily because the evidence is erroneous, but because the logic is not based on evidence at all. Let us consider another example. Kopp postulates the movement of Nazareth from the venerated sites on the hillside (area A) to the valley floor (area B). Empirically, such a movement can be affirmed only if chronologically-fixed evidence from both areas A and B is forthcoming. That should be obvious. There must be earlier settlement in area A (not just agricultural or funereal use, but habitations). Then, there must be evidence for the cessation of settlement in area A. Finally, there needs to be evidence for the later appearance of settlement in nearby area B. If any of these three steps is lacking, then no conclusion regarding the movement of a settlement can be made. In the case of Nazareth, we have not a single one of these three essentials. The Bronze-Iron Age evidence from the hillside does not betray settlement there at all, but agricultural and funerary use. It is therefore clear that *the settlement was always on the valley floor*, where we should expect it—the valley floor is flat and amenable to habitations. That is the only possible conclusion from the evidence unearthed to date.

THE MYTH OF NAZARETH

In this connection, we may look at the case of Japhia which, as we have seen, impinges on the history of Nazareth. Its Roman ruins are three kilometers southwest of the venerated sites of Nazareth. But archaeologists found no Bronze-Iron Age evidence there, though they knew that such a town existed somewhere in the vicinity, for Japhia is mentioned in Jewish scripture. On the other hand, there are demonstrable Bronze-Iron Age remains from the Nazareth basin. Though these are not domestic remains, their termination in the Iron Age shows that the settlement came to an end at that time. In addition, there is no mention of "Nazareth" in the Bible or anywhere else in pre-Christian records. By viewing Japhia and Nazareth synoptically, we are able to satisfy all the evidence, both archaeological and literary. Japhia moved from A to B (from the Nazareth basin to the Roman site) precisely because the evidence in the ground moved from A to B. Finally, that move is also corroborated by the literary record.[25]

Kopp's logic is very different, and begins with scripture:

(1) the inerrancy of scripture demands that Nazareth existed in the time of Jesus;

(2) however, no sign of Greek or Roman Nazareth was found in the Franciscan excavations;

(3) Nazareth must, therefore, have existed *somewhere else*.

The conclusion answers to Church doctrine, which is also the *point de départ* of the argument. Because the logic is not based on evidence in the ground but on scripture, it leads to absurd scenarios whose implications are grotesque. Such doctrine-friendly logic is characteristic not only of Kopp's several articles, but also of the bulk of the Nazareth literature. The scholars who have written on the site have not so much attempted to explain evidence as would a scientist, but have attempted something very different: to vindicate dogma, and to justify scripture. The dominant logic is circular, for its beginning and endpoint are the same: Church belief. In this dogmatic loop evidence is often irritating, at worst alarming, and always irrelevant.

Kopp's hypothesis that Nazareth was at some point in time on the valley floor is an example of illogic fortuitously coming across the correct solution. No excavations have been conducted on the valley floor, but the inference from topography is clear: flat and amenable to habitations, it offers the only possible location in the Nazareth basin for an ancient settlement, while the steep and rocky slope of the Nebi Sa'in, pockmarked with hollows, presents an impossible venue. The fact that habitations and other domestic evidence have never been uncovered on the hillside confirms the obvious. It is clear that the settlement in all ancient periods was situated on the valley floor. At the same time, the evidence from archaeology shows use of the hillside for

---

[25] Chp. 1:36.

agricultural work (grain storage, cisterns, presses, *etc.*) and for tombs. Those were the ancient uses of the Franciscan venerated area. (The location of the ancient village is considered again in Chapter Five.)

In a circuitous way, Kopp's mobile Nazareth scenario explained why no Greek and Roman evidence was found at the venerated sites. But his solution presented a new problem. If the village had moved to the valley floor, as he proposed, then it became necessary to explain why the domiciles of Joseph and Mary were not also on the valley floor, but were on the hillside several hundred meters away.

Undaunted, Kopp proposed a Third Nazareth, one which "moved again towards the south," in the direction of the present Church of the Annunciation.[26] This was the village of Jesus, existing at the new location already some centuries before Christ. However, the unforgiving razor of reason followed the priest's every hypothesis, for his proposal is impossible whether he says aye or nay. If he maintained that the village was at the venerated sites, then he contradicted the newly-revealed evidence of Tonneau and others that no Greek or Roman settlement was there. On the other hand, if he maintained that the village was not at the venerated sites, then he contradicted Church doctrine that Mary and Joseph lived there.

Kopp apparently realizes this dilemma towards the middle of page 190 of his article, and he soon proposes a startling solution: the Nazarenes "loved to live apart." Evidently, the misanthropes were spread out all over the basin. The priest quotes a fourteenth century pilgrim: "The houses are scattered all about" (*domus ejus sunt hinc inde ab invicem dispersae*), and he cites a modern guidebook: "A characteristic of today's town is the isolation of many of the small houses in the outer neighborhoods."[27] Kopp concludes: "The assumption is thus permitted, that in Hellenistic and Roman times one or another house also existed on the southern slope, whose traces have since been obliterated by construction." Those scattered houses (no longer detectable) included the homes of Joseph and of the young Mary. The former was at the site of the present Church of St. Joseph, and the latter at the site of the Shrine of the Annunciation one hundred meters away.

Such was the Church's position at mid-century. The attempt to reconcile doctrinal exigency with the accumulating evidence in the ground, and the surprising lack thereof, led to a complex scenario involving three Nazareths, two moves, and houses "scattered all about." The palpably contrived mobile Nazareth hypothesis ultimately rests on the casual observations of a fourteenth-century pilgrim and of a modern guidebook. Grasping at straws, the tradition went as far as necessary to defend the doctrine of continuous habitation in the face of new archaeological evidence.

---

[26] Kopp 1938:190.

[27] F.J. Scrimgeour, *Nazareth of Today.* Edinburgh and London, 1913, p.1. Kopp 1938:191.

THE MYTH OF NAZARETH

The alternative was unthinkable. To admit the absence of Greek and Early Roman settlement on Franciscan property, plain already in 1931, was fatal to the traditional view of the venerated sites, namely, that Nazareth existed in the time of Jesus. As it had been with the discoveries of Galileo, Copernicus, Darwin, and many others, the Church now was again confronted with a not-so-new yet modern problem: *scientific evidence*.

A changing landscape

Kopp had been a pioneer, attempting a reassessment of Nazareth archaeology in the prewar years, one which sought to accommodate both the newly-emerging data and Church doctrine. But, though the German's intentions were thoroughly Catholic, the Church had difficulty with his work, which proved to be provisional, an aberration, and in the final analysis unacceptable. First of all, Kopp validated Tonneau's dangerous observation that the Franciscan property revealed no signs of settlement (read: *habitations*) at the time of Christ. This was deemed unacceptable. Furthermore, Kopp unwittingly observed that the entire hillside betrayed no signs of an older village.[28] This conflicted with the Church's desire to show that Roman Nazareth was located on the flank of the Nebi Sa'in, precisely where the houses of Joseph and Mary were venerated (see below). Perhaps most disturbing of all, Kopp's publications reviewed damaging evidence of a potentially explosive nature: tombs under the Sanctuary of the Annunciation. Those tombs would require explanation. All this was indeed unsettling.

The exponential growth in scientific knowledge in the twentieth century, particularly during and following the Second World War, had profound effects on all the sciences including archaeology. Vastly greater precision, knowledge, technical expertise, and improved hardware were now available and were creating a flood of new information. In the decades following the war, older views were being revisited, revoked, revised, and rewritten all over the land of Israel.

Besides the scientific revolution, a political one took place. Israel was now a sovereign Jewish state. For the first time in the modern era Jews were able to freely dig in their own beloved terrain, and they approached the task with the alacrity of a husband long away from his beloved. In 1948, as part of the establishment of the state of Israel, the Israel Department of Antiquities and Museums (IDAM) was founded.[29] IDAM continued the function of the former Department of Antiquities of the British Mandate Government, and now coordinated the work of academic entities such as the Israel Institute of Archaeology of the Hebrew University of Jerusalem (the oldest department of archaeology in the land, in existence since 1934). IDAM had a number of functions including curation and storing of the state collection of antiquities,

---

[28] Kopp 1938:190.
[29] The first director of IDAM (1948–1961) was Dr. Shmuel Yeivin.

maintaining a list of registered sites, inspecting newly discovered sites, conducting salvage and rescue operations of endangered sites, maintaining an archaeological library (the state library) and an archive, and publishing results of excavations in three journals: *Alon* of the Department of Antiquities (Hebrew) – now defunct; *'Atiqot* (Hebrew and English) – still published; and *Hadashot Arkheologiyot* (Hebrew and English) – still published, but only on the internet. IDAM also carried out the Archaeological Survey of Israel, and published the results of its work in maps each covering 10 km^2 of the State of Israel. The Israel Antiquities Authority (IAA) superceded IDAM in 1999.

For the first time, Jews were able to control the agenda, methodology, technique, funding, and personnel of archaeological digs taking place on public property. Excavations on non-public property (such as at the venerated sites in Nazareth) became subject to strict laws, regulations, and reporting standards, promulgated particularly in view to the rampant dealing in black market antiquities that has been a perennial problem in the Near East.

The dramatic elevation in archaeological standards after the war, the accumulating evidence in the ground at Nazareth, the conflicting theories regarding that evidence, and the Church's changing posture, were all forcing a new, and hopefully 'definitive' (as far as the Church was concerned) archaeological reassessment of the place. The fundamental problem with the prewar posture was that while Kopp's theories were complex, unverified, and perhaps unverifiable, he *accepted* the newer evidence, and went to endless lengths to accommodate it to Catholic doctrine. The Church, however, perceiving the increasingly hostile implications of the incoming data itself, recognized that the march of science constituted a juggernaut that would not, and could not, be halted. After the war, it adopted a defensive posture regarding the evidence at Nazareth, one essentially characterized by denial.

Father Bellarmino Bagatti

After mid-century, the Catholic Church decided to begin again, as it were. It would conduct a thorough re-excavation of the venerated area, preliminary to building a larger and more impressive monument on the site of the 1730 Church of the Annunciation. The new church would befit its status as a premiere destination of Christian pilgrimage, second only to the most holy sites in Jerusalem. Yet, before a costly and very visible monument to the maiden home of the Virgin Mother was erected, the Vatican desired archaeological validation on two basic counts: firstly, it needed to know that at the turn of the era dwellings did indeed exist in the venerated area. If this were true, then one of those dwellings could well have been that of the Blessed Virgin. Secondly, the Vatican needed validation that there was continuity in settlement at the site – before, during, and after the time of Jesus. Such continuity would prove the existence of an enduring village and would put to rest past 'rumors' concerning the site. Together, these two elements were sufficient to validate both the claims of the Church and of the gospel record, for on the one hand the tradition claims that Jesus' mother grew up at the site of the annunciation (and that the holy child was raised not far away); while on the other hand the gospel states that Jesus came from an already existing and viable town (Gk. *polis*) called Nazareth.

The task of directing the excavations at the venerated sites was given to the Italian priest and archaeologist Bellarmino Bagatti. He was assigned to carry out thorough excavations on behalf of the Custodia di Terra Santa, the body which oversees Roman Catholic properties in the Holy Land. Born in 1905, Father Bagatti entered the seminary of Saint Francis in Tuscany at the age of seventeen. Ordained into the Franciscan order six years later, in 1931 he matriculated to the Pontifical Institute of Christian Archaeology in Rome, where after three years he received the degree of Doctor of Christian Archaeology. In the mid-1930s he began teaching Christian Archaeology at the Studium Biblicum Francescanum (SBF) in Jerusalem, an institute devoted to "the research and academic teaching of sacred scripture and of the archaeology of bible lands."[30] In 1951 Bagatti co-founded the Franciscan journal *Liber Annuus*, in which a number of his subsequent articles appeared. He directed the SBF from 1968–78, that is, immediately following his work in Nazareth. In the course of a long and distinguished career in the Holy Land, Bagatti penned over twenty books and several hundred articles, and was a regular contributor to reference works on archaeological topics. He received a number of honors over the years for devotion both to his students and to his work. Fr. Bagatti passed away in 1990.[31]

To date, Bagatti has been the principal archaeologist at Nazareth. His two-volume work, *Excavations in Nazareth*, appeared in the late 1960s and is the unquestioned primary reference for the archaeology of the site. The Italian also penned a number of articles on Nazareth. Over the years, a number of his claims have been reviewed by other archaeologists and specialists. Those claims have on occasion been corrected and even rejected. Some of Bagatti's pottery datings have been revised, and some of his theories subjected to strident rebuttal by other scholars.

Bagatti published his first major articles regarding the Nazareth excavations in 1955 and 1960.[32] As we shall see in detail later, the Italian denied Kopp's scenario, particularly the hated thesis that the Franciscan property revealed no

---

[30] Per Institute public notice, 2003. We note the priority of "sacred scripture" to "archaeology."

[31] For a complete list of Fr. Bagatti's publications, see *Studia Hierosolymitana in onore del P. Bellarmino Bagatti. I. Studi Archeologici.* Jerusalem: Franciscan Printing Press, 1976, pp. 2–27.

[32] *Liber Annuus* 5 (1955):5–44 and Bagatti 1960.

signs of Greek or Roman habitations ("settlement") – a thesis which was the driving force behind Kopp's reassessment in the first place. More correctly, it is not a thesis but a fact, a fact that Kopp accommodated but which the Church now avoided. Thus, with Bagatti's work the Catholic Church fundamentally leaves the stage of rationalization and enters the stage of denial as regards the true history of Nazareth. Consequently, the history of Nazareth archaeology in the last fifty years is largely a history of obfuscation. This has been abetted by the facts that the Roman Catholic Church owns the properties on which the major excavations have taken place, and has rigorously controlled both the personnel conducting the excavations and the primary publications issuing from those excavations. It is in this light that we must, in turn, adopt a suspicious posture regarding those publications. We cannot merely accept their conclusions at face value, but must continually and methodically refer back to verifiable evidence from the ground.[33] In a sense, we must reconstruct the history of the site from corrupt reports. The ultimate criterion of what is and what is not corrupt, once again, is the verifiable evidence from the ground.

As has been intimated, the work of one archaeologist is not the central issue. So much of the Church's position as regards Nazareth is problematic that we must ever bear in mind the larger clash between faith and fact. The words "Christian Archaeology" perfectly encapsulate that clash. "Archaeology" is the science of determining what (relative to human history) lies in the ground. "Christian" is the dogma concerning a particular god and His Only-Begotten Son, Jesus Christ. Science seeks to determine what is fact, but dogma *already knows* fact – namely, what is important to salvation. The one seeks to discover what it does not know, and the other seeks to prove what it already knows (or claims to know). Between science and dogma resides an unavoidable conflict of presuppositions, and in this conflict one or the other must give way. When discourse is allowed to be free, dogma inevitably yields the field. But free discourse (including that involving the dissemination of these very pages) is a relative rarity in human affairs. When and where discourse is not free, as has been largely the case up until modern times (both in Europe and elsewhere), then fact submits to the dictates of the reigning belief-system, and the unwelcome messenger of reason is—often as not—martyred.

In the Nazareth literature, faith often overrules fact and dogma often trumps science. Even at this preliminary stage in our investigation we have seen that fact plays an essentially secondary role, one that needs to be brought into alignment with faith. This was Kopp's *modus operandi*, even through his solution was not good enough for the Church and is not heard from again. In his 1963 book *The Holy Places of the Gospels*, Kopp makes no mention at all of a moving Nazareth.

---

[33] For a discussion of evidence *vs.* conclusion, see the *Introduction*.

THE MYTH OF NAZARETH

Demolition of the 1730 Church of the Annunciation began in 1954 and was completed the following year. The Vatican was confident it would find the validation in the ground that it sought, and had decided long before any archaeological results were in to proceed with erection of the new structure. It gave Bagatti very limited time to carry out his work before the foundations of the new edifice were laid. Bagatti writes:

> The excavation was carried out with the greatest speed during the months of April-August [1955], with some 150 workers daily, and then the pace slackened. On Jan. 27, 1956, after a report sent to the Dept. of Antiquities, a division of the material found was made with the Director, Dr. Samuel Yeivin.[34]

Ritrovamenti nella Nazaret Evangelica (1955)

As soon as the first archaeological results were determined, Bagatti penned a lengthy and much-anticipated article on the site, "Discoveries in Sacred Nazareth" (*"Ritrovamenti nella Nazaret Evangelica"*). It appeared in the journal *Liber Annuus*.[35] The archaeologist immediately set about allaying the concerns of the Church, and the first page contains the following statements:

> The results thus far determined can be reduced to these: (1) the discovery of the extreme southern border of the village, constructed on a rocky incline already in the Iron Age and continuing even up to our days. (2) Verification that the traditional site of the "house of the Virgin" was surrounded by remains of habitations of an agricultural character, with the exploitation of natural grottos to increase the capacity of the house. (3) A succession of ecclesiastical structures erected according to different aesthetic criteria, yet always on the same site... (Pp. 5-6)

We shall have cause to return to this citation from time to time, for in a few words it contains several fundamental errors: that the village was located on the hillside; that it existed since the Iron Age; and (related to the first point) that ancient habitations were in the venerated area. Entirely correct, of course, is Bagatti's affirmation that there has been a series of ecclesiastical edifices in the venerated area: the present Church of the Annunciation is the fifth structure on the site. It remains to be determined, of course, *when* the first Christian edifice was erected there, a not insignificant point that will be considered in Chapter 6.

What interests us at this juncture is the Italian's assertion that the village existed already in the Iron Age, "continuing even up to our days" (1b). This is the doctrine of continuous habitation, and Bagatti is more explicit at the conclusion of the article:

---

[34] *Exc.* 2.
[35] *LA* (5) 1955:5–44.

74

The Myth of Continuous Habitation

From this brief summary of the remains that have now come to light, the result without any doubt is the continuity of life on the site uninterruptedly across the eras. The opinion, therefore, which suggests movements of the village in diverse epochs, especially the denial of life here in the Roman period, is lacking in archaeological foundation.[36]

Here, for the first time we meet with the word "uninterruptedly," which will figure in a future discussion (see below p. 31). With his last sentence Bagatti explicitly rejects the two prewar theses we have discussed: Kopp's moving Nazareth hypothesis, and the Tonneau-Kopp observation that no settlement existed at the venerated sites "in the Roman period." A footnote to this passage cites: "Kopp, 187–191." Those referenced pages are precisely the ones we have drawn upon in the foregoing discussion, and which created so much consternation for the Church.

In brief, Bagatti's 1955 article announced the new Catholic stance as regards Nazareth. The exact findings were still provisional, and Bagatti would continue to dig for a decade, so this article reveals little new evidence. But that is really not its purpose. For the evidence, we must look to the archaeologist's 1967/69 book, *Excavations in Nazareth* Yet the main lines of the Church's position, those that have endured essentially unchanged to this day, are already set forth in Bagatti's 1955 article.

The article closes with a glowing affirmation of Church doctrine, and with the hope that a new sanctuary, one "truly worthy," would soon rise on the site:

Conclusions. – Having terminated this very limited review of the results of the most recent excavation, we can affirm the acquisition of a quite secure understanding of the place, though it is still imperfect in many particulars. It is now assured that the site, which the ultrasecular [*sic*] tradition has known as the House of the Virgin, is in fact situated in an area that was inhabited in the 1st century of our era. We are now able to lay aside any *doubts generated from* [prior] *hypotheses founded on facts that were examined, necessarily, in a superficial way.* The verification offered here guarantees that the new Sanctuary which will succeed the previous, Christianity's homage to the mystery of the Incarnation, has its reason to exist. We hope that our age will not lag behind those of the past in bringing about something truly worthy. (Emphasis added.)

The "doubts generated from [*prior*] hypotheses" are, once again, an allusion to the prewar Kopp-Tonneau thesis. The Church soon fulfilled Bagatti's hope for a sanctuary of sufficiently stature. Within a year of the article's publication work began on the immense Shrine of the Annunciation, the largest Christian house of worship in the Middle East.

---

[36] Bagatti 1955:23.

THE MYTH OF NAZARETH

The Shrine of the Annunciation

The modern Shrine (also called the Church, or Sanctuary) of the Annunciation is 236 ft. long and 102 ft. wide (72×31 m). Its lofty cupola, covered in gleaming copper and surmounted by a lantern, is in the shape of an inverted lily (a symbol associated with Mary), and reaches to an impressive height of 170 ft. (52 m). The Shrine is oriented west to east on the hillside, so that the ground level under the western entrance is about ten meters higher than under that under the eastern apse (*cf.* Pt. 5, *Illus.* 3). The edifice was designed by the architects A. Barluzzi (preliminary plan) and G. Muzio (final plan). It is the fifth structure built on the spot, not counting occasional renovations.[37] Begun in 1956, the Shrine was essentially completed by 1966, though the formal dedication took place three years later. The decade of construction included the clearing of older structures, floors, and mosaics. During this time, on-site excavations under the supervision of Fr. Bagatti continued.

The Church of the Annunciation (CA) has evoked mixed impressions, ranging from effusive to "ponderous… completely lacking in any grace."[38] Its plan was based on the Crusader church, a three-aisled basilica. The side walls were built on top of the surviving courses of the older walls, and the apses at the east end of the Crusader church were incorporated in the new building. Only at the west end is the modern church shorter than its predecessor. In fact, the Shrine contains two churches. A lower one enshrines the Chapel of the Angel, where in the sixth month (according to the Gospel of Luke) the Archangel Gabriel addressed the Virgin Mary while she was weaving purple and scarlet for the Jerusalem Temple (*Protevangelium of James*). About five meters north of the Chapel of the Angel is a tomb of the kokhim-type (a type prevalent from Hellenistic to early Byzantine times). That tomb has been acknowledged by all, though who was buried there is much debated.[39] This is Bagatti's Tomb 29, and we shall have a good deal to say about it at a later time. Five meters to the west of the Chapel of the Angel is another tomb-complex, also acknowledged by all, containing 4+ burials which have been described by Viaud and Kopp as "kokhim," and by Bagatti as "Crusader."[40] These tombs will be discussed when we consider evidence for the emerging village of Nazareth.

The upper church of the CA is decorated with the work of artists from many different countries, centering on the Marian theme. Behind the altar a huge mosaic shows Christ in glory, with Peter and Mary beside him. Between the upper and lower churches is a large octagonal opening, called

---

[37] For published plans see: Viaud 33, 35, 81, 83; *Exc.* Pl. XI; *DACL* 1043; Finegan 29/47. For the slope of the hillside see Viaud 38, 52, 135; *Exc.* Pl. XI (inset).

[38] *Lonely Planet Guide to Israel*, 1999, p. 288.

[39] Viaud:81 (map); Kopp 1939:88-90; 1963:64; Bagatti *Exc.*:186.

[40] Viaud:35, 81 (maps); Kopp 1939:92; Bagatti 1955:16; *Exc.*:50.

The Myth of Continuous Habitation

the "oculus," from which those above can meditate upon the Chapel of the Angel below, and those below can gaze up into the grand inverted lily-cupola rising heavenwards.

The Dictionnaire de la Bible (1960)

Five years after writing the 1955 article, Bagatti penned a substantial piece on Nazareth for the *Dictionnaire de la Bible*.[41] Unlike the journal *Liber Annuus*, which has a modest circulation principally among Franciscans, the *Dictionnaire* was in its time the pre-eminent Christian reference work in the French language, intended for a broad readership. In Bagatti's *Dictionnaire* article, the archaeologist does not state his position as boldly as in his 1955 writing. The article begins with a one-sentence summation of the Church's position:

> *The ancient village.* On the slope of the hill, between the Church of St. Joseph and that of the Annunciation, abundant and characteristic remains have been found which permit the localization of the ancient village, already existing in Iron II.[42]

It is a complex, calculated, and curious sentence. It is also incorrect. The remains are not "characteristic" of a village, by which Bagatti surely means habitations. The remains are agricultural and funerary, but not domestic. The emphasis upon habitations specifically localized at the venerated sites is a false thesis that will be continually stressed by Bagatti, no doubt in order to substantiate the traditional sites of Joseph's and Mary's dwellings.[43] Those remains do not permit "the localization of the ancient village" on the slope of the Nebi Sa'in, but rather the localization only of its agricultural area and necropolis.

In fact, we do not have "characteristic remains" for Nazareth. Such remains of a village include foundations of houses, hearths, perhaps a city wall, temple, coins, weapons and ornaments, possibly an epigraphic inscription or two. But Bagatti cannot mean these, for none have been claimed at Nazareth prior to Byzantine times. What we have in the published reports is indirect evidence of the pre-Byzantine village culled from the periphery of

---

[41]   *DB* Supplement 6, cols. 318–333.

[42]   Bagatti 1960:318. It is probable that Bagatti here divides the Iron Age into two, not three parts. Thus, his "Iron II" extended to *c.* 600 BCE. Nevertheless, elsewhere he uses Early-Middle-Late Iron nomenclature (EI, MI, LI), *e.g., Exc.* 272. Often his discussion does not subdivide the Iron Period. The argument in this text obtains regardless of which nomenclature Bagatti adopts.

[43]   The possibility of habitations in the venerated area is taken up in Chapter Five, when we discuss the topography of the basin and the more precise localization of the ancient village.

that village, from tombs and agricultural installations. All the ancient pottery, movable objects, and structures that have been found, as far as we can tell, are funereal and agricultural. In other words, it is not possible to speak of "characteristic remains" of the ancient village, for to date no archaeologist has excavated the inhabited part of ancient Nazareth.

Bagatti's statement that the village was "already existing in Iron II" is a mild insinuation of the doctrine of continuous habitation. This, in contrast to the *Liber Annuus* article, where we read explicit statements of a village "already in the Iron Age and continuing even up to our days"; "on the site uninterruptedly across the eras"; and (for good measure) "inhabited in the first century of our era." As we have seen, archaeologists have not offered evidence from the Babylonian and Persian eras. The "abundant" remains mentioned by Bagatti in the above citation are grossly misdated, even if only by implication. They do not follow the Iron Age, but belong to much later times – in fact, to eras beginning with the Middle Roman.

We must now parse more exactly what Bagatti writes. The operative word in the final phrase is "already" (*déjà*). The phrase would be correct without it, for a village was indeed existing in Iron II. Thus the word is incorrect, as might be an erroneous insertion. When a single word is at issue, it can be claimed that we are dealing merely with poor word choice, or perhaps with imperfect translation from the Italian. But this insinuation – that habitation continued uninterruptedly through the centuries – cannot be inadvertent, for it also occurs later in the article. After a discussion of the Iron Age silos, the archaeologist writes:

> "But if, as seems evident, this agricultural character continued until the time of the Lord…" (col. 325). [44]

Here, the operative word is "continued." Once again, it implies the doctrine of continuous habitation, suggested merely as a possibility. If it indeed existed, such continuity of agricultural character would have left evidence dating to the six centuries before Christ. Such evidence clearly exists, for example, in the Iron Age silos discussed in Chapter 1.[45] But that evidence equally clearly comes to an end in the Iron Age. So, without evidence, we must repudiate Bagatti's statement. It does *not* seem evident that the "agricultural character" continued until the time of the Lord.

Because the average reader cannot be expected to examine the evidence contained in the primary reports, both scholar and layperson will naturally take passages such as the above at face value. Reading the above citation,

---

[44] *Mais si, comme il semble évident, ce caractère agricole s'était maintenu jusqu'au temps du Seigneur...* See below pp. 79*ff* for extended discussion.

[45] Chapter 1, pp. 49–50.

one will suppose that the village of Nazareth came into existence either in the Bronze or the Iron Period and continued until the time of Christ. One supposes this even though Bagatti does not speak of a village, but of its "agricultural character." The inference is clear, however: agriculture requires people. This is precisely what the Church wishes the reader to believe. It is the doctrine of continuous habitation, now coyly insinuated.

The remainder of Bagatti's 1960 article (selectively) reviews evidence from the Church of the Annunciation, references to Nazareth in the Church Fathers, and the history of pilgrim accounts. It also offers a short section on "other traditions," in which the author considers "delicate" points such as precisely where Jesus was raised. We shall have cause to return to this article from time to time in our discussion of the Hellenistic and later periods.

A remark is in order regarding the gross chronological error evident in the above discussion. Though only by implication, Bagatti is looking at Roman-Byzantine agricultural installations and suggesting they followed the Iron Period. The error involves over five hundred years. So it is, that the greatest errors are sometimes made in a most casual, almost imperceptible manner. Later, we shall see that Bagatti transposes Roman tombs to Crusader times,[46] and fourth-century CE graffiti to first-century CE.[47] We have already encountered similar chronological confusion in the writings of C. Kopp, who was capable of transposing Middle Roman agricultural installations back two millennia into Middle Bronze times.[48] Such incredible misdating is persistent and rampant in the Roman Catholic literature on Nazareth. It is capable of producing sufficient error that even the Great Hiatus can be covered up – all eight hundred years. Grossly misdated evidence, together with vague generalities (which abound in the literature) can also produce a village in the time of Jesus. Of course, such methodology is unworthy of true scholarship, yet it is unfortunately shared by a number of those who have published on Nazareth. As we have seen, the error is sometimes made obliquely rather than directly, by generality, by implication, by conclusion. No specificity is required, nor desired. In a sense this is safer than the overt misdating of an artefact for, being vague, it is harder to detect. Sometimes Bagatti is capable of vagueness to the point of almost total obscurity. He writes of "agricultural character" and "abundant and characteristic remains." Without specific evidence, however, what do those words mean?

There are a few exceptional cases where Bagatti and others venture to attribute specific evidence to the "lost centuries" of the Great Hiatus. To anticipate the next chapter for a moment, some cases involve the Hellenistic period. Those few attributions – repeatedly stressed in the literature – are

---

[46] *Exc.*50.

[47] See Taylor 1993:262.

[48] Above p.66.

all misdatings. In addition, we shall see that several writers attribute a great deal of evidence to the first century CE, a period laden with meaning for the Church. But we shall find that such evidence is in each case—and without exception—later Roman or Byzantine. This ubiquitous chronological confusion, compounded with error and a penchant for generality, produces a thick, opaque curtain masking the truth of Nazareth.

The antidotes are specificity, precision, systematic analysis, and continual recourse to the finds in the ground, that is, to the primary evidence. With these tools one can address the grotesquely contorted view of Nazareth currently held by tradition, a view based on innumerable imprecise and actually false claims made in the scholarly literature. The purpose of those claims is clear. It is, *in the absence of evidence*, to establish a settlement at Nazareth in the time of Christ. The only way to do this is through invention.

The last several cited statements of Bagatti, taken together, make up the classic formulation of the doctrine of continuous habitation: settlement has existed at and around the Franciscan property in Nazareth from the Bronze Age to the present. In fact, the claim is groundless. But because it is stated by the principle archaeologist at the site, it has been propagated in the secondary literature and assumes a number of forms (see below).

The silos and cisterns

In Palestine, cisterns first appeared in the Early Bronze Age and were usually lined by plaster or stone. They were used for the storage of wine and oil, and for the collection of rainwater in places where there is little naturally-occurring fresh water.[49] They were useful when settling areas that had few springs or that were at some distance from water.[50] Communal cisterns were sometimes large and complex, as those found at Megiddo and some other cities. No communal water system has been found in the Nazareth basin.

It is a pity that careful stratigraphical methods were not employed in the Nazareth excavations for, in their absence, cavities in the ground are difficult to date. An exception is if the archaeologist is lucky enough to find datable pottery and other items inside them (as in Silos 22 and 57, which date those cavities to the Iron Age).

As mentioned previously, a plethora of silos and cisterns exists in the venerated area. The sheer number of these storage hollows (68 under the Franciscan convent alone) has been used as evidence for the doctrine of continuous habitation. Presumably, their great number indicated to Bagatti that people have lived continuously in the area for thousands of years. There is the shade of this suggestion in Bagatti's last-mentioned citation, now expanded:

---

[49] Gophna 29.

[50] *Arch.* 289.

The Myth of Continuous Habitation

La présence de ces nombreux silos ne peut cependant pas nous obliger à accepter l'idée que les parents de Jésus fussent des agriculteurs (Eusèbe, Hist. eccl., III, c. xx), ni à partager l'impression qu'en ressentit l'Anonyme de Plaisance en 570: *Provincia similis paradiso, in tritico et in frugis similis Aegipto, modica quidem, sed praecellit Aegyptum in vino et oleo et poma. Melium extra natura altum nimis, super statum hominis talea grossa* (Geyer, Itinera, 161; Baldi, *Enchiridion locorum sanctorum,* 2ᵉ éd., Jérusalem, 1955, n.5). Mais si, comme il semble évident, ce caractère agricole s'était maintenu jusqu'au temps du Seigneur, il pouvait avoir influé sur le jugement peu bienveillant qu'on portait alors sur les habitants du village (Joa,. I, 46).

The "negative judgment" reflected in the Gospel of John (1:46) can hardly be explained by the simple fact that the Nazarenes were peasant farmers. Something stonger lay behind Nathanael's comment, "Can anything good come out of Nazareth?" We get an indication of it in Luke's account (4:16–30), where the inhabitants of Nazareth attempt to throw Jesus to his death. For now, we shall defer this interesting topic and focus on the archaeological point, namely, that from the mere presence of silos in the venerated area Bagatti sees cause to discuss whether the family of Jesus was involved in agriculture. His logic has taken him far beyond the evidence. Of course, it remains to be proved whether those silos even existed in Jesus' time, whether he grew up in the vicinity, and so on. Thus, the archaeologist bypasses all sorts of evidentiary hurdles on the basis of a preconception, one based on the gospel accounts. If we remove that preconception, then the ridiculousness of his enormous leap of faith becomes apparent: he sees storage pits in the ground and considers whether the family of Jesus was involved in agriculture.

Bagatti similarly rejects this conclusion on literary grounds. He sees that it contradicts the tradition that Joseph was a carpenter (again based on the gospel record—Mt 13:55). It is clear in all this that the Italian is not functioning as an archaeologist, but as a stalwart defender of tradition.

Bagatti's reference to Eusebius is also far afield. In the Church Father's curious story the emperor Domitian (late I CE) summons the poor relatives of Jesus (to Rome?) for questioning and haughtily dismisses them. The church father is writing in the fourth century CE and reporting on an incident over two centuries earlier. What is to prevent this story from being pure fable? According to Eusebius, the relatives told the emperor that they were farmers, thus providing the link (in Bagatti's mind) to the venerated area of Nazareth. But the home village of the relatives is not even mentioned in Eusebius' account. If we take the story at face value, those alleged relatives could come from anywhere at all.

THE MYTH OF NAZARETH

From these disparate strands—the presence of silos, the agricultural character, the poor relatives of Jesus—Bagatti contrives to draw conclusive fodder for the orthodox line: no, Jesus' family was not involved in agriculture (this would conflict with Joseph being a carpenter); the silos do demonstrate continuity in settlement "until the time of the Lord" (thus reaffirming the doctrine of continuous habitation); this agricultural character is supported by Nathaniel's reference in Jn 1:46 (giving Bagatti's theory support even in the gospels). Very possibly, we see Christian Archaeology here at its best.

The prolific number of silos and cisterns under the venerated area is quite adequately explained when we take into account the many centuries in which man has lived in the basin. Let us consider: the first period of habitation in the area was during the Bronze Age. This period lasted eight hundred years (c. 2000-c. 1200 BCE). To this is added roughly five centuries of Iron Age habitation (1200-c. 730 BCE). Finally, we must add the centuries following resettlement of the basin c. 100 CE (Chapter Five). Thus, we have a sum total of at least two thousand years of human habitation during which silos, cisterns, and other manmade changes to the environment were effected in the same ground. In other words, the plethora of silos and cisterns does not indicate *continuous* habitation. It indicates *lengthy* habitation, namely, during the three periods outlined above.

Examination of the photos, drawings, and descriptions of the artefacts at the venerated sites, and itemization of those found in conjunction with the silos and other hollows, shows that some artefacts and related structures date to the Iron age while others relate to later Roman times.[51] A lacuna in the evidence of roughly eight hundred years exists. Together with funereal remains, the agriculturally-related evidence provides a convincing chronology of human presence in the basin during two very disparate eras. This chronology based on the evidence is a very different one from Bagatti's chronology based on extra-evidentiary considerations, noted in the previous section.

Continuous habitation since the dawn of history?

In sum, the tradition maintains that settlement at Nazareth continued unbroken through the eras, quite contrary to the archaeological evidence which establishes a lengthy hiatus in settlement. Essentially an exercise in denial and rationalization of faith, the doctrine of continuous habitation has been affirmed since the 1950s by the Roman Catholic Church, and is also maintained to this day by many non-Catholic scholars. Baldly stated, it affirms that people have continuously lived at Nazareth from the Bronze Age up to modern times.

---

[51] For the Iron Age evidence *cf.* Chapter 1; for the Middle-Late Roman evidence *cf.* Chapters 4–6.

The Myth of Continuous Habitation

It is a most remarkable thesis. According to the doctrine of continuous habitation, the hamlet of Nazareth has been settled uninterruptedly since the time of Abraham. Nazareth, presumably, is in the company of Jerusalem and perhaps a handful of the world's settlements to have enjoyed such outstanding longevity. Hardly any Canaanite towns can make a similar claim. Many ancient and venerable Biblical settlements do not go back to patriarchal times (Gerasa, Hebron). Others ceased long ago (Gezer, Shechem). Yet others were abandoned or destroyed in the course of time, and then re-established at a different location (Gaza, Jericho, Japhia). In short, the tradition's shrill assertion that people continuously lived in the Nazareth basin for the last four thousand years would be, if true, most impressive. Quite apart from any Christian considerations, it would raise the site inestimably in archaeological value. The stratigraphy of the venerated area (for that is where habitation is claimed)[52] would be of the greatest interest. Archaeologists would be able to systematically follow the levels of habitation downwards – as they can at Megiddo – beginning with the upper stratum and progressively exposing older and older settlements. Megiddo offers thirty strata encompassing approximately three millennia.[53] The claim of four thousand years of settlement at Nazareth should reveal something at least remotely comparable, showing human presence all the way back to the Bronze Age. The strata would demonstrate the Medieval village, the Byzantine, then the Roman, Hellenistic, Persian, Iron, and finally the lowest Bronze Age settlement. Four millennia of human presence would be revealed by the archaeologist's spade, each stratum offering evidence such as pottery, wall foundations, coins, seals, ostracae, ornaments, weapons, and so on. After all, the venerated area has been extensively excavated. And so, if the doctrine of continuous habitation were correct, some material evidence would surely have been found to corroborate it. *Some* evidence would be in the ground to tell the tale that the tradition wishes so desperately be told.

But it isn't. For eight hundred years – from the Assyrian conquest to the First Jewish War – the ground is mute. Perhaps recognizing this irritating dilemma, in 1955 Bagatti had a special trench cut a few meters to the East of the Church of the Annunciation. Its purpose was to determine the stratigraphic profile of the venerated area, to once and for all find evidence of settlement in the various periods, and to provide some much-needed vindication of Church doctrine. The trench was dug 5.6 meters (18.4 ft.) down to solid bedrock, and was continued for a length of 12.9 meters (42.3 ft.). Bagatti's description of it is on page 236 of *Excavations*, and is accompanied by a photo. The results, however, disappointed the archaeologist. He writes: "at least where excavated, there were no habitations." He found some Byzantine

---

[52]   The localization of the settlement is considered in Chapter 3.

[53]   See *Appendix 3*: "The Stratigraphy of Megiddo."

sherds, similar to many others in the vicinity. Otherwise, no evidence of human presence was revealed. "All the fill," Bagatti admits simply, "follows normally the declivity of the hill." That is to say, no man-made strata were revealed at all – only virgin earth and rock.

Excavations in Nazareth (1967/69)'

Bagatti's excavations yielded a great deal of new material, which was incorporated into his two-volume opus, *Excavations in Nazareth*. The first volume, with which we are mostly concerned, contains 325 pages and is subtitled *From the Beginning till the XII Century*.[54] We shall simply refer to it as *Excavations* in these pages. The Italian edition was published in 1967 and appeared in English translation two years later.

Excavations claims to be a "complete description of the village" (p. 223), but it falls far short of fulfilling that mandate. Its focus is squarely on the venerated sites, where Bagatti himself excavated and which was an agricultural and funereal area in antiquity. Fully half the volume is taken up with the Shrine of the Annunciation and contiguous terrain (pp. 77–219). With the exception of selected tombs, locations outside the Franciscan property are given perfunctory treatment (*e.g.*, the Jewish Synagogue, p. 233), or none at all (*e.g.*, the Church of St. Gabriel at the northern end of the valley).

The presentation of evidence in *Excavations* is selective and tendentious. Even within the venerated area itself some tombs and certain damaging evidence are ignored, as we shall see. Aspects of the finds that are regarded as supporting the Church's views are emphasized, while those that contradict its views are minimized. For example, Bagatti devotes no less than thirty-three pages (185–218) to the "little grotto No. 29," minutely dissecting and analyzing the graffiti on the walls. He and other Catholic scholars interpret these markings as early signs of Jewish Christian veneration.[55] On the other hand, Joan Taylor has shown them to date to the fourth century CE.[56] Despite Bagatti's lengthy treatment of the grotto, one would hardly suspect that it was once a tomb. Only fleeting mention is made of this fact, couched within a quote of its original discoverer, Brother B. Vlaminck: "in building this trough the workmen had destroyed the original form of the rock, which in former times must have contained a tomb, judging, at least, by the remains of a recess still visible" (p. 186). We shall later have a good deal to say about Tomb 29, and almost nothing to say about the wall markings which are— graffiti. Incidentally, Bagatti renames the chamber "Martyrium of Conon," thus avoiding use of the word "tomb" entirely.

---

[54] Italian title: *Gli Scavi di Nazaret: dalle origini al secolo XII*, 1967.

[55] This theory is taken up in the articles "Nazareth" in OEANE (1997); AEHL (2001), *etc.*

[56] Taylor 1993:262.

The Myth of Continuous Habitation

Despite its limitations, *Excavations in Nazareth* remains to this day the single most important source of archaeological data on Nazareth. We shall refer to it regularly, particularly when we consider the Hellenistic and Roman periods. *Excavations* is now dated, and much of the material it presents has undergone revision by other scholars. The resultant redating has yielded significantly different conclusions from those embraced by the Church.

Scholars too busy to study all 325 pages of Bagatti's tome will appreciate his brief conclusions conveniently set forth in the last two pages of the book. They encapsulate what the Church wishes be known about Nazareth, and there we read a particularly succinct version of the doctrine of continuous habitation:

> ...contrary to what was believed, life did not begin in the place in a recent epoch, but already existed in the Bronze Period, to continue down to our own days.[57]

"[C]ontrary to what was believed" refers to the prewar observations of Tonneau and Kopp regarding the alarming (though correct) lack of Greco-Roman habitations in the venerated area. "[A]lready existed in the Bronze Period" refers to the town of biblical Japhia, located in the Nazareth basin during the Bronze and Iron Ages. "[T]o continue down to our days" denies the existence of a Great Hiatus at Nazareth, plainly evident from the archaeological record and beginning in all likelihood with the destruction of the Northern Kingdom (Israel) at the hands of the Assyrians. Hence, in each and every one of its elements, Bagatti's over-arching conclusion to this "definitive" study on Nazareth is incorrect. It is remarkable that the conclusion of a thick, evidence-laden book is so wide of the mark. It is ironic, too, that much of the data which would correct its errors is provided within the book's own pages. It is sad that scholars have unquestioningly accepted Bagatti's very erroneous historical portrait without examining the underlying evidence. And finally, it is unconscionable that the Church—which has produced, preserved, and protected this false history—claims the moral high ground of infallibility and the possession of ultimate truth.

---

[57] *Exc.* 319. See also *Exc.* 17, 221, 254, 257.

Secondary References to Continuous Habitation

The secondary Nazareth literature of all religious denominations is largely dependent on the primary findings of Bagatti and of a few other Catholic archaeologists working on Church property. Up until the present writing, that literature has not attempted an independent assessment of the primary evidence. Consequently, we should not expect to encounter positions in the scholarly literature that are hostile to the traditional view. Similarly, it should not come as a surprise that many Protestant and Jewish reference works of the last half-century have conformed to Bagatti's interpretations. Nonetheless, the former have adopted a less enthusiastic stance regarding the controversial issues raised in the foregoing pages, most especially as regards the denial of hiatus in settlement at Nazareth. Hence, in the non-Catholic literature, continuous habitation is rarely stated overtly, but is often insinuated according to the model Bagatti himself furnished. Alternatively, the Protestant literature developed a thesis which we shall examine in Chapter 3: the myth of a Hellenistic renaissance.

The doctrine of continuous habitation is voiced in a number of places in the secondary literature. It is not possible to discuss all the relevant passages, and we shall content ourselves with three representative examples. Obviously, evidence from Babylonian and Persian times cannot be cited by those who claim continuous habitation, as there is none. This limitation amounts to an effective prohibition on specificity when it comes to discussing the pre-Christian history of Nazareth. The tack adopted by the orthodox literature, then, is to embrace generalities and vagueness. Conclusions are abundant and, when necessary, data are ignored.

• Jack Finegan's *The Archaeology of the New Testament* (1969, expanded 1992)[58] is a widely-cited book intended for the layperson and non-specialist scholar. Finegan draws heavily on the work of Kopp and Bagatti. The second edition devotes twenty-two pages to Nazareth, and there we read the following:

> In 1970 Bellarmino Bagatti excavated along the north wall of the Crusader church and in some of the grottoes under the wall. When the medieval church was excavated in 1892 much debris was piled here, and in the piles of debris Bagatti found in inverse order (as thrown out in the excavations) pottery fragments *from the Iron Age to the Roman*, Byzantine, and Crusader periods; and in the grottoes likewise he found Roman as well as Crusader pottery, *thus the site was certainly inhabited in the first century B.C. and the first century A.D. as well as earlier and later*. (Finegan 1992:57; emphasis added.)

---

[58] 1969 edition pp. 27–34; 1992 edition pp. 43–65.

We shall see that nothing from this excavation is demonstrably "from the Iron Age to the Roman." This allusion is based on three tiny, allegedly "Hellenistic" shards. Not only does Finegan accept their Hellenistic dating, dubious on several counts (Chapter Three), but he extrapolates therefrom the doctrine of continuous habitation. In addition, his over-the-top conclusion is entirely unfounded. From this small excavation there is no certainty at all that the site was "inhabited in the first century B.C. and the first century A.D. as well as earlier and later." In fact, this is one of the purest statements of the doctrince of continuous habitation in the literature.

He begins his review of the evidence with the following passage:

> The oldest known human life in the region of Nazareth is attested by the skull found in 1934 by R. Neuville in a cave about one and one-half miles southeast of the city, a skull which may be older than that of Neanderthal man. In Nazareth itself a complex of burial caves was found in the upper city in 1963, in which there was pottery of the first part of the Middle Bronze Age (RB 70 [1963], p. 563; 72 [1965], p. 547). *Down in the area of the Latin Church of the Annunciation there was certainly an ancient village of long continuance.* Archeological investigation in and around this church was conducted by B. Vlaminck in 1895, by Prosper Viaud in 1907–1909, and particularly by Bellarmino Bagatti in 1955 when the previously standing eighteenth-century (1730) church was demolished to make way for a new building. The area under and around the church, as well as at the Church of St. Joseph not far away, was plainly that of an agricultural village. There were numerous grottoes, silos for grain, cisterns for water and oil, presses for raisins and olives, and millstones. *While the silos are of a type found at Tell Abu Matar as early as the Chalcolithic Age* (IEJ 5 [1955], p. 23), *the earliest pottery found in them here at Nazareth is of Iron* II (900–600 BC).[59] [Emphasis added.]

This passage contains two overarching errors. The first localizes the ancient village in the venerated area. The second implies the doctrine of continuous habitation, which I shall deal with here.[60] Finegan's statement that "there was certainly an ancient village of long continuance" follows mention of the Middle Bronze Age. The most obvious (though not necessary) implication of this vague declaration is continuation of settlement since Bronze Age times.

Finegan's final sentence is curious. He is referring to silos 22 and 57, the only silos at Nazareth containing Iron Age pottery.[61] Of course, since the *earliest* pottery found in those silos is of Iron II, then the reader supposes

---

[59] Finegan 1969:28; 1992:44–45.
[60] The localization of the settlement is considered in Chp. 3.
[61] Chp. 1:32–33 & 44.

that pottery from later eras was also found in them, leading to the doctrine of continuous habitation.

In fact, the earliest pottery found in those silos was not Iron II but Iron I (1200–1000), and two artefacts found in them may date back even further. The sentence reads much better without the word "earliest," *but it is that word which implies the doctrine of continuous habitation.* Finegan's statement is false on two levels: on the literal level (regarding the earliest pottery), and on the implied level (regarding continuous habitation). Both major errors in this sentence can be laid at the feet of the single word, "earliest."

The insertion of an inappropriate word is little more than a trick. It turns the underlying statement into a falsehood, one that only an expert is able to detect. The average reader, whether scholar or layperson, will be carried along with the general meaning, one which now leads directly to the false doctrine of continuous habitation.

In this context, the insertion of a misleading but useful word is not unique to Finegan, but occurs even in Bagatti's writings. We recall the Italian's 1960 article:

> *The ancient village.* On the slope of the hill, between the Church of St. Joseph and that of the Annunciation, abundant and characteristic remains have been found which permit the localization of the ancient village, already existing in Iron II.

The operative word here is "already" (*déjà*). It is inappropriate and intrusive – Bagatti's statement is correct without it (the village did exist in Iron II). "Already" serves the same purpose as Finegan's "earliest": it changes the complexion of the phrase in a way that directly leads to the doctrine of continuous habitation. This is casuistry. It is literary sleight-of-hand.

The resemblance between the Bagatti and Finegan passages is no coincidence. We can prove direct borrowing through an inadvertent slip of the pen. In his 1960 article, Bagatti (through a French translator) writes:

> On a pu identifier des silos servant à emmagasiner les réserves, des citernes pour l'eau ou le vin, des pressoirs pour le raisin et les olives, des meules de moulin, des grottes et des débris de maçonnerie.[62]

Finegan has retained these elements and their general order, as we see from his text: "...silos for grain, cisterns for water and oil, presses for raisins and olives, and millstones." But the American has mistakenly substituted "raisins" for the French word *raisin*, which in fact means "grape."[63] After all, a press for crushing raisins (dried grapes) makes no sense. This slip

---

[62] Bagatti 1960, col. 318.
[63] *Raisin sec* is French for the English "raisin."

proves direct borrowing by Finegan from Bagatti (obvious in any case). In the next sentence Finegan uses the extra word "earliest," *just as Bagatti had done before him* with "*déjà*." The implication in both cases is the doctrine of continuous habitation, and the underlying literal sense in both cases also becomes false.

The oblique, casuistic, and fundamentally dishonest masking of the hiatus by subterfuge and insinuation finds its way into a number of scholarly publications. The need has existed to make the hiatus altogether disappear from history. But how does one mask *eight hundred years* of non-evidence?

• In the article "Nazareth" from the *Encyclopedia Judaica* (1972), we read:

> Archaeological evidence has shown that the area was settled as early as the Middle Bronze Age, and tombs have been found *dating from the Iron Age to Hasmonean times*.[64] (Emphasis added.)

As far as I know, this is the only claim in the literature specifically dating tombs to the period of the Great Hiatus. No such tombs have been found in the Nazareth basin. In Chapter One we verified that tombs date to the Bronze and Iron Ages. They come to an end with tomb 75, which appeared in the tenth century BCE.[65]

It is unlikely that the *Encyclopedia Judaica* would have invented the above information. Far more probable is that its statement relies on one or another assertion in Bagatti's *Excavations*, such as the following:

> Archaeological proofs of life in the place are the tombs of the Middle Bronze period, and remains of habitations from the Middle Iron period to our days.[66]

This statement of Bagatti, one of his numerous claims of continuous habitation, is demonstrably false: there are no "remains of habitations from the Middle Iron period to our days," despite the Italian's over-the-top claim to have "archaeological proofs" of the same. As regards habitations, their remains have not been found in the Nazareth basin dating either to the Iron Period, nor to the periods following it, nor in fact to any pre-Byzantine eras at all.

Despite the appositeness of the above citation, it is more likely that the author of the *Encyclopedia Judaica* article was misled by another passage from *Excavations*, a seminal summation of Bagatti's findings:

---

[64] *Encyclopedia Judaica*, "Nazareth" (1972) col. 900.

[65] Chp. 1:34-35. Tomb 75 had no artefacts. The latest Iron Age pottery is not funeral, but comes from two silos and from the area around the Church of St. Joseph.

[66] *Exc.* 254.

THE MYTH OF NAZARETH

[a]

(p.29)   Chronologically we have: tombs of the Middle Bronze Period; silos
with ceramics of the Middle Iron Period; and then, uninterruptedly,
ceramics and

*[turn two pages, reviewing a map and two photos
with ancillary data]*

(p.32)
constructions of the Hellenistic Period down to modern times.[67]

I have formatted the passage to reflect the page turns in Bagatti's book,
and call this version [a]. Here we have mention of all the elements in the
Encyclopedia Judaica (EJ) passage: tombs, the Middle Bronze Age, the
Iron Age, and Hasmonean [Hellenistic] times. The author of the EJ article
has evidently misread Bagatti, and through no fault of his own. Bagatti's
statement is a linguistic minefield for a native English speaker, let alone for
one who reads English as a second language. If carefully read *to the very end
of the sentence*, putting all parts together, then the meaning becomes other
than is apparent from a less attentive reading (see below). If one pauses at the
end of page 29, as the pagination forces the reader to do, then the mind will
retain the following:

"Chronologically we have… ceramics of the Middle Iron Period; and
then, uninterruptedly…"

This is the doctrine of continuous habitation. The word order (the
semicolon notwithstanding) invites the supposition that the ceramics begin
in the Middle Iron Period and continue thereafter. Lest I be accused of
imaginatively parsing semicolons, it should be noted that the problem is not
merely pagination, punctuation, and word order. Once again, it is a *misplaced
word*, such as we have already become familiar with in Finegan's "earliest"
and Bagatti's "*déjà.*" The word now is "uninterruptedly," which does not
belong where it is found. The correct reading is as follows:

[b]   Chronologically we have: tombs of the Middle Bronze Period; silos
with ceramics of the Middle Iron Period; and then, constructions of the
Hellenistic Period uninterruptedly down to modern times.

The statement is still false. I wish to make absolutely clear that *no* evidence
has been found at Nazareth dating to Hellenistic times. But Bagatti and others
claim such evidence (Chapter Three), and thus the above statement is entirely
consistent with Bagatti's position as regards the evidence in the ground.

---

[67] *Exc.* 29 and 32.

Version [b] is the only reading which makes both grammatical and archaeological sense, consistent with Bagatti's evidence. Archaeologically, "uninterruptedly" has nothing to do with the Middle Iron Period, but with much later times. It is misplaced and, yet again, changes the complexion of the sentence in a way that strongly suggests the doctrine of continuous habitation. The pagination may or may not be purely coincidental.

One can hardly fault the author of the *Encyclopedia Judaica* article for missing the subtlety of version [b] above, and for not transferring "uninterruptedly" to where it belongs. He did what a reader would do with the muddled sentence in the text, drawing one of a number of possible misinterpretations from the misleading word order, and came up with a statement that would probably have surprised even Bagatti, namely, that tombs at Nazareth date from the Iron Age to Hasmonean times. That statement occurs nowhere else.

In politics there is a term known as 'spin' where an issue, speech or document is interpreted in a tendentious way to serve the interests of one party or another. In religion, unfortunately, that political dimension also exists, with one major difference: the spin is doctrinal. We shall adopt a more respectful euphemism, and call it "interpretive gloss." It infuses the Nazareth literature, not excepting Bagatti's book, *Excavations in Nazareth*. This discussion makes clear that the curious phrasing, lack of precision, incorrect wording, and misleading syntax encountered at certain places in the literature are not entirely the results of coincidence or poor translation.

• *The New International Dictionary of Biblical Archaeology* (NIDBA, 1983), "Nazareth."[68] This single-page article borrows from Finegan's influential treatment of Nazareth examined above. It begins with the same sequence of facts found in that Finegan citation, and also includes the previously-mentioned error regarding the "earliest" Iron Age pottery:

> Recent archaeological evidence shows that Nazareth was inhabited long before as well as during the early Roman period. This is evidenced by the ancient skull found near the town as well as by Middle Bronze-Age pottery from burial caves in the upper part of the city. Also, near the Church of the Annunciation there have been found grain silos of the type that were as early as the Chalcolithic Age but in which the earliest pottery was of Iron II (900–600 BC). Other pottery there consisted of a little from the Hellenistic period, more from the Roman and most from the Byzantine period. Of the twenty-three tombs found *c*. 450 m (500 yd.) from the church most were of the kokim type (*i.e.*, horizontal shafts or niches off a central chamber) known in Palestine from *c*. 200 BC and which became the standard Jewish

---

68   The article is signed "WHM."

type. Two tombs had in them artifacts (lamps, *etc.*) to be dated from the first to fourth centuries A.D. Four tombs sealed with rolling stones typical of the late Jewish period testify to a considerable Jewish community there in the Roman period.

Though the passage reads quite convincingly to one not familiar with the material evidence, it is fairly riddled with errors. The 'interpretive gloss' placed on the data amounts to a *tour-de-force.* With Baroque excess, the author shapes, twists, forces, and contorts the evidence so as to eliminate the slightest suspicion of a hiatus in settlement. Perhaps readers will care to revisit this citation at a later time, after reading this book. They will then find in it half a dozen glaring faults without difficulty. For those who may not wish to wait, I summarize those faults now, sentence-by-sentence, with brief comments.

– "Recent archaeological evidence shows that Nazareth was inhabited long before as well as during the early Roman period." *Comment*: This appears to be an adaptation from Finegan: "In the light of recent archaeological evidence... that Nazareth was an old established site *long before the Early Roman period* and during it..."[69] (emphasis added). In fact, Nazareth was not inhabited in the Early Roman Period. Nor was it inhabited "long before" the Roman period, unless we have in mind the Bronze and Iron Ages and *not subsequent periods* (something neither implied nor obvious from the citation). Thus, both Finegan's and NIDBA's statements are incorrect in one sense and misleading in another. They ignore the possibility of a hiatus in settlement.

– "This is evidenced by the ancient skull found near the town as well as by Middle Bronze-Age pottery from burial caves in the upper part of the city. Also, near the Church of the Annunciation there have been found grain silos of the type that were as early as the Chalcolithic Age but in which *the earliest pottery* was of Iron II..." (emphasis added). *Comment:* The "earliest pottery" claim is now familiar from our dissection of Finegan's article above (pp. 28-30), and this sentence also appears to be borrowed from that source.[70] The final clause is a restatement of the Bagatti-Finegan insinuation of continuous habitation, namely, that evidence at Nazareth postdates the Iron period.

– "Other pottery there consisted of a little from the Hellenistic period, more from the Roman and most from the Byzantine period." *Comment:* As mentioned above, there is no pottery from the Nazareth basin dating to

---

[69] Finegan 27.

[70] It is a resumé of Finegan's section 35 (1969 edition).

the Hellenistic period. This will be shown in Chapter Three. The lack of Hellenistic evidence at Nazareth effectively doubles the hiatus in settlement from four to eight centuries.

– "Of the twenty-three tombs found *c.* 450 m (500 yd.) from the church most were of the kokim type (*i.e.*, horizontal shafts or niches off a central chamber) known in Palestine from *c.* 200 BC and which became the standard Jewish type." *Comment*: We will take up the subject of tombs later. Though the kokim (kokh, pl. kokhim) type of tomb was "known in Palestine from *c.* 200 BC," at Nazareth use of this type of tomb begins much later, as will be proven by the artefacts found in them. They date the kokh tombs to Middle Roman and later times (see next point).

– "Two tombs had in them artifacts (lamps, *etc.*) to be dated from the first to fourth centuries A.D." *Comment*: The Roman tomb evidence is datable to the second century of our era and thereafter. We shall see that most of it is III-IV century CE. The earliest Roman artefacts *may* date to later first century CE.

– "Four tombs sealed with rolling stones typical of the late Jewish period testify to a considerable Jewish community there in the Roman period." *Comment*: Rolling stones are not found in Palestine before 70 CE. The only exceptions are rare monumental examples in Jerusalem (*e.g.*, the tomb of Queen Helena of Adiabene).[71]

Thus, every sentence of the above passage has inaccuracies, some egregious. The cumulative effect of all these errors, large and small, is an entirely false history of the site.

In a sense, Kopp's prewar moving Nazareth hypothesis was safer for the Church than the continuous habitation doctrine first promulgated by Bagatti in 1955. The former was complex and difficult to comprehend – indeed, incomprehensible. Yet, an incomprehensible position is not immediately testable by evidence at hand. Since mid-century, the Church's position has been verifiable, largely through evidence that Bagatti himself unearthed. The archaeologist rejected complexity, and chose to take the bull by the horns, as it were. He opted for the simple, direct solution, and for the grand line: Nazareth has existed since the dawn of history.

Taking the bull by the horns is a most precarious maneuver, and the slightest error often proves fatal. Yet, the Church's position rests on not one, but twin horns, both dangerous to its interests. One horn is the evidence in the ground – or rather, the lack thereof – during the centuries following the Assyrian conquest. Bagatti himself must have recognized the sheer impossibility of the

---

[71] Kloner 1999:25–28. We shall discuss rolling stones in Chapter Four.

doctrine of continuous habitation the very year he first announced it. That was in 1955, the year he also dug the stratigraphic trench.

The second horn is a pattern of deception and invention in the literature, one which we have begun to reveal in these pages. That pattern includes global errors such as wholesale misdatings of evidence, as well as subtler errors such as cunningly-placed (and misplaced) words like "already," "earliest," and "uninterruptedly" at strategic places in the literature. All these stratagems serve a simplistic, unrealistic, and even ludicrous position: Nazareth has continually existed for the past four thousand years.

There was no continuous habitation at Nazareth. The valley was empty of human settlement beginning with the Assyrian conquest in the late eighth century BCE, and it remained empty for many centuries thereafter. On fundamental issues of archaeology, Bagatti and the Church have planted themselves squarely and stridently on the wrong side of the fence. Understandably, they have done so for deeply-held doctrinal reasons. But a bull does not turn aside for doctrine, and nor should a reasoning reader. We have a right to know the facts about Nazareth, and the Great Hiatus is one of those facts.

Chapter Three

The Hellenistic Renaissance Myth

The Great Hiatus: Part II
(332–63 BCE)

The Hellenistic Renaissance Myth

The Hellenistic Period

Chronology 332– 63 BCE

332 BCE	Conquest of Palestine by Alexander the Great.
301	Battle of Ipsus decides control of Syria-Anatolia.
301–201	Palestine under the Ptolemies.
201–198	Wars for conquest of Palestine.
198–166	Palestine under the Seleucids.
166	Desecration of the Temple and beginning of Maccabean revolt.
141	Simon Maccabeus expels the Seleucid military garrison from Jerusalem.
141–63	Second Jewish Commonwealth. Simon makes foray into Galilee (1 Macc 5:23).
104	Judas Aristobulus I converts Galilee to Judaism at the point of the sword.
94–88	Pharisees revolt against Alexander Janneus, and a six-year civil war ensues. 800 Pharisees crucified.
63 BCE	The Roman general Pompey conquers Jerusalem.

The fact that no hard evidence from the Babylonian and Persian Periods was found at Nazareth, despite much searching, led in some circles to the eventual abandonment of the continuous habitation doctrine. Towards the end of the twentieth century non-Catholic scholars began to suggest another possibility, one less fraught with difficulties, more consistent with the archaeological evidence, and also fully compatible with the gospel account. The Hellenistic renaissance doctrine, as I call it, acknowledges a hiatus in settlement at Nazareth but proposes that the hiatus ended several centuries before the time of Christ. This doctrine comes to grips with the lack of evidence following the Iron Age, as well as with the lack of mention of the village in the Old Testament, and in these ways it is more historically correct. At the same time, the Hellenistic renaissance doctrine conforms to the gospel assertion that Jesus came from Nazareth, and thus it upholds the inerrancy of scripture. Today, this view is widely held in Protestant circles. Yet, these pages will show that the Hellenistic renaissance doctrine has as little basis in fact as does the doctrine of continuous habitation.

Many scholars divide the centuries following Alexander the Great's conquest into two parts: the Hellenistic Period (332–*c*.166 BCE) and the

THE MYTH OF NAZARETH

Hasmonean Period (*c.* 166–63 BCE).[1] However, in this work the Hellenistic era encompasses both these periods, which are sometimes differentiated as "Early" and "Late" Hellenistic. When confusion might otherwise arise, I will date the century intended or use the word "Hasmonean." Otherwise, "Hellenistic" is used generally to signify pre-Roman times in Palestine, namely, from the conquest of the land by Alexander to the Roman conquest under Pompey (332–63 BCE).

Thus, the Hellenistic period in Palestine comprises three successive political regimes: the Ptolemaic hegemony of the third century (301–201), several decades of Seleucid domination (201–166), and the fractious Hasmonean era (166–63). The Hellenistic Period is, of course, not synonymous with Greek influence which was known in the Levant long before Alexander and survived well after the first century BCE.

Ptolemaic times

In the early fifth century Persia represented the largest empire the world had ever known, stretching from India (Pakistan) to Libya. Accustomed to victory, the Achaemenids under Darius the Great suffered the first of many defeats at the hands of the Greeks in the Battle of Marathon (490 BCE). Xerxes, Darius' eldest son, made a concerted attempt to revenge his father's defeat, and though his armies managed to invade Greece and even to burn Athens (480), his fleet lost the Battle of Salamis, and his general, Mardonius, was defeated in the decisive battle of Plataea. The enormous effect of these victories on Greek society cannot be overestimated. "The Greeks," writes Helmut Koester, "had successfully withstood the onslaught of an eastern superpower. The consciousness of the superiority of Greek education, Greek culture, and of the Greek gods formed not only the Greek mind, but also that of other nations, later including even the Romans, although they were to become the masters of the Greeks."[2]

The golden age of classical Greece followed upon the defeat of Persia, but the Peloponnesian Wars (431–404) were enormously destructive and costly to both Sparta and Athens. The fourth century witnessed increasing impoverishment of the Greek population. In 338 Philip of Macedon conquered Athens and brought an end to its glory, as Demosthenes noted at the time. The conquest of Persia beckoned, and Isocrates, then ninety years old, told Philip: "Once you have made the Persian subject to your rule, there is nothing left for you but to become a god."[3]

---

[1] An alternate dating ends the era a generation later, with the accession of Herod the Great (37 BCE).
[2] Koester *History*:2.
[3] Koester *History*:9.

The Hellenistic Renaissance Myth

Philip was murdered in 336, and the lot of conquering Persia fell to his son, Alexander the Great, who was immediately proclaimed king of the Macedonians at the age of twenty. Alexander, a profound student of Greek ways, was educated by Aristotle himself. Within a year Alexander had suppressed revolts in Greece and crossed the Bosporus into Asia Minor, thus beginning his legendary conquests. In 333 he defeated the Persian King Darius at Issus (between Asia Minor and Syria), and then swept down the eastern Mediterranean seaboard easily conquering all in his path, with the exception of the island city of Tyre, which required an extended siege. In 332 Alexander conquered Palestine, and he may have visited Jerusalem. Egypt submitted to him without a battle, and the founding of Alexandria at the mouth of the Nile marked the creation of a vibrant new center of commerce and culture. In 331 Alexander defeated Darius a second time at Gaugamela (east of the upper Tigris), and this allowed him access to Mesopotamia. By 327 the conqueror had reached India. In 323 Alexander fell ill in Babylon and died, not yet thirty-three years old.

Alexander the Great failed to leave an heir and successor, and his vast kingdom fractured into three principle parts ruled by his Macedonian successors, the "Diadochi": Greece under the Antigonids; Persia under the Seleucids; and Egypt under the Ptolemies. Syria, Palestine, and Phoenicia were of especial importance to the Seleucids, for they furnished strategic access to Mediterranean sea trade. In the two decades after Alexander's death Palestine was repeatedly the venue of battles between the Diadochi, until in 301 BCE Ptolemy I Soter succeeded in annexing the land.

The seeds of deep divisions within Judaism were planted in the Ptolemaic period, divisions that came to a head in subsequent Seleucid and Maccabean times. One problem was monetary: the critical right to collect taxes in Judea on behalf of the Ptolemies was purchased in the mid-third century (and retained) by traditional enemies of Jerusalem, namely the Tobiads.[4] This family possessed ancestral lands in 'foreign' territory, namely in Ammon east of the River Jordan, and were allied with the anti-Jerusalem Samaritans.[5]

A second problem was more broad: the increasing tension between Hellenism and Judaism (see next section). This also involved the Tobiads, who were thoroughly Hellenized, and had become related by both marriage

---

[4]   The Tobiads were of priestly lineage (Schalit 96) yet originally were inveterate enemies of Jerusalem (Neh 2:10; cf. Isa 7:6). As early as Persian times the Tobiads insinuated themselves into high priestly affairs through marriage (the High Priest Eliashib, c. 450 BCE, was related to a Tobiad—Neh 13:4). They played a decisive role in the divisions leading up to the Maccabean Revolt and proved the biblical writer wrong: "but you [Tobiah and other foreigners] have no share or claim or historic right in Jerusalem" (Neh 2:20; cf. 6:1–14; 13:4–14).

[5]   Cf. Josephus Ant. XII.168.

and financial interests to the leading priestly families of Jerusalem.[6] It is fair to say that the upper stratum of Jewish society in the third century was markedly Hellenized, a fact that eventually made the office and choice of High Priest highly contentious not only in the religious, economic, and political dimensions, but also in the cultural.

Our knowledge of the Galilee in Ptolemaic and Seleucid times is very limited. Strong promoters of Hellenism, the Ptolemies established a few *poleis* in Palestine after the Greek pattern. Attributes of the *polis* included the adoption of the gymnasium, athletic contests, temples honoring Greek divinities, and governance by a *boulé* (association of leading citizens). The citizens of the *polis* had rights of property ownership and inheritance, freedom from some obligations, and the right to mint coins. Except for Philoteria (Beth Yerah) on the southern end of the Sea of Galilee, no new *poleis* were founded in Palestine by the Ptolemies. On the other hand, a number of towns already settled in Persian times were raised to the status of *polis*. These were not in the interior of the Galilee, but on its periphery, and included Ptolemais (Acco), Jaffa, Ascalon, Dor (later) and Gaza on the coast. Albrecht Alt terms this a *Städtegürtel* in the territories surrounding Galilee, namely, on the Mediterranean coast and in the Decapolis.[7] Philadelphia (Amman), Pella (Tabaqat Fahil) and Dion (Tell el-As'ari) were *poleis* east of the Jordan River. A Macedonian military colony was established in Samaria.[8] In all, few Palestinian settlements were founded or refounded in Hellenistic times. We must bear this in mind when we come to consider the thesis of a Hellenistic refounding of Nazareth (below, pp. 136*ff.*). New Hellenistic settlements tended to be military (Ptolemais, Philoteria, possibly Scythopolis).[9] Though we cannot be sure of the scale of immigration into Palestine by Greek colonizers during this era, Kuhnen points to a substantial increase in population, but no evidence of movement of peoples and, significantly, no repopulation of the interior highlands of Galilee.[10]

The fertile Beth Shan and Lower Jezreel Valleys to the south and east have revealed no less than 73 sites dating to the Hellenistic period.[11] This appears an impressive number, yet it is a substantial decline from the 117 sites similarly noted in Persian times. Chancey affirms that "No cities were founded and no colonists settled in the interior of Galilee."[12]

---

[6]   Tcherikover reviews the career of the Tobiad Joseph at 131*ff*; *cf.* Koester I:210.

[7]   Alt 385.

[8]   Kuhnen:33. Schürer also notes the *poleis* of Hippus and Gadara East of the Jordan (I.1.196). It is possible that Beth-Shan also became a polis during Ptolemaic times.

[9]   D. Graf, "Palestine," in OEANE:225–26; Arav: 98, 99.

[10]   Kuhnen:33.

[11]   Arav 102.

[12]   Chancey 35–36.

The Hellenistic Renaissance Myth

This was already suspected in the 1950s, when Albrecht Alt penned his "Hellenistic Cities and Regions in Galilee" (1959).[13] It begins:

> Only in the time of Alexander the Great does the Galilee gradually emerge from darkness, insofar as its fate under the rule of the Assyrians, Babylonians, and Persians is hidden to us. Even then and for a long time thereafter we have scarcely any reports except of individual sites; the region as a whole... clearly re-emerges only after its annexation to the Hasmonean state towards the end of the second century before Christ. Out of this heterogeneous heritage it is necessary to recover a portrait of the settlement history of Galilee in Hellenistic times and, where possible, its relationship to the preceding period.
>
> The characteristic feature of the new age is, in almost the entire Near East, the well-known elevation of discrete settlements to the rank of cities in the Hellenistic sense of this word... [A]s regards the formation of towns, the plains were much preferred to the hilly country. Galilee, too, was no exception to this rule; for while the high massif in its interior does not once offer [*aufweist*] an urban site in the last and ripest stage, already at the beginning of the Hellenistic age we encounter the first cities on its low-lying periphery...[14]

"Admittedly," writes E. Barnavi, "there were some larger Jewish enclaves inhabiting the eastern Galilee and the Jezreel valley, but the vast majority of the Jewish population of Palestine remained concentrated in the Judean hills and in Jerusalem."[15] In sum, the third and second centuries BCE appear to have been a low point in the interior of the Galilee.

The Seleucids and the Maccabean revolt

The third century BCE witnessed no less than four wars for control of Palestine and, after three years of warfare, Antiochus III finally succeeded in bringing the region under Seleucid control in 198 BCE.[16] The tax system of the region and trade continued much as before. However, many names changed, and in Jerusalem and some other towns the Hellenists assumed unchallenged control. Surprisingly few new *poleis* were created in the region in Seleucid times, including Antiochia to the north (near Paneas, at the mouth of the Jordan River), and Seleucia in the Golan.[17] In the Galilee only Scythopolis (Beth Shan) has been proposed as emerging in this period, and Gerasa in the Decapolis, but even they are not certain.[18]

---

[13]   A subsection of "Galiläische Probleme," in Alt's *Kleine Shriften zur Geschichte des Volkes Israel*, vol 2.
[14]   Alt 1959:384.
[15]   Barnavi 1992:34.
[16]   Schalit:79–80.
[17]   Freyne 1980:113–114.
[18]   Kuhnen:34. Polybius (5.86) notes that the people of Coele-Syria (Palestine-Phoenicia) favored the Ptolemies over the Seleucids. *Cf.* Josephus *Apion* II.iv.5.

THE MYTH OF NAZARETH

It was during the fairly short period of Seleucid control over Palestine that the conflict between Judaism and Hellenism came to a head. That conflict had both religious and extra-religious dimensions. It is self-evident that the worship of foreign gods was anathema to Judaism. Practically speaking, only Jews who embraced Greek ways could rise to positions of power in the *polis*. One of the major aims of Antiochus IV (175–164 BCE), was to foster unity by spreading Hellenism throughout his extensive dominions, but violent conflict soon followed upon his choice of Jason, an ardent Hellenizer, as High Priest. Jason paid a large sum of money to Antiochus for the position, and vowed he would pursue a policy of vigorous Hellenization among the Jews. Ever mercenary, however, Antiochus soon favored yet another candidate, Menelaus, who offered the king a much larger sum for the High Priesthood (II Macc. 4:24). Some scholars have suggested that Jason or Menelaus was the "Wicked Priest" of the Dead Sea Scrolls.

Having been replaced by Menelaus and thinking Antiochus dead, Jason raised an army and laid siege to Jerusalem. Antiochus appeared, attacked Jerusalem, despoiled the Temple treasury, and placed an uncompromising tyrant in command of the city. Antiochus was in a particularly vicious mood after being humiliated by the Romans in Egypt (168 BCE), and on his return trip through Palestine he decided that Jerusalem should be destroyed and repopulated by Greeks. Most of the male inhabitants of the city were in fact killed, and many of the survivors rallied to Judas Maccabeus in the countryside. Thus began the Maccabean Revolt.

Antiochus IV was surnamed Epiphanes ("the manifest [God]") by his partisans and Epimanes ("the mad") by his detractors. He proceeded to institute anti-Jewish regulations against Sabbath observance, circumcision, and food laws, on pain of death. He then had an altar to Zeus set up in the Temple (this was probably the "abomination that makes desolate" of Dan. 11:31). His intention was nothing less than the eradication of the Jewish religion.[19] As alluded to above, many inhabitants of Jerusalem as well as faithful Jews were put to death, and open rebellion finally broke out in 167 BCE, when the Hasmonean priest Mattathias killed the king's envoy. Numerous *Hasidim* ("pious ones") rallied to the revolution, which went from victory to victory notwithstanding the opposition of large Syrian armies. In the white-hot heat of revolt, an inspirational and apocalyptic tract was penned: the book of Daniel. Judas Maccabeus, son of Mattathias, eventually conquered Jerusalem and reinstituted proper observance in the Temple (on 25 Chislev [December], 165 BCE). Antiochus died a year or two later while campaigning in Parthia.

---

[19] Schürer I.i.207.

The Hellenistic Renaissance Myth

The Hasmonean Age

For roughly one tumultuous century the Jewish state achieved independence under Maccabean (Hasmonean) leadership. The exploits of Judas Maccabeus ("Judah the hammer") and his family—champions of Yahweh and quintessential liberators of the Jewish people—are enshrined in the books of Maccabees I-IV. Though Hellenism was a critical element of the Hasmonean revolt, and though that war was largely a reaction against paganism and the excesses of Greek ways, it should also be recognized, as L. Schiffman has pointed out, that:

> ...the Hasmonean descendants of the Maccabees themselves acquired the trappings of Hellenism. They began to conduct their courts in Hellenistic fashion and were estranged from Jewish observance. This transition went way beyond the need of any monarch at that time to make use of Hellenistic-style coinage, diplomacy, and bureaucracy. The Hasmoneans employed foreign mercenaries to protect them from their own people.[20]

It is understandable, then, that the century of Hasmonean hegemony is sometimes referred to as the Late Hellenistic Period. We know comparatively little of the Galilee in the second century. In mid-II BCE Simon Maccabeus "withdrew the Jews of Galilee and Arbatta (exact location unknown) to Jerusalem."[21] The late second century BCE witnessed the decline or abandonment of a number of major sites in northern Palestine.

Galilee was annexed to the Hasmonean state in the reign of Aristobulus I (104–103). A resurgence in settlement finally followed in the early first century BCE. An archaeological survey conducted by M. Aviam shows that new sites sprang up in the Galilee during the reign of Alexander Janneus (103–76 BCE):[22]

> The appearance of new sites in the Late Hellenistic era suggests that new settlers moved into Galilee, the most likely candidates being Judean colonists. Perhaps they came to reclaim ancestral territory, or perhaps they were attracted by Galilee's climate and arable land. In any case, the expanded settlement which began in the Late Hellenistic period continued into the Roman period.[23]

Some scholars who cleave to the existence of Nazareth in pre-Christian times have noted the expanded settlement patterns in Galilee in the Late Hellenistic period, and also the rejuvenation or refounding of nearby

---

[20] Schiffman:101–02.

[21] Chancey:37. *Cf.* I Macc. 5:23.

[22] Aviam, "Galilee," NEAEHL, vol. II, 453.

[23] Chancey:47.

THE MYTH OF NAZARETH

Sepphoris at this time (below, pp. 136*ff.*). They have suggested that Nazareth experienced a similar refounding during this epoch. However, we shall see that there is no archaeological substantiation for this opinion. A careful review of the excavation reports shows that there was no human presence in the Nazareth basin during Hellenistic times. The few alleged "Hellenistic" shards invariably prove, upon examination, to belong to later Roman times, or alternately, to the Iron Age. In addition, there exists a striking lack of attestation for entire categories of Hellenistic evidence which we should expect to find, such as wall foundations, coins, and common forms of Hellenistic pottery. For example, M. Aviam notes that a coarse form of pottery, which he terms Galilean Coarse Ware (GCW), "was used extensively during the Hellenistic period." This ware can today be accurately dated,[24] but none has been claimed or found in the Nazareth basin. Again, Chancey (p. 35) writes: "Ptolemaic and Seleucid coinage almost invariably appears in the Hellenistic strata of Galilean sites..." No Hellenistic coins have been found at Nazareth.

Nevertheless, there have been a number of claims in the literature trumpeting the existence of Hellenistic evidence at Nazareth. These claims fall into two basic categories. The first involves movable evidence and tends to be specific. It generally concerns one or more "Hellenistic" oil lamps or pottery shards. These itemized claims occur almost entirely in the primary literature, and in each and every case they are spurious, often for revealing reasons.

A second type of claim involves structural evidence, usually of a vague, non-specific nature. It occurs almost entirely in the secondary literature and points to the existence in the Nazareth basin of tombs, silos, cisterns, wine and olive presses, some of which it labels "Hellenistic." In a way, this type of claim is more difficult to deal with, for all these structures were used in Palestine in both Hellenistic and Roman times. However, we shall discover a pronounced tendency among certain Christian archaeologists to backdate later Roman evidence into earlier times, in order to substantiate a village before the time of Jesus. The most egregious example is labeling certain tombs and oil lamps "Herodian" when they are in fact Middle and Late Roman. This problem in nomenclature, recurrent in the Nazareth literature, will be taken up in detail in Chapter 4.

In the following pages we shall determine that the "Hellenistic" evidence claimed at Nazareth, both specific and general, is erroneous. We begin with the itemizable artefacts.

---

[24] Aviam:46.

The Hellenistic Renaissance Myth
Claims of Specific Hellenistic Finds

Ultimately, an accurate history of Nazareth can be determined only on the basis of datable material excavated on site. Is there, then, specific material in the Nazareth basin that substantiates human presence there in the pre-Christian centuries?

To answer this question, we shall begin with an examination of the two most referenced "Hellenistic" claims in the literature. They involve a group of six oil lamps on the one hand, and part of a single oil lamp on the other. These claims lie at the heart of pre-Christian Nazareth. The amazing and almost inexplicable sagas that accompany these finds are an eye-opener to the researcher, and reveal that the very heart of Nazareth archaeology is terribly flawed.

The Richmond report

In 1930, while laying the foundations for a private house in Nazareth, a tomb was discovered approximately 320 m southwest of the Church of the Annunciation.[25] As is customary in the Holy Land, work was immediately suspended and the Department of Antiquities was notified. An inspector came to the site, and subsequent excavation uncovered a rectangular underground chamber with nine shafts (*kokhim*) radiating outwards from three sides. The tomb is Bagatti's number 72 (*Illus.2*).[26] It contained human bones and some artefacts, including six oil lamps, a juglet, beads, and small glass vessels. These finds were summarized in a brief report published in the 1931 issue of a new journal, *The Quarterly of the Department of Antiquities in Palestine*.[27] The report, entitled "A Rock-cut Tomb at Nazareth," consists of a mere half-page of prose, followed by three pages of diagrams and photographs. It is signed "E.T.R."

Born in 1874, Ernest Tatham Richmond joined the Royal Asiatic Society in 1910 and served as a functionary of the Ministry of Public Works in Cairo when Egypt was a British Protectorate (1914–22). He authored a number of articles on Egypt. and was subsequently appointed Director of Antiquities in Palestine. His signed 1931 report on this Nazareth tomb may have been authored by Richmond himself after a personal visit to the site, or it may be based on information received from his inspector, Naim Effendi Makhouli.

---

[25] *Maps*: Kopp 1938:193, marked number "3"; DB Suppl. 6 (1960) cols. 319–20, number "2"; Bagatti *Exc*:28, Fig 3 (unmarked, in quadrant D1). *Discussion*: Kopp 1938:192, 194; Bagatti *Exc*:242. *Notes*: The tomb is Bagatti's number 72. The scale on the DB map is faulty (shortened by one-third). Richmond locates the tomb "about 250 m. south-west" of the Church of the Annunciation.

[26] *Exc*. 242. This is Kopp's tomb no. 3 (Kopp 1938:192–94).

[27] QDAP Vol 1, No. 2, pp. 53–54.

THE MYTH OF NAZARETH

The report itself is unremarkable except for one word in the final sentence:

> *Tomb No. 10.* Two glass vessels (Pl XXXIII.5, third and fourth from left), six Hellenistic lamps (Pl. XXXIV.2), and iron, glass, and pottery fragments.
> E.T.R.

This is the first mention in the Nazareth literature of specific Hellenistic evidence. If Richmond were correct, and if six Hellenistic oil lamps were indeed found only a few hundred meters from the venerated area, then the case for Nazareth existing in the time of Jesus would be virtually assured. Such is the awesome importance of the single word "Hellenistic" in this brief and obscure report.

However, a glance at the photo (*Illus. 3.1*) shows to even an amateur that none of the lamps signaled by Richmond is Hellenistic. The two in the upper row have been specifically dated by Israeli specialists to between "the second half of the first century A.D." and the third century,[28] that is, Middle-Late Roman times. Two of the lamps (lower left and lower right) are of the bow-spouted type, which will be studied in Chapter Four. They are dated in Galilee from *c.* 25 CE to *c.* 135 CE.[29] The remaining two lamps are Late Roman (see below). In other words, all six oil lamps date to the common era.

A more precise dating for several of the lamps in the Richmond report can be ascertained from an invaluable 1978 publication, *Ancient Lamps in the Schloessinger Collection.* It itemizes over five hundred Hellenistic and Roman oil lamps from Syria, Palestine, and Arabia. Authored by Renate Rosenthal and Renee Sivan, this compendious work contains a description and photo of each lamp, together with a note on provenance, condition, dating, type, ornamentation, and a comparison with similar specimens found elsewhere. Rosenthal and Sivan are aware of Mr. Richmond's report and specifically date two of his six lamps (upper left and upper right) to between 50/70 CE and 200 CE.[30] They date the lamp at the lower right to *c.* 100 CE,[31] which corresponds to the Middle Roman period. The remaining three lamps consist of an undecorated bow-spouted lamp (lower left) dating to the latter half of I CE, and in the lower middle, two rather unusual lamps with stubby nozzles.

---

[28] R. Rosenthal and R. Sivan: 85 (discussion), and 89 (bottom right), following P. Kahane.

[29] V. Sussman (1985:53) writes that these lamps made their first appearance in Palestine "after the reign of Herod [the Great]." A few years must be allowed for their dissemination to the Lower Galilee, hence, 25 CE is an approximate *terminus post quem* at Nazareth.

[30] Rosenthal & Sivan: 85, 89.

[31] Rosenthal & Sivan: 85. It is a "Darom-type" bow-spouted lamp, as described in Sussman 1982:15–19.

Parallels to these latter have been variously dated III–VI CE.[32] Since we are using 70 CE as the beginning of Middle Roman times, all six oil lamps in *Illus. 3.1* are Middle Roman, Late Roman, or Early Byzantine.

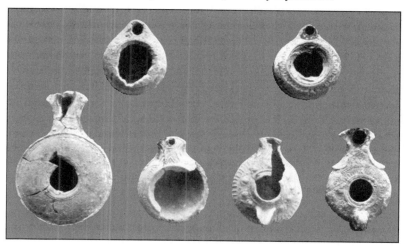

Illus. 3.1. Six oil lamps of the Roman period found in Tomb 72.
(Photo from QDAP 1931, Pl. XXXIV.2)

One can only speculate how the word "Hellenistic" entered Richmond's report. The discrepancy in dating is huge, amounting to between three and five centuries. No expert would be capable of such a mistake.[33] Nor would he treat these six lamps as a group, for they represent strikingly different types. It is remarkable that this egregious error survived the scrutiny of the Department of Antiquities of Palestine, in whose *Quarterly* the report was published. But then, Richmond was himself Director of the Department.

These six Richmond oil lamps underwent a second stage of misrepresentation a few years after the publication of Richmond's report. Fr. Clemens Kopp, whom we have previously met,[34] penned his first installment of *"Beiträge zur Geschichte Nazareths"* in 1938. He commented on Richmond's "Hellenistic" assessment as follows:

---

[32] *Cf.* the following, all with small wick hole and stubby nozzle: (a) Sellers and Baramki fig. 41:63 & 74. This is their type VIII, which they date "4th or early 5th century A.D." (b) Mazar, *Beth She'arim* vol. III, pl. LXXI:32. He considers the lamp uncommon and its date uncertain, but notes a parallel "in a sixth-century context" (p. 190). (c) Mazar, *Beth She'arim* vol. I, fig. 23:3 (III-IV CE).

[33] For descriptions, photos, and sketches specifically of Hellenistic oil lamps see Sussman 6–7; Bailey 18; Goodenough I:140 (chart at vol. II #253), and Rosenthal & Sivan.

[34] Chapter 2, pp. 65–70.

> R[ichmond] classifies 6 lamps by date very generally as "Hellenistic," according to the accompanying photographs of the finds they must surely go back at least to 200 BCE.[35]

This statement goes considerably beyond Richmond's error of the single word "Hellenistic," which denotes a period continuing into the first century BCE. Fr. Kopp supplies a much earlier date: "at least... 200 BCE," *i.e.*, the third century BCE. This magnifies the previous mistake, and we can only wonder what made the German choose a date that has not the remotest relevance to the lamps in question. Even an amateur collector would not be so misled, much less an antiquities dealer, not to mention a writer on archaeological matters such as Fr. Kopp. To date this group of Roman-Byzantine oil lamps before 200 BCE is a monstrosity—it errs in some cases by over five hundred years. There is no question of an inadvertent slip, for the priest claims to have examined the accompanying photographs himself and appeals to his own expertise. The only possible conclusion, then, is that deception is heaped upon deception.

The priest's *modus operandi* is transparent. Kopp fabricates Hellenistic evidence in an attempt to bolster the case that Nazareth existed before the time of Christ. At the same time, he undergirds the Church's position by providing a false Hellenistic claim, one readily available for subsequent citation in the Nazareth literature.

In his 1963 book, *The Holy Places of the Gospels*,[36] Kopp continues the same line as in his work of a generation earlier: "Two kokim sites, untouched by plunderers, have been discovered in Nazareth recently. The contents show that one belongs to the period about 200 B.C., the other to the first century A.D." The first of these sites must refer to the Richmond tomb, for nowhere else does Kopp claim II BCE evidence. A few years later Bagatti corrected this misdating.[37] As for the "first century A.D." site (Tomb 70), Kopp is probably correct—some oil lamps from that tomb may date to the latter part of I CE, as we shall see in Chapter Four.

It is self-explanatory that if the village of Nazareth existed in the time of Jesus, then it came into existence sometime before the turn of the era. For the tradition, then, Nazareth must have been either born or already in existence in Hellenistic times. Thus, one epoch depends on the other: the existence of a viable village at the turn of the era (one with a synagogue and crowd that could accompany Jesus, Lk 4:16–30) depends on its existence already in Hellenistic times.

---

[35] *"nach den beigegebenen Bildern der Funde muss man wohl mindestens bis auf 200 v. Chr. heraufgehen."* Kopp 1938:194.

[36] English translation of *Die heiligen Stätten der Evangelien* (Regensburg, 1959).

[37] *Exc.* 242.

The Hellenistic Renaissance Myth

This appears to be the inspiration behind Kopp's dissimulation of evidence. The shocking lack of finds of a Greco-Roman settlement in the basin, already noted by Tonneau in 1931,[38] placed an enormous burden on the tradition to materially demonstrate that Nazareth existed in the Hellenistic era.

The kokh tomb

In his 1938 Nazareth report, Kopp also considers the tomb in which the Richmond artefacts were found. Technically, this is known as a kokh tomb. We shall briefly consider this type of Jewish burial before returning to what Kopp has to say about the Richmond tomb. *Kokh* literally means "grave, cave for burial" in Mishnaic Hebrew. The plural is *kokhim*.[39] Probably imported from Egypt and first noted in Palestine about 200 BCE,[40] the kokh tomb "virtually became the canonical form of the Jewish family grave" from about 150 BCE to 150 CE.[41] This form of burial continued in use well into Byzantine times.[42] The exact layout of the tomb, the dimensions of each kokh, and the number and placement of kokhim are specified in the Mishna.[43]

The typical kokh tomb had a central square chamber, often with a pit dug into the floor that allowed a man to stand upright. From each side (all except the entrance) one to three kokhim were hewn horizontally into the rock, radiating outwards from the central chamber.[44] Each kokh was about one meter high and two meters long, and was designed to accommodate a single body.[45]

Illus. 3.2 shows the plan of the Richmond tomb (Bagatti's no. 72), a typical kokh tomb. Over twenty tombs of this type have been found in the basin, and a number have probably not been discovered.[46] Most were robbed

---

[38] *Revue Biblique* XL (1931) p. 556. See Chapter 2, pp. 65*ff.*.

[39] Also spelled *kok,* plural *kokim.*

[40] Kuhnen:73; Hachlili:790; Galling, "Nekropole," *Palästina Jahrbuch* 1936, p.76; Goodenough I:66.

[41] Finegan 1969:185.

[42] This will be detailed in Chp. 4. Later examples of kokhim tombs are at Beth She'arim (III-IV CE) and Silet edh-Dhahr (to VII CE). *Cf.* Mazar; Sellers and Baramki.

[43] Mishna, *Baba Bathra*, 6.8;Babylonian Talmud, *Bava Bathra* 100b–102b.

[44] Hachlili:789; Finegan:189, etc.

[45] Hachlili, "Burials," ABD I:789. *Loculus* (pl. *loculi*) is another name often used interchangeably with *kokh* (Hachlili 789, Finegan 189). However, with some authors (*e.g.* Goodenough I/66, 88) *loculus* refers to what has been called the 'shelf' tomb (see Finegan/184). Because of its non-uniform use, the term *loculus* is avoided in this book.

[46] Residents of the modern town claim the existence of tombs which have never been excavated. In his 1992 edition, Finegan counted 18 kokh tombs in the Nazareth basin (p. 46). The tombs are itemized in Chapter 5.

in antiquity, but three kokhim tombs at Nazareth fortunately contained movable finds at the time of discovery.[47] Mostly pottery, such finds include jars, oil lamps, glass, and metal objects dating to Middle Roman and later times. These critical artefacts—most especially the oil lamps—allow us to date the birth of Nazareth.

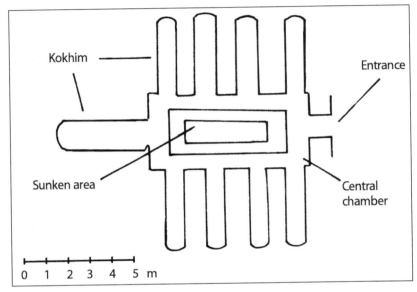

Illus. 3.2. **Plan of a Jewish kokh tomb.**
(The "Richmond" Tomb 72. Redrawn from QDAP 1931:54.)

Seeing that Richmond's tomb is of the kokh type, Kopp dates it incomparably early by recalling the very first kokh tomb known in all of Palestine, that at Marisa far to the south.[48] This tomb, the German conjectures, was hewn already in III BCE—itself an improbably early date. In any case, the oil lamps should have sufficed to show that his analogy is grossly in error, for the Marisa lamps have typically long Hellenistic nozzles and are very different in form. They have nothing in common with the lamps found in the Nazareth tomb.[49]

Immediately following his citation above, Kopp continues:

---

[47]   Tombs 70, 71, and 72.

[48]   Kopp 1938:194.

[49]   For diagrams of oil lamps from Marisa see Goodenough, vol. II, fig. 254 (discussion p. 143).

Kokh tombs emerge first in Alexandria and the towns of Phoenicia. The earliest example in Palestine is the tomb of Apollophanes in old Marisa. Its inscriptions begin in 198 B.C. It must therefore have been cut already in III BCE. The type could not have reached Nazareth so quickly from the south, [and so] we must certainly look to Phoenician burial installations for inspiration [als Pate]. Even as Phoenician colonizers first used this type of tomb in Marisa, so one may suppose that non-Jews were also the pathfinders in Nazareth.[50]

This series of speculations derives from one error: that the lamps in the Richmond report are Hellenistic. From that seed, Kopp concludes that the tomb itself must date to early Hellenistic times. This in turn leads to his analogy with the earliest kokh tomb in the land, that at Marisa far to the south, though the Nazareth lamps have nothing at all in common with the former. In fact, the Richmond lamps are closely related to those found in a much nearer kokh tomb, at Silet edh-Dhahr in the territory of Manasseh, used I CE–VII CE.[51] But Kopp cleaves to the conviction that the Nazareth lamps are early Hellenistic, and from this false conviction ultimately ensues his adventurous proposition that the inhabitants of Hellenistic Nazareth were not Jews but Phoenicians—this, because the kokh form of tomb could not have moved so quickly from south to north, and therefore must have come from Phoenicia.

Kopp's thesis of a Hellenistic-Phoenician Nazareth quickly disappeared from the literature. Bagatti does not take it up, and it is never heard of again. Whatever we may say of the German's speculations, their purpose is transparent: to make the case that Nazareth existed before the time of Christ.

This is not the end of the story regarding these six "Hellenistic" oil lamps first brought to our attention by Richmond's short report. In his 1969 *Excavations in Nazareth*, Bagatti acknowledges Richmond's error and correctly redates the lamps to II-III CE. Having removed one error, however, he then introduces another equally damaging. We shall take up that problem, which involves the term "Herodian," when we deal with Early Roman times in Chapter Four.

The infamous "Hellenistic" nozzle

As we noted in Chapter Two, a major conclusion of Bagatti's *Excavations in Nazareth* is the Church's doctrine of continuous habitation:

---

[50] Kopp 1838:194.

[51] Specific parallels at Silet edh-Dhahr to two Richmond lamps date IV–VI CE (Sellers & Baramki: 8, 29, 44). They will be reconsidered when we take up the Roman period.

> ...contrary to what was believed, life did not begin in the place in a recent
> epoch, but already existed in the Bronze Period, to continue down to our
> own days.[52]

Of course, a settlement existing from the Bronze Period "down to our
days" implies a settlement also during Hellenistic times. On the same page,
however, Bagatti offers a terse admission:

> We have met with only few traces of the Hellenistic period, but there are
> many elements of the Roman period.

This is surprising. A "few traces of the Hellenistic period" are, of course,
far less than one would expect of a settlement in Hellenistic times, one
already in existence for almost two millennia. The Italian does not offer an
explanation for the paucity of Hellenistic finds, and we are left to suppose
that the remains of the Greek village have either evaded the archaeologist's
spade, or that the village was at a low ebb during the Hellenistic period.

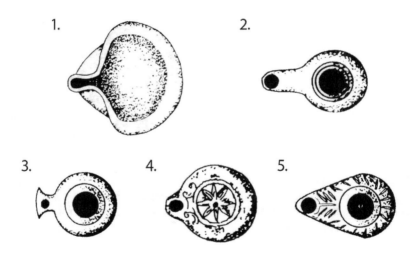

***Illus.3.3.* Typical Palestinian oil lamps.**
1. Late Iron age   2. Hellenistic   3. Bow-spouted ("Herodian")
4. Roman   5. Byzantine

Nevertheless, the existence of even a "few traces"—if they existed—
would be of monumental importance as regards the pre-Christian history of
Nazareth. We must therefore ascertain what those Hellenistic traces consist of,
describe and itemize them, and thence arrive at a conclusion regarding a pre-

---

[52] *Exc.* 319. For discussion see Chapter 2, pp. 84–85.

The Hellenistic Renaissance Myth

Christian settlement. We have already addressed one claim—the six oil lamps mentioned by Richmond and then by Kopp—and have found those lamps to be Roman rather than Hellenistic.[53] Indeed, Bagatti corrects Richmond's error, but he still mentions the word "Hellenistic" upwards of a dozen times in his *Excavations*—rarely, however, in connection with identifiable evidence. A careful review of his tome shows that there are astoundingly few artefacts involved:

> The only pieces which seem to indicate the Hellenistic period is [*sic*] the nozzle No. 26 of Fig. 233, and 2 of Fig. 235, a bit short for the ordinary lamps, but not completely unusual. (Pp. 309–10.)

This is a second surprise. We note, first of all, the incorrect English grammar. The subject is plural and two examples are given, but the verb is singular. It is of no moment whether the faulty grammar is due to the author or to the translator, for—since Bagatti nowhere claims Hellenistic structural remains—we here have the remarkable admission that *the entire Hellenistic period at Nazareth is represented by only two pieces:* an oil lamp nozzle, and number "2 of Fig. 235." In contradiction to the above statement, a careful review in fact shows that Bagatti alleges other Hellenistic shards in his *Excavations*.[54] He has evidently ignored these latter instances in his above summation which concludes his book. Certainly, two pieces are precious little upon which to base the existence of a village. Apparently, however, they constituted the sum total of pre-Christian evidence at Nazareth as of 1967, the publication date of *Excavations* (Italian edition). Such staggering importance is therefore placed on "the only pieces" from Nazareth witnessing to Hellenistic times, that they merit the most careful scrutiny.

A third surprise meets us when we compare the two artefacts. Incredibly, they are two versions of one and the same piece—represented once in a photo (Fig. 233 #26), and once again in a sketch (Fig. 235 #2). This may explain the singular verb *is* in Bagatti's statement: the two pieces *are* one.

What, then, is this transcendently important bit of clay? What, by the archaeologist's own admission, is this solitary proof of pre-Christian Nazareth? What, indeed, is this artefact upon which the entire Christian story depends?

It is the broken nozzle of an oil lamp. Examination of photo and diagram shows that we are dealing with a shard approximately 3 cm long by 2 cm in depth, that is, about the size of an adult's thumb from mid-joint to tip (*Illus. 4:1*).[55] It was discovered in Silo 24, immediately east of the Church of the

---

[53] The six lamps will be itemized and individually dated in Chapter Four.

[54] In a 1970 article Bagatti offers additional Hellenistic claims (see below, pages 28–31).

[55] A scale accompanies *Exc.* Fig. 235, located in the lower left quadrant. Presumably,

Annunciation,[56] and was found among artefacts from the Iron, Roman, and Byzantine periods.[57] This in itself should raise suspicion, for we are dealing with an outlier, a solitary chronological exception in the assemblage. In any case, upon this small shard rests the fate of pre-Christian Nazareth, as far as the principal source is concerned.

Is the shard Hellenistic? The nozzles of Hellenistic lamps were typically long with a rounded tip (*Illus.3.3:2*),[58] though shorter ones were not unknown.[59] Bagatti's "Hellenistic" nozzle is not particularly long and has a flattened tip. The border of the discus is discernible in Bagatti's photo, showing us that the nozzle was no longer than diagramed in *Illus.3.4:1*. This is where the fracture occurred, and thus we can see that the nozzle was shorter than the common Hellenistic types.[60] Even Bagatti had qualms in this regard, for he wrote that it is "a bit short for the ordinary [Hellenistic] lamps, but not completely unusual." We are dealing, then, with an *atypical* Hellenistic oil lamp.

To support his thesis, Bagatti offers several "Hellenistic" parallels in a footnote.[61] One parallel is to a nozzle found at the Mount of Olives near Jerusalem.[62] Comparison of the two shards, however (placed side-by-side in *Illus. 3.4:1* and *3.4:2*), shows that they are quite different: the Nazareth nozzle has almost parallel sides, a flat tip, and large wick hole. On the other hand, the Jerusalem example has a triangular shape with strongly slanting sides, a rounded tip, and small wick hole. Though the scales may not match precisely, the shapes are clearly dissimilar.

In fact, it is not likely that the Jerusalem parallel is itself Hellenistic. Without wishing to open yet another can of worms, I note that Bagatti claims on p. 117 of his book, *Gli Scavi del Dominus Flevit* (from which the Jerusalem parallel is drawn), that "nn. 1–7 of fig. 25" belong to the Hellenistic period. This claim is hardly tenable.[63] No. 1 is a small folded lamp of the Early

---

all 43 artefacts in Bagatti's figure are drawn to the same scale, though we cannot be sure. Some of the representations are of poor quality.

[56] *Exc.* 301 (No. 26), 44, 48; Pl. XI.

[57] *Exc.* 44, 46. Artefacts from Silo 24 include figs. 225:6, 8; 227:19–20; 230:2.

[58] *Cf.* Goodenough 1953, vol. II, figs. 254-255; J. Hayes 165–6; Sussman 7. Galling 14*f.* delineates five types of Hellenistic lamp, all with the long nozzle.

[59] *E.g.*, Rosenthal & Sivan Nos. 325–327.

[60] *Exc.* Fig. 233, No. 26. The photo shows that the diagram at *Exc.* fig. 235:2. has been poorly drawn. The wick hole of the artefact is larger and round (not oval), and extends almost the entire width of the nozzle. *Illus. 3.4.1* is the rendering in *Excavations in Nazareth*.

[61] Exc. 310, note 43.

[62] *Gli Scavi del Dominus Flevit*, Fig. 25: 2. The book is essentially by B. Bagatti. J. Milik contributed the chapter on inscriptions.

[63] Paul Lapp also redates much of Bagatti's *Dominus Flevit* material to Roman rather than Hellenistic times. See P. Lapp:112.

Roman period;[64] nos. 3–5 date I BCE–I CE;[65] and nos. 5-8 are bow-spouted ("Herodian"), that is, I CE–early II CE.[66] All these lamps are of the Early Roman period. Only Bagatti's no. 2 is indeterminate—it is too fragmentary to tell. It is precisely this shard that the Italian uses as a "Hellenistic" parallel to the Nazareth nozzle. The nozzles are quite different, in any case, as we readily see in *Illus. 3.4.*

Another parallel offered by Bagatti is to a 1964 article on Hellenistic pottery written by Nancy Lapp.[67] Lapp's photo presents not one, but three nozzles from Shechem (*Illus. 4:3*). All three are quite distinct, and only her middle example has a flattened tip and approximately the same proportions as the Nazareth shard. But it is not a close parallel—the Shechem example is noticeably wider at the base than at the tip. Lapp calls these "plain, wheel-made delphiniform lamps" whose "nozzles are rounded and carelessly formed."

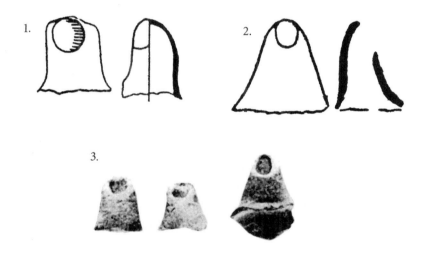

Illus. 3.4. The "Hellenistic" nozzle and its alleged parallels.
(1) The "Hellenistic" nozzle (2) The Jerusalem parallel (3) The Shechem parallels
(i. *Exc.* Fig. 235:2; ii. Bagatti-Milik, Fig. 25: 2; iii. N. Lapp 1964, Pl. 1:29–31)

---

[64] P. Lapp's Type 81, which he dates 75–4 BCE (P. Lapp 1961:192). Bagatti's example has the red slip and fine walls of such lamps (cf. Smith 1964:122).
[65] *Cf.* Goodenough vol I:145; vol. II, pl. 257; Strange 1975, Fig. 16:5.
[66] Bow-spouted lamps are discussed in Pt. 4.
[67] N. Lapp 1964: Plate I, Nos. 29–31.

THE MYTH OF NAZARETH

Bagatti did not realize that his "Hellenistic" lamp nozzle is related to a lesser-known type indigenous to the Galilee in Roman times. He needn't have gone as far afield as Shechem and Jerusalem for parallels. In 1983 the Spanish scholar F. Fernandez published a book-length treatment of the Roman pottery of Galilee, *Ceramica Comun Romana de la Galilea*. The Spaniard reviews a considerable number of Bagatti's finds and sometimes reaches different conclusions. Fernandez mentions *Exc.* Fig. 235:2 (the "Hellenistic" nozzle) in a footnote, and includes it in his lamp-type L1, which he calls the product of a "local pottery tradition."[68] The body of type L1 has a strikingly elevated rim around the filling hole which forms a small bowl sitting atop the lamp (readily seen in profile). The nozzle of this curious lamp ranged between two extreme forms, shown in *Illus. 5A* and *5B*. We shall see below that there were also intermediate variants in which we can locate the "Hellenistic" nozzle under discussion. The bowl on top of the lamp is an elaboration of the ridge around the filling hole, commonly seen in the bow-spouted lamp.[69]

Variant A. Bagatti discovered three examples of lamp type L1-A (= *Illus. 3.5A*) in Tomb 70 at Nazareth. He calls them "very unusual."[70] Four more examples were discovered in 1980–81 by Israeli archaeologist Nurit Feig when she excavated a number of tombs 2.6 km from the Church of the Annunciation.[71] These tombs are beyond the eastern edge of the basin, on the far side of the hill called Jebel el Maskaub (summit 438 m). Lamp type L1-A was also found in Roman contexts of nearby loci in Southern Galilee, such as Tiriah (only 200 m south of the Feig tombs), Afula, and Mishamar Haemek.[72] All the aforementioned examples are of variant L1-A, in which the nozzle has inwardly slanting sides and a small, rounded tip,[73] similar to Bagatti's Hellenistic parallels found in Jerusalem and Shechem (above, *Illus. 3.4:2* and *3.4:3c*). Feig perceptively notes the potential to confuse this variant with Hellenistic examples. Like Fernandez, she points out that this lamp is the product of a local tradition:

> The lamps in illustration 9:10–11 and 11:2 [all of Type L1-A] have a long nozzle similar to typical Hellenistic nozzles. The raised rim, however,

---

[68]   Fernandez: 63 (note 1 and discussion).

[69]   Bailey 1972:Pl. 6c; Smith 1966:4 and 1961:60–61. A precursor of type L1 may be the Hellenistic "Ephesus" lamp (Szentleleky 51).

[70]   *Exc.* fig. 192:15, and discussion pp. 239–40.

[71]   The Feig tomb is located at map. ref. 1808/2335. The archaeologist's report (in Hebrew) was published in *'Atiqot* 10 (1990) pp. 67–79. The four lamps of type L1 (all from tomb M) are her figs. 9:10–11 & 11:2.

[72]   Feig 73 and note 12 (Hebrew). Fernandez (p. 32) itemizes examples also from Karm er-Ras (near Cana), and Capernaum. Sussman notes the type at Abu Shusha and with the Galilee boat discovered at Ginnosar (see below).

[73]   Fernandez L1:1 & 4; Feig fig. 9:10–11; fig. 11:2 (photo).

resembles Roman lamps like those found at Ephesus. The base of the lamp is flat and thick, and around its opening a small bowl is moulded. The lamps were carefully made on a potter's wheel, and their firing is intermediate. This type, of which 4 examples were found in Tomb M, was probably the product of a local pottery tradition. According to all the finds from this tomb, it is possible to assume that it dates from the middle of the first century [CE] to the middle of the second century CE.[74]

Because they lie outside the immediate Nazareth settlement area, the Feig tombs have not been used in this work as evidence of settlement in the basin.[75] Nevertheless, those tombs cast welcome light on aspects of the archaeology of Nazareth. Lamp-type L1 is a case in point.

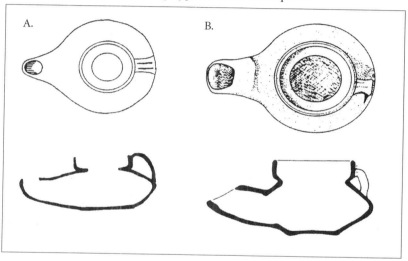

***Illus. 3.5.* Oil lamps of a local pottery tradition in Roman times.**
(Fernandez Type L1.) A. From Nazareth, Tomb 70; B. From the Galilee boat.
(Redrawn from *Exc.* Fig 192:15; Wachsmann:98.)

---

[74] Feig 74.

[75] It is difficult to know exactly how far the Nazareth settlement area extended. I have chosen the 400 meter contour line as the boundary, in that it stretches from peak to peak and defines the Nazareth basin (see Chapter. 1, *Illus. 1.3*). All tombs and artefacts within that contour line have been included in the primary data for this study. Tombs and artefacts beyond that line, or more than two kilometers from the CA, were probably in the spheres of neighboring settlements such as Japhia, Afula, Reina, or Sepphoris. Feig supposes that the tombs she excavated belonged within the sphere of Nazareth (her note 27). I find this unlikely, as those tombs are more than one kilometer beyond the crest of the hill. In any case, including the Feig tombs in the primary Nazareth data would not alter the conclusions of this study.

Ms. Feig found a fifth lamp of related type, wheel-made like the others, in tomb B. The archaeologist compares it to a lamp found in Shimron "dated by [Paul] Lapp to the first century CE."[76]

Context is certainly an important factor in cases like this, where we are dealing with an unusual lamp of limited geographic dispersion. We shall see that, in all cases, the context secures a Roman dating for the L1-type lamps found in the Nazareth basin and in the surrounding area, including those examined by Feig, Fernandez, and Bagatti.

With the above in mind, we note that Feig dates the tombs she excavated, and their associated artefacts, to Middle-Late Roman times:

> From these facts and from the findings it is possible to relate the use of these tombs to a period of time between the middle of the first century (M) to the third century CE (D). [77]

Fernandez also affirms a Roman dating for the assemblage in which the three Nazareth examples of lamp type L1-A were found (Tomb 70, not far from the Church of the Annunciation):

> The type [ejemplar] from Nazareth, n.1, does not betray any date, and the rest of the published material from the same [tomb] is certainly no earlier than the second third of the first century after Christ.[78]

Thus, Fernandez assigns Tomb 70 a *terminus post quem* of 33–67 CE. This is approximately the *terminus* Feig assigned to the nearby tombs she excavated, namely, post-50 CE. These two loci represent all the lamps of type L1 in the immediate Nazareth area, and it is evident that this "local pottery tradition" is not Hellenistic but Roman. This is clear from both context and typological parallels.

Nevertheless, Bagatti's "Hellenistic" lamp nozzle is not similar to variant L1-A at all. It is, rather, much like Fernandez' type L1-B. The latter lamp is slightly larger, and its nozzle has almost parallel sides, a wide and flat tip, and a large wick hole—quite like the "Hellenistic" nozzle.[79] Type L1-B is less well represented than the other. What can we discover regarding its dating?

---

[76] Feig 74; Fig. 9:10. In footnote 7, the archaeologist notes Hellenistic precursors that lack the distinctive raised rim around the filling hole. *Cf.* O. Broneer, *Ishthmia III*, Princeton, 1977, p. 18. Pl. 17:133–135; D.M. Robinson, *Excavations at Olynthus II*, Baltimore, 1930, p. 143, nos. 89–90, fig. 307; P. Baur, *The Excavations at Dura-Europos*, vol. 4, Pt. III, p.5.

[77] Feig 79. Feig's 1990 conclusion, as cited, is more conservative than her first published dating, communicated in the *Israel Exploration Journal* of 1983:116–17: "The finds in the *kokhim* and on the floor-level of the caves are dated to the second-third centuries C.E."

[78] Fernandez 63.

[79] On this variant see Fernandez L1:2 & 3, both found near Cana; Feig fig. 11:2; and the Galilee boat lamp (Sussman 1990). We recall that the wick hole in Bagatti's "Hellenistic" nozzle is larger than is shown in the drawing of *Illus. 3.4:1*. See above note 57.

The Hellenistic Renaissance Myth

The Galilee boat

In the winter of 1986, two young men from the nearby kibbutz of Ginnosar were walking along the shore of the Sea of Galilee. The water level was particularly low for the area had experienced several years of drought, with the result that the two could walk on land that was normally under water. They noticed the outline of a boat in the mud, and when experts examined the discovery it was determined that an ancient boat had been found dating to the turn of the era. The boat was preserved in a laborious process that took several years, and is now in the Yigal Allon Museum of Kibbutz Ginnosar.

A single intact oil lamp was found in the boat. It is of the type L1-B, and is diagrammed above in *Illus. 3.5-B*.[80] We particularly note the nozzle, which is slightly longer than usual, has almost parallel sides, a flattened tip, and a large wick hole. It shares these characteristics with the "Hellenistic" nozzle of Bagatti, and furnishes a closer parallel than any furnished by the Italian. The only difference is in the underside of the nozzle. When one compares the profiles of *Illus. 3.4:1* (above) with *Illus. 3.5-B*, one notices that the former has a more pronounced curvature, with the wick hole in a more superior position. This too, however, is readily explained. The curvature of the Bagatti shard matches the underside of three examples of type L1 found in tomb 70 at Nazareth, whose form is diagrammed in *Illus. 3.5-A*, above. It is evident, then, that the Bagatti lamp nozzle is a hybrid of the two variants: the underside is modeled with the curvature of *Illus. 3.5-A*, while the outline is in the form of *Illus. 3.5-B*. Several similar hybrid lamps were found by Feig in her tomb M nearby,[81] and these represent the closest parallels to the Bagatti shard.

In 1990, Varda Sussman published a study of the Galilee boat lamp. She commented on its dating as follows:

> Both the shape and the ware have a great deal in common with oil lamps and other vessels dated to the Early Roman and Herodian periods, ranging in date from the mid-first century BCE to the mid-second century CE.[82]

Thus, all the datings that we have assembled for this Galilean local tradition—lamp type L1—are Roman, not Hellenistic. It is all but certain that the Bagatti shard belongs among them, as seen from its form and from the presence of a number of nearby examples in and around the Nazareth basin. A chronological review of the local results for this lamp type follows:

---

[80] The side view shows a curve in the Bagatti example (*Exc.* Fig. 235:2) most closely paralleled by Fernandez L1 no.1 (p. 42)—*i.e.*, the lamps from Tomb 70.
[81] Feig 73-74, diagrammed in her Fig. 9:11.
[82] Sussman 1990:97.

Locus	Artefact(s)	Type	Assemblage date
Nazareth Tomb 70	3 lamps	L1-A	c. 33 CE + [83]
Feig, Tomb M	4 lamps	L1-A/B	50 CE–150 CE[84]
Feig, Tomb B	1 lamp	L1-A	I CE (P. Lapp)[85]
Galilee boat	1 lamp	L1-B	50 BCE–150 CE[86]

According to these results, seven of the above nine lamps date c. 33 CE–c. 150 CE. The other two lamps are compatible with this range, and it is clear that late I CE to early II CE was the favored era for this local lamp tradition. We shall see in Chapter Four that this is also the earliest time when one can speak with certainty of the resumption of settlement in the Nazareth basin. The dating of the lamp nozzle we have been considering is entirely compatible with that time.

Bagatti's so-called "Hellenistic" oil lamp nozzle, now identified as a shard from Fernandez' Roman lamp type L1, is the most prominent of several small pieces of pottery that comprise the sum total of alleged Hellenistic evidence from the Nazareth basin.[87] This lamp nozzle alone is responsible for multiple mentions of the word "Hellenistic" in *Excavations in Nazareth*.[88] When we remove it from consideration, as we can now do, then the case for Nazareth in Hellenistic times is weakened beyond repair, for the remaining shards are more easily dismissed.[89]

The Church of St. Joseph material

In August, 1970, Bagatti excavated a 6×15 meter area next to the Church of St. Joseph. The express purpose of this excavation was to verify the existence of traces of settlement at the turn of the era—more particularly, traces of the house of the Holy Family itself. As Bagatti writes in the following passage, such traces had evaded prior attempts:

> *Scavando la chiesa medievale, per ricostruirla col titolo di S. Giuseppe a Nazaret, nel 1892 i francescani si limitarono a ricavare la pianta dei muri senza preoccuparsi dei piccoli oggetti. In questo modo restarono visibili dei resti: a) crociati con alcuni ricorsi della chiesa; b) bizantini*

---

[83] Fernandez 63.

[84] Feig 74.

[85] Feig 73 and her note 7.

[86] Sussman 1990:97.

[87] A summary of the alleged Hellenistic evidence is found in *Illus. 3.6.*

[88] *Exc.* 300, 304, and 309

[89] See the next section, points A, B, and C.

con porzioni di pavimento musivo, una vasca quadrata ed una cisterna a pera; precristiani con grotte e sili riuniti con corridoi. Mancava, proprio, la testimonianza archeologica del periodo principale, del I secolo, a cui la tradizione raccolta dal P. Quaresmi nel 1620 e ripristinata dal P. Viaud, voleva far risalire l'abitzione della S. Famiglia.

È vero che lo studio-storico-teologico del P. Testa mostrava l'ambiente come un luogo abitato dai giudeo-cristiani, e quindi dava appoggio alla tradizione mantenuta nell'ambiente familiare, però la prova archeologica mancava. Per costatare la permanenza della vita sul posto è stato intrapreso lo scavo nella zona adiacente alla chiesa stessa, sul lato di nord. Esso è stato tenuto nel mese di Agosto del 1970, previo permesso del Dipartimento delle Antichità di Israele.[90]

Thus begins Bagatti's article, "Scavo Presso la Chiesa di S. Giuseppe a Nazaret." We shall put aside the Bagatti-Testa claim "that the area was settled by Jewish-Christians," a thesis convincingly rebutted by Joan Taylor in her book, *Christians and the Holy Places.* On the other hand, we shall concentrate on the archaeological evidence Bagatti brings forward in this excavation, namely, one hundred small pottery shards. They date to many periods, including the Iron and the Byzantine, and most are no larger than 3–4 inches at their maximum extent (no scale is provided).

It is important to note that this was a *re-excavation* by Bagatti of a site first dug in 1892. As a result, the area was greatly disturbed and *no stratigraphy was either possible or attempted.* A further compromising aspect is that the small finds came from a pile of material evidently discarded by the first diggers. Older finds were sometimes above more recent ones, and the archaeologist states that some of the objects described may not even have come from the area in which they were found. Bagatti writes (p. 6):

---

[90] "Excavating the medieval church prior to its reconstruction as the [Church] of St. Joseph of Nazareth, in 1892 the Franciscans limited themselves to determining the plan of the walls without preoccupying themselves with the small objects. In this way, the [following] remains were exposed: a) Crusader, with some church remains; b) Byzantine, with portions of the Moslem pavement, a square basin and a pear-shaped cistern; c) Pre-Christian, with grottos and silos connected by corridors. Lacking, properly-speaking, was archaeological evidence from the principal period, the first century [CE], a tradition indebted to P. Quaresmius in 1620 and reasserted by P. Viaud, which sought to uncover the domicile of the Holy Family.

"To be sure, P. Testa's historical and theological study showed that the area was settled by Jewish-Christians, thus giving support to the tradition regarding the domesticity of the site, but the archaeological proof was lacking. In order to verify continuity of settlement at the place, the excavation was undertaken in an area adjoining the church itself, on the northern side. This was carried out in the month of August, 1970, with the authorization of the Department of Antiquities of Israel." (Bagatti 1971a:5.)

> It was out of the question to find intact [stratigraphic] levels with characteristic objects since the zone [of the excavations], at least in part, was disturbed [*manomessa*]… [I]t was not possible to discern distinct levels, but only an accumulation of material coming *in great part* from the area of the church itself. For this reason, sometimes older remains were found in higher positions than more recent ones. (Emphasis added.)

Given these untoward circumstances, it is indeed hazardous to attempt any conclusions based on the finds from this excavation. Bagatti claims that three of the recovered shards are Hellenistic. We will contest that claim below, but here it can be noted that their presence in the assemblage would be exceptional, for the remaining ninety-seven shards are Iron Age, Middle-Late Roman, Byzantine, and Medieval. Furthermore, the three fragments in question are "mutilated" and far too small to provide a reliable reconstruction of complete artefacts, even for an experienced eye. Their form must remain entirely conjectural—the three shards may be parts of pots, jars, craters, or other vessels, with or without spouts, *etc*. Nevertheless, Bagatti claims both a reconstruction and a Hellenistic dating for two (or possibly all three) of the shards.

Other problems attend Bagatti's presentation. The photos accompanying the text are poor, and shadow obscures the greater portion of the visible surfaces of the objects portrayed. This renders it impossible for the reader to obtain a clear idea of the artefacts. An additional, but less grievous impediment is that the description, drawing, and photograph numbers do not correspond with one another. For example, photo 13:1 = drawing 17:15. When applied to one hundred objects, one can appreciate the unwieldiness of this Byzantine presentation. Regarding the three "Hellenistic" shards, Bagatti writes:

> *Del periodo ellenistico si notano le pentole col labro rientrante nell'interno (fig. 13, 2–3). Dell'ultimo ellenistico o romano è la base verniciata (fig. 13,1) sfortunatamente molto mutila.*[91]

We will ignore the "greatly mutilated" shard, itself sufficient reason to disqualify it as evidence for any period. In addition, Bagatti admits that it could be Roman. As regards the other two pieces, it is well known that vessels with incurved rims—though common in Hellenistic ware[92]—were not unique to that period. This too disqualifies these pieces as demonstrably Hellenistic evidence. Incidentally, it is surprising that the archaeologist's descriptions do not match the diagrams, for the drawings of the two objects in question do not show a "rim turned inwards."

---

[91] "Of the Hellenistic Period the pots with rim turned inwards are noted (fig. 13, 2–3). Late Hellenistic or Roman is the painted base (fig. 13,1) unfortunately greatly mutilated." Bagatti 1971a:23.

[92] P. Lapp:46–47.

The Hellenistic Renaissance Myth

Most decisive, however, is the fact that the diagrams provided for the two artefacts show the upper portions of characteristic *Roman* cooking pots, with small handles set close to the rim and thin walls that facilitated the rapid transmission of heat. The photo corresponding to one shard (*Scavo* 13:2 = 17:1) also shows the "sliced" handle typical of such Roman ware. Hayes dates the appearance of this type to *c.* 100 CE.[93]

Ancillary problems, touched on above, make it difficult to use any of the hundred shards from this excavation as evidence for any period:

1. The area of the excavation was disturbed
2. The shards may have come from outside the area
3. No stratigraphy was determined
4. The recovered pieces are often too small to establish the form, type, and dating for the artefacts from which they came

In addition, we have mentioned that the diagrams of the objects at critical points do not match the descriptions. Finally, Bagatti provides no typological parallels. These are all reasons enough to disqualify these small pieces as "Hellenistic" evidence. Over-riding all these considerations, however, is the fact that there is nothing demonstrably Hellenistic about the shards. Bagatti seems to realize this, for in a *Communication* regarding this excavation (published in the *Revue Biblique* later that year), he surprisingly omits mention of the Hellenistic age and includes only the Iron, Roman, Byzantine, and Crusader eras in his results:

> *On trouva d'abord un niveau moderne; puis commencèrent à apparaître des tessons de l'époque du fer, certains autres des époques romaine et byzantine, enfin ceux d'époque croisée immédiatement sur le rocher. On obtint ainsi une stratification inversée, ce qui montrait clairement que le remplissage provenait bien de l'église.*[94]

Even though the word "Hellenistic" is not present in the above passage, it had again entered the primary literature of Nazareth through the main article, to which the *Communication* is but a footnote, as it were. We indeed read of Hellenistic finds in Bagatti's subsequent references to the St. Joseph site. Thus, the *Encyclopedia of Archaeological Excavations in the Holy Land* (1977): "Potsherds from the Israelite, *Hellenistic*, Roman, and Byzantine periods and the Middle Ages were also found" (emphasis added).[95] An identical assertion is made in the Italian's 1993 NEAEHL article, "Nazareth."[96]

---

[93] Hayes 76–80. For *Scavo* 13:1 *cf.* Hayes Fig. 31:3; for *Scavo* 13:2 *cf.* Hayes Fig. 33:1.
[94] RB 78 (1971):587.
[95] EAEHL, "Nazareth," p. 921.
[96] NEAEHL, "Nazareth," p. 1104.

THE MYTH OF NAZARETH

In a passage we have already considered, Finegan goes a step farther and uses Bagatti's indeterminate results to support the doctrine of continuous habitation:

> In 1970 Bellarmino Bagatti excavated along the north wall of the Crusader church and in some of the grottoes under the wall. When the medieval church was excavated in 1892 much debris was piled here, and in the piles of debris Bagatti found in inverse order (as thrown out in the excavations) pottery fragments *from the Iron Age to the Roman*, Byzantine, and Crusader periods; and in the grottoes likewise he found Roman as well as Crusader pottery, *thus the site was certainly inhabited in the first century B.C. and the first century A.D. as well as earlier and later.* (Finegan 1992:57; emphasis added.)

Compounding error upon error, Finegan's statement has moved levels of magnitude beyond the slim evidence, which is now used as witness of settlement "from the Iron Age to the Roman," and as proof of habitation at and around the turn of the era. It is stunning when we recall that all these claims go back to none other than the three so-called "Hellenistic" shards discussed above. We have seen that these artefacts are by all appearances Middle to Late Roman. Even if we put aside the other compromising elements of this excavation as listed above, there is nothing recovered which demonstrates eras "from the Iron Age to the Roman."

In summary, let us review the interesting history of this small excavation site next to the Church of St. Joseph:

• In 1892, the Franciscans excavated the area. They were primarily interested in structural remains (pre-medieval wall foundations and pavements) and, indeed, were ultimately focused on discovering evidence from the time of Christ. Despite that pre-scientific age in archaeology, these early diggers surprisingly ignored the small artefacts and simply piled them to one side.

• In 1970 Bagatti re-excavated this pile of small finds and itemized precisely one hundred of them. He noted that no stratigraphy was possible because the site had been disturbed by his predecessors, and that in the pile of debris older finds were *sometimes* above more recent ones (later, Bagatti claimed to detect an "inverse" order in the pile). Among these hundred artefacts the Italian claimed that three were Hellenistic—this is the key point. However, there is nothing demonstrably Hellenistic about these shards at all, and all three appear, in fact, to be Roman.

The Hellenistic Renaissance Myth

• From the non-evidence presented by the three questionable shards, Bagatti claimed evidence from the Hellenistic Age, the Roman Period, and—by inference—the time of Christ. He noises this claim in his 1971 publication and in several dictionary articles. The archaeologist also (arbitrarily, I would suggest) associates the shard-pile with the adjacent Church of St. Joseph. All this is transparently directed at one goal: to use the St. Joseph excavation as evidence for habitation at the turn of the era and, indeed, for evidence of one particular habitation: that of the Holy Family. This linking of the St. Joseph excavation with the nearby Church and with the "Roman Period" (read: *the turn of the era*) occurred to the archaeologist after publication of his 1970 article, and appears in his *Communication* of 1971. Ultimately, however, the fact that no Hellenistic and *Early* Roman evidence exists in the shard-pile invalidates all of Bagatti's conclusions.

• In 1992 Finegan (cited above) overtly stated what Bagatti had merely implied, namely, that pottery fragments from the shard-pile dated "from the Iron Age to the Roman [Period]." Thus, once again the Great Hiatus in settlement is obliterated, as later Roman evidence appears Hellenistic and also from the time of Christ. Finally, Finegan cannot refrain from stating in black and white what Christian archaeologists from the beginning have wished to state: that "the site was certainly inhabited in the first century B.C. and the first century A.D. as well as earlier and later." This over-the-top statement is of course erroneous, for it is still based on the same three *later Roman* shards.

The reader should keep in mind that two- and three-inch fragments of pottery vessels are a precarious basis indeed for fixing the type and date of an artefact. Bagatti's resorting to such small fragments time and again is hardly salutary either for his method or for his conclusions. In the best of circumstances and with larger shards, the possibility for confusion is still significant, even by professionals.

If we honor Bagatti's diagrams, then these shards are parts of Roman cooking pots (see above). Because there is a non-correspondence between the diagrams and the descriptions, however, we are in an impossible position. If one were to honor the descriptions alone, then I would suggest that the two St. Joseph fragments belong to the Iron Age. "Two rims were at first considered Hellenistic counterparts of the Iron II holemouth jar rim," writes Paul Lapp. "... Actually, they are from craters and have Iron II parallels. Their ware is definitely Iron II and not Hellenistic..."[97] Such reevaluations to the Iron Age are not rare, and Bagatti already assigns no less than twenty-eight shards from the St. Joseph excavation to the earlier epoch. Four of those Iron

---

[97] P. Lapp:43, n.194.

Age fragments have "rims with ridges"[98] as, arguably, the brief description implies ("*col labro rientrante nell'interno*").

Regardless of how we treat Bagatti's contradictory presentation, the shards in question are probably Roman, possibly Iron, and certainly not Hellenistic.

A few more revealing observations can be made regarding this small excavation site. First of all, we wonder at the very existence of the shard-pile. Does it not betray a categorically unscientific attitude, even for 1892? After all, why were these pieces not placed carefully in a museum, or in some place for safekeeping? Why were they simply discarded to the side? It is as if the Franciscans, intent upon finding structural remains from Roman times, despoiled the remainder. This reminds one less of priests venerating a holy site as of Egyptian tomb robbers hunting for gold, smashing up masks and funerary objects and simply strewing them to the side.

Bagatti's inconsistency is also noted. In 1970 he writes of a pile with no order, and a year later of an "inverse" order. Surely his first observation is correct, for the building of a rubbish heap (which is essentially what the shard-pile originally represented) is rarely done with care, and much mixing and scattering inevitably take place.

It can also be noted that in this excavation Bagatti had no way to know what came from where, nor even if the material in the shard-pile had been excavated at the site or had been brought in from somewhere else.

It is of course not possible to expect modern scientific methods from the earlier Franciscans, nor even from Bagatti. Today excavation is conducted with the stratigraphic position of everything (sometimes even pollen!) being carefully documented. Thus, it is possible to create a three-dimensional diagram showing the original positions of all material at a site. Though such scientific rigor was never expected of the Franciscans, we do have every right to ask why they did not use the proper care and correct methods available at their time. Sloppiness, too, can be useful, as when the desire exists that certain facts *not* see the light of day. In this case confusion and disorder are a tool. We have already noted (Chapter Two) a chronological confusion, a "cavalier" approach to dating, under which the tradition has labored in dealing with the archaeological evidence from Nazareth. With so much to hide—indeed, the entire eight hundred year hiatus—is it any surprise that the Franciscans have chosen not rigor, but laxity in their archaeological work?

Remaining material represented as Hellenistic

In the preceding pages we have reviewed the three principal cases in which Nazareth evidence was labeled Hellenistic in the primary literature.

---

[98] *Scavo* Fig. 12:7–10. See Pt. 1:Ap. 2, "Itemization of the Iron Age Artefacts."

These cases are notable because the conclusions based upon them have been enormous, though the shards themselves are sometimes very slight. We now turn our attention to the few remaining Hellenistic claims of specific material in the ground.

- **A.** On page 183 of Bagatti's *Excavations in Nazareth*, we read:

> We give (figs. 144–5) the principal pieces of pottery found in the earth over the Grotto. Evidently they appertain to different periods, and *from the oldest shards we can establish with certainty the presence of life there several centuries before Christ.* (Emphasis added.)

This eminently quotable and self-assured statement places us squarely in the evidentiary gap following the Iron Age, the gap that I have termed the Great Hiatus (Chapter Two). In the last sentence Bagatti insists upon the incontrovertible existence of evidence from (presumably) the Hellenistic period. Of what does that certain evidence consist?

The archaeologist himself eliminates from contention ten of the eleven shards in the accompanying photo (p. 184), for in the itemization and discussion we read that Nos. 1–7 are from the Iron Period; No. 11 is Byzantine; while Nos. 9 and 10 are unspecified. This means that shard no. 8 bears the full weight of Bagatti's certainty regarding "the presence of life there several centuries before Christ." It is a triangular shard, approximately three inches long (no scale is given). The description reads:

> 8: Fragment of vase, exterior view, with white colour below and black above. On the inside (5 mm. thick) it is black, although the outside is leather coloured.

Remarkably, on the immediately following page the archaeologist admits that he is not certain whether the shard is early at all. In contrast to his previous conviction, he now mildly suggests that it may be Roman or Hellenistic:

> "The black varnish given to No. 8 reminds us of the custom in such products during Hellenistic-Roman times." (P. 185).

Of course, black varnish was used in many epochs. Though Bagatti appears to be suggesting "Hellenistic-Roman times" for the shard, his statement is a monument of ambiguity which may refer only to the varnish. In any case, the archaeologist is merely offering a suggestion, not a rigorous typological comparison—the varnish simply "reminds" him of a custom during Hellenistic-Roman times, that is, between 330 BCE and 330 CE, a period of no less than six and one-half centuries! The word "Hellenistic"

THE MYTH OF NAZARETH

appears entirely gratuitous. There is nothing uniquely Hellenistic about the shard, and the Italian offers no parallels in a footnote. We must conclude that his certainty regarding the "the presence of life there several centuries before Christ" has no material basis.

Judging from the context, no. 8 is probably not a Hellenistic outlier, but comes from the Iron Age or possibly from Roman times, as Bagatti himself intimates. There is no reason at all to consider it Hellenistic.

Bagatti's *modus operandi* is transparent. On the one hand an archaeological statement is made with conviction, a statement which is eminently quotable and which establishes the Church's position regarding Nazareth. Such statements are amenable to citation in the secondary literature. Then, however—in the 'fine print' as it were—the former conviction is modified, reduced, or even annulled. In every case involving Hellenistic evidence, inadequate (or no) substantiation is given for the prior certainty.

As regards the St. Joseph's shard, Bagatti's self-contradictory presentation suggests that he has merely engineered an opportunity to introduce the word "Hellenistic" into his tome. It had the desired effect. For example, in reference to this very passage from Bagatti's *Excavations*, Joan Taylor writes: "Sherds found in rock fissures within the grotto date from Hellenistic to Byzantine times."[99] Other authors have been similarly misled.

• **B**. On pages 136–37 of *Excavations in Nazareth*, we read:

> The Objects found under the pavement give us the remains of several periods, but as far as we know nothing beyond the 5th century. The oldest fragment appears to be the big vase Fig. 79, No. 1, with a small lip on top, which has parallels in Hellenic times and also earlier. Considering their fragmentary nature,[100] it is not easy to be precise, but the type is clear. Equally Hellenistic is the concave collar, No. 4, of which there are samples from the 1st century B.C.

(i) Two claims of Hellenistic ("Hellenic") evidence are made by Bagatti in these lines. The first is to a fragment of a "big vase [i.e., jar] Fig. 79, No. 1." The description at *Exc.* p. 132 describes the fragment as follows: "rim of a wide open vase of clay of a leather colour outside and black inside…" A black and white photo of the shard is offered (fig. 80:1). It appears to be approximately 1 x 3 inches (no scale is given). Bagatti writes (above) that it has parallels in Hellenistic times "and also earlier." In a footnote he gives two parallels—both to the Iron Age. If the shard were Hellenistic, one can be sure the archaeologist would have provided Hellenistic parallels, for that is the era he claims for it. Bagatti freely admits that the shard could be "earlier." This is

---

[99] Taylor 1993:254.

[100] The English reads: "Considering their fragments nature…"

128

The Hellenistic Renaissance Myth

confirmed by the parallels provided, and we shall accordingly consider that it comes from the Iron Age. There is nothing particularly Hellenistic about the artefact, and the word "Hellenic" may again be gratuitous.

(ii) The second reference to Hellenistic evidence occurs in the last sentence of the above citation and regards "the concave collar, No. 4." Unfortunately, Bagatti's text and diagram supply only the most general idea of this shard. No photo is provided, and we do not even know the size of the piece in question. The pertinent description (*Exc.* 132) reads simply: "mouth of a vase of yellowish clay, well fired, made in haste." Bagatti claims there are "samples from the 1st century B.C.," by which he seems to mean that this shard has similarities with artefacts of I BCE from elsewhere in Palestine. He offers a footnote with parallels. It is tempting to explore those parallels here[101] and to verify whether they are indeed first century BCE. But that does us little good. Though we can learn all we wish about the parallels he furnishes, we are supplied with insufficient information to match or not match the Nazareth shard against them. Finally, Bagatti's wording is not a rigorous typological match, but simply a similarity. In sum, we cannot admit the shard as evidence of anything, for we know too little about it. This Hellenistic claim must be rejected as unverifiable.

• **C.** On page 285 of *Excavations* we read of a shard that Bagatti apparently ascribes to the Roman period, and in whose description we also find the word "Hellenistic." It is the neck of a cooking pot, "maroon outside, black inside":[102]

> The oldest element of these cooking pots appears to be No. 1 of fig. 224, whether the pieces are parts of one sole vase, or two. The neck, with the splayed mouth, recalls the Hellenistic-Roman custom for these artifacts. At least from the designs given it is rare to note the thinning of the clay towards the rim, *but in reality it exists in many vases of the Roman period*, even though not in such a pronounced manner. [*Emphasis added.*]

In a footnote, Bagatti provides only Roman parallels for this shard. Similar to the preceding case, the word "Hellenistic" in this description is misleading and entirely gratuitous.

Unsubstantiated Hellenistic claims
We have now reviewed all the material evidence that the primary Nazareth literature presents as "Hellenistic," and have found that the little that in fact

---

[101] S. Saller *Excavations in Bethany* pp. 200–202; P. Lapp *Palestine Ceramic Chronology,* p. 146; and Kraeling, *Gerasa* p. 553.
[102] *Exc.* 282 and fig. 224:1.

exists has invariably been misrepresented. We began with the Richmond oil lamps, considered the "Hellenistic nozzle," the St. Joseph material, and finally the few remaining artefacts that Bagatti claimed belonged to the Hellenistic period. In each case we discovered that the Hellenistic claim was unfounded. Only in the case of one shard (C, above), was there not enough information to arrive at a conclusive opinion. But, given what we have learned in the foregoing discussion, it is all but certain that this shard, too, is not "Hellenistic." It appears to be yet another pretext to introduce that word into Bagatti's book.

We now come to a different class of assertion: those Hellenistic claims made by Bagatti and others that are not backed by any discrete evidence at all. Numerically, such abstract claims preponderate, for they are very easy to make. They are found in both the primary and secondary literature on Nazareth, and are particularly damaging for they are often eminently quotable. These empty "Hellenistic" claims are found in virtually all the reference works on the place, including Bagatti's own reports. We now look at several such general declarations in *Excavations*. They are simply claims, not tied to any material evidence at all, and are prominent in the text, usually being found at the head of a section or in its closing summary.

• **D.** On pages 29 and 32 of *Excavations* we read the following critical conclusion, which we have previously encountered:

> Chronologically we have: tombs of the Middle Bronze Period; silos with ceramics of the Middle Iron Period; and then, uninterruptedly, ceramics and constructions of the Hellenistic Period down to modern times.

This assertion was carefully analyzed in Chapter Two in reference to the doctrine of continuous habitation.[103] It mentions "ceramics and constructions of the Hellenistic Period," but I wish to emphasize that nowhere does Bagatti discuss any actual "constructions" (wall foundations, tombs, agricultural installations) of that period. Had he done so, I would mention it now and would itemize those passages here. There are none. The only pre-Christian structural remains in the basin that Bagatti discusses are Bronze and Iron Age tombs and silos (Chapter One). In the next chapter we shall consider Roman and later structural evidence. Nowhere does Bagatti (or anyone else) discuss any actual "constructions" from the centuries of the Great Hiatus at Nazareth, *i.e., c.* 700 BCE- *c.* 100 CE.

In light of this situation, the word "Hellenistic" in the above citation simply does not belong. Bagatti's last phrase should read: "and then, ceramics and constructions of the *Roman* Period uninterruptedly down to modern times."

---

[103] Chapter 2, pp. 90–91.

However, the statement as published had great effect. It helped establish the doctrine of continuous habitation (Chapter Two), and introduced the 'certainty' of Hellenistic evidence at Nazareth. It was requoted or paraphrased in the *Encyclopedia Judaica* and other reference works.[104] Even with no evidence whatsoever to back it up, a sentence such as the above can be especially damaging, for a scholar need only read it once in order to assure himself that the village of Nazareth existed in Hellenistic times. Indeed, that is why the statement was thus worded.

An echo of the above citation begins the section in *Excavations* entitled, "Pottery of the Hellenistic [*sic!*] Roman and Byzantine Periods":

> In dealing with the excavations around the venerated Grotto we have treated also many shards because they served to suggest a date. As we have said, some shards belong to the Hellenistic period, others to the Roman and many to the Byzantine.[105]

Direct paraphrases are found in NIDBA and in Jack Finegan's *The Archaeology of the New Testament*.[106] Of course, we have systematically seen that the "Hellenistic" shards Bagatti claims invariably belong either to the Iron Age or to Roman times.

• E. Related to the preceding is the following overall summary by Bagatti:

> We have met with only few traces of the Hellenistic period, but there are many elements of the Roman period.

The location in the concluding remarks of *Excavations in Nazareth* assure that this sentence has been widely read. Also in the same vein is a 1977 assessment by Bagatti (*EAEHL*, "Nazareth," p. 921):

> Potsherds from the Israelite, Hellenistic, Roman, and Byzantine periods and the Middle Ages were also found.

The above statement would correspond to the evidence in the ground if the word "Hellenistic" were removed.

• F. "Hellenistic" occurs in passing in the opening sentence of "The Necropolis of Nazareth," also from Bagatti's *Excavations* (p. 237):

---

[104] *EJ*, "Nazareth" col. 900. See Pt. 2:30.

[105] *Exc.* 272. This claim was first made by Bagatti in his 1960 article, "Nazareth," for the *Dictionnaire de la Bible* (col. 324).

[106] Paraphrases are found in *NIDBA*, "Nazareth," p. 330, col. 1; Finegan 1992:45.

> The necropolis of the Bronze Period was found, at least in part, in the
> zone of our excavations and also during the construction of shops near the
> Tiberias road. That of the Iron Period, as those of the Hellenistic, Roman
> and Byzantine periods, are all outside the Franciscan area.

Coherent with the evidence found in them, the kokh tombs at Nazareth
(discussed above) must themselves be dated to Roman times. In short, there
was no Hellenistic necropolis at Nazareth.

• **G.** Finally, mention can be made of two Hellenistic claims published in
short reports authored by Yardenna Alexandre. During May 1998 a small
excavation was conducted *c.* 100 m NW of the Church of St. Joseph. A brief
report (unsigned) was published in *Hadashot Arkheologiyot.*[107] The pertinent
sentence reads: "Sherds from the Iron Age, *Hellenistic*, Roman, Byzantine,
Mamluk and Ottoman periods were found on the bedrock" (emphasis added).
No description, itemization, or diagram is furnished and the number and nature
of these shards is not known. In a personal communication to this author the
archaeologist wrote that the finds were minimal and that she has nothing to add
beyond the published report. Given the lack of even rudimentary information
on the shards, we must consider this an unsubstantiated Hellenistic claim.

Ms. Alexandre conducted another excavation in 1997–98 in the Fountain
Square and adjacent St. Gabriel's Square of Nazareth (next to Mary's Well).
This excavation was under the auspices of the Israel Antiquities Authority
and Government Tourist Ministry, in the context of the Nazareth 2000
development program (an ambitious initiative designed to stimulate tourism).
According to personnal correspondence with the archaeologist, a short report
on this excavation is scheduled for publication in *Hadashot Arkheologiyot.*
Ms. Alexandre graciously shared an advance copy of the report with me.
Unfortunately, it again lacks specificity as regards description, itemization, or
illustrations of discrete finds, which constitute the requirements of verification,
so important in this context. Ms. Yardenna writes:

> The main excavations were carried out under the modern 1960s
> concrete Fountain House, which was demolished with the aim
> of reconstructing the ruined Ottoman stone Fountain House. The
> archaeological remains exposed dated from the Roman, the Crusader,
> the Mamluk and the Ottoman periods. From the Roman period part of a
> covered dressed stone channel was exposed, as well as some wall stubs
> and Middle Roman pottery.

As we shall see in subsequent chapters, these results accord perfectly
with the settlement of Nazareth in Middle Roman times. However, in the final
sentence of the report, Ms. Alexandre adds:

---

[107]   Alexandre 2000.

Some fragmentary stone walls and floors were cut by the vaulted reservoir, thus indicationg that there was some occupation here in the Hellenistic, Crusader and Mamluk periods.

It is a mystery how the archaeologist can date "fragmentary stone walls" to Hellenistic times, particularly since the associated pottery was later Roman at the earliest (see above). A request to the archaeologist for specifics (number, description, and diagram of Hellenistic artefacts) produced no reply and thus, once again, this Hellenistic claim must be reckoned as unsubstantiated. It is clear that with the contentious issue of Nazareth archaeology, evidence should only be admitted which is verifiable, for numerous claims have been made which cannot be substantiated.

The popular literature (newpaper articles and the Internet) has mooted the existence of a "Roman bath-house" dating to the time of Christ, one connected with the Fountain House near Mary's Well in Nazareth. The suggestion has even been made that a Roman resort existed at Nazareth, one rivalling nearby Sepphoris. We need not consider such opinions seriously, for Ms. Alexandre dates the extensive underground waterworks to very late times:

The excavations revealed a complete vaulted reservoir with four well openings in a row, overlain by a stone-paved courtyard. This vaulted reservoir or cistern was in use in the 18th-early 19th centuries. Two large stone channels were exposed here, the ancient of which seems to have been part of the Crusader channel that originally transported the water from the source, under and past the St. Gabriel's church and down to the water house. . .

It is clear that the waterworks Ms. Alexandre describes are very late— eighteenth to early nineteenth centuries, with a stone channel which goes back to Crusader times. There is nothing here at all to suggest the time of Christ, much less the Hellenistic Period.

Summary

The preceding pages show that the actual physical evidence at Nazareth attributed to the centuries before Jesus amounts to no more than a group of mislabeled oil lamps and a few equally mislabeled fragments of pottery. In all, these oil lamps and pottery shards total fourteen artefacts. Ten of these artefacts are clearly not Hellenistic (nine are Roman or Byzantine, and one is from the Iron Period). Thus the entire case for Hellenistic Nazareth rests on four pottery fragments that can easily fit in the palms of two hands.[108] Two of these fragments are fully compatible (by their diagrams) with Roman times and do not fit the description offered, the third fragment is "greatly

[108] These four shards are marked by a (•) in *Illus. 3.6.*

mutilated," and the fourth is not sufficiently characterized to even permit an opinion. There is not the least reason to suppose that any one of these shards is Hellenistic. *Illus. 3.6* lists the fourteen artefacts found in the excavations that constitute the sum total of alleged Hellenistic evidence at Nazareth.

Armed with such non-evidence as presented in the foregoing pages, Bagatti peppers his writings on Nazareth with the word "Hellenistic." The average reader will certainly be misled. Thus, the caption to Fig. 233 of *Excavations* reads: "Lamps of the Hellenistic and Roman period in various places." The caption to Fig. 235 reads: "Pottery of the Bronze, Hellenistic and Roman periods found in various places." On p. 309, in the concluding section of the book, we read the following bold statement: "[F]rom the Hellenistic to the medieval period one can follow the continuous development, with several examples from each century." Of course, this is categorically untrue, not only as regards the Hellenistic Period but also regarding the Early Roman Period which followed. There was no "continuous development," and we can now affirm that there are no "examples" at Nazareth from III BCE, II BCE, or I BCE.[109]

Briefly stated, there was no pre-Christian Nazareth.

---

[109] The present analysis is compatible with a recent study by D. Hamidovic: "On the one hand, between the end of Iron I [*c.* 1000 BCE] and the Roman Period it is not certain that the site was occupied, or perhaps the site was very sparsely populated, according to the recovered archaeological material. Doubt is permitted as regards the Hellenistic II era (*c.* 200–63), on the other hand nothing [*aucun élément*] can assure occupation in the Iron III or Persian eras (539–332) nor in the Hellenistic Period (*c.* 332–200)" (Hamidovic:102). The facts presented in these pages show that Hamidovic is too tentative.

Description	Archaeologist	Page	Era claimed	Actual era
6 oil lamps	Richmond, Kopp	105–9	Hellenistic	Middle-Late Roman
1 nozzle of bow-spouted oil lamp	Bagatti	111–20	Hellenistic	Early-Middle Roman
• 2 3″ fgmts. (St. Jsph.)	Bagatti	120–26	Hellenistic	Middle-Late Roman, or Iron
• 1 fgmt. (St. Jsph.)	Bagatti	122	Hellenistic	Unverifiable ("greatly mutilated")
1 3″ triangular fgmt.	Bagatti	127–8 Section A	Hellenistic-Roman	Roman
1 3″ fgmt. of "big vase"	Bagatti	128–9 Section B	Hellenistic	Iron Age
• 1 "concave collar"	Bagatti	129 Section B	Hellenistic	Unverifiable (insufficient data)
1 neck of cooking pot	Bagatti	129–30 Section C	Hellenistic-Roman	Roman

(•) See footnote 109.

Illus. 3.6. **Summary of the alleged Hellenistic evidence from Nazareth**

THE MYTH OF NAZARETH

General Hellenistic Claims

The preceding pages form the core of this study, in that they systematically demonstrate that no material evidence from the Nazareth basin dates to Hellenistic times. The foregoing review of evidence has not been based merely on finds from the venerated area, as might be supposed, but has also encompassed the results from numerous other loci in the basin, most particularly twenty-seven ancient tombs that have thus far been excavated in many other parts of the basin.[110] The reason none of those many tombs has been mentioned in the preceding pages is that none contained any Hellenistic evidence. We can now affirm with confidence that the settlement of Nazareth did not come into existence during the Hellenistic Period, and that the basin was entirely devoid of human habitation during that era. This unambiguous conclusion is here enunciated for the first time.

This is, of course, not the view one reads in the published literature. Despite the archaeological record, the virtually unanimous view among both Catholic and Protestant scholars is, understandably, to the contrary. After one century of excavations, this state of affairs is sufficient proof that those writings have responded to the exigencies of doctrine rather than to those of fact.

We shall now consider the mere assertions of a Hellenistic settlement at Nazareth. On the basis of the foregoing pages we can affirm, *a priori,* that all such claims are empty. They tend to be brazen, vague, superficial, and often quite remarkable. They assert in one form or another that the settlement of Nazareth preceded the time of Jesus. The most egregious proposal of this nature asserts nothing less than a refounding of the village in Hellenistic times and the existence of a thriving settlement in the second century BCE. I call this the "Hellenistic renaissance myth."

The Hellenistic renaissance myth

We have seen that Alt and more recent scholars have delineated two settlement patterns in pre-Hasmonean Galilee. On the one hand, a number of *poleis* existed on the periphery of the region, namely, on the Mediterranean coast and in the Jordan Valley. On the other hand, the hilly interior, including the Nazareth range, was notably bereft of settlement (above, p. 5). In apparent conflict with this consensus, however, in the later twentieth century two American scholars—Eric M. Meyers and James F. Strange—proposed that the inland village of Nazareth emerged in early Hellenistic times and grew into a thriving settlement already in that era.

This is, in fact, the case with Sepphoris, approximately 7 km (4.3 mi) north of Nazareth. Interestingly, both Meyers and Strange excavated extensively at

---

[110] These tombs are itemized and described in Chapter 5.

Sepphoris and have published widely on that town. They jointly led the Meiron Excavation Project in 1976, which "recognized the importance of Sepphoris for further work in Galilee."[111] In 1983 Strange organized a Sepphoris survey team under the sponsorship of the University of South Florida (USF), where since 1972 he has been a professor of Religious Studies. From 1983–1989 Strange directed annual excavations at Sepphoris, and he has returned to the site more recently to continue excavations. Concurrently, Eric Meyers and others organized a bi-national project sponsored by Duke University of North Carolina and the Hebrew University of Jerusalem, which sponsored five campaigns at Sepphoris beginning in 1985.

Besides his writings on Sepphoris, Strange has authored scores of archaeological reference articles on many ancient sites in Palestine—indeed, so many that his contributions read like a gazeteer of ancient Palestine.[112] He has published extensively on Nazareth, perhaps most noteworthy being two articles entitled "Nazareth": one in the *Anchor Bible Dictionary* (1992), the other in the *Oxford Encyclopedia of Archaeology in the Near East* (1997).[113] Other than Bagatti, Strange is arguably the most cited scholar on Nazareth. This is curious for two reasons: (a) unlike Bagatti, Strange received no academic degree in the field of archaeology. His training includes a B.A. in Philosophy (Rice University), a Master of Divinity (Yale Divinity School), and a Ph.D. in New Testament Studies (Drew University); and (b) Strange himself has never dug at Nazareth, nor has he authored a report dealing with material remains from the Nazareth basin.[114]

---

[111] Meyers, Netzer, and Meyers 1.

[112] Strange contributed 182 articles alone to The *Macmillan Dictionary of Judaism in the Biblical Period* (1996).

[113] Strange's bibliography on Nazareth includes: E. Meyers and J. Strange, *Archaeology, the Rabbis, & Early Christianity*. Nashville: Abingdon, 1981; J. Strange, "Diversity in Early Palestinian Christianity: Some Archaeological Evidences," *Anglican Theological Review*, vol. LXV (1983), pp. 14–24; "Some implications of archaeology for New Testament studies," in *What has Archaeology to do with Faith?* pp 23–59. Harrisburg: Trinity Press Int'l, 1992; "Archaeology and the New Testament," *Biblical Archaeologist*, vol. 56 (Sept. 1993), pp. 153–157; "First century Galilee from archaeology and from the texts," in *Archaeology and the Galilee*, pp. 39–48. Atlanta: Scholars Press, 1997; "The sayings of Jesus and archaeology," in *Hillel and Jesus*, pp. 291–305. Minneapolis: Fortress Press, 1997; "Ancient texts, archaeology as text, and the problem of the first-century synagogue," in *Evolution of the Synagogue*, pp. 27–45. Harrisburg: Trinity Press Int'l, 1999; and articles entitled "Nazareth" in the *Encyclopedia of Archaeology in the Biblical World* (1991), *The Anchor Bible Dictionary* (1992), the *Macmillan Dictionary of Judaism in the Biblical Period* (1996), and the *Oxford Encyclopedia of Near Eastern Excavations* (1997).

[114] Strange has excavated at Tell er-Ras, French Hill in Jerusalem, Kh. el-Kom, Caesarea, Kh. Shema, and Sepphoris. (*Biblical Archaeologist* 56:3 [1993] p. 153.)

THE MYTH OF NAZARETH

Though very influential, Strange's contributions to the scholarly Nazareth literature are limited to brief summaries of the site's archaeology and history in reference articles and books. He is not in a position to offer us any new material evidence, and thus his opinions lie entirely within the range of the secondary Nazareth literature. Nevertheless, his views have radically departed from those of Bagatti and the Church, and have moulded the prevailing attitude in non-Catholic circles regarding Nazareth. The alleged link between early Sepphoris and Nazareth has led to avenues of inquiry recently explored in print, such as the possibility that Jesus and/or Joseph may have worked at Sepphoris, that Jesus may have become acquainted there with urban Greek and Roman ways, and even that Jesus may have frequented the theater at Sepphoris, influencing his use, for example, of the word *hypocrite*, so frequently encountered in the gospels.[115]

Perhaps the first expression of the Hellenistic renaissance doctrine at Nazareth is found in the 1981 book of Strange and Eric Meyers, *Archaeology, the Rabbis, & Early Christianity*. It devotes a mere one and one-half pages to Nazareth, and in that brief space we read the following remarkable statement:

> It is in the second century B.C.E. that extensive remains [in Nazareth] are to be found, which suggests that this is the period of the refounding of the village.[116]

The claim of "extensive remains" from Hellenistic Nazareth is nothing less than amazing. We have scoured the literature and the material evidence from the basin in the preceding pages, and have found a total of fourteen oil lamps and shards claimed as Hellenistic, of which none in fact came from that era. The originality of the above citation is breathtaking.

It is also unusual in a number of respects. We should note, first of all, that the view of a Hellenistic "refounding" does not accord with the Catholic doctrine of continuous habitation (see Chapter Two). Officially, at least, Catholicism asserts that Nazareth has existed continuously since the Bronze Age.[117]

Secondly, the chronology of this "refounding"-*cum*-"extensive remains" is contrary to what we know of the Galilee in Hellenistic times. As we have noted, surveys show a marked *decrease* in the number of sites from the Persian

---

[115] Strange 1997; Batey 1992:59; 2001. *Hypocritês* in Greek had two meanings: (1) an actor, and (2) a dissembler. The second meaning is apparently intended in the canonical gospels, but Strange and others suggest the first as a possibility in the New Testament. Incidentally, it has recently been shown that the theater at Sepphoris was constructed *after* the time of Christ, namely, not before mid-first-century CE.

[116] Meyers and Strange 57.

[117] Bagatti 1955:5–6, 23; *Exc.* 319, *etc.* Discussion in Chp. 2:7–28.

to the Hellenistic eras, as well as the abandonment and decline of many sites. The period III-II BCE was a low point in the region (above, pp. 5-6). Paul Lapp writes: "a number of major sites were abandoned or substantially declined in the last half of the second century B.C. or shortly thereafter."[118] He adds that almost constant warfare and unsettled conditions in Hellenistic times led to a decline in prosperity, reflected in the poor quality of the pottery.[119]

Thirdly, the claim of "extensive remains" flatly contradicts the archaeological results of Bagatti, who concludes his *Excavations in Nazareth* with the statement: "We have met with only few traces of the Hellenistic period."[120]

Certainly, "extensive remains" would leave ample traces, both in the ground and in the published literature. Wall foundations, hearths, pottery, coins, tombs, agricultural installations—these are the sorts of evidence that attest to a flourishing settlement in Hellenistic times. It would be impossible that such a village left no archaeological trace of its existence over many generations and centuries.

For the purposes of comparison, we may consider the town of Marisa, a thriving settlement in the Hellenistic era—the same town that Kopp supposed to be contemporary with the kokh tombs at Nazareth (above, p. 15). Located in southern Judea, Marisa was a Canaanite city already in Biblical times (Jos 15:44). Excavations there have demonstrated the following:

> Within the inner wall [Marisa] is roughly divided into blocks by streets, and the houses and buildings are built on the streets and around open courts within the blocks. The relatively regular plan and also the objects found, including pottery, coins, and Greek inscriptions, indicate a town of the Hellenistic period. The middle stratum of the excavations may be assigned to the third and second centuries BC, the upper stratum to the first century BC and later.[121]

This is precisely the era for which Meyers and Strange claim extensive remains at Nazareth. But nowhere at Nazareth has such Hellenistic evidence been reported, neither streets, nor houses, nor courts, and so on. There are no archaeological strata, inscriptions, or coins, as we find in the Judean town. Such Hellenistic evidence from Nazareth has never been published. We have only

---

[118] P. Lapp 1961:230. The author enumerates Gezer, Samaria, Beth-Shan, Shechem, Beth-zur, Lachish, "and possibly also Bethel, Dothan, Shiloh, and Tell Zakariyeh" as abandoned or in major decline in II BCE.

[119] P. Lapp 1961:230. Nancy Lapp notes that the "workmanship of the cooking pots in the second century B.C. had deteriorated considerably. Ware is thinner and less durable; most pots are carelessly made." (N. Lapp 1964:22.)

[120] *Exc.* 319.

[121] Finegan:188. In fact, Marisa was destroyed by the Parthians in 40 BCE and never rebuilt. Today, it is the location of modern Tell Sandahannah.

the "few traces of the Hellenistic period" reported by Bagatti, traces we have invalidated. Indeed, the general lack of Hellenistic evidence has been keenly felt by the tradition for a long time. Fathers Bagatti and Kopp suggested that man-made wall foundations and other domestic structural evidence have long since disappeared, and have pointed to the fact that the Nazareth basin has been built over, thus rendering the necessary evidence unavailable. Yet such a convenient explanation cannot be claimed at the venerated area, which has been intensively excavated. Bagatti cleared away the later structures and excavated far into the ground, sometimes down to solid bedrock.[122] But where he dug, no remains such as we read above at Hellenistic Marisa were found.[123]

Interestingly, though the Hellenistic renaissance thesis has no applicability to the Nazareth basin, it has every relevance for nearby Sepphoris, so well known to both Strange and Meyers.[124] Strange has asserted that Nazareth "was surely a dependency of ancient Sepphoris, the capital of Lower Galilee in the Roman period."[125] Given this attitude, and firmly convinced that Nazareth existed in both Hellenistic and Early Roman times, it may be understandable that with the rise of Sepphoris he might also suppose that Nazareth came into being and flourished during those eras. Unfortunately, the lack of evidence from the basin has not impacted his judgment.

A close connection between Nazareth and Sepphoris is unlikely for another reason: Nazareth and Sepphoris are on different sides of the east-west ridge which forms a divide in Lower Galilee.[126] When it finally came into being, Nazareth was naturally oriented to the southwest towards Japhia (which once was in the basin itself), not to the north.

Even given the belief in a close connection between Nazareth and Sepphoris (a belief generally held in Christian circles today), it is surprising that archaeologists of the stature of Meyers and Strange would take a position in diametric opposition to the conclusion of the principal archaeologist at Nazareth, B. Bagatti. A remarkable feature of the Nazareth literature is that it has accommodated strikingly varied positions, none of which are dependent upon the archaeological record at all.

---

[122] *Exc.* 236.

[123] The Church has also claimed the ancient Nazarenes liked to live in caves, which presumably would remove much evidence of habitations. Against this view, see Chapter 1, p. 36; Aviam 2004:90; Chapter 2, p. 66.

[124] See J. Strange, "Six Campaigns at Sepphoris: The University of South Florida Excavations, 1983–1989," in Levine, pp. 339–351 (bibliography in his note 1). Also, E. Meyers and J. Strange, "Survey in Galilee, 1976," *Explor* 3 (1977), 7-18; E. Meyers, J. Strange, and D. Groh, "The Meiron Excavation Project: Archaeological Survey in Galilee and Golan, 1976," *BASOR* 230 (1978), 1–24.

[125] J. Strange, "Nazareth," in OEANE, p. 113.

[126] Chapter 1, pp. 19–22.

The Hellenistic Renaissance Myth

Roughly a decade after the publication of *Archaeology, the Rabbis, & Early Christianity*, the six-volume *Anchor Bible Dictionary* (*ABD*) appeared. This standard reference work in American biblical scholarship contains a two-page article entitled "Nazareth," authored by James Strange. Its conclusion is as follows:

> The general archeological picture is of a small village, devoted wholly to agriculture, that came into being in the course of the 3d century B.C. Although there are traces of earlier Bronze Age or Iron Age occupation, none of these suggests a continuity of more than a generation at a time. It is the late Hellenistic period that gives life to Nazareth, as it does with many other sites which have been surveyed or excavated in the Galilee. People have continued to live in Nazareth from the 3d century B.C. to the present day.[127]

Several aspects of this passage are notably in error. Strange asserts the existence merely of "traces" of a Bronze or Iron Age settlement. He apparently does not realize that over one hundred artefacts have been identified in the basin from those early periods, itemized by Bagatti in 14 pages of his *Excavations in Nazareth*.[128] The Bronze-Iron evidence has been comprehensively reviewed in Chapter One and attests to a "substantial settlement," one I have suggested was in fact the town of biblical Japhia.[129] Nevertheless, Strange's minimalist view is mirrored in other secondary literature. Regarding the Bronze and Iron Ages at Nazareth, J.D. Crossan writes: "The remnants from those earlier occupations are, however, quite limited…"[130] Elsewhere, Crossan and J. Reed write: "There is some evidence, mostly ceramic, not architectural, for [Nazareth's] occupation in the Middle Bronze and Iron Age…"[131] All this is rather curious, particularly the assertion of no "architectural" remains, for in Chapter One we discussed no less than six substantial Bronze-Iron Age tombs.[132] Perhaps Crossan and Reed do not consider tombs to be "architectural" remains. It matters little, for the material from those early periods is not scant, and suggests that the American scholars have not bothered to familiarize themselves with the primary literature, or have chosen to ignore its findings.

In the above citation, Strange asserts that "It is the late Hellenistic period that gives life to Nazareth, as it does with many other sites which have been

---

[127] ABD (1992), "Nazareth," p. 1051.

[128] *Exc.* 258–272.

[129] Chapter 1, p. 53*ff*. The Bronze and Iron periods are not elsewhere mentioned in Strange's article.

[130] Crossan 16.

[131] Crossan and Reed 32.

[132] See Chp. 1: *Illus. 5*.

surveyed or excavated in the Galilee." Typically, "late Hellenistic" refers to early II BCE (pre-Hasmonean), in which case this view coheres with Meyers' and Strange's earlier opinion of a II BCE "refounding" of the town. It fact, the archaeological evidence points to a burgeoning of settlement in the Galilee a century later, i.e., during the time of Alexander Janneus.[133] Sometimes the Hasmonean era is included in the "Hellenistic period," in which case Strange's view would have more support from the surrounding region. A migration of Jews northwards from Judea accompanied and followed the expansion under Hyrcanus and his sons, Antigonus and Aristobulus. Aviam writes that "By the time of King Janneus [c. 100 BCE], the Galilee was almost fully inhabited by Jews."[134] This contrasts with the situation that obtained in Galilee in earlier Hellenistic times, when the region was sparsely populated.[135] Nevertheless, since no I BCE evidence has been discovered in the Nazareth basin, it would appear that Strange's position is at best an extrapolation from the general situation in the Galilee. In addition, the view of a Nazareth renaissance in Hellenistic times coheres only with what is known from nearby Sepphoris, a town the American has extensively excavated. We have already noted that he views ancient Nazareth as having been a dependency of Sepphoris.

Despite the claim of a thriving Hellenistic village at Nazareth, one scours Strange's 1992 *ABD* article in vain for Hellenistic evidence, whether structural or movable. The lack of any such evidence is confirmed by the stratigraphic trench which Bagatti cut to the East of the Church of the Annunciation. The trench, we recall, yielded no results of habitations or of any sign of human presence other than a few Byzantine shards.[136] It might be objected that the trench was simply poorly positioned. But we must keep in mind that the burden of proof is on those who argue *against* the evidence (or lack thereof). Bagatti, Strange, and other exponents of the tradition argue the existence of a village when the ground is entirely mute in that regard. Such exponents ultimately have recourse to the doctrinal statements in the gospels, which mandate a village of Nazareth in the time of Jesus. But these canonical assertions can carry no weight *prima facie*, for they themselves require substantiation. Ultimately, the history of Nazareth devolves upon the material record in the ground, as revealed by the archaeology of the site.

One element of Strange's 1992 article that could conceivably lend weight to a village at Nazareth in the Hellenistic era is the author's mention (twice) of "Herodian" tombs. We shall consider the term "Herodian" carefully in the

---

[133] Above, p. 103.

[134] Aviam 2004:54.

[135] Above, pp. 100, 103.

[136] *Exc*:236. On the stratigraphic trench, *cf.* Chapter 2, p. 83*f.*

next chapter. Here, I wish merely to note that Strange uses it as evidence for a "pre-Herodian" (*i.e.*, Hellenistic) village:

> As inferred from the Herodian tombs in Nazareth, the maximum extent of the Herodian and pre-Herodian village measured about 900×200 m, for a total area just under 60 acres.

We shall see that there is no Herodian evidence at all from Nazareth. What Strange terms the "Herodian" tomb is the kokh-type tomb, discussed above (pp. 13–16). The type was in use as late as Byzantine times in Palestine and, on the basis of their form alone, there can be no justification for assuming that these tombs date as early as the Herodian or even pre-Herodian periods. That they date to the second, third, or fourth centuries after Christ is proven by the artefacts found in those tombs, as also by ancillary structural evidence (the presence of rolling stones, arcosolia, and trough graves in association with some of the Nazareth tombs) which we shall discuss when we take up the Roman period.

The 'backdating' of the kokh tombs at Nazareth to "pre-Herodian" (read: "Hellenistic") times effectively makes the III CE necropolis appear III BCE—a difference of half a millennium. This recalls Kopp's backdating of these same tombs to the time of their first appearance in Palestine.[137]

From the foregoing discussion we can see that there is no basis to infer either a Hellenistic or Herodian dating from the kokh tombs at Nazareth. The artefacts found in them are Middle to Late Roman, the tombs sometimes have rolling stones, and no Hellenistic or clearly Herodian evidence has been found anywhere in the basin.[138]

Point-by-point

After the Strange-Meyers hypothesis in the early 1980s of a Hellenistic renaissance at Nazareth, two views came to dominate the literature: the continuous habitation doctrine espoused by the Church, and the Hellenistic renaissance doctrine adopted principally by American Protestant scholars. These contradictory views regarding the pre-Christian history of Nazareth led to some confusion in the literature. For example, the article "Nazareth" from *The Dictionary of Judaism in the Biblical Period* (1996) presents both positions:

---

[137] Above, p. 110.

[138] Three kokh tombs at Nazareth (numbers 70, 71, and 72) had quantities of datable pottery and oil lamps. All the post-Iron Age artefacts date to Middle Roman and later times (Chapter 6). The several kokh tombs excavated by N. Feig confirm this dating. The latter are not used in the primary data for this work, however, as they lie outside the immediate Nazareth basin.

THE MYTH OF NAZARETH

> Excavations beneath the modern Church of Saint Joseph showed that there was village occupation at Nazareth from the period of the Israelite monarchy. Excavations beneath the Church of the Annunciation, however, showed that the period of continuous occupation began in the second century B.C.E.[139]

The attentive reader will be understandably perplexed by this passage, for the two churches discussed are only 100 m apart. If one locus showed habitation from II BCE, then it would seem curious that the other showed habitation from 700 BCE. The author of the *DJBP* article does not attempt to harmonize these two scenarios, and simply presents them side-by-side. We have seen that neither is correct. Yet, of these two theories, the conclusion cited above from Strange's 1992 Nazareth article (*ABD*) encapsulates the prevailing view today regarding the ancient settlement, at least outside of Roman Catholic circles. It is sufficiently significant that we shall now consider it point-by-point:

A. The general archaeological picture is of a small village.
B. The village was devoted wholly to agriculture.
C. The village came into being in the course of the 3d century BC.
D. The traces of earlier Bronze Age or Iron Age occupation do not suggest a continuity of more than a generation at a time.
E. It is the late Hellenistic period that gives life to Nazareth, as it does with many other sites which have been surveyed or excavated in the Galilee.
F. People have continued to live in Nazareth from the 3d century BC to the present.

It may first be observed that each of these six statements requires a good deal of evidence in order to be substantiated. They are conclusions, not evidence. 'Evidence' and 'conclusion' are confounded in the Nazareth literature, as if a scholar's opinion itself could stand in lieu of evidence. This is never the case, yet the evidence in the ground (or the lack thereof) at Nazareth is sometimes forgotten, sometimes suppressed, and sometimes simply ignored (as with the Great Hiatus), on the basis of statements similar to the six enumerated above. We have already noted that several American scholars writing about Nazareth seem unaware of the evidence unearthed by Bagatti, and have adopted conclusions contrary to his. Their statements often stand in lieu of evidence, despite evidence, or even contrary to the evidence. What they have to say is particularly dangerous because the average layperson and non-specialist scholar turns not to the primary literature for information about Nazareth, but to tendentious reference articles written by a very few scholars.

---

[139] *DJBP*, "Nazareth," p. 449.

Fortunately, the reputation of even the greatest archaeologist does not remove the need for evidence. To state the obvious, archaeological evidence is of a material nature. Though indeed subject to interpretation regarding character, age, location, function, value, and other considerations, as a physical entity it is subject to description and categorization, itemization, and to being photographed or drawn. It is demonstrable, verifiable, and its existence provable. On the other hand, a conclusion does not lie in the ground but is entirely the opinion of the author. The determination whether that conclusion is correct or incorrect devolves upon a single question: does it demonstrably accord with the material evidence? In other words: *is it provable?*

We are now aware that the Nazareth literature is rife with unwarranted conclusions, many of which are not compatible with the material record. There is such great doctrinal pressure to validate the gospel message that even ludicrous conclusions in accord with that message have entered the literature. The evidence is, in fact, viewed with suspicion, for it often poses a threat to catholic doctrine. The result is a general downgrading of evidence and a concomitant upgrading of the messenger. Both laypersons and scholars tend to forget that the messenger is only that: one who brings *evidence*. It is the evidence that properly determines the message, not the other way around.

We will begin with Strange's point D, that "The traces of earlier Bronze Age or Iron Age occupation do not suggest a continuity of more than a generation at a time." In Chapter One we determined the contrary: there was continuity in settlement for hundreds of years during the Bronze and Iron Ages. The 117+ artefacts schematized in *Illus. 1.5* showed only two apparent dislocations in settlement. The first was towards the end of the Middle Bronze Period (*c.* 1500 BCE), when the Egyptians invaded Palestine following the expulsion of the Hyksos from their country. The use of Tombs 7 and 80 ceased about this time, while the evidence from Tomb 1 is scant. A second dislocation in settlement may have occurred between the Late Bronze and the Iron Age (twelfth century BCE). At that time Tomb 1 ceased to be used. Other than these two instances, there appears to have been continuity of settlement for lengthy periods within the Middle Bronze, Late Bronze, and Iron Period.

As for Strange's point C—perhaps the most egregious of all—we have seen that his backdating of the kokh tombs to Hellenistic times effectively turns III CE evidence into III BCE evidence. How much difference a single letter makes! We are speaking here of an error of five hundred years. Such gross distortion of chronology is already familiar to us from the writings of Kopp and Bagatti.[140] Strange now joins their company, so that in every generation the scholarly Nazareth literature is marred by wholesale chronological misinformation.

---

[140] See Chapter 2, pp. 65, 71.

THE MYTH OF NAZARETH

Of course, there is no published evidence to substantiate the assertion that a village came into being at Nazareth in the course of the third century BCE. If true, that Ptolemaic refounding would be authenticated in some way, whether by coins, pottery, habitations, tombs, or other evidence. As already shown, no such evidence exists in the Nazareth basin, as it does at Marisa, for example. We have also noted that archaeological surveys show a marked decline in the number of settlements in Lower East Galilee from the Persian to the Hellenistic period.[141] Finally, we recall that "The interior of the Galilee... was still relatively sparsely populated on the eve of the Maccabean campaigns."[142] In sum, contrary to the situation in Lower Galilee, and lacking any evidence at all from the ground at Nazareth dating to Hellenistic times, it is preposterous to suppose that a village came into being there in III BCE.

Strange's chronological error cannot be imputed to mere imprecision, to an error of one or two generations, for we cannot suppose that the Seleucids, a century later, were any more aggressive than the Ptolemies in colonizing Galilee:

> Seleucid colonists, typically consisted of Greeks, Macedonians, people from Asia Minor, and locals, but we have no indication that any such colonists were ever brought to Galilee. The Seleucid foundations and colonies seem to have been limited to the surrounding territories...[143]

We now turn to Strange's point E: "it is the late Hellenistic period that gives life to Nazareth." This refers to Hasmonean times, but here again, the assertion is not substantiated by movable or structural finds in the ground. There are indeed a number of *claims* that such evidence exists (considered in the foregoing pages), but when these claims are checked they prove false, for the underlying data (when it exists) never proves to be Hellenistic.

Strange appears to be uncertain as to the exact Hellenistic century in which Nazareth was refounded. In 1992 he proposed III BCE (point C), while a decade earlier he and Meyers proposed II BCE (p. 138, above). At the conclusion of his ABD article, Strange writes that "It is the late Hellenistic period [*i.e.*, I BCE] that gives life to Nazareth." Many categories of evidence are notably lacking for any of these proposals. Coins are a case in point. "Hasmonean coins," writes Chancey, "are ubiquitous in the Hellenistic and Roman strata of sites in both Lower and Upper Galilee." He adds: "Numismatic finds shed some light on what occurred in Galilee after the Hasmonean conquest."[144] Chancey notes that such coins had a lengthy circulation stretching well into I CE. They are totally absent from the Nazareth basin even through Roman

---

[141] See above, pp. 100–101.
[142] Chancey:36.
[143] *Ibid.*:36.
[144] Chancey:46.

times. The earliest recovered coin is of the emperor Constantius, who ruled 337–361 CE.[145]

Strange's points C and E assert that Nazareth came into existence in III BCE and was thriving *c.* 100 BCE, "the late Hellenistic period." In 1997 the archaeologist had also modified this view, positing the highpoint of Nazareth a century later, that is, about the time of Christ: "Nazareth exhibits archaeological remains from the Middle Bronze II, Iron II, and late Hellenistic periods, but its heyday was in the Early Roman period."[146]

The evidence Strange offers for an Early Roman "heyday" of Nazareth consists entirely of "Late Hellenistic to Early Roman caves with domestic installations, some used as late as the Byzantine period."[147] This is a reappearance of the discredited troglodyte theory that we first encountered with Kopp in the 1930s.[148] It continues to be mooted in more recent literature,[149] and has been reinforced by the discovery of part of a wall on the Franciscan property, as well as by "depressions" that Bagatti surmised were from erstwhile walls. We will consider the domestic cave theory more closely in Chapter Five.

Strange's point F is simply a bald, unsubstantiated, and irresponsible claim: "People have continued to live in Nazareth from the 3d century BC to the present." We have rebutted this overarching conclusion in the foregoing pages, and have carried out an extensive analysis of what underlies the various "Hellenistic" claims in the Nazareth literature.

As for points A and B, we shall see that they are entirely correct—if placed in a later Roman context. There was a village of Nazareth, and it was agricultural, *in II CE and thereafter* (Chapters Four–Six). Here we see again the recurring problem of backdating later Roman evidence into periods of the Great Hiatus—to the "Herodian" period, to the "time of Christ," to the "Hellenistic" Age, *etc.* The many cisterns and storage silos that have been found in the venerated area, the wine presses and agricultural installations, the pottery, oil lamps, and tombs—these witness to a busy village in later Roman times. The thriving village of Nazareth was a fact four centuries after the Hellenistic period and well after the time of Christ.

Cave-dwelling aside, one cannot avoid the general observation that though Strange's Hellenistic renaissance-*cum*-heyday in Early Roman times

---

[145] Bagatti writes "Constans" (*Exc.* 210), Roman emperor in the West from 337–350. His brother Constantius II reigned in the East. *Cf.* Taylor 255. The coin was found embedded in the plaster of Locus 29 under the CA.

[146] OEANE, "Nazareth," p. 113.

[147] OEANE, "Nazareth," p. 114.

[148] Chapter 1, pp. 23*ff.* The adaptation of caves to agricultural (rather than domestic) use will be taken up in Part Four.

[149] See, *e.g.*, Crossan and Reed 2002:34–35.

THE MYTH OF NAZARETH

has no relevance to Nazareth, it has every relevance to nearby Sepphoris, where the American assiduously excavated.

Sepphoris

The site of the ancient town has been identified with the present day Moshav Zippori, located on a roundish hill 285 m high (935 ft.) overlooking the Beth Netofa Valley.[150] *Zippori* in Hebrew means "bird," and the town may have been so named due to it's perched position on a hill. Sepphoris is about seven kilometers (4.3 miles) northwest of the Nazareth basin. Late Iron II remains attest to a settlement there in VII–VI BCE. Some scattered pottery shards, including a fine animal-shaped rhyton (drinking horn), date from the Persian and Hellenistic periods, but there are no structural remains before III–II BCE, unless we count a basalt grinding stone found in a nearby field. Firm confirmation of structural remains, numerous coins, and other movable finds have been found at Sepphoris dating to that era. Jewish presence there also began no later than Hasmonean times.[151]

In Hasmonean times Sepphoris came into its own. It was a prestigious city, "probably the administrative center of the whole of Galilee."[152] Josephus recounts that about 100 BCE the ruler of Cyprus invaded the mainland and besieged Ptolemais, captured Asochis, and made an unsuccessful bid to capture Sepphoris.[153] The town at this time must have been a walled settlement of considerable strength. Indeed, Josephus writes that it had been "the strongest city in Galilee." In the first century BCE, "For all intents and purposes, Sepphoris had already become the capital of the Galilee."[154]

A considerable amount of pottery dates to the centuries between I BCE and III CE.[155] In 57 BCE, the Roman proconsul of Syria chose Sepphoris as his administrative headquarters for the Galilee. The town's prestige continued after the turn of the era. For Josephus, Sepphoris is "the ornament of all Galilee."[156] The city sided with Rome during the First Jewish Revolt and was under Jewish local government until the Second Revolt (132–135 CE). At that time it was renamed Diocaesarea. Towards the end of the second century CE Sepphoris served as the headquarters of Rabbi Judah the Prince and of the Sanhedrin, at which time and place the Mishna was redacted. This may have been its most brilliant period. Thereafter the city declined in importance, though it continued to be inhabited through Crusader times.

---

[150] Map ref. 176.239. NEAEHL "Sepphoris," 1324; Meyers, Netzer, Meyers: 3.
[151] Meyers, Netzer, and Meyers:10.
[152] Z. Weiss, NEAEHL, "Sepphoris," p. 1324.
[153] Ant. 13.12.5.; War 2.5.10*f.*
[154] E. Meyers, "Roman Sepphoris" p. 323.
[155] HA 8/5/2005, p. 117.
[156] Ant. 18.2.1.27.

148

The Hellenistic Renaissance Myth

From the foregoing brief résumé of its history, we can appreciate that Sepphoris fulfilled many of the requirements Strange proposes for Nazareth: a "birth" (or re-birth) in III–II BCE; a "heyday" in Hasmonean times; a flourishing settlement at the turn of the era; and continued habitation from III BCE onwards.

We have already noted how the Nazareth basin is not oriented towards Sepphoris, but towards Japhia and the Jezreel Valley to the south.[157] The connection between these two settlements was probably not close even when they were both in existence after Middle Roman times, for the Nazareth Ridge constitutes a significant geographical separation.

The reader of the foregoing pages is now wiser: Nazareth has not existed since the dawn of history, multiple "Hellenistic" claims are unfounded, and the scholarly Nazareth literature is replete with chronological distortion on a massive scale. The purpose is patent—to support the story as told in the canonical gospels. Yet archaeology tells a different story with clarity: there were no people living in the Nazareth basin during the seven centuries before the turn of the era. Not a single structure, tomb, coin, oil lamp, or shard speaks to the contrary.

We have now reached the end of the road leading to a pre-Christian Nazareth, explored the last footpath leading to a settlement before the time of Christ. The tradition, with its myths of continuous habitation and Hellenistic renaissance, ultimately leads one into a poisonous bog of misinformation. The conclusion derived from the material at hand is irrefutable: *no people lived in the Nazareth basin in the centuries before the birth of Jesus*. The implication is equally irrefutable: *if there was no Nazareth before his birth, then Jesus did not come from Nazareth*.

The many citations examined in these pages, and shown to be false, demonstrate a persistent effort on the part of the tradition to obscure data and alter history. Distortion of fact and a fundamental betrayal of trust have been the price paid to protect the story related in the canonical gospels. Wearing priestly robes and affecting scholarly mien, the wolves guard a precious idea that now appears in great jeopardy: Jesus of Nazareth.

In our investigation into the history of Nazareth, the time of Christ remains to be examined. In the next chapter we shall determine whether Jesus of Nazareth was indeed a fiction, a creation of the storytellers whose writings the Christian world holds in such high esteem.

---

[157] Chapter 1, *Illus. 1.2.*

Chapter Four

The Time of Christ

The Great Hiatus: Part III
(63 BCE – 70 CE)

The Time of Christ

The Time of Christ

Chronology 63 BCE – 70 CE

BCE

63 — Pompey conquers Palestine; Hyrcanus II (63–40 BCE) retains control of Judea and Galilee; Julius Caesar restores port of Jaffa and a few other territories to Jewish control; appointment of five regional councils.

48 — Pompey killed in Egypt

44 — Julius Caesar assassinated in Rome

37 — King Antigonus II is beheaded, and with him the Hasmonean line comes to an end. Accession of Herod the Great

7 — Herod kills his two sons, offspring of his Hasmonean wife Mariamne, after first killing her.

4 — Death of Herod; general uprising in Palestine; Judas the Galilean, son of Hezekiah, inspires the zealots (*sicarii*) or 'fourth order' among the Jews and raids Sepphoris; crucifixion of 2,000; Accession of Herod's son Archelaus as ruler of Greater Judea (Judea, Idumea, Samaria).

CE

6 — Archelaus deposed by the Romans; census of Judea by Quirinus; Judas the Galilean's second revolt is suppressed.

6–37 — Roman government of Judea via prefect in Caesarea Maritima.

c. 30 — Putative crucifixion of Jesus.

44 — Roman annexation of Judea.

c. 35–60 — Putative conversion and ministry of Paul of Tarsus.

41 — Emperor Caligula attempts to desecrate the Jerusalem Temple.

44–66 — Roman government of Palestine via procurators.

64–68 — Persecution of Jesus-followers in Rome under the emperor Nero

66 — Beginning of Jewish War.

70 — Destruction of Jerusalem.

c. 65–75 — Compilation and first edition of the Gospel of Mark, possibly in Rome

66–70 — First Jewish War, fall of Jerusalem and destruction of the Second Temple.

The Hasmonean period in Jewish history effectively ended in 63 BCE with the entrance of Pompey into Jerusalem and his bloody siege and conquest of the temple mount, in which the last adherents of the Hasmonean king Aristobulus II were barricaded. Though Hyrcanus II, the brother of Aristobulus, was placed on the Judean throne (with the title of *ethnarch* rather than *king*), he had to pay tribute to Rome and ruled at the latter's wish, subject to the supervision of the Roman proconsul of Syria. In fact, the

153

Romans preferred to deal with the Idumean royal house to the south, ruled by Antipater, who was officially dubbed "friend and ally of the Roman people" by Julius Caesar. Antipater had for a long time promoted Roman interests in Palestine. During the waning decades of Hasmonean rule, actual power was in Antipater's hands. At first he was advisor to Hyrcanus II and governor (στρατηγος) of the southern province of Idumea, but then made procurator (επιτροπος) of Judea.

Antipater managed to get his two sons, Phasael and Herod, appointed governors of Judea and Galilee respectively. This was accomplished against the wishes of the Hasmonean-friendly Jewish aristocracy, who were successful in having Antipater poisoned in 43 BCE. Rebellion broke out across the land against the Idumean overlords, but the capable Herod was able to quell these through both military and diplomatic measures. The populace was divided, and Herod was supported principally by non-Jewish elements in the land.

Palestine was invaded by the Parthians in 40 BCE, and Herod was forced into exile. The Hasmoneans were restored to power, but in Rome Herod was immediately named King of the Jews by the Senate. He returned to Palestine and, with much Roman help, regained the throne in 37 BCE for good. One of his first acts was to execute Antigonus, the last Hasmonean monarch. Herod continued his anti-Hasmonean policies, and eventually exterminated all that blood line—including most of his own family for, in order to gain acceptance in Judean circles, he had married Mariamne, granddaughter of Hyrcanus II.

During Herod's long reign (37–4 BCE) he aggressively pursued vast building activities which ameliorated the economic situation by lowering unemployment. The Temple was greatly expanded, Caesarea Maritima (the Roman headquarters) was essentially created from the ground up, including its impressive harbor, and many other cities were refurbished.

At Herod's death renewed rebellion broke out against Idumean hegemony. This was the beginning of a long period of brigandage, messianic movements, and general unrest which climaxed in the destruction of Jerusalem in 70 CE. In the north, Judas the Galilean[1] raided the armory of Sepphoris and inspired the people to resist. Josephus credits him with founding the "fourth sect" of the Jews (in addition to Pharisees, Sadducees, and Essenes), namely, the Zealots or *Sicarii* ("violent revolutionaries and assassins with religious motivation").[2] Like the Maccabees, Judas' sons and grandsons were revolutionaries, but unlike the Maccabees, they all met a violent and unsuccessful end.

In the process of reducing Judas' rebellion, the Romans under Varus put Sepphoris to the torch and sold its inhabitants as slaves. Thereafter, the city

---

[1]   This was the son of Hezekiah the "robber chief" whom the twenty-five year old Herod put to death *c*. 47 BCE (Schürer I.i:383).

[2]   IDB II:1006.

no longer opposed Rome—in the First Jewish Revolt Sepphoris had coins minted bearing the legend *Eirenopolis*, "City of Peace."[3]

After the general pacification of the land, Herod's kingdom was divided between his three sons. Galilee and Perea (across the Jordan) fell to Antipas; Judea, Samaria, and Idumea to Archelaus; and parts of southern Syria to Philip. Schürer describes the character of Antipas (known simply as "Herod" in Josephus and the New Testament) as "sly, ambitious, and luxurious, only not so capable as his father."[4] Antipas rebuilt Sepphoris and other cities in his realm. In an effort to protect his domains in Perea, he allied himself with Aretas, the Nabatean king, by marrying his daughter. This, however, led to much difficulty for him *vis-à-vis* Aretas, when he later divorced his wife (her name is not known) to marry a relation, Herodias. John the Baptist was preaching at this time and, according to the New Testament (Mk 6:14*ff.*) the prophet took exception to the royal liaison which resulted in John's imprisonment and death. More probable is that the sly monarch feared the prophet's growing influence, and slew him as a precaution (as Josephus relates).[5]

Aretas retaliated to the casting aside of his daughter by invading Herod's realm and inflicting a great military defeat on him in 36 CE. The Roman emperor Tiberius, seeing his empire invaded, ordered Vitellius, his general in Syria, to take Aretas dead or alive. However, the emperor suddenly died, releasing Vitellius from his obligation.

Meanwhile, Herod Philip had died (34 CE) without issue, and after three years his tetrarchy in Southern Syria passed to Agrippa I. This Agrippa also inherited Antipas' holdings when the latter was banished to Gaul in 39 CE (apparently a victim of Caligula's suspicious temperament).[6] Galilee remained in the hands of Agrippa I (who died in 44 CE) and then Agrippa II until the First Jewish Revolt.

Many causes have been proposed for that revolt, and like all great debacles, the causes can probably be divided between those that were endemic and longstanding, on the one hand, and immediate precipitants on the other. We have mentioned the unsettled nature of the times, the activity of zealots in the land, the hegemony of the half-foreign Herodians, not to mention of the fully-foreign Romans. Certainly, one immediate precipitant was the looting of the Temple in 66 CE by Gessius Florus, the Roman procurator. Josephus paints this Florus in the most vile terms, as one who—enlisting the aid of common rogues—was accustomed to plunder cities and communities at will and without reason.[7] It would appear that this man was insensitive to

---

3   Schürer I.ii:4; Meyers, Netzer, and Meyers 11.
4   Schürer I.ii:18. *Cf.* Lk 13:32.
5   Jos. *Ant.* 18.5.2; Schürer I.ii:23.
6   Schürer I.ii:36; Jos. *Ant.* 18.7.1–2; *Wars* 2.9.6.
7   Schürer I.ii:190; Jos. Ant. 20.11.1; Wars 2.14.2.

the explosive possibilities of the times, and helped precipitate the ultimate catastrophe.

A tumult arose among the inhabitants of Jerusalem at the despoiling of the Temple. Florus marched on the city (his headquarters was Caesarea) and gave orders to his soldiers to plunder one quarter. A large number of citizens were crucified on May 16, 66. Revolutionaries seized the fortress of Masada. The High Priest refused to make the daily offering to the emperor—"equivalent to an open declaration of revolt against the Romans" (Schürer). The die was cast.

With few Roman soldiers, Jerusalem fell to the rebels. After prolonged preparations, Cestius Gallus, the governor of Syria, entered Palestine with the twelfth legion and many auxiliaries. Soon Titus and Vespasian arrived with more troops, so that the Romans had three legions, 23 auxiliary cohorts, and many cavalry on Palestinian soil. Thus began seven years of war, which space does not permit us to review in detail here. We note, however, that the Galilee was not spared, with the exception of Sepphoris, which handed itself over to the Romans and became their strong garrison city in the north. Jotapata (15 km north of Nazareth), defended by Josephus himself, was taken by siege (July, 67 CE) and with it Galilee fell to the Romans.

In August of 70 CE Jerusalem was besieged and conquered. The Temple burned down in a general conflagration, despite the orders of Titus. The rebels held out in part of the city and then finally in the mountain stronghold of Masada. There they were commanded by one Eleasar son of Jairi, a descendant of Judas of Galilee. This virtually impregnable bastion also capitulated in April, 73 CE after a prolonged and famous siege. The Romans found only seven women and children alive, and 953 bodies of rebels who had committed suicide.

A note on method

The turbulence of the First Jewish War was accompanied by much dislocation in settlement patterns, as towns were destroyed and people displaced. One of the results, as we shall see, was the establishment of the small Jewish town of Nazareth in Lower Galilee.

The incipience of a village is not equivalent to the arrival of the first settlers at a site. No village springs up overnight. It requires a certain amount of time—perhaps a generation or two—to come into existence. Most encampments do not become villages, but are transient as people move on after a few years. In order for an encampment to become a named village two things must take place: (1) settlers must stay at the site; and (2) their number must be augmented sufficiently that the place merits a name. In other words, permanence and population are the factors that can transform an encampment into a village. A stable population, of course, will soon begin constructing edifices and tombs, and will make major agricultural alterations to the surrounding landscape.

The presence of tombs indicates both permanence and population, and it is strongly suggestive of a "village." Thus, *the earliest tomb* at Nazareth is a significant clue regarding the existence of a village. Determining its date will be an important goal of these pages. The period of tomb use can be revealed by dating funerary artefacts found *in situ*.

Even as a village worthy of a name is not contemporaneous with the first settlers, so it may not be contemporaneous with the earliest artefacts found at a site. Those artefacts may be extra-funerary and may predate the first tomb. We can suppose that a named village comes about at least 1-2 generations after the first settler. This represents a lag-time of at least 25-50 years, one which could be added to the "earliest" estimates we will be discussing. On the other hand, certain counterbalancing factors conspire to weight the evidence in an earlier direction, such as the possibility that the earliest evidence from a site has not yet been found—and may never be found. Thus, there are mutually offsetting biases affecting the limited Nazareth evidence, and we will therefore treat that evidence at face value, according to the time spans that the most recent scholarship has determined.

The Time of Christ, as these pages are entitled, by convention refers to the turn of the era. Though I know of no scholars who claim that Jesus lived later than the turn of the era, a few have proposed a considerably earlier time for him.[8] Some have identified Christ with men other than Jesus,[9] and others have denied his existence altogether.[10] In this work *The Time of Christ* denotes the time span from the Roman conquest of Palestine (63 BCE) to the fall of Jerusalem in the First Jewish War (70 CE). That era is called the Early Roman Period, though other ways of dividing Roman chronology are extant.[11]

It is not my intention here to question the conventional understanding of Christian origins, that a man by the name of Jesus (Yeshua, Joshua) lived in Palestine in the early first century CE and inspired the religion we now call Christianity. Yet at the beginning of the third Christian millennium these axiomatic tenets are coming under increasing scrutiny by a number of scholars. Mindful of this, I use *The Time of Christ* for expedience, without thereby ascribing to any historical assumptions implied. We shall take up questions

---

[8]   *E.g.*, W.B Smith 1906; Ellegård 1999.

[9]   Recent proposals include, among others: the Teacher of Righteousness, Menahem the Essene, John the Baptist, and James the Just.

[10]   Doherty, Zindler.

[11]   The Roman chronology used in this series is as follows:
Early Roman: 63 BCE–70 CE
Middle Roman: 70–180 CE (death of Marcus Aurelius/accession of Commodus)
Late Roman: 180–337 CE (death of Constantine I).

THE MYTH OF NAZARETH

associated with the historical Jesus in a second volume, *A New Account of Christian Origins*. In *The Myth of Nazareth* I restrict consideration to the archaeology of Nazareth, with the purpose of showing that the provenance of Jesus, as set forth in the gospels, is not historical.

Roman burial customs in Palestine

The kokh tomb

In Chapter Three we discussed the kokh-type tomb in connection with six oil lamps which were claimed to be Hellenistic but which are in fact Roman.[12] A score of kokh tombs have been discovered in the Nazareth basin. These tombs are the principal source of our evidence from Nazareth, and we must now consider their chronology more carefully. The discussion which follows is indebted to the analysis of Hans-Peter Kuhnen, published in 1990.[13]

Scholars of Galilean archaeology have been greatly influenced by the archaeology of Jerusalem and its environs. A large city, the center of Judaism and home of the Temple of Yahweh, and commanding political and military power in the region since time immemorial, the Judean capital has understandably served as an archaeological reference for the rest of the land. Certainly, many archaeological innovations in Palestine are first detectable in Jerusalem, and only later in other parts of the Holy Land. As regards Nazareth, the failure to completely appreciate a lag time between the appearance of kokh tombs and bow-spouted oil lamps in Jerusalem and their appearance in the Galilee has generally resulted in an early chronology for the site. For example, in 1969 Finegan writes:

> At Jerusalem, the great majority of ancient tombs are of this [*i.e. kokh*] type, and date approximately from 150 B.C. to A.D. 150. It may fairly be said that this type of tomb virtually became the canonical form of the Jewish family grave.[14]

Finegan's statement may be true, but it would still be a mistake to suppose that the kokh tomb simultaneously appeared in the Galilee and Jerusalem. Kuhnen writes:

> Kokh tombs [*Schiebestollengräber*], which under the Hasmoneans gradually replaced the older chamber tombs, also dominated the graveyards of [Jerusalem] almost with exclusivity after the accession of

---

[12] Chapter 3, pp. 105–109 (*Illus. 3.2*, p. 110).
[13] Kuhnen, *Palästina in Griechisch-Römischer Zeit* (1990), pp. 253*ff.*
[14] Finegan 1969:185.

158

Herod… Under Herod and his heirs, the kokhi type of grave also appeared in the Jewish-populated surroundings of Jerusalem, for example, in Tell en-Nasbe and in el-'Ezriye (Bethany)… Apparently only later, from approximately the middle of the first century after Christ, did people begin to build kokh tombs in other upland regions of Palestine, as seen in Galilee at Huqoq, Meron, H. Sema and H. Usa… So it is evident that during the first century after Christ kokhim came into fashion in all parts of the land west and east of the Jordan…[15]

From this we see that kokh tomb use begins *c.* 150 BCE in Jerusalem, comes to prevail in that city after Herod's accession, and spreads to Galilee only after *c.* 50 CE.[16] Thus, M. Aviam has noted that "no Jewish tombs from the Hasmonaean or Early Roman periods have yet been excavated in the Galilee."[17] In all, there is a 200-year delay between the first beginnings of kokh use in Jerusalem and its appearance in Galilee. The delay is even greater if we consider that the first kokhim in Palestine may date as early as III BCE.

We are now able to deal with a false assumption frequently encountered in the Nazareth literature: that the presence of kokh tombs in the basin automatically attests to human presence there in Hellenistic times, or in the time of Christ, or even in Early Roman times. Thus, already in the 1930s, Fr. Clemens Kopp considered the Nazareth tombs to be as early as III BCE[18]—by comparing them to possibly the earliest kokhim known in Palestine (those at Marisa). His error amounts to no less than three centuries. The same assumption persists even to the present day. For example, in a 1998 German reference article on Nazareth, we read: "Grabfunde bezeugen eine Besiedlung seit dem Ende des 3 Jh. v C"[19] Such a view has fueled the false Hellenistic Renaissance doctrine, disproved in Chapter Three.

---

[15] *Schiebestollengräber, die unter den Hasmonäern allmählich die älteren Kammergräber ersetzt hatten, beherrschten auch nach der Thronbesteigung des Herodes fast mit Ausschliesslichkeit die Friedhöfe der Stadt… Auch im jüdisch besiedelten Umland Jerusalems entstanden unter Herodes und dessen Erben Gräber des Schiebestollentyps, beispielsweise in Tell en-Nasbe und in el-'Ezariye (Betanien)… Anscheinend noch später, etwa ab der Mitte des 1.Jh. n.Chr., begann man in den anderen Bergregionen Palästinas Gräber mit Schiebestollen anzulegen, was für Galiläa Huqoq, Meron, H. Sema und H. Usa… belegen.*
Somit ist anzunehmen, dass Schiebestollengräber während des 1.Jh. n.Chr. in allen Landesteilen westlich und östlich des Jordan in Mode kamen… (Kuhnen 254–55).
[16] This view is very different from that which posits the general adoption of the kokh tomb throughout the Semitic world already in Hellenistic times. (See, *e.g.,* Hachlili and Killebrew:110.)
[17] Aviam 2004:306.
[18] Chapter 3, p. 110.
[19] *LTK,* "Nazaret," 710.

Similar examples are readily encountered: "Of the twenty-three tombs found *c* 450 m (500 yd.) from the [Church of the Annunciation] most were of the kokim type... known in Palestine from *c* 200 BC and which became the standard Jewish type"[20] This is true enough yet, as Kuhnen reveals, there is no connection between the kokhim tombs of 200 BCE and those at Nazareth.

Again, in another dictionary article on Nazareth we read: "The location of the tombs of the first century BCE to the first century CE disclose that the occupied area extended hardly 300 by 100 meters."[21] In fact, this is not at all the case. The Galilean kokhim tombs, as we have just seen, were not "of the first century BCE to the first century CE." We can now say that, *at the earliest, the Nazareth tombs date to the latter half of the first century CE.* As regards the emplacement of the ancient village, we must defer that interesting question until Chapter Five, when we consider scriptural demands to locate the village on the hillside.

Contrary to the implications found in much Nazareth literature, the many kokhim excavated in the basin are evidence neither of Hellenistic times nor of Early Roman times. Per Kuhnen's analysis, they postdate 50 CE, and probably 70 CE. A Middle Roman beginning for kokh tombs at Nazareth accords with the dating arrived at from other data in the basin, including pottery, rolling stones, arcosolia, trough graves, and stone vessels.

The so-called "Herodian" tomb

An interesting complication of the above discussion—and one that has led to a good deal of confusion—is the fairly recent designation of the kokh tomb as "Herodian." Only one archaeologist, to my knowledge, has taken up this identification, but he is quite influential. We shall see that "Herodian" is problematic not only in connection with tombs, but in connection with the bow-spouted oil lamp, a type which also figures importantly in the Nazareth evidence (see below).

As a valid archaeological designation for the turn of the era, "Herodian" came into currency in the 1930s with the work of Kathleen Kenyon and others. Though Bagatti often refers to "Herodian" oil lamps, he never calls the kokh-type tomb "Herodian."[22] Nor did Kenyon. The first such attribution that I have been able to discover is in James Strange's 1992 article "Nazareth" from the *Anchor Bible Dictionary*:

> As inferred from the Herodian tombs in Nazareth, the maximum extent of the Herodian and pre-Herodian village measured about 900×200 m, for a total area just under 60 acres.

---

[20] *NIDBA*, "Nazareth," 330.

[21] DJBP, "Nazareth," 449.

[22] Bagatti often refers to "the period of the kokhim tombs" (though he nowhere defines that period). *Cf.* Bagatti 1967:7; *Exc.* 240, 313, 318, *etc.*

The type of tomb Strange designates by the term "Herodian" is revealed later in the same article:

> Beneath the convent of the Dames de Nazareth about 100 m W of the Church of the Annunciation are remains of houses, a tomb of the Herodian period, and other underground working spaces typical of those found beneath the other churches.

The "tomb of the Herodian period" is Bagatti's tomb 73, which contained at least seven kokhim. In fact, there are two chambers under the convent, both of the kokh type. They may at one time have been connected, forming a single large tomb complex. If so, then they subsequently became divided by intrusive secondary constructions.[23]

Yet, some scholars have proposed that the kokh tomb ended in the first or second centuries CE. This is especially the case with Catholic scholars. R. Smith wrote in 1961:

> Various viewpoints on the use-span of the kok type of interment are brought together by H. Vincent in [*Revue Biblique*], XLIII (1934), pp. 564–67. Vincent expresses a preference for the round dates of 200 B.C.–A.D. 200… J.T. Milik informs me from his wide knowledge that kok burials definitely came to an end by A.D. 135. The late date formerly given probably arose from instances in which tombs cut prior to 135 were re-used after that date.[24]

The view of Father Milik is neither tenable nor universally held. We now know that the kokh type of burial endured in Northern Palestine through Roman and into Byzantine times. Kokhim have been found in Sepphoris dating to III CE,[25] in the catacombs of Beth Shearim dating to III–IV CE,[26] and in a burial cave at Kafr Kanna (7 km NE of Nazareth) dating to IV CE.[27] In the hill country of Manasseh, a particularly late example was excavated with ten kokhim in a "IV–VI CE" context.[28] Knowledge of kokhim use through Roman times has been known for a long time. Thus Goodenough writes, in 1953:

---

[23] For the tombs see *Exc*:242–244 and Bagatti's figs. 193–194. Older bibliography on these tombs includes *Histoire des decouverts faits chez les Dames de Nazareth* (Beyrouth, 1936); *Studi Franciscani* (1937), pp. 253–258; *Les Fouilles de Nazareth* (Paris, 1954), all by Bagatti.

[24] R. Smith 1961:59, n.18.

[25] NEAEHL, "Sepphoris," p. 1328.

[26] Mazar, vol. 1, p. 134, fig. 5, pl. XVI, *etc*; Hachlili:793.

[27] Berman:107–08.

[28] Chamber B at Silet edh-Dhahr (Sellers & Baramki: 8, 29, 44). See also Goodenough I:66 and 88.

THE MYTH OF NAZARETH

In the centuries which followed the fall of Jerusalem, however, the dominant Jewish convention of burial was that of the chamber tomb with kokim. This is the form stipulated in the Mishna, and the type most commonly found.[29]

An early end to kokhim use, espoused by some Catholics, tends to backdate Middle and Late Roman evidence into Early Roman times. As has been mentioned, this is a recurring problem in the Nazareth literature.

We are now able to construct a chronology of kokh tomb use in Palestine (*Illus. 4.1*).

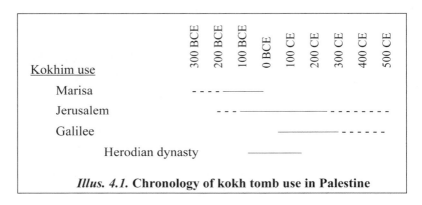

***Illus. 4.1.* Chronology of kokh tomb use in Palestine**

It can be seen from the above chart that there was a particularly early period of kokh tomb use—already in Hellenistic and Hasmonean times—exemplified by the tombs at Marisa in the south of the land.[30] The type came to Jerusalem in II BCE and endured there for many centuries. Finally, in the middle of I CE kokhim use arrived in the northern part of the country. Like Kopp, who linked kokhim use at Nazareth with tombs at Marisa, other writers seem oblivious to the slow and gradual spread of the kokh tomb northwards. Thus, Finegan again:

> Eighteen of the tombs [at Nazareth] are of the kokim type, which was known in Palestine from about 200 B.C., and became virtually the standard type of Jewish tomb.[31]

This is, of course, literally true, though the number of known kokh tombs in the basin has now risen to at least twenty-one. But Finegan's statement has no relevance to Nazareth, for the tombs there do not date to "200 B.C." In other words, the implication is entirely false. Yet Finegan's influential

---

[29] Goodenough I:88.
[30] Marisa was destroyed in 40 BCE and never rebuilt.
[31] Finegan 1969:28 = 1992:46.

The Time of Christ

assessment has been emphasized in subsequent scholarly literature. In the section on Nazareth from his 1991 book, *The Historical Jesus: The Life of a Mediterranean Jewish Peasant*, J. D. Crossan writes:

> The use of such multishafted burial chambers is quite significant because, as Jack Finegan observed, "from about 200 B.C. [they] became virtually the standard type of Jewish tomb," so that it may fairly be said that this type of tomb virtually became the canonical form of the Jewish family grave.[32]

Once again, this ignores the 250-year delay in arrival of the kokh tomb to Galilee. Thus, the Nazareth literature routinely backdates 20-odd tombs by a substantial period of time. To the unwary and non-specialist reader, the result is that much post-Jesus evidence is effectively transformed into pre-Jesus evidence. A false chronology results. This is exacerbated by emphasis on the *first appearance* in Palestine of tombs, oil lamps, etc. That emphasis is misleading, for the first appearance of a type at some remote location has little or no necessary relation to when a tomb, oil lamp, *etc.*, was actually hewn or used elsewhere. The presence of kokhim at Nazareth does not mean they were contemporary with the first such tombs in Palestine, any more than readers of printed books today are contemporaries of Johann Gutenberg.

Terminology also plays a role in the false chronology that has governed Nazareth for several generations. We see from *Illus. 4.1* that it is clearly misleading to call the kokhim tombs "Herodian." The Herodian dynastic period was but a small part of the eight centuries between 300 BCE and 500 CE, "the era of the kokhim tomb."[33] In addition, the kokh tomb came to the Galilee long after the reign of Herod the Great and towards the end of the Herodian dynasty, with the result that this term has virtually no applicability to the Nazareth tombs.

We have seen that Strange designates kokh tombs "Herodian." In a 1997 article, he explicitly connects the "Herodian" tomb with the Early Roman period:

> Nazareth exhibits archaeological remains from the Middle Bronze II, Iron II, and late Hellenistic periods, but its heyday was in the Early Roman period. Judging from the locations of its Early Roman (Herodian) tombs (which must have been located outside the village according to Jewish law), its size then must have been about 900 m from the southwest to the northeast and 200 m southeast-northwest.[34]

---

[32] Crossan 1991:16. See also NIDBA (1983), "Nazareth," 330.

[33] The phrase occurs several times in Bagatti's *Excavations*. The last Herodian was Agrippa II, who ruled largely gentile areas in Syria, Perea, and Galilee He lived in Rome from 75 CE on, and died *c.* 100 CE.

[34] OEANE, "Nazareth," 113.

Thus an attempt has been made, in a two-step process, to identify kokh tombs (which had a lifespan of many centuries) exclusively with the Early Roman period. This is not true anywhere in Palestine, much less in the Galilee where the kokh tomb arrived in mid-I CE.

Bagatti also implicitly (but not explicitly) associated the kokh-type tomb with Early Roman times—*e.g.*, by contrasting the "period of the kokhim tombs" with II-III CE, later Roman times, *etc.*:

> We, therefore, have three glass vases well-known at the period of the kokhim tombs, then a jug of the Late Roman period (No. 5); 18 lamps of which 7 with enlarged nozzles are "Herodian"; 7 round ones with flat bodies of the 2nd-3rd centuries; 3 with saucers, not later than this time, and one heart-shaped with reliefs, not prior to the 7th century, 2 pots usually found in kokhim tombs and a pan and a juglet evidently later. (*Exc.* 240)

The juglet Bagatti mentions in the last sentence is typical Roman ware, which Fernandez dates *c.* 100-*c.* 275 CE.[35] Yet, for Bagatti it is "evidently later" than material "usually found in kokhim tombs." Evidently, Bagatti supposes that kokhim use ended *c.* 100 CE—a grave error that undermines his entire chronology. In fact, kokhim use was only then *beginning* in the Galilee. From this we see how artificial are the Italian's chronological assumptions. He is so inured to this way of thinking that he often uses "the period of the kokhim tombs" as a substitute for "I CE." In fact, *all* the material from Tomb 70 (and, indeed, from Nazareth) arguably falls into Bagatti's "later" category, and much of it—*e.g.*, the items mentioned in the above citation—was found in kokh tombs. The principal question, as we shall now see, is whether *any* of this material predates 100 CE.

The earliest Nazareth evidence

More than two dozen tombs have been discovered in the Nazareth basin dating to the Roman period. Their exact number is debatable, because it will be shown (Chapter Five) that one or more exist under the venerated area, and that several tombs (such as those under the Sisters of Nazareth convent) may in fact be a single tomb with subsidiary chambers. These tombs are all of the kokh type, which we have seen postdate *c.* 50 CE. The kokh-type tomb gave way in Roman times to other forms of burial—such as the arcosolium and trough grave. All these types of burial are represented in the Nazareth basin.

---

[35] Both the pan and juglet are specifically itemized by Fernandez. The juglet (*Exc.* Fig. 192:20) is Fernandez no. 198, Type 8.3, pp. 115, 149, and 229. It dates *c.* 70-*c.* 300 CE. The pan is Fernandez no. 481, Type 15.3, dating *c.* 250 CE+. (*Cf.* Appendix 5.)

Four of the roughly twenty kokh tombs yielded movable finds *in situ*, such as pottery, oil lamps, glass perfume bottles, *etc*. They are tomb numbers 70, 71, 72, and one excavated in 1995 in El Batris Street, about 525 m NW of the Church of the Annunciation—a tomb not known to Bagatti.

Thus, the following affirmation is now possible: *all of the funereal finds from Roman Nazareth date after the time of Christ.* They do so because they all come from kokh tombs.

If the tombs did not predate 50 CE, is it possible that the village of Nazareth did?

We shall review all the known Roman evidence from Nazareth in the remaining chapters. Here it may be mentioned in advance that the greatest quantities of movable evidence date to the third and fourth centuries CE, and then again to medieval times. Moving back in time, we can say without doubt that a number of oil lamps and pieces of pottery also date to the second century of our era. However, *not a single artefact can be dated with certainty prior to 100 CE.* That astonishing statement will become clear in the following pages.

Archaeologists are rarely granted certainty. They are very pleased to find eminently datable artefacts, such as coins or inscriptions with a name or date. Nazareth, surprisingly, has divulged no coins of the Roman period. Oil lamps constitute the most datable find in the basin. Palestinian oil lamps have been well studied and can sometimes be dated to within a quarter of a century. We shall make much use of them in our investigation, for many oil lamps have been discovered in the Nazareth basin. Jars, jugs, cooking pots, pans, plates, glass bottles, and small items (beads, metal pins), complete the catalogue of movable finds, which we shall consider later.

The ancient oil lamp

"The oil lamp," writes Varda Sussman, "provided movable, protected and controllable light to the world for thousands of years, really until the advent of electricity and the electric light bulb."[36] The typical oil lamp was a hand-held clay vessel small enough to be carried in the palm of the hand. The earliest lamps that have been discovered date to the third or perhaps the fourth millennium BCE. They are simply bowls or saucers with telltale burn marks on the rim. Towards the end of the third millennium, the rim of the bowl was pinched to form a spout, thus producing the first dedicated oil lamp. About 1300 BCE, the rim began to be turned outwards rather than inwards (*Illus.4.2:1*). This basic type was very long-lived, continuing with minor changes for about a millennium, until the end of the Persian period.

---

[36] Sussman 1985:43. In this section I am indebted to Varda Sussman's article, "Lighting the Way Through History" (*BAR*, Mar–Apr 1985).

A new type, imported from Greece, first appeared in Palestine in the seventh century. The form consisted of two parts: (a) a true nozzle (spout) that terminated with the wick hole; and (b) a round, open saucer. The nozzle was fully enclosed, like a short tube, which the potter attached to the saucer. By the fourth century the sides of the saucer had "closed up" on top to form a large filling hole, one through which the oil was poured. The Greek lamp nozzle was distinctively elongated (*Illus.4.2:2*). Palestine was flooded during the Persian Period with imports of this kind. Early Greek potters continued to fashion lamps out of two parts (nozzle and body), but eventually potters began working from a single piece.

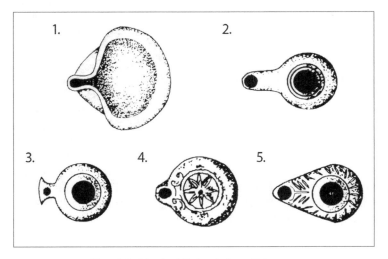

Illus.4.2. Typical Palestinian oil lamps.
1. Late Iron age 2. Hellenistic 3. Bow-spouted ("Herodian")
4. Roman 5. Byzantine

The closed lamp afforded room for decoration, especially on the top surface, called the *discus*. Imported lamps could be highly decorated. However, Palestinian lamps were generally less so, commensurate with the Jewish commandment forbidding any "graven image, or manner of likeness" (Ex 20:4-5). We shall see that decorated oil lamps did come into vogue after the destruction of the Second Temple. But their ornamentation is comparatively restrained, avoids depiction of the living creatures altogether, and consists of geometrical patterns, fruit, olive branches, and the like.

At first oil lamps were hand-made, then wheel-made, and finally mould-made. From II BCE onwards almost all oil lamps were mould-made. This type of lamp was fashioned from upper and lower moulds which at first were virtually identical. A thin layer of clay was applied between the moulded halves to fuse them. A wick hole and filling hole were then cut into the top, and the lamp was finally fired in a kiln.

The bow-spouted ("Herodian") oil lamp

Of particular interest for our purposes is a lamp type well known in Palestine during the first and early second century CE. It had several varieties, and is most immediately recognized by a distinctively bowed spout or nozzle (*Illus.4.2:3*). A number of these lamps have been found in the Nazareth basin. Though it is often termed "Herodian," this designation—as with the tomb of the same name (see above)—is a misnomer. We shall shortly see that this lamp type was not contemporary with the reign of Herod the Great, and that it outlived his dynasty. Perhaps realizing this, Paul Lapp used an alternate name for this lamp in his classification,[37] one which we adopt in these pages: the bow-spouted lamp.

At least nineteen bow-spouted oil lamps have been found at Nazareth.[38] There are probably many more, represented by small shards. "With some rare exceptions," writes Bagatti, "the lamps came to us in fragments."[39] Naturally, fragments do not always permit a clear typological determination, and therefore some smaller fragments have not been used in my tally.[40] Nineteen is probably a conservative estimate for the total number of these lamps.

Fourteen of the Nazareth bow-spouted lamps are made on the potter's wheel and are quite plain, with very little (or no) ornamentation. The type is often called "Herodian," and the Nazareth examples are itemized in *Illus. 4.3*, numbers 1–14. The remaining five bow-spouted lamps belong to a distinctive variety which appeared briefly between the two Jewish revolts.[41] Called Darom ("Southern") by Varda Sussman,[42] this subtype is mould-made and decorated, with a number of characteristics not shared by its plainer cousin (*cf.* Appendix 5).

For a long time, scholars had only the vaguest notion of the dating of the bow-spouted oil lamp. In 1914, H. Walters dated its appearance in Palestine to IV-III BCE, through false association with Greek and Hellenistic lamps[43]—

---

[37] P. Lapp 1961:193.

[38] This tally does not include lamps found near Nazareth but outside the basin, *e.g.*, in the Feig tombs 2.6 km East of the CA (Feig 1990). *Illus. 4.3* nos. 14–16 are the lamps of the local pottery tradition discussed in Chapter 3, pp. 117*f.*

[39] *Exc.* 299.

[40] E.g., Bagatti 1971b, fig. 15:1–3.

[41] Sussman 1982:16; Rosenthal and Sivan 82.

[42] Darom lamps were produced in the region of Beth Guvrin, southwest of Jerusalem. (Sussman 1982:17.)

[43] H.B. Walters, *Catalogue of the Greek and Roman Lamps in the British Museum*, 1914, pl. XL. See R. Smith 1961:53, n.3.

thus erring by several centuries. In the 1920s and 30s G. Fitzgerald maintained that the bow-spouted lamp was a type "common in the Hellenistic Period, but which is also well-known in Byzantine times." He dated some specimens as early as III BCE.[44] A decade later it became evident that the type appeared in Early Roman times. Hence the name "Herodian."[45] However, studies in Israel since mid-century, and an increasing fund of published parallels—often in carefully controlled stratigraphic contexts—have inexorably moved the *terminus post quem* for this lamp later and later. In 1961 P. Lapp wrote that undecorated bow-spouted lamps were current "75 B.C.–A.D. 70."[46] In that same year, however, R. Smith tentatively dated the type from *c.* 37 BCE (the accession of Herod the Great). Smith even considered a later beginning for this lamp possible.[47] He offered the following explanation of the designation:

> The name "Herodian," originally intended to designate the period of the reign of Herod the Great (37 to 4 B.C.), seems to have been used as a Palestinian equivalent for the term "Augustan." The narrow use-span of the lamp which the term originally implied cannot be maintained, but the term "Herodian" is still useful if we take it to include the period of the entire Herodian dynasty, which ended with the death of Herod Agrippa II in presumably A.D. 100.[48]

This view is now also out of date. In 1976, Yigael Yadin noted that the bow-spouted lamp was not found in a representative I BCE assemblage in Jerusalem. Yadin estimated its appearance there to "the middle of [Herod's reign *or even later*"[49] (emphasis added). In 1980 J. Hayes wrote that such lamps were common in Jerusalem in early I CE.[50] In 1982 Varda Sussman dated the appearance of this type in Judea to "the reign of Herod." A few years later, however, she was able to conclude: "Recent archaeological evidence suggests that their first appearance was somewhat later, *after the reign of Herod*"[51] (emphasis added). We will adopt the latter view in these pages.

Thus, we can now date the first appearance of the bow-spouted lamp in Jerusalem to *c.* 1–25 CE.[52] Because a few years must be allowed for the

---

[44] FitzGerald 1931:40 (regarding his Pl. 36:1) and FitzGerald 1930:15, Pl. L, No. 26.
[45] Sukenik considered the lamp to date *c* 100 BCE–*c* 50 CE. See Sukenik 1947 and Goodenough I:145.
[46] P. Lapp 193.
[47] R. Smith 1961:58–59, 65, and n. 17.
[48] R. Smith 1961:53 n.1.
[49] Yadin 45.
[50] Hayes 1980:13.
[51] Sussman 1982:14; 1985:53.
[52] Sussman notes that the earlier phase of this lamp is evidenced in burial caves in Judea, especially in Jerusalem (Sussman 1982:14). R. Smith notes that the bow-spouted lamp "appears to have had its origin in the vicinity of Jerusalem... From there it spread widely throughout Palestine" (Smith 1961:53, n.2). This view is questioned

spread of the type to the rural villages of the north, c. 15–c. 40 CE is the earliest probable time for the appearance of this type in Southern Galilee. Accordingly, we shall adopt 25 CE as the *terminus post quem* for the bow-spouted oil lamp at Nazareth.

Use of these lamps continued for over a century, and specialists are unanimous that they were in use until 135–150 CE.[53] "For practical purposes," writes Smith, "…we may take A.D. 135 as the *terminus ante quem*" for this type of lamp.[54] The time span, then, for the bow-spouted lamp in Lower Galilee is slightly over a century: c. 25 CE to c. 135 CE.

In 1961 R. Smith published a study of the plain bow-spouted ("Herodian") lamp of Palestine. He attempted to differentiate two subtypes. The earlier variety—which we shall call Type 1—went out of fashion in the middle of I CE. At that time, a related Type 2 appeared, first in Jerusalem and then throughout the land.[55] Smith identifies five characteristics that differentiate these two subtypes,[56] as listed in *Illus. 4.4.*

Twelve of the earliest Nazareth lamps are Type 2, which according to Smith postdates c. 50 CE. Only one lamp is Type 1 and *may* predate 50 CE by a few years.[57] Thus, we see that virtually all the oil lamps at Nazareth

---

(without countervailing evidence) by Fernandez: 66. We note that Fernandez in general adopts an earlier chronology than most of the other cited researchers, yet his reasoning and methods are not entirely convincing. He relies largely on Loffreda's results from Capernaum (many of which have been questioned) and Fernandez' Nazareth data are quite incomplete (he includes only two of Bagatti's 12 plain bow-spouted lamps in his book). Fernandez divides these "Herodian" lamps into four subtypes (versus the two of R. Smith) and suggests an equal number of chronological periods (p. 66), but his ambitious typology seems arbitrary. His data are included in *Illus. 4.3* for completeness.

[53] R. Smith notes that bow-spouted oil lamps continued to be made and used well into the second century (R. Smith 1961:59). Feig writes: "The lamps in Illustration 9:6–9 are among the "Herodian" lamps of the first century A.D., but in the Galilee these lamps are also typical of the second century A.D" (Feig 1990:73). Sussman considers that these lamps were used "till the mid-2nd century A.D.," a position shared by Rosenthal and Sivan (Sussman 1982:14; Rosenthal & Sivan:80).

[54] R. Smith 1961:59.

[55] R. Smith 1961:64 (for dating); 1966:4 (for geographical diffusion). The results also are presented in R. Smith 1966:15.

[56] R. Smith 1961:60–62.

[57] *Exc.* fig. 233:1 (discussion p. 299). Not included in this tally is a lamp shard which Bagatti curiously suggests is "Herodian." The diagram (*Exc.* 235:35) does not match the discussion (p. 306) which speaks of "cuts" in the handle. Bagatti mentions this lamp shard in an apparently Late Roman context at *Exc.* 309. An uncommon bow-spouted lamp (Fernandez type L. 4) had a sliced handle, and perhaps this is Bagatti's referent and his diagram is poorly drawn. Incidentally, Fernandez considers this subtype "proto-Herodian" (p. 81) and backdates it to I BCE, misinterpreting R.

[* = Found in kokh tomb]

No.	Exc. fig.	Findspot	Description	Smith Type	Fernandez	Date
1-14		BOW-SPOUTED (Plain):				
1.	233:1	VA (L. 51c) 20m N of CA	Shard (nozzle and neck)	1	(3.1 or 3.2)	c. 25 CE–c. 135 CE
2.	233:2	VA (L. 51a) 20m N of CA	Shard (nozzle)	2	(3.4b)	c. 25 CE–c. 135 CE
3.	233:3	CA (L. 26) Byz. atrium	Shard (nozzle and neck)	2	3.4b	c. 25 CE–c. 135 CE
4.	233:4	CA (L. 46)	Shard (nozzle and neck)	2	(3.4b)	c. 25 CE–c. 135 CE
5.	233:5	VA (L. 48f) 20m N of CA	Shard (part of discus)	2	(3.4)	c. 25 CE–c. 135 CE
6.	235:3	VA (unspecified)	Shard (nozzle)	2	(3.4c)	c. 25 CE–c. 135 CE
7.	235:4	VA (unspecified)	Shard (nozzle and neck)	2	(Not included)	c. 25 CE–c. 135 CE
8.	235:5	VA (unspecified)	Shard (part of discus)	2	(3.4c)	c. 25 CE–c. 135 CE
9.	235:8	VA (unspecified)	Shard (part of discus)	2	(3.4c)	c. 25 CE–c. 135 CE
10.	192:6	T. 70 (30m S of CA)	Plain bow-spouted	2	3.2(b)	*c. 25 CE–c. 135 CE
11.	192:11	T. 70 (30m S of CA)	2 Lamps	2	(Not included)	*c. 25 CE–c. 135 CE
13.	—	T. 72 (350m SE of CA)	Richmond photo lower left	2	3.4	*c. 25 CE–c. 135 CE
14.	—	El Batris (500m NW of CA)"	Herodian" lamp	?	—	*c. 25 CE–c. 135 CE
15-19.		BOW-SPOUTED (Darom)	5 Lamps (see Chp. 5)	—	8	*c. 70 CE–c. 135 CE
20-22.		LOCAL TRADITION	3 Lamps (*Exc.* 192:15) Found in T. 70. *Cf.* Chp. 3:22f.			*c. 50 CE–c. 150 CE
23-29.		ROMAN	7 Lamps (Broner XXV; Loeschke VIII)		9.1	*c. 50 CE– III CE

192:13-14 = 5 lamps from T. 70; Richmond photo upper left & rgt. = 2 lamps from T. 72

Illus. 4.3. **The earliest Nazareth oil lamps**

postdate mid-I CE, as do the tombs. The convergence of tomb evidence and oil lamp evidence makes it amply clear that—per Smith's typology, at any rate—the entire evidentiary profile for Roman Nazareth is post-50 CE. Only a single outlier (one oil lamp) *might* date a few years earlier, but no other evidence from the emerging settlement could be dated so early.[58]

The above having been said, it bears mention that Smith's typology is not universally recognized. Thus, Rosenthal and Sivan write in 1978:

> There have been attempts by Kahane (1961) and Smith (1961) to divide the Herodian lamps into chronological and typological groups. The latest excavations, however, seem to indicate that all the variations occur simultaneously.[59]

	Type 1	Type 2
a) Neck	Acutely curved	Less curved
b) Ridge around filling hole	Wide border ("flange")	Little or no flange
c) Nozzle	Acutely spatulated	Slightly spatulated
d) Wick hole	Medium size, oval shape	Large, round or wide
e) Decoration	None	May have circles and bands

Illus. 4.4. R. Smith's two subtypes for the plain bow-spouted oil lamp.

Smith (1966:14) who suggested a mid-I CE date and considered it a development of other types.

[58] Of course, that single oil lamp could also have been brought into the basin twenty, thirty, or even fifty years after it was made, in which case it would not truly constitute early evidence, but merely represent a "holdover" from a past generation—much as today, every household has at least one or two items that are quite old. On the other hand, the lamp might very well date after 50 CE, in which case it is not an outlier at all.

[59] Rosenthal and Sivan 80.

If Rosenthal and Sivan are correct, then the outlier[60] is contemporaneous with the remaining plain bow-spouted lamps, and *all* of those lamps (nos. 1-14 in *Ilus.* 3) may date as late as 135 CE or as early as 25 CE. This moves the *terminus post quem* back a quarter century.

In conclusion, the data clearly show that settlers did not come into the basin before *c.* 25 CE. In the "early" scenario, a few people entered the basin in the second quarter of I CE and began building tombs about mid-century.

On the other hand, the evidence equally supports a "late" scenario, whereby people came into the Nazareth basin not before the beginning of the second century CE. After all, the *terminus ante quem* for the nineteen bow-spouted Nazareth lamps is *c.* 135 CE.[61]

Both scenarios—early and late—satisfy the 85 to 110-year time span during which people must have settled the basin.[62] Of course, these are extremes. The totality of evidence cannot be arbitrarily weighted towards the earliest or towards the latest possible date. More probable—indeed, most probable—is a "middle" scenario which equally credits the late and early views: people started to come into the Nazareth basin towards the midpoint of this time span. In other words, our best hypothesis—judging from the tombs and from the earliest datable Roman evidence at Nazareth—is that settlers started to come into the basin about 80 to 90 CE.

Though it is routinely termed "Herodian" by many archaeologists (see below), I wish to reaffirm that the bow-spouted oil lamp dates from about 25 CE in the Galilee *at the earliest*. We recall that twelve of thirteen plain bow-spouted lamps found at Nazareth are Smith's type 2, which is the *later* variety (*Illus. 4.3*). If we accept Smith's chronology, these most likely appeared in the latter part of the time span for such lamps, namely, from 75–100 CE onwards.

An overall conclusion now emerges with great clarity. After the protracted Jewish Revolt the country lay ravaged, the temple destroyed, and Jerusalem in ruins. People were in motion, seeking a fresh start, and the birth of Nazareth was one result of this momentous chapter in Jewish history. The

---

[60] A careful review of Bagatti's drawings shows that three lamps (*Exc.* 192:6 and 11 [2 examples]) display the oval and medium-size wick hole of Smith's Type 1, while having all the remaining characteristics of Type 2. These lamps may be examples of the 10% which Smith calls "transitional" and which he dates to mid-I CE. Then again, they may be misdrawn. Fernandez, who examined the lamps in Nazareth, noted that "the drawings [in *Excavations in Nazareth*] are not always entirely correct" (Fernandez 29).

[61] *Illus. 4.3*:1–14, and the five Darom lamps that date between the two Jewish revolts. To these can be added the three lamps of the local pottery tradition (*Illus. 4.3*:15–17), whose *terminus ante quem* is *c.* 150 CE.

[62] The shorter time span of 85 years (50–135 CE) would obtain if all the lamps came from kokh tombs.

evidence indicates quite clearly that the first settlers moved into the Nazareth basin in the generation following the First Jewish Revolt.

Regardless of which scenario we follow—early, middle, or late—one thing cannot be doubted: the emergence of Nazareth was after the time of Christ.

"Herodian"

The first reference to artefacts of "the Herodian period" from Nazareth appears to be a reference in a 1951 article by Father A. Médebielle. We recall that already in the late 1930s Fr. Kopp noted with astonishment that recent excavations under the Franciscan Convent had revealed "no trace of a Greek or Roman settlement" (quoting Fr. Tonneau from a few years before).[63] Apparently over-reacting to this evidentiary lacuna, Médebielle wrote: "The pottery *of the time of Herod* betrays modest circumstances..."[64] (Emphasis added.) Bagatti later corrected Médebielle's assessment: "The excavations of 1955 made more precise the date of the 'primitive' habitations, because the pottery is far earlier that [*sic*] the 'Herodian' period."[65] In fact, Bagatti was the first to identify Bronze and Iron Age remains, which he did not realize were from ancient Japhia.[66]

Médebielle's choice of Herod (the Great) in reference to Bronze-Iron Age finds was a portent of things to come. "Herodian"—a term so laden with chronological implications—would be used by Bagatti himself, and by many others, in reference to the tombs and oil lamps at Nazareth. We have seen that, in the former case the "Herodian" period is a small fraction of the lifespan of kokh-type tombs, while in the latter case the bow-spouted oil lamps appeared in the Galilee only towards the end of Herodian times.

Looking 'past' the designation "Herodian" allows us to recognize that the underlying structural and movable finds at Nazareth have nothing to do with the turn of the era. On the other hand, we will surely be misled if terminology guides our thinking, as it did Strange when he incorrectly thought that the 20+ kokh tombs (which he calls "Herodian") were evidence for a "Herodian and pre-Herodian village."[67]

Finally, we may note that these two major errors—misuse of "Herodian," and misdating of kokh tombs—generally relate to one another. In the 1990s James Strange overtly identifies kokhim and "Herodian" tombs.[68] With

---

[63] Kopp 1938:188-89. See Chapter 2, pp. 65*ff.* Tonneau's original words are also at *Exc.* 220.

[64] A. Médebielle, *Studia Anselmiana* 27–28, Rome (1951), p. 313.

[65] Bagatti p. 220, n. 5.

[66] See Chapter 1, pp. 53–55.

[67] ABD, "Nazareth," 1992.

[68] See above discussion, p. 161..

Bagatti, this identification must be 'teased' out, as it were. Yet, it becomes clear if the reader follows up sometimes vague, obscure, and difficult references—with which the Italian's writings seem laden. On page 52 of *Excavations*, for example, the archaeologist writes:

> We noticed [*in the Chapel of the Angel*] many sherds of very thin walls and well fired, and we have extracted, among other things, a flat handle characteristic of the "Herodian" period (see Chapter 5).

No page reference is given. The reader, presumably, is expected to examine sixty pages of text (which make up Chapter Five of *Excavations*) in order to find the "flat handle" of which Bagatti speaks. It is, I venture, on p. 280:

> The last jug described with spherical body and flat handle is well known from finds in kokhim...

The identification is made: what is "characteristic of the 'Herodian' period" is, for Bagatti, "well known from finds in kokhim."

The reader also wonders at the arcane challenge to find "the last jug described with spherical body and flat handle"—a reference number would certainly be helpful. A search eliminates several jugs (no mention of a spherical body...), but towards the top of the same page, we discover the object (*Exc.* fig. 220:9):

> 9, a jug with spherical body rebuilt from pieces. Leather coloured clay. From the zone to the east of the Crusader church, No. 68a.

The corresponding diagram shows a jug with a handle identical to those of two neighboring jars. Bagatti considers this jug characteristic of the "Herodian" period (above). However, Fernandez (who typically espouses an early chronology) dates this jug from *c.* 60 CE–*c.* 200 CE.[69] The reference Bagatti himself furnishes points to parallels "of the Roman and Byzantine periods."[70]

The Italian is entirely correct in asserting that many artefacts are typically found in kokh tombs. The problem is that this general fact alone hardly signals a I CE dating in Galilee or anywhere else. Kokhim continued to be used for many centuries, as we have seen. Bagatti either did not realize this or he refused to acknowledge it. As a result, he arbitrarily transposes a wealth of later material back to the first century CE—"the Herodian period."

---

[69] It is Fernandez no. 224, type 9.2.2a (pp. 116, 150, and 230)

[70] *Gli Scavi del "Dominus Flevit"*, I, pp. 129–131, fig. 30, 1–3. The description reads: "Of these jugs No. 1 comes from a kokhim tomb, and is well-known in such locales as much for the narrow neck, the ribbon handle, thin walls, and accurate workmanship, as for the pointed base." The caption reads "Jars... of the Roman and Byzantine periods."

Furthermore, the references which the archaeologist himself provides contradict his chronology. When followed up, those references inevitably lead to later Roman and even to Byzantine times.

This *modus operandi* cannot exist without an irreverent, almost cavalier approach to chronology.[71] Unfortunately, "Herodian" is now almost universally applied to bow-spouted lamps. Yet, that is not the most extreme case—Bagatti has even been known to call such lamps Hellenistic.[72]

Some perceptive Jewish and Christian archaeologists have begun avoiding the term "Herodian" altogether. Alternatively, they put the designation in quotes—sometimes with an explanation to the effect that the tombs or oil lamps in question date later than the time of Herod the Great.

Other alleged evidence from the first century CE

Pottery

We have seen how two elements common in the Nazareth literature present a false impression of I CE evidence—the "Herodian" label applied to certain oil lamps, and phrases like "the age of the kokhim tombs," so frequent in Bagatti's writings. These elements have helped produce a false—and early—chronology of the place. Their misuse has facilitated the backdating of twenty kokh tombs, as many oil lamps, and associated artefacts—in other words, *virtually all of Roman Nazareth*. For, once the early chronological implications are established, these two elements can then be used to misdate other evidence by association. After all, a panoply of evidence from Nazareth was found in kokh tombs, and much of it was also in the company of bow-spouted ("Herodian") oil lamps.

The strategy of dating to I CE by association with "Herodian" lamps is found already in Bagatti's 1955 article "Ritrovamenti nella Nazaret evangelica."[73] The priest offers a photo of nine fragments (some very small) of cooking pots from the venerated area, briefly describes them, and remarks:

...All these characteristics match those noted in ceramics which have to do with [*che si aggira sul*] the Herodian Period—in some cases earlier as well, in some cases later—to which these pieces can be ascribed without difficulty.

This attribution is confirmed, among other things, by the discovery of so many fragments of "Herodian" lamps... [74]

---

[71] Chapter 2, pp. 78*f.*
[72] *Gli Scavi del "Dominus Flevit,"* p. 117. The passage is discussed in Chapter 3, p.114.
[73] This article is discussed in Chapter 2, pp. 74–75.
[74] Bagatti 1955:20.

Perhaps Bagatti forgot this passage when fifteen years later he included the same photo in *Excavations in Nazareth*, fig. 225, but failed there to mention the Herodian Period at all. Curiously, his information on dating (*Exc.* 285) omits all mention of fig. 225 and entirely discusses fig. 224 ("Cooking pots"). The relation between the two figures becomes apparent only when the following equivalences (presented in the fine print, as it were) are made:

$$
\begin{array}{rcl}
\textit{Exc. fig.} \quad 225{:}4 & = & 224{:}6 \\
225{:}6 & = & 224{:}4 \\
225{:}1a & = & 224{:}7
\end{array}
$$

All this needless complexity presents a sure obstacle to anyone seeking to make sense of Bagatti's presentation, and perhaps one could be forgiven for avoiding such tedium and simply taking the archaeologist at his word, as most people have obviously done. Let us not be dissuaded, however, but see if we cannot determine what Bagatti is actually saying, at least in this particular instance.

We learn that the *earliest* of the cooking pots is "No. 1 of fig. 224" which recalls "the Roman period" (*Exc.* 285). This vague "Roman" assertion itself jeopardizes any necessary relationship between these objects and the Herodian period. But then, confusion reaches an altogether new level when we note that a few pages earlier Bagatti assigns that very shard to the Iron Age! His arcane cross-referencing has evidently gotten the better of the archaeologist himself. The details are:

• On page 269 of *Excavations*, item 215:7 is identified as **"the rim of the vase in fig. 224,1."** This item is included in "Pottery of the Iron Period." Bagatti continues: "Other elements of the Iron Period were found in silo 57…"
    → *I.e.*, 215:7 = 224:1; "rim of vase"; Iron Period.

• On page 282 of *Excavations*, "fig. 215,7" is identified with **artefact 224,1, "neck of cooking pot."** This is included in the section "Pottery of the Hellenistic Roman and Byzantine Periods," subsection "Cooking pots."
    → *I.e.*, 215:7 = 224:1; "neck of cooking pot"; Hellenistic-Roman-Byz. Periods.

• Finally, on page 285 of *Excavations*, we read: "The oldest element of these cooking pots appears to be No. 1 of fig. 224, whether the pieces are parts of one sole vase, or two. The neck, with the splayed mouth, recalls the Hellenistic-Roman custom for these artifacts. At least from the designs given it is rare to note the thinning of the clay towards the rim, *but in reality it exists in many vases of the Roman period*, even though not in such a pronounced manner." (Emphasis added.)

The upshot of all this is that the careful reader is left in complete perplexity. Bagatti's earliest cooking pot turns out to be possibly Hellenistic, vaguely "Roman," and elsewhere identified with the Iron Age. It can have absolutely no evidentiary value for the "Herodian" period, as he originally insisted in his 1955 article.

Given evidence of this sort of dissimulation, we are faced with the need *in every case* for independent scholarly assessments of the artefacts found at Nazareth, as well as for their typology and dating. The tendentious nature of Bagatti's writings on Nazareth is clear, with the result that it is impossible to accord those writings the respect normally granted to scientific investigation. To ascribe an artefact on one page to the Iron Age, on another to the Roman period, and yet to use it as evidence for a village in the time of Christ, beggars all explanation. In fact, there is one and only one possible conclusion: in Bagatti's writings we are dealing primarily not with archaeology, but with faith.

Except for individual oil lamps, there exists no objective study of pottery artefacts from Nazareth. This is a desideratum. We have already shown, in any case, that much of this pottery (that from kokhi tombs) must postdate *c.* 50 CE. The general Nazareth evidence, as determined above, also points to a late-I CE beginning for the settlement. The pottery, glass objects, metal, etc., from the basin must certainly accord with these results. Indeed, Bagatti himself dates a great deal of the Nazareth material to Middle Roman, Late Roman, and Byzantine times (Appendix 6). The critical issue examined in these pages is the *early* evidence—the movable and structural finds that Bagatti and others claim is I CE. As far as the movable finds are concerned, these principally amount to a score of oil lamps, lamps which we have determined date as late as 135 CE.

Bagatti's dating for the bow-spouted ("Herodian") lamp seems at least partly a matter of convenience. On the one hand, he is aware that these lamps continued in use into II CE:

> The second century is indicated by the round lamps with concave surface (6–7), associated with the "Herodian" lamps...[75]

On the other hand, the Italian considers the "Herodian" lamp to be a purely first century CE phenomenon, evident from the following passages which relate to the finds in Tomb 70:

---

[75] *Exc.* 310. In Bagatti's terminology, lamps with a "concave surface" describe typical Middle Roman lamps, *e.g.*, at *Exc.* 242, in connection with lamps in T. 72, (dated *c.* 50 CE–III CE by Rosenthal and Sivan, p. 89). Such Roman lamps were round with a concave discus. Other Nazareth examples are at *Exc.* fig. 192:13–14 (five examples from T. 70). For discussion and plates see Rosenthal and Sivan 85; Bailey Pl. 12 *f.* Bagatti's translator variously uses "concavity" and "concave."

THE MYTH OF NAZARETH

> Small pieces of "Herodian" lamps found at the threshold and a little inside show clearly how this place was in use already in the first century. (*Exc.* 46)

> The first century is represented by the Herodian lamps, found entire in a tomb not far from our excavations (see above pp. 238-40)... (*Exc.* 310)

Furthermore, the archaeologist can consider those lamps evidence of a pre-70 CE village:

> In fact side by side with the "Herodian" lamps, you find those round ones with a cavity [= *concavity*] in the upper part, and others more recent. From this we can argue that the village, even though it ran into difficulties in the war of 70, was never abandoned. (*Exc.* 237)

The presence of II and III CE Roman lamps ("round lamps with a cavity") can only be post-70 CE—as Bagatti is aware. Therefore, his only evidence for pre-70 CE in the above passage is the "Herodian" lamps. Their presence in the same assemblage with II-III CE Roman lamps should have at least alerted the archaeologist to the possibility of contemporaneity. But Bagatti here prefers to see a sequential deposition in the tomb—bow-spouted lamps first, then Roman. His scenario is not possible for the same three reasons given previously. Firstly, the "Herodian" lamps postdate the time of Christ. Secondly, they were found in a kokh tomb, which postdates the middle of the century. Thirdly, the totality of early lamp evidence suggests a post 80-90 CE date for entry of the first settlers into the basin (above, p. 21). In other words, the data Bagatti furnishes indicate not a pre-70, but a post-70 assemblage. The tribulation and survival of a I CE "village" during the First Jewish Revolt can only be described as mythical.

In asserting that Nazareth "was never abandoned," though it may have run into "difficulties" in the First Jewish War, Bagatti is in fact defending a favored thesis of the Church, namely, that there was an unbroken lineage of Jewish-Christians in Nazareth since the time of Christ. Bagatti needed to put this in print because Kopp, only a few years before, had insisted that Nazareth was entirely wiped out:

> In this year 67, the Roman soldiers passed through Nazareth more than once on plundering raids and during the assault of Japha. Those of Nazareth's inhabitants who had been able to flee to Japha, either fell there by the sword or were taken into slavery. Perhaps all perished, perhaps a few found a haven somewhere or other. It is certain that the Nazareth of the gospels was utterly wiped out in this warfare. Only caves in the rocks, used either for graves or dwellings, were able to survive these storms.[76]

---

[76] Kopp 1963:53.

Four of the 20+ kokhim at Nazareth contained movable artefacts at the time of discovery. They are tombs 70, 71, 72, and a tomb about 650m northwest of the Church of the Annunciation, located on El Batris Street. These tombs will be briefly considered in turn.

An important assemblage was found in Tomb 70, located 30 m south of the Church of the Annunciation.[77] This single-chambered tomb contained thirteen kokhim and has yielded more artefacts than any other Nazareth tomb. They are diagrammed at *Exc.* fig. 192. Seventeen oil lamps were found there, including seven bow-spouted (three plain, four Darom), three of a local pottery tradition, five dating to Middle Roman times, one Late Roman, and one Byzantine. Eight pottery and glass vessels beginning with those "usually found in kokhim tombs" (*Exc.* 240) complete the inventory.

The artefacts from T. 70 share the same page of *Excavations in Nazareth* with artefacts from another tomb, T. 71, which is located outside the venerated area, approximately 650 m southeast of the CA. Bagatti's tally from T. 71 is probably incomplete, since no oil lamps are represented and since the archaeologist's information came not from his own excavations but from the Nazareth museum, which no doubt had a selection (24 artefacts in all).

Bagatti writes: "From this you can see that the tomb [T. 70] was in use for many centuries" (*Exc.* 240). This is of course correct. Nothing, however, in either tomb 70 or 71 need predate 100 CE, as one scholar observes:

Les objets recueillis dans les tombes côtées 70 et 71 ne seraient pas à dater avant le milieu de la période romaine, c'est-à-dire environ au IIe siècle de notre ère. Le matériel de la citerne 51 est daté entre le IIe et le IVe siècles.[78]

T. 72 is the third Nazareth tomb that contained artefacts.[79] This kokh tomb, located approximately 350 m SE of the CA, was considered in Chapter

---

[77] The proximity of this tomb to the CA is a delicate matter. "30 metres" is the distance from the CA given by Asad Mansur in his 1923 description of the tomb (Mansur 90), and is the distance used in these pages. Given the Jewish prohibition against living in the vicinity of tombs, this was evidently too close for Bagatti who misdirects his reader to quadrants "C 1–2" of his map (*Exc.* 237 and fig. 3). The interface of quadrants C1 and C2 locates the tomb approximately 300 m from the CA. Interestingly, Bagatti's map does not even show this tomb, yet marks others more distant from the CA. The omission of several tombs near the CA is likewise to be observed in Finegan's map (Finegan 1969:27; 1992:44). Kopp 1938:193 provides a more accurate map. *Illus* 5.2 sites all the known Roman tombs.

[78] Hamidovic 2004:99, n. 32.

[79] See Richmond 1931; *Exc.* 242.

Three in connection with the six oil lamps it contained.[80] E. Richmond and C. Kopp claimed that those lamps were Hellenistic. However, Bagatti reassigns them to the "2nd-3rd cent."[81] Some interesting glass and metal objects were also found, but nothing that indicates a date earlier than Middle Roman times. In his short treatment of this tomb, Bagatti wrote that it contained "a glass pendant with a lion and *according to Richmond* other 'Herodian' objects" (emphasis added). Richmond, however, does not use the word "Herodian" anywhere in his brief report—it is Bagatti's invention. The latter's wording also suggests that the "glass pendant with lion" dates to the Herodian period, though no such dating has ever been established for the artefact.

The fourth and last tomb in the basin to yield artefacts is one located near the crest of the Nebi Sa'in, presently located on El Batris Street northwest of the CA. A half-page report on this tomb was published in 1998.[82] A number of chambers with kokhim were discovered, but only "sparse ceramic finds," some of which are diagrammed. Z. Yavor, the report's author, notes "fragments of a cooking pot, a juglet and a store jar (Fig. 59:1–3), as well as of a bowl and a Herodian lamp." Many glass and stone beads, a bronze spatula, and fragments of three glass bottles complete the inventory. Yavor assigns the date of the tomb "to the 1st century CE." If he is correct, then this tomb would date to the latter part of I CE, compatible with Kuhnen's 50 CE+ date for kokhim use in Galilee. Even if it were one of the first kokh tombs in the Nazareth basin, it is unlikely that its use did not continue into II–III CE, particularly as it appears to have contained several burial chambers.

There was also a quantity of material discovered in the venerated area that was, apparently, not associated with tombs. We shall have more to say about the exact provenance of some of this material in Chapter Five. For now, it is sufficient to point out those artefacts which Bagatti claims to be I CE. There are few. One is on p. 46 of *Excavations*, where the author writes that in locus 24 (an area of silos next to the CA) artefacts from many periods were found. Those periods include the Iron, Roman, and Byzantine. Bagatti writes: "Also, a glass perfume bottle with a form well known in the 1st cent. (see Ch. V) was found." A check of Chapter Five shows a very typical perfume bottle (Fig. 237:1), approximately 10 cm high and of "bluish" glass. Its form—which is entirely generic—was well known in many centuries, not only the first. On p. 313 Bagatti writes that this bottle was "common in the period of the kokhim tombs"—which for the author signals I CE. Again he is correct. The form *was* common in the first century CE—and in many other centuries besides. Bagatti tells us nothing about this bottle that indicates I CE.

---

[80]   Chapter 3, pp. 105*ff.*

[81]   *Exc.* 242. A photo of the lamps is found at Chapter 3: *Illus. 3.1.*

[82]   Yavor in ESI vol. 18 (1998), p. 32.

Before passing on to other considerations, it can be noted that the movable finds at Nazareth are treated in a number of places in the primary literature. The major sources of information on those finds are listed here in chronological order:

- Bag. 1955:18–23 —Preliminary finds. This is superceded by *Excavations*.
- *Exc.* 132–38 —Much material found "under the mosaics" of the CA.
- *Exc.* 184 —Eleven shards from the venerated grotto.
- *Exc.* 237–42 —Itemized material from tombs 70 and 71.
- *Exc.* 258–318 —Chapter Five entitled "The small objects" (pottery, glass, metal, and stone objects). This is the principle source.
- Bag. 1971a —Material from the St. Joseph excavation.

All the above passages are from Bagatti's writings. Other scholars have studied the oil lamps (Rosenthal and Sivan, Sussman, R. Smith, *et al.*) and their results are also incorporated in these pages. The excavations of Nurit Feig (regarding several Middle Roman tombs), though entirely compatible with the results of this study, lie outside the Nazareth basin and are not incorporated in the primary data used in this book.[83] With the exception of Yavor's contribution discussed above, several recent short reports (*e.g.*, from *Hadoshot Arkheologiyot*) have not included itemizations, photos, or diagrams of additional material from Nazareth. Lacking such itemization, their statements (which also accord generally with the conclusions of this study) are not included in the primary data for discussion.[84]

Stone vessels

After the beginnings of pottery production in the Neolithic period, the use of stone vessels was limited to grinding and crushing. However, an exception occurred towards the turn of the era in Palestine:

> In the late Second Temple period, from the first century BCE to the second century CE, there was a stone vessel industry in the Jerusalem region whose products were used for storage and measurement. These stone vessels were made for observant Jews who observed the laws of purity strictly since, according to rabbinic halachah, stone vessels remain pure.[85]

The manufacture of stone vessels continued into the second century:

---

[83] Feig 1990.

[84] In writing this book it has been my strict policy to include in the primary evidence only artefacts verifiable by description, photo, and/or diagram in the published literature. Time and again this policy has proven judicious on account of innumerable dubious claims.

[85] Eshel 2000 (first paragraph).

THE MYTH OF NAZARETH

[T]he zenith of the stone vessel industry was reached, with a variety of lathe-turned and hand-carved vessels, between the end of the first century B.C.E. and 70 C.E. The manufacture of lathe-turned stone vessels seems to have terminated with the fall of Jerusalem, but hand-carved vessels persisted into at least the early second century C.E.[86]

Roland Deines studied these vessels, and writes:

> The geographical dispersion [*of handworked stone vessels*] was greater than the lathe-turned types, and their use can be followed up to the time of Bar Kokhba.[87]

Bagatti unearthed four pieces of two stone vessels. He devotes a short passage to these artefacts at the end of his book. I cite it here in full:

> *Stone vases*. There are preserved only 4 fragments of white, soft stone, like to that usually used in burial chambers for ossuaries. A first fragment, coming from silo 36, is the wall of a big vase of 26 cm. diameter outside, adorned on the outside with two lines. The walls are 12 mm. thick.
> A second fragment represents the lower part of a vase, which could be the same as the preceding, since it was found in the same place and has the same thickness.
> The other two are handles, which can be of the same cylindrical vase of 3–9 cm. in diameter, inside, wall 11–12 mm. They come from the Byzantine atrium. They are rectangular with a hole in the middle. Both, because all the pieces are fragmentary and because they are well known, we omit reproducing them, especially as they were not found in any sealed place.
> On account of the similarity with vases found in kokh tombs we believe they belong to the Roman period.

Deines concurs:

> [From] Nazareth come four stone vessel fragments, which were found in the Franciscan area of excavations... Each two fragments belong together. We are dealing with a not too large stone vase, with an external diameter of 26 cm. and a thickness of 12 mm; as well as with a two-handled goblet. (Deines 45)

The vase (*eine nicht allzu grosse Steinvase*) comes from Silo 36, on the north side of the Church of the Annunciation. Deines, relying on Bagatti's scant information, does not categorically state whether this vessel is wheel-

---

[86] Gibson 187. The author adds: "Complete mugs...are usually dated to the first century C.E. but are known to continue in use into the early second century C.E. (p. 185).

[87] Deines 45.

or hand-made. Both types, he writes, were produced at the stone workshop in the Tir'an Valley nearby (see below).

The stone goblet was found under the CA, in an area which we shall discover contained Roman-period kokhim tombs (Part Five). Thus, the goblet may have been funerary. This is not ruled out even if, as both Bagatti and Deines point out, we are dealing with fill from Crusader times. For when the Crusaders built their Church over the Byzantine structure they had no hesitation in clearing away the old in order to construct walls, *etc.*, where they deemed appropriate (*Exc.* 44). Such clearing, however, would not have brought in debris from far away. We can be confident that the ancient fill, though it may contain several eras jumbled together, contains finds from the immediate vicinity—including tomb finds.

The hand-made stone goblet is represented by Deines in a diagram and two photos. Regarding its dating, the author writes:

> Their geographical dispersion [of hand-made stone vessels] was greater than that of wheel-made types, and their use can be followed until the time of Bar Kochba.[88]

The stone goblet fragments found at Nazareth may well date to the first part of II CE. According to S. Gibson, stone vessels "are usually dated to the first century C.E., but are known to continue in use into the early second century C.E." Elsewhere he notes: "The manufacture of lathe-turned stone vessels seems to have terminated with the fall of Jerusalem, but hand-carved vessels persisted into at least the early second century C.E."[89] H. Eshel concurs with this latter dating: "In the late Second Temple Period, from the first century BCE to the second century CE, there was a stone vessel industry in the Jerusalem region whose products were used for storage and measurement."[90]

Thus we are left with the distinct possibility that these stone vessels were produced about 100 CE or slightly later, perhaps in the vicinity of Nazareth. This is consistent with the other evidence which points to Middle Roman settlement of the basin, that is, after the First Jewish Revolt.

The two stone vessels found at Nazareth are part of the early evidence from the site. They must be added to lamps 1–22 of *Illus. 4.3*, as remains of the earliest stage of Nazareth's history, namely, the settlement that was born between the two Jewish revolts.

The stone vessels have an additional significance. They may suggest that the community was founded by Torah-observant Jews. We must keep in mind that in the earliest stage of the village relatively few people were

---

[88] Dienes 45. Diagram p. 51 + Photos 2a and 2b.
[89] Gibson 185, 187.
[90] Eshel: first paragraph.

involved—probably less than one hundred. After all, this was the *beginning* of the settlement. Everyone certainly knew everyone else very well and, indeed, it is probable that the earliest settlers (and the later ones?) were related by blood. The discovery of two stone vessels amongst the earliest remains of the village—vessels which are intimately related to Jewish purification laws—signifies, I would suggest, that the first settlers, and indeed the entire village, was composed of Torah-observant Jews.

Certainly, we cannot place too much emphasis on two artefacts that were, in Bagatti's words, "not found in a sealed place." But it would be difficult to explain how these fragments came to be where they were discovered unless they were once used by inhabitants of Nazareth. Thus, the probability is great that we are dealing with a Jewish village.

This observation is supported by the fact that the ornamentation of the twenty-two above-mentioned oil lamps is entirely in accord with the Jewish proscription against the graven image.[91] On not one of the lamps do we find a pagan representation of a person or an animal. In fact, a review of all the pottery and oil lamps from Nazareth during Roman-Byzantine times demonstrates that this is consistently the case.[92]

A stone vessel workshop has been identified three kilometers north of the Nazareth basin, near Reina.[93] According to Deines, it produced both wheelmade (lathe) and handmade vessels. Its existence shows that Torah-observant Jews lived in Southern Galilee before the Second Jewish Revolt, and also in the vicinity of the Nazareth basin. Proximity suggests that the Nazareth vessels were produced at this or possibly some other workshop in Southern Galilee,[94] but as yet we cannot rule out that they may have been brought by the first settlers from Judea. We know of several stone vessel industries in the neighborhood of Jerusalem.[95] A scientific assessment of the Nazareth stone fragments, their color and composition, could be helpful in shedding light on the character and perhaps provenance of the earliest settlers.

---

[91] For a typical assemblage of lamps from a pagan site, see Aviam 83.

[92] In contrast we note the childish, poorly executed (and probably post-Byzantine) graffiti in Tomb 70, which includes two incised heads (photos at *Exc.* 245). In tomb 72 a small Phoenician glass pendant with lion and star was found (Richmond Pl. XXXIII:4).

[93] For location information see Y. Alexandre, "En Rani," *Hadashot Arkheologiyot* 117 (2005), dated 11/4/2005.

[94] Aviam:315 mentions a possible stone vessel industry at Bet Lehem HaGelilit, 7 mi. NW of Nazareth.

[95] See Gibson:1983 on the stone vessel industry at Hizma; Eshel:2000 on those found at Qumran; Bagatti and Milik 1958:164-65 on some vessels found in the "Dominus Flevit" excavations.

Many "stone quarries" were noted by Bagatti in the venerated area.[96] It has recently been suggested that the stone vessels found nearby were produced on site. However, Bagatti identifies all these rock cuttings with Crusader work, judging from the dimensions of the cuts. In one case (L 34) "the cutting in the rock is later than the press" (*Exc.* 49). Hence this quarry cannot belong to the earliest phase of settlement, which would be required were it used in stone vessel production (which ended *c.* 135 CE).

The Nazareth stone quarries are a good example of how the imagination can overlook chronological indicators, leading to extreme scenarios. In these stone quarries one scholar is ready to see evidence of a village in the time of Jesus:

> ...Moreover, recent excavations in Nazareth itself suggest that the assumption that Jesus and members of his family would in all probability (and perhaps of necessity) have worked in nearby Sepphoris is no longer so obvious. It appears that Nazareth had its own thriving economy— including building, if the evidence of the stone quarries tells us anything, the commercial and economic activities of Nazareth were more than adequate to keep the local residents fully occupied, with little need to seek out-of-town employment.[97]

Although the quarries have nothing to do with the stone vessels, and though Nazareth was not yet in existence at the time of Jesus, the above citation is probably correct in claiming that the Nazarenes need not have depended upon Sepphoris, and that the inhabitants had their own viable economic base. These are evident from the impressive agricultural installations that have been excavated.

Roman oil lamps

It is possible that some of the Roman oil lamps found at Nazareth date to the second half of I CE. The seven lamps itemized at the bottom of *Illus.* 3 are the earliest such lamps found in the basin. The nozzles of such oil lamps were shorter than their Hellenistic predecessors and could be either rounded or triangular, often possessing volutes, that is, "collars" on each side of the neck. A low base, sometimes ring-shaped, supported the lamp.[98]

---

[96] *Exc.* 43, 48-49 and figs. 5 (#18), 6 (#2), 13, 21. These are at loci 17-19, 24, 26, in front of 34 (a wine press), and to the east of the CA apse (*Exc.* fig. 5, #18). The finished medieval blocks are pictured at *Exc.* fig. 19.

[97] Evans 2004.

[98] For a study of Roman oil lamps in Palestine see Rosenthal and Sivan (*op. cit.*), and smaller studies such as Neidinger, Wexler and Gilboa, etc. For Roman lamps in general see Szentléleky 1969.

THE MYTH OF NAZARETH

The seven early Nazareth examples are all variants of a Roman type common throughout the region (*Illus. 4.2:4*).[99] They may have been manufactured in Palestine itself or imported from Egypt, Cyprus, Asia Minor, *etc.* By 100 CE in Palestine, writes R. Smith, "lamps of predominantly Roman form became the dominant type."[100] Many Roman lamps had pictorial representations of people and animals that would have been offensive to religious Jews. The Nazareth examples, however, either sport no decoration or have simple floral patterns, double axes, etc. Examples of this lamp-type have been found in pre-destruction levels of Jerusalem, and Kahane dates the type's appearance to the second half of the first century CE. This agrees with other evidence from Nazareth that we have gathered thus far, and supports a late-I CE entry into the basin of settlers. Use of this Roman lamp-type continued well into the third century, so we have no way of knowing whether these lamps came with the first Nazareth settlers or whether they were brought in later.

"Rolling stones"

It is occasionally suggested that the presence of round blocking stones at the mouths of kokh tombs is evidence of the time of Christ. Regarding Nazareth, one author writes that "Four tombs sealed with rolling stones typical of the late Jewish period testify to a considerable Jewish community there in the Roman period."[101]

A. Kloner, however, has shown that funerary "rolling stones" did not occur before 70 CE, except in a very few royal and aristocratic examples in Jerusalem (notably the tombs of Herod the Great and of Queen Helen of Adiabene):

[I]n Jesus' time, round blocking stones were extremely rare and appeared only in the tombs of the wealthiest Jews.

[M]ore than 98 percent of the Jewish tombs from this period, called the Second Temple period (*c.* first century B.C.E. to 70 C.E.), were closed with square blocking stones. Of the more than 900 burial caves from the Second Temple period found in and around Jerusalem, only four are known to have used round (disk-shaped) blocking stones.

In later periods the situation changed, and round blocking stones became much more common. Dozens of them have been found from the late Roman to Byzantine periods...[102]

---

[99] Broneer type XXV, Loeschke XIII. See Rosenthal and Sivan 85*ff.*; R. Smith 1966:24–25.

[100] R. Smith 1966:25.

[101] NIDBA (1983), "Nazareth," p. 330. Signed, "WHM."

[102] Kloner 1999:28, 23, 25.

Several tombs at Nazareth had rolling stones. One covered the entrance of tomb 70, located 30 m south of the CA, and another rolling stone sealed the tomb under the Dames de Nazareth convent approximately 100 m from the CA.[103] According to Kloner, such tombs postdated 70 CE and were common in later Roman times. Thus, it is noteworthy that Strange uses the Dames de Nazareth tomb as evidence of the "Herodian period"[104]—its rolling stone clearly disqualifies it from that era.

According to local tradition St. Joseph was buried in the tomb under the Dames de Nazareth convent. Bagatti demurs: "there is no archaeological proof for this. The form can only indicate a possibility, because ancient literature… says that it was excavated in the rock and the type brings us to the time of the death of the saint" (*Exc.* 243).

However, the presence of a rolling stone is one more reason to discount this pious tradition.

Ossuaries

The practice of secondary burial entailed the collection of the bones of the deceased after a period of time (perhaps one year) and their placement in bone boxes (ossuaries). Though there is scholarly disagreement regarding the chronology of secondary burial in ossuaries, it is universally held that the custom was current in the Early Roman period in Palestine. In 1970–71 James Strange excavated a group of ossuary tombs which he considered "characteristic of the Herodian period."[105] Hachlili and Killebrew note that "a complete change in burial customs occurs during the beginning of the first century A.D. along with the change in the political status of Judea, which became a Roman province." They ascribe the emergence of secondary burial to this time. This is close to the opinion of Kloner, who dates the introduction of ossuaries to the last third of the first century BCE, and Rahmani to *c.* 20–15 BCE. This is true for Judea but, significantly, Aviam has determined that stone ossuaries did not appear in the Galilee until II CE.[106]

The practice of secondary burial continued through the Roman period, and ossuaries have been found at locations quite distant from Jerusalem "as late as the fourth century CE."[107] No ossuaries have been found in the Nazareth basin. However, Bagatti did note some ossuary fragments at some remove from the CA. He has the following to say on the subject:

---

[103] In fact, there may have been two kokh tombs under the convent (*Exc.* 243). Its rolling stone is pictured at *Exc.* Fig. 195.

[104] ABD, "Nazareth," p. 1051.

[105] Strange 1975:46. For Strange, the Herodian period includes I CE and extends back to 75 BCE (pp. 61, 63).

[106] Hachlili and Killebrew 129; Kloner 1980:252–253 and XIII–XIV (English summary); Rahmani 1994:21; Aviam 316.

[107] "Ossuary" in OEANE (signed B. McCane).

> In the controlled excavations no ossuaries were seen, like those found, *e.g.*, in Jerusalem. But since the excavations are very limited we cannot deny that in other tombs a second burial might have taken place in ossuaries. It is certain that at the "Fright" of the Greek Orthodox there are thrown about many pieces of soft stone with ornaments which belonged to one or more ossuaries. The walls have 3 cm. of thickness and are well worked on the outside, but a little rough on the inside. Nearby are grottos and one might assume that ossuaries were in use therein. The place is much frequented, which explains the breaking of the ossuaries.[108]

The "Fright" is the reputed spot from where the Virgin Mother observed the angry Nazarenes when they attempted to throw the Savior off a cliff (Lk 4:29).[109] It is located 1.2 km south of the CA. If the archaeologist is correct, then it would appear that there were one or more kokhim tombs at the "Fright" with Middle-Late Roman ossuaries. Those kokh tombs have not been discovered, but several "grottos" exist at the site which could long ago have been transformed.

The fragments Bagatti describes belong to decorated chalk ossuaries, one of three subtypes described by Aviam.[110] If those fragments at the "Fright" were from a kokh tomb—as seems entirely probable—then they must have postdated mid-I CE, as did such tombs themselves. They suggest comparison with ossuary fragments found in the excavation of a nearby tomb complex at Nazrat Illit, 2.6 km east of the CA, conducted by Nurit Feig in 1980–81. Feig dates those ossuaries to the second-third centuries CE.[111] Aviam has generally dated ossuary use in Galilee to the "second to fourth centuries CE."[112] Thus, the ossuary fragments described by Bagatti are not evidence of I CE.

Sarcophagi

Four sarcophagi are mentioned by Bagatti on pp. 246–47 of *Excavations*. Two survive—one for an adult and one for a child (the other two were last attested in the 1800s). The photo provided shows a sarcophagus festooned with garlands. Sarcophagi have been known since time immemorial (*cf.* ancient Egypt). Goodenough discusses several turn-of-the-era examples from the "Tomb of the Kings" in Jerusalem. Recently, Aviam has offered a comprehensive review of Galilean sarcophagi.[113]

---

[108] *Exc.* 247.

[109] The site is also called the Jebel Qasr el Mutran.

[110] Aviam 277.

[111] Feig 72–73 (Hebrew). Aviam:277 also describes ossuaries from nearby Sepphoris and Mashhad.

[112] Aviam 311.

[113] Aviam 271–76.

Bagatti describes the larger Nazareth sarcophagus as "of Roman appearance." He notes that the plaque bears no inscription and supposes that it may have faded. However, it was quite common to leave the inscription blank, for sarcophagi were (like kokhim) used for a succession of burials.[114] The decoration is similar to that found on sarcophagi at Beth Shearim,[115] and this suggests a Middle-Late Roman dating.

The adult Nazareth sarcophagus found in the Crusader cemetery appears to belong to a large group of Sepphoris sarcophagi. The Crusaders included several virtually identical ones into the wall of their grand tower on the hill.[116] It is probable that this and the other sarcophagi were brought to Nazareth from outside, perhaps as an ornamental addition to the sacred sites long frequented by pilgrims.[117] These massive stone objects are aesthetically pleasing and quite imposing.

To my knowledge, no one has suggested that a Nazareth sarcophagus dates before II CE. In any case, the original findspots of these objects now seem beyond proof. They are discussed here simply for completeness.

Inscriptions

Bagatti treats a number of inscriptions. We shall here consider only those which he or others have claimed go back to I CE. They are two:

(1) A tablet currently at the Bibliothèque Nationale in Paris carries a Greek inscription and is sometimes called the "Edict of Nazareth" or "Ordinance of Caesar." The inscription outlines the penalty of death for those who violate tombs or graves, and similar ones are well known from late antiquity.[118] Its date and provenance are uncertain, though it was shipped from Nazareth to Paris in 1878. Yet, this inscription continues to be cited in the Nazareth literature as evidence of a I CE settlement there. For example, from a 1992 publication we read the following: "The tombs of Nazareth are less known among students of Early Roman Palestine than the famous Greek inscription found there, probably dating to the mid-first century CE, of an imperial decree prohibiting grave-robbing."[119]

---

[114] Goodenough, vol. I:137.

[115] Aviam 272.

[116] Photo at Aviam 272. The Nazareth example is also reminiscent of a sarcophagus from a Jewish cemetery in el-Jish described by Avi-Yonah, with "pendant ribbons curving down from tops of wreaths." (Cited with discussion in Goodenough, vol. I:136.)

[117] This has been a problem with other Nazareth evidence. A I CE stone inscription (see below) was "found" in Nazareth, though it came from elsewhere.

[118] The inscriptions often contained a curse on anyone who would disturb the body or open the tomb. See ABD, "Palestinian Funerary Inscriptions."

[119] Levine 84.

Bagatti does not use it as evidence. He writes: "we are not certain that it was found in Nazareth, even though it came from Nazareth to Paris. At Nazareth there lived various vendors of antiquities who got ancient material from several places."[120] C. Kopp is more definite: "It must be accepted with certainty that [*the Ordinance of Caesar*]... was brought to the Nazareth market by outside merchants."[121] In addition, the inscription may be a forgery or may date much later than mid-I CE. All these facts disqualify the Ordinance of Caesar as evidence from Nazareth in I CE.

(2) Kopp reports on an Aramaic funerary inscription now in the Franciscan Museum of Nazareth.[122] In the scholarly literature this inscription is sometimes attributed to I CE, or even before.[123] It reads: "So'em, son of Menahem. Rest on his soul!" The inscription is incised on a fragment of marble about three feet high and one foot in diameter. Bagatti writes: "Paleographically it is judged as a late Hebrew inscription, of the 4–6 cent."[124] E. L. Sukenik dated the inscription to IV–V CE.[125]

Remarkably, many references in the secondary Nazareth literature consider this Byzantine sepulchral inscription as evidence for an early dating of the village. Thus:

> There are no public inscriptions [from Nazareth] whatsoever, instructive of the level of illiteracy and lack of elite sponsors. The only inscription from [*the*] *pre-Christian period* is an Aramaic funerary inscription found in the tombs (CII 2.988). [126] [*Emphasis added.*]

The wild misdating by some of this Byzantine inscription to much earlier times might suggest that, in dating it "4–6 cent." (above), Bagatti has misconstrued BCE for CE (he includes no reference to era). The difference, of course, is at least six centuries.[127] However, I know of no one who has

---

[120] *Exc.* 249.

[121] Kopp 1938:206, n.1.

[122] Kopp 1938:205–06.

[123] The inscription uses the Aramaic *bar* for "son." It is pictured in *Exc.* fig. 201, discussion p. 248. Bibliography on this inscription is found in J.-B. Frey, *Corpus Inscriptionum Iudaicarum*, vol. II (1952), No. 988, p.173.

[124] *Exc.* 248.

[125] *Monatsschrift für Geschichte und Wissenschaft des Judentums*, LXXV (1931), pp. 462*ff.*

[126] Reed 2002:132. *Cf.* also Taylor 233.

[127] Levine 1992:84. The effective substitution of "BCE" for "CE" has also occurred with the theory of a renaissance of Nazareth in the second century BCE. Such a statement would be correct for II CE. When I first read the BCE suggestion, I supposed that the author had simply made a typological error of "CE" instead of "BCE." But his accompanying discussion of an alleged Hellenistic revival in the village proved

suggested that this marble fragment dates to the Babylonian or Persian periods. From what we have learned in Part Two of this series that is, in any case, quite impossible. Bagatti himself settles the matter with his assessment of the inscription as paleographically "late Hebrew." Its Byzantine dating accords well with the flourishing Jewish village that we will see existed during the fourth to sixth centuries CE.

Graffiti

It is natural that a site so fabled in Christian lore as Nazareth should over the centuries attract a quantity of pious etchings, as those who travel far choose to leave their mark at the hallowed place before returning home. Fathers Bagatti and Testa have analyzed a profusion of these marks of every description—some perhaps not Christian—in a laborious effort to show that, already in the early centuries after Christ, Nazareth was venerated by Jewish Christians.[128] This is of great importance to the Church, whose authority in Nazareth can best be authenticated by demonstrating an unbroken lineage of veneration extending back to the first apostles.

It makes no sense to examine the Byzantine graffiti here, where we are concerned with the basin before 70 CE. I mention them only because Bagatti, Testa, and other Catholic scholars have claimed that some of these marks may date to I CE. The reasoning is contrived, even curious. Bagatti writes:

> Note in the second line the cross which has attached to the right arm a line which has the appearance of the Hebrew letter waw [*it is a short vertical line*], which is a symbol of Christ. From the palaeographic aspect the two last letters are noteworthy; the first for its rather unusual form which finds parallels in inscriptions from the 1–4 centuries, the second for its great height which also has parallels in inscriptions on Palestine ossuaries. The small transversal stroke in the first line is also a motif known from the ossuaries.[129]

Taylor, who has examined the graffiti on site, notes that ossuaries are irrelevant in this case and that Bagatti's palaeographic observations are "cursory."[130] She shows in a number of ways (not limited to epigraphy) that the graffiti under discussion "should be dated to the period when Christian

otherwise. (See the discussion of the Hellenistic Renaissance thesis in Chapter 3).

[128] *Exc.* 146–69 and 190–218 regarding graffiti under the CA; pp. 244-45 for Tomb 79; Byzantine markings pp. 105-114; Christian and other markings 123-132; III CE Greek funerary inscription 248-49; Hebrew funerary inscription *Exc.* 247; Edict of Nazareth Exc. 317. Testa carried out most of the interpretation of these graffiti on behalf of the Church in *Il Simbolismo dei Giudeo-cristiani*, Jerusalem 1962; and "Le grotte mistiche dei Nazareni e I loro riti battesimali," in *Liber Annuus* XII (1962), 4-45. See *Exc.* 4, n. 13 for further bibliography on Testa's work.

[129] *Exc.* 158. See also Bagatti 1967b.

[130] Taylor 259.

pilgrims first came to Palestine from outside, that is, some time in the fourth century."[131] Thus, Bagatti's estimate regarding dating, "1–4 centuries" is untenable except with regard to the end of that period. The long dating range which, in this case, includes I CE is quite gratuitous, but not atypical.

A similar case exists with a marble stone inscribed with lettering, possibly Aramaic.[132] Bagatti writes:

> Since the writing is very rough we may well consider it the work of a pilgrim who wrote on marble, which was visible as, for example, a sceen [sic]. Yet the direction of the words, on the opposite side, make us think of marble that could be turned. Fr. Testa, by palaeographic comparisons, dates the inscription to the end of 1st or beginning of the 2nd century A.D. and reads on on [sic] side ובִיר גווייה proposing two possible translations.

Testa translates the recto: (a) "And a well is his body (or: his inside or belly). (b) "And a well is within her (or: within him)." The verso: "In place of the prune the cypress will arise."[133] He considered that the letters were from an Aramaic targum of Isaiah. Furthermore:

> [Testa] holds that this fragment is an archaeological witness of the first order not only on account of the monumental documentation of ideas on the "wells", but in particular on account of the rapport it has with the place where was venerated the Incarnation of the Word.[134]

This is, of course, a great deal of weight to place on a few possibly Aramaic characters of uncertain meaning. If Testa were right and these graffiti have Christian religious evocations, then they certainly do not predate the arrival of Christian pilgrims to Nazareth in IV CE. This despite the fact that Bagatti and Testa hold to a theory that Nazareth was continually venerated by Jewish-Christians from the time of Christ. Taylor has convincingly rebutted that thesis in her book.

On the other hand, it is possible (but likely?) that early Jews of Nazareth inscribed graffiti on their agricultural installations, in Aramaic alluding to the Isaiah targum. However, this fragment is of marble, and Taylor notes that nearby marble fragments come from "relatively modern masonry near the Byzantine convent."[135] There is no reason to doubt that this marble fragment-cum-inscription, too, dates to the same late, post-Byzantine period. Of course, this impugns Testa's palaeographic dating of I–II CE, which should be revisited. In any case, even were he correct regarding such an early dating, then these graffiti were executed by the Jewish inhabitants of Nazareth

---

[131] Taylor 262.

[132] Exc. 170–71, including photos of the graffiti, recto and verso.

[133] Testa 1967:99–104. Bibliography at Exc. 170, n. 113.

[134] Exc. 171.

[135] Taylor 257.

between the two Jewish Revolts. No one has suggested that they are earlier than 70 CE.

"Domestic installations"

In the reference article "Nazareth" from the *Anchor Bible Dictionary*, James Strange writes:

> In chronological order, the occupational sequence in this area appears to have included: (1) detached caves of indeterminate (perhaps domestic) use, dating before the 3d century…

Five years later, in his article for the *Oxford Encyclopedia of Archaeology in the Near East*, Strange adopts an earlier chronology:

> (3) Late Hellenistic to Early Roman caves with domestic installations, some used as late as the Byzantine period…

Strange is the scholar most associated with the Hellenistic Renaissance doctrine, which posits "the refounding of the village" in II BCE and "extensive remains" from that time.[136] In Chapter 3 we examined this doctrine in detail and found it to entirely lack evidentiary foundation—there is no evidence at all of human presence in the Nazareth basin dating to Hellenistic times.

These pages have shown that evidence in the basin does not begin before *c.* 25 CE (oil lamps) and 50 CE (kokh tombs) *at the earliest*. Strange's proposal of "Late Hellenistic to Early Roman caves with domestic installations" is fanciful. It is, in fact, a resuscitation of the old troglodyte theory already encountered in Part Two. There, we noted the words of M. Aviam that the caves of Galilee "are wet or damp from December to May."[137] During those months they are uninhabitable, and no one has suggested that the Nazarenes were cave dwellers one part of the year and lived in houses the other part.

We have also noted that the flank of the Nebi Sa'in, on which the venerated area is located, is far too steep, rocky, and pockmarked to support habitations.[138] It is eminently possible, of course, that one or more grottoes and agricultural installations of Middle Roman-Byzantine times was covered by a roof, perhaps even enclosed by walls against the weather or for protection. This is probably why Bagatti detected one or two doorways in the venerated area, some walls, steps, etc.[139]

---

[136] Meyers and Strange 57. See Chp. 3:37.

[137] Aviam 2004:90, Chapter 2, page 66.

[138] This will be taken up in more detail, with its important implications for the tradition, in Chapter Five.

[139] *Exc.* 46 notes a flight of stairs, the threshold of a door, a small section of wall, depressions indicating walls, *etc.*

Most of the walls Bagatti discusses in *Excavations* belong to the various Church edifices raised on the site (pp. 80-97). On pages 115-18 he claims remnants of pre-Byzantine walls, but the most evidence for this that he can muster are numerous pieces of mortar found in a basin, blocks reused in the later Byzantine structure, and two fragments of a wall *in situ*. In the photo (*Exc.* fig. 69), large blocks produce a grand wall which hardly appears domestic, at least not for a humble dwelling.

In Bagatti's masonry evidence it is impossible to get farther back chronologically than the fourth century CE. Joan Taylor, who carefully studied the structural evidence at Nazareth, notes: "The remains indicate that the entire area was used for agricultural processing activity. Domestic buildings may have been constructed over the complexes."[140] If such structures were domestic (a debatable issue) they were certainly from Late-Roman-Byzantine times.

The critical issue of chronology has been quite ignored in the traditional literature. Thus Finegan:

> Of the numerous grottoes at least several had served for domestic use, and had even been modified architecturally for this purpose. One of these, where walls were built against a grotto to make a habitation, had already been found by Viaud under the convent adjoining the Church of the Annunciation and is shown in the photograph.[141]

No evidence exists to date these structural remains before Middle Roman times. The simplest explanation is that the few remnants of walls in the venerated area are late evidence of agricultural activity, as mentioned above.

In fact, Bagatti is on most tenuous ground when he attempts to date the little masonry evidence in the venerated area to the Early Roman era. All the accompanying movable evidence is Middle Roman and later. This is sufficient proof that the structural evidence should be similarly dated. A separate issue is whether those masonry remains are domestic or agricultural, an uncertainty which is reflected in the secondary literature:

> In the rock-cut cavities [*under the CA*] it was possible to detect traces of houses. Some uniform depressions apparently held the foundations of walls. The remains of these structures vanished when the bishop's palace was built.[142]

Taylor writes: "It is now possible to conclude that there existed in Nazareth, from the first part of the fourth century, a small and unconventional

---

[140] Taylor 231–33.
[141] Finegan 1969:28; 1992:45.
[142] EAEHL: 922.

church which encompassed a cave complex."[143] Yet, a wine press, collecting vat, cisterns, and silos are in the immediate area. The "cave complex" Taylor describes was surely related to these. When we factor in the sloping and rocky terrain, and the ubiquitous pits in the ground, we see an area quite unsuitable to habitation. In sum, the ceaseless literary refrain of 'domestic caves' comes neither from archaeological evidence nor from topography.

The reference literature is capable of gross exaggeration in regard to the few masonry findings in the venerated area:

> Excavations revealed the remains of a wall from a large public building dating to the 1st century AD.[144]

Perhaps the author was influenced here by the accounts of Jesus preaching before many in the synagogue of Nazareth (Mk 6:2) However, no one has detected any evidence of such a "large public building" in the venerated area dating earlier than the first Christian structure, erected in Byzantine times.

Basins

In 1960 Bagatti wrote of a stepped wine collecting vat under the Church of St. Joseph.[145] He radically altered his opinion a few years later, however, and referred to it as a basin for Jewish-Christian initiation or ritual immersion. The latter occurs in the 1967 Italian edition of *Excavations*, where he also writes of a similar basin under the CA (discovered too late for his 1960 article).[146] In fact, Bagatti's former impression was correct. Taylor has convincingly shown that these basins were collecting vats used in winemaking.[147] This is evident both from their proximity to wine presses and to the fact that a *mikve* with a mosaic in the floor is extremely improbable. Bagatti dates the basins to Late Roman-Byzantine times.[148] In this case he could be too late. Given that the village of Nazareth was established in Middle Roman times, these agricultural vats could be as early as second-century CE.

A II CE dating is arrived at (through a different reasoning) by Strange, who considers the "ritual bath" under the CA to be "perhaps as early as the 2d century but not after the 3d, perhaps for Jewish-Christians."[149] Yet, in 1997 Strange writes that the ritual bath is "third-century CE, or later."[150]

---

[143] Taylor 265.

[144] AEHL, "Nazareth."

[145] Bagatti 1960:235.

[146] Mosaic 1 was removed in July 1959, to reveal the vat under the CA (*Exc.* 115). The mosaic is pictured at *Exc.* Pl. VI (top). Viaud called the basin under the CJ simply a "*vasque à fond de mosaïques*" (p. 141, *cf.* LeClercq 1038).

[147] Taylor 249 *ff.*

[148] *Exc.* 232.

[149] ABD, "Nazareth," 1051.

[150] OEANE, "Nazareth, p.114.

THE MYTH OF NAZARETH

Nowhere does Bagatti use the words *mikve* or *mikvaoth* to describe these basins. Nevertheless, these words have crept into the literature with the insinuation that those ritual baths are evidence of a Jewish village already in Second Temple times. It is unnecessary to cite these claims, [151] for the basins in question were not *mikvaoth*, and nothing suggests they date to Second Temple times.

Coins

The earliest coin in the Nazareth basin is one of Emperor Constantius II (*r.* 337–51 CE).[152] It can be noted that in 1889, Schumacher made a vague reference to undated coins found under the Dames de Nazareth convent, "which must have an ancient Jewish origin" (*monete trovate, devono avere un'antica origine giudaica*).[153] No subsequent mention is made of those alleged coins.

The assertion of I–IV CE coins by Bagatti in a 1993 encyclopedia article is also vague and entirely gratuitous: "Two loculi graves [*at Nazareth*] found intact contained lamps, pottery, glass vessels, and beads—objects usually found with coins of the first to fourth centuries CE."[154] This is another example of introducing 'I CE' via a long dating range, where only the termination of that range is applicable (see "Graffiti," p. 191 above). Though Bagatti's statement may be valid for some other places, I CE coins have certainly not been found in the kokhim (loculi) at Nazareth.

Representative passages from the secondary literature

Repeatedly in the Nazareth literature, we find claims of a settlement either in Hellenistic times or at the turn of the era, claims which invariably rest on later Roman evidence that has been backdated into the time of Jesus, or even earlier. As we have seen for the Hellenistic Period, so also for the Early Roman Period there is no evidence that must be dated to the turn of the era—neither tombs nor oil lamps, pottery, inscriptions, coins, *etc.*

Nevertheless, there is great pressure to date much of the Nazareth material to the time of Christ. We have examined how this has taken place through one device, namely, by designating oil lamps and kokh tombs "Herodian." Other structures, such as wine and olive presses, silos, and cisterns, span multiple

---

[151] Crossan and Reed 36; DJBP, "Nazareth," p. 449, col. 2; Strange in OEANE, "Nazareth, p.114.

[152] The coin was found in the plaster of locus 29. Taylor 255 shows that it was erroneously ascribed by Bagatti to Emperor Constans (*Exc.* 209). A coin dating 238–44 CE was found at the "Fright" (2 km south of the CA—*Exc.* 251).

[153] Bagatti 1937:256, citing Schumacher 1889. It is unknown what became of these alleged coins which, to judge from the others found in the Nazareth basin, date III–VII CE.

[154] NEAEHL 1103, col. 2.

196

eras. In these cases, such longevity has facilitated their backdating to the time of Christ because it is virtually impossible to prove that these structural elements did *not* exist at the turn of the era, particularly in the absence of a rigorous stratigraphic method, as has been the case with Nazareth archaeology. The main recourse left for dating, then, becomes the movable finds associated with those structures. In all cases except the two stone vessels, those finds *must* postdate the turn of the era. On the other hand, the stone vessels could be considered contemporary with the turn of the era, *at the very earliest*. This is the conclusion of our foregoing analysis of the Nazareth evidence.

We cannot consider all the passages in the secondary literature that make claims of a village in the time of Christ. They essentially rely upon the evidence we have considered in the foregoing pages and dismissed. We shall consider a few representative passages.

A. In Finegan's influential *Archaeology of the New Testament*, we read: "The findings already referred to (No. 35) provide positive evidence of the existence of a town at Nazareth in the time of Jesus."[155] Finegan specifically notes the following:

1. an agricultural village
2. "numerous grottoes, silos for grain, cisterns for water and oil, presses for raisins [*sic*] and olives, and millstones."
3. pottery of the Roman period
4. several grottos adapted for domestic use
5. eighteen tombs of the kokhim type
6. pottery and other artefacts from two kokhim tombs dating "probably from the first to the third or fourth centuries of the Christian era."
7. four kokhim tombs sealed with rolling stones

Using the results of our analysis of the evidence in the foregoing pages, we see that there is virtually nothing in the above list which is categorically false. The settlement was agricultural, there were indeed "numerous grottoes," the pottery was Roman, *etc*. Point 6, with its nebulous "from the first to the third or fourth centuries," is in fact correct. The pottery (*cf.* the oil lamps) does date from I–IV CE (and beyond)—but none of it *requires* a I CE dating. All the oil lamps, *etc.*, could date to early II CE.

The fourth point above is false—the grottos were not adapted for domestic use, but for agricultural use. Finally, point 5 is an underestimate of the number of kokh tombs simply because a few have been discovered since publication of Finegan's book.

Though only one of the above points is arguably false (domestic use of the installations), Finegan's overall conclusion is wholly incorrect:

---

[155] Finegan 1969:29; 1992:46.

these points do *not* "provide positive evidence of the existence of a town at Nazareth in the time of Jesus." A careful reading shows that none of the above points favors a settlement at the turn of the era. In fact, they all are entirely compatible with later Roman times. As we have seen, the "pottery of the Roman period" (point 3) is Middle-Late Roman, as are the kokhim and the agricultural structures Finegan mentions in point 1. The conclusion that these somehow date to the time of Jesus simply does not derive from the evidence. It is an example of global backdating.

B. Crossan and Reed write:

> Like the rest of Galilee, which lay relatively uninhabited until the Late Hellenistic Period, Jews settled [*Nazareth*] under Hasmonean expansionist policies.[156]

When authors declare that Nazareth came into existence in Hellenistic times, the natural inference is that the settlement continued into Roman times and subsequently until today. Reading the above citation, no one would suppose that Nazareth was abandoned in Roman or later times. We similarly encounter a number of cursory statements in the literature which claim Hellenistic beginnings for the village. They are oblique, yet strong, endorsements of settlement at Nazareth in the time of Christ.

On the same page as the above passage, Crossan and Reed allude to various general categories of evidence:

> [B]eginning in the late second century BCE, numerous settlements appear across Galilee with coins from the Jerusalem-based Hasmoneans in their foundations and with a material culture similar to that of Judea. Pottery forms and types were similar; both Judea and Galilee used stone vessels; villages contained stepped, plastered pools, or ritual baths; the people's diets avoided pork; and they practiced secondary burial as bones were gathered into ossuaries, or bone boxes.
>
> The people of Nazareth at the time of Jesus were Jews, very likely the descendants of Hasmonean colonizers or Jewish settlers who migrated there over a century earlier.

This passage speaks of "Nazareth at the time of Jesus" and mentions several categories of evidence that we have discussed—stone vessels, ritual baths, and ossuaries. No ossuaries were found in the Nazareth basin and, in any case, ossuary use dates only from the turn of the era—too late to validate a village already in the time of Christ. The "ritual baths" were wine collecting vats dating to Middle Roman times and thereafter. The stone vessels were

---

[156] Crossan & Reed:32.

indeed current at the turn of the era, but their use continued into II CE—quite compatible with our scenario of a post-70 beginning for the settlement. The fact that "people's diets avoided pork" is not a criterion for dating. It cannot even enter into a discussion of the character of the settlement—Jewish or gentile—because from our current knowledge and from the rather poorly-conducted excavations, there is simply no way to determine what the early Nazarenes ate.

Crossan and Reed also write that "Numerous settlements appear across Galilee with coins from the Jerusalem-based Hasmoneans in their foundations." This fact has no specificity to Nazareth. Hasmonean coins have indeed been found in Galilee, but the earliest coin in the basin is Late Roman (mid-IV CE).[157] We have no evidence at all that the Hasmoneans settled Nazareth.

Finally, the statement that *"Pottery forms and types at Nazareth were similar to those in Judea"* lacks any chronological reference (as do the other points above). In fact, the pottery forms and types found at Nazareth are not Hellenistic-Early Roman, but Middle Roman and later.

Thus, there is no justification at all for Crossan and Reed's concluding remark: "The people of Nazareth at the time of Jesus were Jews, very likely the descendants of Hasmonean colonizers or Jewish settlers who migrated there over a century earlier."[158] None of the above points offers evidence for settlement at Nazareth at the time of Christ, let alone during Hellenistic times.

C. Fairly recently, conflicting information has appeared in the scholarly literature regarding stone vessels (above, pp. 181*ff*). J. Reed considers the Nazareth vessels "particularly significant" Early Roman evidence:

> The publications of the limited Franciscan excavations at Nazareth cite four stone vessels and a *miqweh*, and the tombs outside the ancient village are *kokhim* style, with many ossuary fragments strewn about... The finds of stone vessels are particularly significant. Since they went out of use in the first century, their fragmentary presence in Middle or Late Roman Period fill indicates their use at the site in earlier periods.[159]

The logic and data in this passage are faulty. As we have seen, the "four stone vessels" are four fragments of two vessels, a stone jar and a stone goblet. Reed's categorical statement that stone vessels went out of use in the first century CE is also incorrect. Specialists are unanimous that handmade stone vessels continued in production and use well into the second century CE—at least until the Second Jewish War.

---

[157] *Exc.* 46; Taylor 255.

[158] Crossan & Reed 32.

[159] Reed 2002:50–51.

The presence of stone vessels in Middle Roman Period fill does not indicate or even suggest use of the site in earlier periods, as Reed states. On the contrary, it is entirely compatible with the settlement of Nazareth beginning after 70 CE, *i.e.*, in Middle Roman times. Elsewhere, the same author writes:

> At Reina, a few kilometers from Nazareth and Sepphoris, a stone-vessel manufacturing site has also been found at a calcite outcropping; based on matches found in first-century contexts at Sepphoris, it certainly dates to the first century B.C.E. or C.E.[160]

Once again Reed misdates the stone vessel industry. It began toward the turn of the era and continued until the Bar Kokhba revolt. Consistent with the other early evidence, the stone vessel fragments found at Nazareth date between the two Jewish revolts.

D. In Part Three we discussed an assemblage of approximately 100 shards excavated by Bagatti in 1970 adjacent to the Church of St. Joseph.[161] By Bagatti's own admission, multiple problems attended this excavation. The area was "disturbed," the shards may have come from outside the area excavated, and no stratigraphy was attempted. In his article, "Scavo presso la chiesa di S. Giuseppe a Nazaret," the archaeologist claimed that two of the shards were "Hellenistic."[162] Our analysis showed that they have no demonstrable Hellenistic traits. In fact, it is impossible to tell what the shards are, for they are mutilated, very small, and not even in agreement with the diagrams furnished.[163]

Jack Finegan refers to this excavation but entirely omits mention of the Hellenistic period, referring instead to the turn of the era:

> In 1970 Bellarmino Bagatti excavated along the north wall of the [*Church of St. Joseph*] and in some of the grottoes under the wall. When the medieval church was excavated in 1892 much debris was piled here, and in the piles of debris Bagatti found in inverse order (as thrown out in the excavations) pottery fragments from the Iron Age to the Roman, Byzantine, and Crusader periods; and in the grottoes likewise he found Roman as well as Crusader pottery, *thus the site was certainly inhabited in the first century B.C. and the first century A.D. as well as earlier and later.*[164] (Emphasis added.)

---

[160] Reed 1999:101.

[161] Chapter 3, pp. 120*ff.*

[162] *Liber Annuus* v. 21 (1971), pp. 5–32.

[163] Chapter 3, pp. 120*ff.*

[164] Finegan 1992:57.

Finegan's linking of this evidence to the turn of the era is as untenable as was Bagatti's linking of it to the Hellenistic period. There are two primary reasons: (1) Both conclusions are dependent on a manifestly flawed excavation (the site was disturbed, no stratigraphy attempted, the shards tiny, the documentation incorrect).[165] (2) The only movable finds from this excavation between the Iron Age and Middle Roman times (and hence those used by Finegan also for his conclusion) are the two questionable "Hellenistic" shards, mentioned above.[166] Finegan's claim of "pottery fragments from the Iron Age to the Roman" is the doctrine of continuous habitation discredited in Part Two. It is based on two tiny shards from St. Joseph, for other than those shards there is *nothing* in the excavation upon which Finegan's overarching conclusion could rest.

When one realizes how slight is the actual evidence upon which such grand Nazareth conclusions reside—"continuous habitation," "the time of Christ," "the Hellenistic Age," "Early Roman times," "from the Iron Age to Roman times," *etc.*—then one recognizes the absurdity of placing confidence in those conclusions. The two shards that underlie both Bagatti's and Finegan's evidence for approximately eight hundred years *could not be more tenuous.*[167]

E. Though this entry is not strictly from the "secondary" literature (it was authored by Bagatti), it reviews Richmond's short 1931 report[168] and hence is included here. Regarding the six oil lamps which Richmond incorrectly called "Hellenistic," Bagatti acknowledges Richmond's error and correctly redates the lamps to II–III CE. Having removed one problem, however, he then introduces another which is equally inappropriate:

> Tomb No 72 (fig. 3 D1). In this place there are several kokhim tombs, but the plan of one only is given with a description of the objects, by the one time Director of Antiquities in Palestine T. Richmond. It had lamps, which are round and have a concavity; they were in use in 2nd-3rd cent.; a glass pendant with a lion and according to Richmond other "Herodian" objects. (*Exc.* 242)

Bagatti does not mention the word "Hellenistic," and his dating "2nd-3rd cent." can only mean "CE" (an interesting omission, for the four centuries between II BCE and III CE are precisely the issue at stake). The archaeologist's quaint terminology—"lamps, which are round and have a concavity"—is

---

[165] See Chapter 3, pp. 143*ff.* for an explanation of each of these points.

[166] A third shard was "greatly mutilated," and is not included as evidence.

[167] The bits of clay are in all probability Middle Roman or later—as is arguably all the post-Iron Age material from the venerated area.

[168] Richmond 1931:53. See Chapter 3, pp. 105*ff.*

his customary euphemism for a common Roman lamp type. Typical mould-made lamps of Middle-Late Roman times are round and have a concavity or depressed area towards the center of the discus.[169] It is not a firm rule. In fact, Bagatti's description does not pertain to the Richmond lamps, an issue we have already treated.[170] We are most interested here in the final phrase: "*according to Richmond* there were other 'Herodian' objects" (emphasis added). This is Bagatti's invention, for Richmond does not use the word "Herodian." Bagatti is essentially placing words in the other's mouth. He has, in effect, expunged "Hellenistic" and substituted the equally incorrect "Herodian." Both terms are highly-charged when associated with the Nazareth evidence. They are particularly prized by the tradition, for both firmly support the orthodox view that the settlement existed in the time of Christ. When it became obvious to Bagatti that the one term ("Hellenistic") was not defensible, he substituted the other ("Herodian"), which is somewhat easier to defend.

As we have seen, "Herodian" is a misnomer when associated with a good deal of the Nazareth evidence—kokhim tombs and oil lamps. We have dated the incipience of bow-spouted ("Herodian") lamps at Nazareth to between *c.* 25 CE and *c.* 135 CE. This is too late for the time of Jesus, and it effectively removes these lamps—the earliest datable Roman artefacts—as evidence for a village at the time of Christ.

Other considerations

The site of the "casting down"

Much ink has been spilled regarding where exactly the ancient Nazarenes took Jesus and attempted to cast him to his death (Lk 4:29).[171] Some scholars have written of "unsurmountable topographical difficulties."[172] Others have pointed out that not far from the venerated area, about 350 m to the north, is a sheer cliff. It is on the flank of the Nebi Sa'in and is popularly called the Mensa Christi, a great rock outcropping near the Maronite Church. Perhaps the site is appropriate, though its steep slope is no greater than twenty meters.[173] Perhaps, again, the site is not impressive enough, for today the casting down is memorialized at the Jebel Qafza ("Mount of the Leap"), over 2 km south of the Nazareth basin. Perhaps this roundish hill was chosen because it is visible from all directions. All these considerations primarily refer to the scriptural story and not to archaeology. E. Robinson, when he visited Nazareth in 1841, wrote:

---

[169] Sussman 1985:50.

[170] Chapter 3, pp. 105*ff.*

[171] See Chapter 1, pp. 24*ff.*

[172] K. Schmidt, *Der Rahmen der Geschichte Jesu*, p. 41.

[173] Dalman 73.

The monks have chosen for the scene of this event the Mount of the Precipitation, so called; a precipice overlooking the plain of Esdraelon, nearly two miles South by East of Nazareth. Among all the legends that have been fastened on the Holy Land, I know of no one more clumsy than this; which presupposes that in a popular and momentary tumult, they should have had the patience to lead off their victim to an hour's distance, in order to do what there was an equal facility for doing near at hand.[174]

Other spots in and outside the basin have been selected, and the topic is often animated among tourists. Such speculation can have little relevance to the matter considered in these pages. Whether there was or was not an appropriate spot in the basin for the casting down does not add to our evidence of a settlement at Nazareth in the time of Jesus. As regards the account in scripture, there are many problems associated with the authenticity of the Lucan pericope (which Bultmann showed was a rewriting of Mark),[175] quite outside topographical considerations.

A synagaogue of the first century CE?

From the foregoing review of the movable and structural evidence in the basin, it is clear that the presence of an imposing manmade structure dating to the turn of the era is an impossibility. As shown above, we have no oil lamps from the alleged time of Jesus, no pottery, no tombs, no coins, and so on. The frequent allusions to a synagogue at Nazareth in Early Roman times must rest entirely on extra-archaeological considerations, namely, on the gospel accounts, most particularly that of Luke (4:16 ff.).

Despite the above, claims have been made for not one, but *two* synagogues in Roman Nazareth. This complexity is an unforeseen result of the Church's longstanding desire to authenticate its presence at Nazareth. That desire led to the thesis that Jewish Christians lived in Nazareth continuously from apostolic times. However, it soon became evident that *minim* would not have been welcome in Jewish synagogues, as the Gospel of John already makes clear:

"Ask him; he is of age, he will speak for himself." His parents said this because they feared the Jews, for the Jews had already agreed that if any one should confess him to be Christ, he was to be put out of the sysagogue. (Jn 9:22; cf. 12:42–43)

Thus, the tradition proposed one synagogue for the Jewish Christian followers of Jesus, and another one for the Jews. Bagatti suggests that the former was under the Church of the Annunciation itself (*Exc.* 145–46). He duly notes signs of a Byzantine ecclesiastical structure there, and then

---

[174] Robinson 187.
[175] Bultmann 1963:31–32.

suggests "Pre-Byzantine buildings" of the second to fourth centuries CE. "Other chronological considerations," he writes, "will be derived from the graffiti." However, Taylor has shown that neither the masonry evidence nor the graffiti are earlier than IV CE.[176]

In another passage (*Exc.* 111) Bagatti suggests that "high bases [*of columns*] were reused because they are of the same kind as the stones found under the mosic pavement of which we shall speak." Here again, however, the mosaic is of a late date (V CE), and the stones under it belong to the first ecclesiastical structure constructed in IV CE. Bagatti suggests that the stylobate wall between the nave and the southern aisle of the basilica was reused in the Byzantine church (*Exc.* 84–85, 115), but this wall also certainly formed part of the IV CE construction. Finally, the Italian suggests that two marble columns were part of the early structure, but Taylor writes that these belong to "relatively modern masonry." She notes that the original structure had an east-facing apse, and that "synagogues were oriented toward Jerusalem and churches to the east." "The form of the building ...bears no resemblance whatsoever to a synagogue. It is an unconventional structure designed to encompass the cave complex in a practicable manner."[177]

Bagatti's second synagogue, "that of the Jews" (*Exc.* 233–34) was located about 150 m northwest of the Church of St. Joseph. Indeed, there is evidence that such a structure existed in later Roman and/or Byzantine times, one which served the Jewish population of Nazareth. The structure was converted to Christian use after the Jews were expelled in the seventh century.[178] Four column bases of white calcite were found at this location (*Exc.* 233). There are Hebrew mason's markings of a *lamed, dalet*, final *mem* and a *tet* which is "curiously more similar to Nabataean than the usual Jewish script" (Taylor). Interestingly, the arguable presence of Nabatean has led some to propose an Early Roman dating for the columns and hence for the entire synagogue (on the false basis that Nabatean script was necessarily early, or even decisive in this case). However, there is no reason to suppose that the columns, and the Jewish synagogue that once stood at the site, predated Byzantine times.

The neighborhood of Nazareth

For completeness, mention can be made of two tombs not far from the Nazareth basin but outside the scope of this study. One is located 2.3 km NE of the Church of the Annunciation, on the far side of the Jebel en-Namsawi (peak 500 m). The only published material on this excavation is a half-page article titled "Nazareth."[179] At least fourteen kokhim were revealed, together with a quantity of pottery (including "Herodian" lamps) which the

---

[176] Taylor 1993: 235–43; 255, 267.

[177] Taylor 1993:257.

[178] Taylor 1993:265.

[179] ESI, vol. 16 (1997) p. 49; plan p. 50.

authors—A. and N. Najjar—attribute to "the 1st century CE." No itemization is offered, and I have made no attempt to verify the dating of this tomb, for it probably came within the ambit of the settlement of Hirbet Tirya.

Those responsible for hewing the foregoing tomb may also have used a tomb complex 2.6 km east of the CA, excavated by Nurit Feig in 1981 and also considerably outside the Nazareth basin.[180] I have studied the results of the four Feig tombs which—though damaged and robbed in ancient times—divulged a considerable quantity of artefacts, including a number of bow-spouted oil lamps. Ms. Feig dates the complex to "between the middle of the first century and the third century A.D." (p. 79). This entirely accords with the archaeological results from the basin, and shows that material remains in a wider radius from the CA were contemporaneous with the settlement of Nazareth. It is entirely possible that these more distant tombs were also connected with the people who settled Nazareth in the latter half of I CE, or with their descendants.[181]

Conclusions

Taking scripture as their guide, most scholars reflexively assume that Nazareth existed in I BCE and—in all likelihood—also in Hellenistic times. Few have given the matter much thought, preferring instead to defer to reputed experts who, as we have seen, have been less than honest with the data of archaeology. Both expert and non-specialist scholar have danced to the same piper, cleaving to the scriptures that they hold dear. The evidence in the ground, however, clearly contradicts those ancient writings. We can now affirm that *not a single post-Iron Age artefact, tomb or structure at Nazareth dates with certainty before 100 CE.*

The critical oil lamp information, collated above, shows that human presence in the basin postdated *c.* 25 CE. The beginning of kokh tomb use in the Galilee (*c.* 50 CE) further demonstrates that the settlement came into being not before the middle of the first century of our era.[182] All the other

---

[180] Feig 1990 and "Communication" of 1983.

[181] Mention can be made of the *Nazareth Village* project, whose purpose is to recreate the town of Jesus approximately 1 km west of ancient Nazareth. During April 1997 a survey was undertaken in an area of *c.* 0.5 sq km south of Nazareth Hospital, prior to development. Agricultural terraces, three watchmen's booths, a wine press and other structures were discovered. According to the published report (HA 110 [1999] p. 90) "Sherds, mostly dating to the Late Roman period (2nd–4th centuries CE), were scattered on the surface." The published scholarly literature does not support claims made (*e.g.*, on the Internet) regarding I CE evidence associated with this project.

[182] What has *not* been found also supports the conclusions of this study. For example, no radial oil lamps were discovered in the basin. They are a type of lamp which "came into use sometime during the first half of the first century BCE and continued in use until at least the early part of Herod's reign" (Vitto 2000:84), *i.e.*, *c* 75–*c* 25 BCE. They

evidence, both movable and structural, is compatible with a beginning of settlement in the years following the First Jewish Revolt.

The nineteen bow-spouted oil lamps from Nazareth—the earliest post-Iron Age lamps from the basin (above, *Illus. 4.3*)—can all be dated between the two Jewish revolts. A number of them (the Darom lamps) *must* be so dated. Hence, the decades between the two Jewish revolts are the earliest in which we can speak with certainty of the reappearance of people in the basin. Before 70 CE such presence is questionable. Certainly, the possibility exists that some settlers came into the basin as early as 25 CE. This view, however, requires that we abandon an impartial stance regarding the evidence and adopt an "early" scenario.

2 stone vessels	20+ kokhim tombs	9 bow-spouted oil lamps	5 bow-spouted oil lamps	5 darom oil lamps
I BCE – c. 135 CE	c. 50 CE – c. V CE	c. 25 CE – c. 135 CE	c. 50 CE – c. 135 CE	c. 70 CE – c. 135 CE
		Context uncertain (*Illus.* 3:1–9)	In kokh tombs (*Illus.* 3:10–14)	(*Illus.* 3: 15–19)

Illus. 4.5: A summation of the earliest datable evidence from Nazareth

We have seen that the label "Herodian" has caused great damage. It h We have seen that the label "Herodian" has caused great damage. It has been misapplied both to oil lamps and tombs, with the result that much later evidence has been insinuated into the time of Herod the Great. This "backdating" of evidence is pervasive in the Nazareth literature.

Two stone vessels could be dated to I BCE, and the first oil lamps as early as *c.* 25 BCE—but all of these 'earliest' Roman artefacts, without exception, could equally well date as late as II CE. We shall see (Chapter 6) that the great bulk of Roman evidence dates to the second century CE and thereafter.

Given the fact that it takes a generation or two to establish a village, it is certainly not possible to envisage a named settlement of Nazareth (Semitic *Natsareth*) before 70–135 CE. The approximate midpoint of this range is 100 CE, and that is the date I suggest for the beginning of the "village" of Nazareth as a named place. Though people may have begun to enter the basin a generation or two earlier, we cannot speak with confidence of a village before the second century of our era. This is the only reasonable conclusion to be derived from an impartial view of the evidence.

are notably lacking from the Nazareth finds.

Of course, this analysis turns prior theories of the genesis of Nazareth on their head:

> First-century Nazareth was a small Jewish settlement with no more than two to four hundred inhabitants. Like the rest of Galilee, which lay relatively uninhabited until the Late Hellenistic Period, Jews settled it under Hasmonean expansionist policies.[183]

We can now affirm that the settlement of Nazareth was much later than the period of the Hasmoneans. It was indeed Jews who settled the basin, but they did so towards the end of the first century of our era, following the momentous cataclysm of the First Jewish War.

---

[183] Crossan and Reed 32.

Chapter Five

Gospel Legends

The location and size of the ancient village

Competing literary traditions

The traditional view regarding the location of Nazareth in Jesus' day rests on three fundamental errors: (1) that habitations existed on the hillside known today as the Nebi Sa'in; (2) that one of those habitations, now under Church of the Annunciation, was the maiden home of the Virgin Mary; and (3) that the residential portion of the village lay higher up the slope.

All these beliefs are ancient, and they ultimately stem from the localization of Mary's dwelling in the present venerated area, which measures approximately 100 by 60 m. As early as IV CE the spot was marked by a small Christian edifice.[1] The Roman Catholic Church has maintained that tradition ever since. We may ask: why was this inauspicious site identified with Mary's maiden dwelling? The area, after all, was hardly appropriate for dwellings until modern times, being rocky, cavernous, and sloping (see below).[2]

In answer to that question, we note that the first Christian pilgrims to Nazareth apparently associated the humble dwelling of Mary with a cave, of which there are many on the hillside.[3] We should not demand logic from such associations, which derive from piety and thrive largely outside the realm of reason. Perhaps, in locating Mary's dwelling in a cave (or contiguous to one), the original tradition conflated her dwelling with the nativity scene in the cave of Bethlehem (Lk 2:7 *ff*). Both have merged in the pilgrim's mind, as in this Medieval account:

> Then we went to Nazareth... There beside the city is the site of the Annunciation, and this is an underground cave, which is very like that of Bethlehem where Christ was born...[4]

In pious traditions such a conflation of elements is not rare. For example, today the Christmas story juxtaposes Matthew's magi and Luke's shepherds. In choosing a cave for the Annunciation, the early pilgrims were perhaps also influenced by the humility of Mary, for which the simple setting of a cave is uniquely appropriate. In any case, today the alleged domicile of Mary lies in

---

[1]   Taylor 267.

[2]   A small *wadi* (stream), dry much of the year, bisects the southern slope of the Nebi Sa'in. According to *Exc.* p. 7 (Fig. 2, caption), the area to the south of it was uninhabited at least until medieval times.

[3]   According to another tradition, the first ecclesiastical structure at the site was built by Count Joseph of Tiberias in IV CE. See Chapter 6.

[4]   Frescobaldi *et. al.*: No. 51, dating to 1384 CE.

the "venerated grotto," at the lowest level of the Church of the Annunciation (CA). At the mouth of that cave is a modest area measuring 5×10 m known as the Chapel of the Angel. There the angel Gabriel spoke to the virgin.[5] However, this association to Mary's youth may not have been the earliest. A competing story is presented in the *Protevangelium of James*, an immensely popular text of the early Christian centuries. Related to the romance in style, the *Protevangelium* has survived in many versions, languages, and under a number of titles, such as "The Story of Mary." The work chronicles the miraculous birth of the Virgin to wealthy parents, her upbringing (in the Jerusalem Temple, no less), her purity and betrothal to Joseph, and the immaculate conception of Jesus. Its last paragraph states that the apostle James wrote down the text, hence the title. This work was particularly prized in Eastern Christendom, but condemned by the Roman Church as early as IV CE.[6]

Though the *Protevangelium* assumed its present form after 150 CE, it contains a number of even older traditions which, however, it fails to harmonize with complete success (see below).[7] Many of its characterizations and events are at first blush entirely unbelievable—except perhaps to an already deeply committed Christian. For example, Mary is raised in the Jerusalem Temple (PrJa 8.1–2), and the census affects only the inhabitants of Bethlehem (PrJa 17.1). In all fairness, however, the canonical birth stories are hardly more believable.

The *Protevangelium* artfully focuses the reader's attention upon the mysterious nature of the divine child which Mary bears in her womb. Joseph is, understandably, entirely suspicious of this anomaly which he had nothing to do with. He is unsure of Mary's status, which gains literary force in view of the imminent census (*cf.* Lk 1:1–7). "How shall I enroll her?" he asks. "As my wife? I am ashamed to do that."[8] "Or as my daughter? But all the children of Israel know that she is not my daughter." Joseph resigns himself to God: "The day of the Lord itself will do as the Lord wills" (PrJa 17.1).

The geography of the *Protevangelium* reflects a southern, or Judean, tradition: the elderly Joseph lives in Bethlehem of Judea (8.3; 17.1),[9] and all events take place in and around that town. The *Protevangelium* does not know Nazareth, nor does it once mention Galilee. This scenario is closer to that of Matthew than Luke. According to Matthew, the Holy Family resides

---

[5]   Exc. 174, 178.

[6]   The *Protevangelium* is listed among rejected titles in the *Decretum Gelasianum* (VI CE), which represents decisions that can be traced back as far as Pope Damasus I (366–383 CE).

[7]   NTA (1991) I.423–24.

[8]   The *Protevangelium* (16.2) makes it clear that Mary's perpetual chastity had been entrusted to Joseph for safeguarding.

[9]   PrJa 8:3; 17:1. Coincidentally, Julius Africanus locates Nazareth in Judea (Euseb. *Eccl. Hist.* I.7).

in Bethlehem of Judea (Mt 2:1) where Jesus is also born. Herod the Great exterminates the male babies of Bethlehem (2:16), and no mention is made of Galilee until after the Holy Family's flight to Egypt (2:22–23). This southern tradition survived for many centuries, as we see in the following account of a Medieval pilgrim visiting Nazareth:

> Some say the Virgin was born in this city, but wrongly and out of ignorance they say so, *for, as I told you above, she was born in Jerusalem*... The real house, then, of the Blessed Virgin is cut in the mountain [*of Nazareth*], which is of tuff rock, and is underground, sixteen braccia square, of two small rooms, one beside the other, in one of which Joseph lived and in the other the Blessed Virgin. And that same house that was there at the time of the Annunciation is there at present.[10] [Emphasis added.]

This house "cut in the mountain," where Mary allegedly lived after her betrothal, is the grotto presently under the Basilica of the Annunciation.

In contrast to the above account and that of the *Protevangelium*, the Gospel of Luke presents the more familiar northern tradition, in which both Mary and Joseph are originally from Nazareth (Lk 1:26–27; 2:4). Like Matthew, however, Luke seems aware that the Messiah should hail from Bethlehem, according to scripture:

> But you, O Bethlehem Ephrathah,
>> who are little among the clans of Judah,
> from you shall come forth for me
>> one who is to rule in Israel,
> whose origin is from of old,
>> from ancient days.   (Micah 5:2)

Luke accordingly uses the device of the census to place the birth of Jesus in the messianic city of Bethlehem (Lk 2:1–7; *cf.* Mt 2:6).[11] For several reasons, such a census cannot have been historical. Galilee was not within the area of direct Roman jurisdiction but was administered by the puppet ruler, Herod Antipas. In addition, the Romans would hardly have required people to return to their birthplace—a curious recipe for social chaos with no practical purpose.[12] Then again, we know that the nearest census was in 6 CE, too late to accommodate the traditional chronology of Jesus.

My interest is not to delve deeply into the pious literary traditions regarding Jesus' provenance. I touch on those traditions because they have decisively shaped the history of Nazareth. They have determined the location

---

[10] Suriano 160.

[11] Both Luke and the *Protevangelium* have the manger. But in the latter, Jesus is placed in a manger to hide him from the soldiers of Herod (22.2). Luke lacks the massacre of the babies.

[12] See Koester I:395.

of the holy shrines, present as early as the fourth or fifth century, and have
guided the interests of the Church, the archaeology of the basin, and the
thoughts of pious pilgrims through the ages. Indeed, the venerated texts have
forcefully asserted themselves to the exclusion of the very evidence in the
ground.

The Christian literary traditions are, however, not monolithic.
Incompatibilities have led to curiosities such as competing venues of worship.
For example, in Nazareth there are two Churches of the Annunciation
separated by one-half kilometer. To the Greek Orthodox, the Annunciation
as well as the place where the Holy Family lived are directly above Mary's
Spring. A church has marked the spot since Byzantine times. It has been
variously called the Church of St. Gabriel, the (Greek Orthodox) Church of
the Nutrition, and the (Greek Orthodox) Church of the Annunciation.

The rationale behind this alternate site can be traced back to the
Protevangelium of James.[13] As mentioned above, in this text Mary was raised
in the Jerusalem Temple, "and the whole house of Israel loved her" (PrJa
7.3; 10.2). At the age of twelve Mary was placed in the care of the elderly
and widowed Joseph, who lived in Bethlehem of Judea (17.1). In the Greek
tradition, then, the Virgin's maiden home (after her stay in the Temple) and
the home of Joseph are identical. The *Protevangelium* gives the following
account of the Annunciation:

> And [*Mary*] took the pitcher and went forth to draw water, and
> behold, a voice said: 'Hail, thou that art highly favored, the Lord is
> with thee, blessed art thou among women,' And she looked around
> on the right and on the left to see whence this voice came. And
> trembling she went to her house and put down the pitcher and took
> the purple and sat down on her seat and drew out (the thread).
>
> And behold, an angel of the Lord (suddenly) stood before her
> and said: 'Do not fear, Mary; for you have found grace before the
> Lord of all things and shall conceive of his Word.' When she heard
> this she doubted in herself and said: 'Shall I conceive of the Lord,
> the living God, [*and bear*] as every woman bears?'
>
> And the angel of the Lord came and said to her: 'Not so, Mary;
> for a power of the Lord shall overshadow you...[14]

We notice that there are *two* auditions in the *Protevangelium*. The first
is at the spring (or well), where Mary went to draw water, and the second is
at her home—which, as we have seen, was also Joseph's home. Thus, for
the Greek Orthodox, several elements are united in one site: Mary's home,

---

[13] NTA v. 1, pp. 421 *ff.*
[14] *Ibid.* p. 430.

Joseph's home, the (second) annunciation, and also the place where Jesus was reared.[15]

The Eastern Church has quite ignored that this account belongs to the southern Judean tradition. Obviously influenced by the canonical accounts, which emphatically place Jesus' youth in Nazareth, pilgrims early on transposed the above-mentioned events from Bethlehem of Judea to Nazareth of Galilee. Yet they conserved many of the elements in the story from the *Protevangelium*. Thus, according to the Eastern Rite, Mary had two auditions. The first took place at the spring which the Nazarenes duly dubbed "Gabriel's Spring." The name did not sit at all well with the Latins across the basin, who believed that Gabriel visited the Virgin on their property. Kopp writes:

> The Name "Gabriel's Spring" remained uncontested until the beginning of the Middle Ages, when the Latins dislodged it through silent yet energetic opposition. It was renamed after "Jesus and Mary" or simply "Mary," and today even the Greek Orthodox call it "Mary's Spring."[16]

The Nazareth basin offers only one proper site where Mary could have gone to draw water, and the Greek Orthodox constructed an edifice directly upon it in Byzantine times. Today this is known as the Greek "Church of the Annunciation," to be distinguished from the better-known Franciscan church bearing that name. Not sure whether the holy domicile was to the left or to the right of the spring, the Greek tradition has simply constructed its shrine on arches over the water source itself. This edifice is probably the only church in existence constructed over a fully functioning spring. It was already visible when the pilgrim Arculf visited in the year 670.

The Eastern Rite was not so much claiming possession of the spring as primacy of certain traditions enshrined in the *Protevangelium of James*. After all, that text asserts that Mary experienced her first angelic audition when she "went forth to draw water." Kopp considers the possibility with typical Germanic thoroughness:

> Topographically it is possible that immediately next to the spring, left and right on the elevations of the narrow watercourse, Jewish dwellings once stood, which were removed between 630 and 670 with the construction of the [Greek Orthodox] basilica.[17]

Presumably, Mary went a few paces outside her dwelling to draw water. Others supposed that she lived in a cave right over the spring, and did not need to go out to draw water. Thus, Peter the Deacon writes in his *De Locis Sanctis* (XII CE):

---

[15] Kopp 1939–40:117. The German offers an extended review of the history of the Church of St. Gabriel at Kopp 1939:253–285.

[16] Kopp 1963:258.

[17] Kopp 1939:261.

> The cave in which she lived is large and most luminous, where an altar has been placed, and there inside the cave itself is the place from which she drew water. Inside the city, where the synagogue was where the Lord read the book of Isaiah, there is now a church. But the spring from which Mary used to take water is outside the village.[18]

So, once a church was over the site, pilgrims assumed that the holy family lived over the spring itself. Thus, Arculf notes that "the house in which our savior was raised" was over the village spring. Pious tradition considered this colorful scene, and was pleased to imagine that Jesus drew water for his mother. A fully-functioning pulley, with rope and bucket, was visible within the Greek church already in 1283 CE.[19] Apparently, the entire village came to Jesus' home for water and, indeed, no more apt reification of the Johannine saying is possible: "Whoever drinks of the water that I shall give him will never thirst; the water that I shall give him will become in him a spring of water welling up to eternal life" (Jn 4:14).

Determined to get to the bottom of this tradition, one day Fr. Kopp took it upon himself to discover the actual source of the spring. He proceeded to crawl on his belly along the narrow underground passageway which feeds water from the mountain to the church, and verified that the source is "about thirty-two and a half feet underground."[20] The passageway is about eighteen meters long and, to his great embarrassment, Kopp got stuck. He subsequently complained (to the Greeks?) of the narrowness of the conduit and in his 1963 book writes tartly, "The way ought to be opened and kept open by a slight excavation." We may imagine that some inside the church (or perhaps startled passersby) heard muffled yells coming from an unknown quarter deep within the rock, and upon investigation discovered the begrimed priest stuck fast in the dark tunnel and quite soaked with holy water. In fact, no better metaphor can be found for a soiled tradition, one that has for two millennia been stuck fast within the narrow and dark confines of unreasoning faith.

Kopp has few charitable words for the Church of St. Gabriel and writes of the "wrong path" [*Irrweg*] taken by the Greeks.[21] He is only half-right. Both competing Latin and Greek venues for the site of the annunciation are founded on very creative, incompatible and, at bottom, fantastic literary traditions.

The preceding discussion alerts us to the fact that the greatest interest over the centuries has focused on two sites that are in fact peripheral to the actual Jewish settlement. The Franciscan venerated area is located in a cemetery, which was *ipso facto* outside the inhabited part of the village. The Greek

---

[18] Geyer 1898:112.
[19] Kopp 1939:264.
[20] Kopp 1963:75. A plan of this waterworks is at Kopp 1938:257.
[21] Kopp 1939:276, 277.

Church of the Annunciation is located at the 360m elevation halfway up the northern slope. Topography indicates that it was also outside the settlement. Though Nazareth did not yet exist at the turn of the era, we have not addressed where precisely in the basin the Jews of later Roman times built their habitations. In itself the question is scarcely important, and the answer, in any case, seems obvious—topography indicates that the people lived on the valley floor. The question bears closer investigation, however, simply because the tradition has made such persistent, contrary, and extravagant claims regarding the venerated area and the steep hillside of the Nebi Sa'in. There are three basic reasons why those claims are false, that is, why the hillside could not have been inhabited at the time of Jesus. They can be summarized in three words: chronology, topography, and tombs.

We have already considered the chronology *in extenso*. The material evidence shows that Nazareth came into existence after the First Jewish Revolt (Chapter Four).

As regards topography, it is remarkable that the tradition locates the entire Roman settlement on the slope of the Nebi Sa'in and above the 350 m contour line.[22] The area could hardly be less conducive to ancient dwellings. Bagatti labels the traditional location on a map accompanying his 1960 article, "Nazareth" (marked in *Illus. 5.2* with the words "Bagatti's village").[23] The rocky, steep, and cavernous nature of the limestone hillside is self-evident and, besides, the archaeologist was quite aware that a number of tombs dotted the hillside.[24] In the face of all these negative elements, there must have been some overriding reason that demanded a hillside location. Why, indeed, has the Church since IV CE insisted upon a hillside location for Nazareth?

As with so much in the tradition, the answer ultimately lies in scripture. We recall the Lukan passage where Jesus shocks his neighbors—indeed, insults them—by insinuating that the Nazarenes rank below foreigners in the eyes of God:

> When they heard this, all in the synagogue were filled with wrath. And they rose up and put him out of the city, and led *him to the brow of the hill on which their city was built*, that they might throw him down headlong. But passing through the midst of them he went away. (Lk 4:28–30)[25] [Emphasis added.]

---

[22] We shall consider the detailed topography of the venerated area below.
[23] Bagatti 1960:319 (fig. 599).
[24] Bagatti knew the Jewish tomb prohibition, for he mentions it already in 1937. See Baldi-Bagatti 1937:245 [23].
[25] A strident anti-Nazareth stance is reflected in all four canonical gospels. The hillside venue of the village is discussed at Bagatti 1955:24.

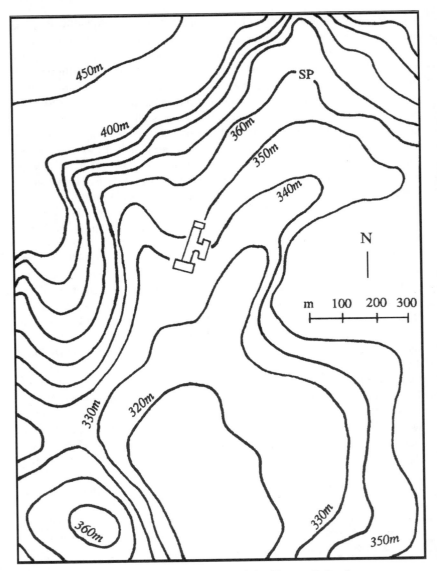

Illus. 5.1. **The topography of the Nazareth basin.**

Accordingly, from the time Christian pilgrims first came to Nazareth until the present day, they have expected (even insisted) that the settlement be on a hill. Through the centuries, the Church has accommodated this expectation and faithfully located the domiciles of Joseph and Mary on the hillside. Already in IV CE the first ecclesiastical structure was built in the venerated area. Until relatively modern times the uneven, sloping terrain, and the cavernous nature of the ground have conspired to prevent the construction of private dwellings on the mountainside. But the unfavorable characteristics of the area did not prevent the construction of ecclesiastical structures, a fact which attests to the power of tradition to overcome almost all obstacles.

The Franciscan Church of the Annunciation (and its predecessors) memorializes an habitation that was never there. It is not a monument to any humble dwelling, but a monument to a cherished *idea* embodied in scripture. That idea is grand, and the church standing there today is fittingly massive, imposing, and grand. It has nothing to do with the Jewish village of later Roman times. It has everything to do with ideas, ideas enshrined in the New Testament scriptures. In turn, the *expectations* of pilgrims have been fully met: there is a town on the hillside, as Luke wrote. There is a cave associated with the Holy Family, as pious tradition imagined. There is even the humble "workshop of St. Joseph" (the CJ) nearby, where he plied his trade as a carpenter (Mt 13:55). Thus, the venerated structures reflect scriptural requirements quite to the exclusion of evidentiary or historical considerations.

The tombs of the Roman era

The third basic reason, mentioned above, why the hillside could not have been inhabited at the time of Jesus is the presence of tombs. In Judaism, man was created in the image of the divine (Gen 1:26). God breathed the spirit (*ruach*) into Adam, making him a living being (Gen. 2:7). That spirit is a gift and returns to the Lord at death (Eccl. 12:7). Thus, the dead person is ritually impure, and contact with a corpse must be avoided.[26] Uncleanness was infectious, so that a person could become unclean through contact (Lev. 5:3). According to Torah, three forms of uncleanness were serious enough to exclude the infected person from society: leprosy, bodily discharges, and impurity resulting from contact with the dead:

> The LORD spoke to Moses, saying: Command the Israelites to put out of the camp everyone who is leprous, or has a discharge, and everyone who is unclean through contact with a corpse; you shall put out both male and female, putting them outside the camp; they must not defile their camp, where I dwell among them. (Num 5:1–3).

Impurity from contact with a corpse lasts seven days (Num 19:11). Elaborate rituals are necessary to remove the impurity. Thus, the Talmud mandates that habitations be a minimum distance ("fifty ells," or about seventy-five feet) from the nearest tomb.[27] The ell (Heb. *ammah*) is a unit of

---

[26] Num 9:6; 19:11, 16, 18; 31:19.
[27] *Midrash Bava Batra* 2:9.

length derived from the human body, typically measuring six handbreadths.[28] Calibrating 3 inches for each handbreadth ("the width of four fingers"), then 50 ells = 300 handbreadths = 900 in = 75 ft = 25 yds = 23 m. Thus, tombs had to be outside the town, and at least this distance from the nearest habitation. Hence, the presence of tombs automatically disqualifies the existence of ancient habitations at the same sites, at least as regards Jewish settlements. And we know that ancient Nazareth was indeed Jewish. This can be inferred from the following facts: (a) the arrival of the priestly family of Hapizzez in II CE; (b) the recorded Jewishness of the village in accounts of the Church Fathers and others; [29] (c) the presence of stone vessels among the earliest evidence; and (d) the consistent lack of pagan symbolism on the pottery finds.

No less than twenty-five later Roman tombs have been excavated in the Nazareth basin. Most are of the kokhim type. More tombs doubtless exist, for only a small part of the basin has been excavated. Not infrequently a tomb is discovered during the construction of a house, and rumors are common regarding the existence of ancient tombs here and there in the basin. In addition, we shall soon consider a number of tombs that have been documented in one form or another but whose existence is contested by the tradition. In any case, the score or more kokh tombs must postdate 50 CE, as we have seen.[30] Given the Jewish prohibition against habitation in the vicinity of the dead, the emplacement of these Roman tombs furnishes a clue as to the location of the ancient settlement. A glance at *Illus. 5.2* shows that they exist on both the western and the eastern slopes of the basin. From this it is quite clear that the ancient settlement was between the two slopes and on the floor of the basin. Topography confirms this. In contrast to the hillsides, the valley floor offers several advantages for the construction of dwellings: it is relatively flat, it is less rocky and has greater depth of soil, and it is not encumbered with caves, hollows, and pits.

Yet Bagatti and the tradition do not view the topography of the basin in this way. Indeed, they ignore the tombs to the east and claim to see a ring of tombs on the hillside itself. The tradition, of course, has been concerned with demonstrating that the residential portion of the settlement included the area of the venerated sites. This is the subject of the first major section of Bagatti's 1960 article "Nazareth," in the *Dictionnaire de la Bible*. The article was written towards the midpoint of the archaeologist's decade-long excavations.

---

[28] The ell contained two spans (*zeret*), each made up of three handbreadths (*efa*) of four fingers (*eba*). A slightly larger ell is also mentioned at Ezek 40:5 and 43:13 (one handbreadth larger than the traditional ell).

[29] *E.g.*, Epiphanius: "Until the reign of Constantine Nazareth had only Jewish inhabitants" (*Haer.* 1.136). Points (a) and (b) are discussed in Chapter 6; points (c) and (d) in Chapter 4.

[30] Chapter 4, pp. 158*ff.*

In French, it takes up no less than twelve columns of text and includes a full-page topological map of the Nazareth basin. Like the author's 1955 writing, the article is provisional and makes no pretense towards completeness. (For example, the Bronze Age is nowhere mentioned.) It is divided into three parts. The first, entitled "The Ancient Village," begins as follows:

> THE ANCIENT VILLAGE. On the slope of the hill, between the Church of St. Joseph and that of the Annunciation, we have discovered abundant and characteristic finds which permit the localization of the ancient village, *already existing in Iron II.* This is all the more important in that occasional excavations carried out in the environs and recently well-studied have made us aware that *similar finds do not exist elsewhere, thus excluding some other localization [of the settlement].* We were able to identify silos serving to warehouse stores, cisterns for water or wine, presses for grape and olive, millstones, grottos, and masonry debris.[31] (Emphasis added.)

In Chapter One we verified that the settlement (probably Japhia) existed in Iron II but did not continue after that period. As for the claim that "similar finds do not exist elsewhere" in the basin (that is, outside the putative hillside area marked for settlement by the tradition), in his 1960 article Bagatti attempts to substantiate this by reporting on four digs made during construction activities in various parts of the basin.[32] The problem is that all four of those excavations were conducted above the 350 m contour line, thus ignoring the most obvious localization of settlement—the valley floor. After all, no one should expect to find ancient habitations on the hillsides, nor is it surprising that Bagatti did not find any there. He is eerily silent about the valley floor. In other words, the archaeologist looked where he needn't, and where he should have looked—he didn't.

Elsewhere in the same article Bagatti writes:

> The necropolis. – The map given [*in*] fig. 599 locates the ancient remains of Nazareth: one notes there the ensemble of the Annunciation, at the center, and in the environs, marked in black, a series of tombs to the north, to the west and also some to the south. These are the remains actually known of the ancient necropolis...[33]

In contrast, a glance at *Illus. 5.2* shows that the tombs to both east and west of the valley floor form a larger "ring" that is eminently more probable than the one perceived by Kopp and Bagatti. Those tombs localize the settlement

---

[31] Bagatti 1960:318. See Chapter 2, p. 77.
[32] Bagatti 1960:328. The four soundings are: (a) 150 m from the Virgin's Fountain on the Tiberias Road; (b) higher up the hillside next to Mary's Well; (c) to the west of the Convent of the Dames de Nazareth; (d) south of the last-mentioned (exact location unspecified).
[33] Bagatti 1960:326.

on the valley floor, not on the hillside, and not in the venerated area (which itself contains tombs).

Very little of the Nazareth basin has ever come under the archaeologist's spade, and most of the area is now thoroughly urban and built over. It is not impossible that other, undiscovered, tombs of the Later Roman period exist in the very hillside area that Bagatti signals as the *ville antique*.

A generation before Bagatti, Fr. Clemens Kopp strove mightily to reconcile the many tombs that dot the hillside with scripture. Yet he, too, contrives to locate the village on the slope:

> The chain of tombs is an important thread with which to gauge the placement of Jewish Nazareth. According to Jewish law, a tomb had to be at least 50 ells outside the town. Now, the kokhim tombs wind around the spring practically like a wreath. Here, then, must also have been the natural center of the second, the Jewish, Nazareth. The terrain roundabout is fairly flat, and would on this account also initially invite settlement.[34]

This citation is factually incorrect: the area is not at all flat—the slope at this point rises from 340m to 400m, a steep 15-25% grade.[35] It should be noted that the spring Kopp refers to is not Mary's Spring at the north end of the basin, but the lesser known 'Ain ed-Jedide ("New Spring"), a seasonal water source with low volume located near the Mensa Christi church. This spring is marked in *Illus. 5.2* by a dot near tomb K8. Kopp has relied for his argument on Gustav Dalman, who in 1935 proposed the 'Ain ed-Jedide site as the central locus of Jesus' settlement. Dalman admitted that this was "an almost insecure, even unfavourable position."[36] Kopp fully concurs:

> Where was the second Nazareth, which was also the town of Christ? It was certainly not built over the first; no pre-Byzantine masonry feature [*Mauerzug*] has thus far been found in the area. Its wealth lay in the natural grottos, easily formed and enlarged artificially out of the soft limestone. Precisely for this reason the place is a poor candidate for house building. In addition, the reaches [*Ausläufer*] of the Nebi Sa'in—which at a height of 488m form the Nazareth boundary—steeply fall here to the valley floor, which lies at an altitude of 343 m. The attentive observer has always wondered that the town... "sits most uncomfortably on practically a sheer cliff."[37]

---

34 Kopp 1938:207.
35 Calculated from Tomb 73 to the 400 m contour line.
36 Dalman 65.
37 Kopp 1938:189.

The attentive observer may wonder at the remarkable obstinacy of the Church as it maintains such an unlikely venue for the town of Nazareth. The tradition would have the Torah-observant Jews of ancient times living among tombs and on a steep slope—while the open valley floor beckons below. In any case, *Illus. 5.2* shows that tomb K8 fairly ruins the "wreath" of tombs proposed around that spring, lying as it does in the midst of the area both Kopp and Dalman propose for the village.

Yet the scholarly Nazareth literature to this day attempts to squeeze the village of Jesus among the hillside tombs. Thus one dictionary article states:

> The location of the tombs of the first century B.C.E. to the first century C.E. disclose that the occupied area extended hardly 300 by 100 meters.[38]

We shall see, however, that any attempt to locate a settlement on the slope of the Nebi Saʻin places it not *between* tombs but *among* tombs.

In Kopp's view Nazareth moved about, while in Bagatti's view the ancient town existed since the time of Abraham in a narrow space on the hillside. First mapped in the Italian's 1960 article "Nazareth,"[39] this area is contiguous with the venerated area (as demanded by tradition) and is marked "Bagatti's village" in *Illus. 5.2*. It places the houses of Mary and Joseph at the southern edge of the village—an interesting proposition, for the venerated area was in fact at the village's *northern* edge.

Bagatti recognized the necessary boundary set by the tombs further up the hillside, and he accordingly placed the limits of the village at roughly the 360 m contour line. This would still locate habitations on an inhospitable slope. On the positive side, his village situated the inhabitants near Mary's Spring—no doubt correct.

It is very possible that other (as yet undiscovered and unverified) tombs exist in the sloping areas where Kopp, Bagatti, and others have located the town of Jesus. These areas have not been systematically excavated, for they lie outside Franciscan property. The suspicion of additional tombs is not entirely an argument from silence, as we see from several interesting claims made by Asad Mansur, who authored a whole book on the history of Nazareth in the 1920s.[40] Kopp was familiar with Mansur's work, and writes:

> A. Mansur mentions (*ta'arich* p. 164) graves "in the form of kokhim" in the hollows under the Greek Bishop's residence.[41] But a structure is not there—the hollows significantly differ in length and breadth from kokhim.

---

[38] "Nazareth," DJBP:449.

[39] Bagatti 1960:319 (fig. 599), marked "Ville antique."

[40] Asad Mansur (Saʻd Ibn Mansur), *History of Nazareth: From its Remotest Times to the Present Days*. Cairo: Al Hillal, 1924 (338 pp., Arabic).

[41] See *Illus. 5.2*.

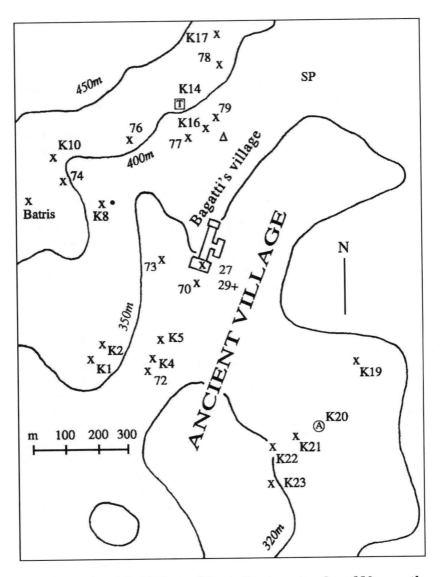

Illustration 5.2. **Middle and Late Roman tombs of Nazareth.**

x kokhim	SP Mary's Spring
Ⓐ arcosolium	• "New Spring" (seasonal)
T trough grave	△ Greek Bishop's residence

He also considers natural protrusions under the Church of St. Joseph to be kokhim, as well as the bulging extension west from the Grotto of the Annunciation (ibid. p. 33). When he therefore also signals graves "in the form of kokhim" [*near a dwelling on the hillside*], caution is required.[42]

Despite Kopp's ardent desires to defend the tradition against the onslaught of science and rationalism, these pages have shown him to be egregiously in error on a number of occasions as regards the Nazareth data.[43] One wonders now how much credit to accord his uniform denials of Mansur's findings. It is possible, of course, that Kopp is right and Mansur wrong regarding every putative tomb claimed by the Arab. On the other hand, it is possible that one or more of these allegations indeed represent Roman tombs situated in the area traditionally claimed for the village. I have deemed it unnecessary to verify every rumor of a tomb on the hillside, simply because the traditional scenario is adequately invalidated by chronology and topography.

It should be mentioned that none of the traditional localizations of the village (by Bagatti, Kopp, or Strange) takes into account the five Roman-era tombs on the eastern side of the basin (K19–K23). Those tombs also signal a village boundary. They show that the settlement was on the valley floor, between the hills (and tombs) to east and west. In postulating a hillside village, the Nazareth literature routinely ignores these more remote tombs—another indication that the tradition proceeds not from evidence, but from convenience.

The size of the village

The Mishna mandates a minimum distance ("50 ells," or about 25 m) from the nearest habitation, which means that theoretically a ring of tombs could signal the periphery of a village. However, the mishna stipulates neither a maximum distance of habitations from tombs nor a specified distance. Thus, no village periphery is ascertainable merely from the locations of tombs. Those locations can determine only two things: (a) where habitations were *not* (they were not at or near the tombs); and (b) the *general* position of a village. In the case of Nazareth a tomb perimeter (not village perimeter) is obvious, particularly to the east where the five Roman tombs are in an almost straight line. To the west, also, five tombs are in a straight line (including the tombs under the CA). These east-west boundaries tell us not the precise location of the village houses, but the general location of the ancient settlement—on the valley floor. That valley floor, incidentally, has never been excavated.

---

[42] *Wenn er darum in einer Höhle rechts vom Eingang vom Grundstück von U.L. Frau vom Schrecken ebenfalls Gräber "von der Art der Kokim" signalisiert, so ist Zurückhaltung geboten.* Kopp 1938:207, n. 2.
[43] See Chapter 2, pp. 65ff; Chapter 3, 107f; and above p. 222.

THE MYTH OF NAZARETH

The tombs nearest to the basin floor are low on the hillside and below the 350 m contour line. This indicates that the Roman village was not on the hillsides. Much less did it creep up them. Evidently, the 500 m between tombs to east and west left plenty of room for the village, so that the ancient Nazarenes at first saw no point in scaling the heights to bury their dead. We can conjecture that the inhabitants hewed tombs gradually farther and farther away as the village grew, and as lower areas on the slopes became used up (not only by tombs, but also by agricultural installations). According to this scenario, the first tombs were those nearer to the valley floor. This is, however, a conjecture.

The valley floor is very spacious, measuring 1.5×0.5 km. All of Jerusalem could fit into that area, and there is no way to gauge how much of that space was empty in antiquity. As alluded to above, from the number and locations of tombs alone we cannot tell how large or small the village was.

It is also hazardous to attempt a population estimate from the number of extant tombs. We recall that the kokhim type of tomb was used for several centuries after its arrival in Galilee. During those centuries the Nazarenes may have constructed new tombs higher up on the Nebi Sa'in, rather than have reused older tombs closer by. In this case, the village population may have stayed fairly small and constant. On the other hand, if virtually all the tombs represented in *Illus. 5.2* were in use at the same time (an improbable scenario) then, certainly, the settlement was more than a village, and its inhabitants numbered well into the hundreds.

Regarding the size of the Roman village, we can thus say with a fair degree of confidence only that a substantial settlement existed there during Middle to Late Roman times. This is evident from the great number of kokh tombs in the basin. We can, furthermore, conclude that the settlement was located on the valley floor. Its precise population and dimensions must remain a mystery, barring extensive excavations under modern Nazareth. We cannot say whether the ancient domiciles were scattered about or grouped together, how many there were, nor where on the valley floor they were concentrated. In sum, it is evident that the Nazarenes built tombs on the slopes to the northwest and the southeast, that they numbered perhaps a hundred or more, that they lived on the valley floor, and that they were Jewish. Beyond these few facts we cannot venture.

In light of the preceding discussion, it is interesting that the principal writer on Nazareth in the last several decades, James Strange, has claimed knowledge both of the number of inhabitants and of the square footage of the village at the time of Christ. In a book co-authored with Eric Meyers and published in 1981, he writes:

Judging from the extent of its ancient tombs, Nazareth must have been about 40,000 square meters in extent, which corresponds to a population of roughly 1,600 to 2,000 people, or a small village.[44]

This curious passage poses a number of problems. First of all, it is obvious that Strange and Meyers are not considering the valley floor in their calculation, but suppose that some other plot of land was the locus for the village. This is clear because the relatively flat, habitable area of the valley floor (roughly below the 340 m contour line and between tombs to east and west) encompasses a much larger area than calculated in the above citation—approximately 36 hectares (360,000 square meters or 89 acres), which is the aggregate equivalent of a square with sides extending well over half a kilometer. In comparison, Strange's figure of 40,000 square meters corresponds to a modest plot of land 200 m square. Not coincidentally, perhaps, this corresponds to the area of Bagatti's village between the venerated area and tombs 77, K16, and 79 (*Illus. 5.2*), while allowing a buffer ("50 ells") between habitations and tombs.

Approximately a decade later, however, Strange arrived at a radically different solution:

As inferred from the Herodian tombs in Nazareth, the maximum extent of the Herodian and pre-Herodian village measured about 900×200 m, for a total area just under 60 acres. Since most of this was empty space in antiquity, the population would have been a maximum of about 480 at the beginning of the 1st century A.D.[45]

Several elements of this passage are noteworthy. First of all, "900×200 m" measures an area equivalent to just under 45 acres (44.48 acres = 18 hectares),[46] not 60 acres. Secondly, the area Strange now proposes for habitation is many times larger than his 1981 estimate (180,000 square meters *vs.* 40,000 square meters), yet it is still only one half the habitable area of the valley floor as inferred above. Thirdly, the archaeological remains offer no clue at all as to how much "empty space" there may have been in antiquity. The only area systematically excavated has been the venerated area, which measures under one hectare, not the 18 hectares that Strange implies. It is a complete mystery how, from the modest area that has been excavated, he can arrive at "a maximum of about 480" people for the entire village. We also note that though the area he now considers for habitation is over four times larger than in 1981, his population estimate is four times smaller ("1,600 to 2,000" vs. 480). Finally, we are at a complete loss as to how Strange links his

---

[44]   E. Meyers and J. Strange 1981:56.

[45]   ABD, "Nazareth," p. 1050.

[46]   1 hectare = 10,000 square meters (the area of a square with sides of 100 m) = 2.471 acres.

population estimate to "the beginning of the 1st century A.D." All this might be of little consequence were Strange not the most cited archaeologist on Nazareth of the last generation, and were his 1992 ABD article not the first (and often only) scholarly source for information about Nazareth.

In the above two citations, Strange has insisted upon precision where Bagatti was originally much more cautious:

> Limits of the ancient village. – By observing the common rule which excluded tombs from places of habitation, one arrives, by the discovery of sepulchral chambers, at delimiting in some sense the extent of the ancient village.[47]

This passage is from the Italian's article "Nazareth" in the *Dictionnaire de la Bible,* written midway in his excavation of the venerated area. In principle, Bagatti is entirely correct. One can, through the emplacement of the tombs, delimit "in some sense the extent of the ancient village." In fact, this is what we have done above, and we have seen that the village was *on the valley floor.* We have determined this by considering all the tombs in the basin, including those to the east, and by also taking into account the character of the hillsides.

Though Bagatti's affirmation above is correct in principle, its application amounts to nonsense, for the archaeologist thinks that the venerated area was itself part of the ancient village, which stretched astride the mountain. We have critiqued the questionable "ring of tombs" that he, Kopp, and others propose on the hillside, and from which they think to delimit a village. That location defends the idea that the venerated area was the site of Jesus' home. That idea, in turn, ultimately derives from the fourth chapter of Luke, where Nazareth is located on "the brow of a mountain upon which their city had been built."[48] This notion was already very familiar to the first pilgrims. Indeed, it was probably their only "hard" fact about Nazareth. Yet, where exactly on the hillside the Holy Family lived was for a long time in dispute— and still is. We have seen that there are dual traditions. The Greek Orthodox follow the *Protevangelium of James* and locate the dwelling of Mary over the spring at the north of the basin. This seems to have been the earliest tradition. For example, the sixth-century visitor known as the Anonymous of Piacenza supposed that the spring had to be "in the middle of the city."

In the 1930s, the redoubtable Fr. Clemens Kopp attempted to harmonize these competing traditions. Seeing that the Roman Church venerated an area at some remove from the spring, yet at the same time acknowledging the more ancient tradition, Kopp proceeds from the assumption that the town was indeed centered at the spring and extended as far as the Franciscan venerated area:

---

[47] Bagatti 1960:328.

[48] ἕως ὀφρύος τοῦ ὄρους ἐφ᾽ οὗ ἡ πόλις αὐτῶν ᾠκοδόμητο.

The two basilicas are separated from one another by a [*substantial*] distance. That over the spring is "in the middle of the city," that of the Annunciation must then, to avoid contradiction, have lain either outside the settlement or on its rim... As has been already mentioned, Jewish Nazareth must—on account of the graves [*under the Franciscan venerated area*]—have been situated at the spring. Presumably it moved from thence southwards along the western side of the valley, reaching the [*present-day*] Moslem cemetery, since according to well-attested tradition it was here that in 570 the synagogue [*noted by the*] Anonymous of Piacenza stood.[49]

Thus, Kopp again proposes that Nazareth moved. We recall his mobile Nazareth hypothesis relating to the Bronze and Iron Ages. This later movement permits accommodation of the two traditions, one centered about the spring, the other about the venerated area. Of course, his argument completely ignores the valley floor, the unwelcome topography of the slope, as well as the presence of tombs on the other side of the valley—tombs which Kopp himself mapped. The *raison d'être* of Kopp's argument is to accommodate the Franciscan zone on the hillside. We shall now examine more closely that zone, and why it could not have been the dwelling place of Mary, Jesus, and Joseph.

The venerated area

The area owned by the Custodia di Terra Santa, an arm of the Roman Catholic Franciscan order, has been the locus of most of the archaeological work in the Nazareth basin and is of necessity the focus of this study. The visitor today will find the venerated area situated in a densely populated urban area. Since 1620 CE (when the Druse emir Fakr ed-Din permitted Christians back into Nazareth) the Franciscans have owned a roughly triangular plot of land 100×150 m at its greatest extent, on which are now several structures: (1) the Church of the Annunciation (CA) to the south; (2) the Church of St. Joseph (CJ) to the north; (3) the long Franciscan monastery between them; and (4) the monastery school (*Illus. 5.3*). Bagatti's excavations in the decade from 1956–66 were focused on the southern portion lying under and around the CA (the convent and CJ were already standing). The results of those excavations are described in the archaeologist's two-volume *Excavations in Nazareth*.

In the following pages, measurements will be computed from the nearest wall of the Church of the Annunciation. Thus, Mary's Well is 800 m northeast of the CA, and Tomb 70 is 30 m south of the CA.[50]

---

[49] Kopp 1938:260.

[50] For the locations of the CJ and CA within the Nazareth basin, see Chapter 1, *Illus. 1.3*.

THE MYTH OF NAZARETH

The slope

The eastern side of the Nebi Saʻin rises from 320m at the valley floor to a peak of 495 m, an average grade of 14%—steep by any account. The sections to the left and below *Illus. 5.3* depict the slope of the venerated area and are redrawn from Bagatti's *Excavations in Nazareth* (Plate XI). According to the diagram, the average slope of the venerated area from north to south is 8%, but the archaeologist describes a somewhat steeper grade in the text:

> As for the nature of the terrain, now that we are at the level of the rock a steep incline from north to south is noted (9.8m within the excavated area of 70 m), which continues towards the north, resulting in *c.* 14 m of difference with the Church of St. Joseph. Roughly the same steep incline exists to both east and west…[51]

"9.8 m within the excavated area of 70 m" is equivalent to a 14% grade—similar to that of the hillside in general. This information places a curious passage of Kopp in relief:

> Before the slope, running southwards from [*the*] Nebi Saʻin on the north, comes to an end in the valley, there is a fairly level rock plateau. Here the Church of the Annunciation stands.

Photograph courtesy of gallery.tourism.gov.il

Photograph of the modern Roman Catholic Church of the Annunciation, apparently the fifth shrine to be built at this location. Believed by many to mark the home of the Virgin Mary and the place where the Archangel Gabriel delivered the original 'Hail Mary,' the church is built over tombs of an ancient necropolis.

[51] Bagatti 1955:6.

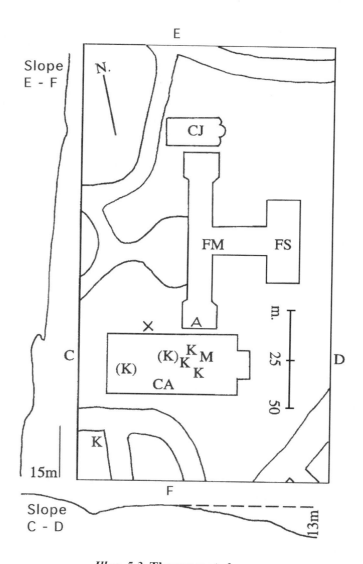

***Illus. 5.3.* The venerated area.**

The slope of the hill is given in section to the left (north-south A–B) and below the
diagram (east-west C–D). Principal modern streets are indicated.

CA = Ch. of the Annunciation CJ = Ch. of St. Joseph
FM = Franciscan Monastery FS = Franciscan school
K = kokhim tomb M = alleged house of Mary
A = "The Virgin's Kitchen"
X = Possible habitation of the Holy Family according to Viaud

"A fairly level rock plateau" is scarcely an appropriate designation for the venerated area. The difference in elevation, for example, between the two ends of the Franciscan Monastery is roughly 10 m. This caused problems during the building's construction in 1930. The entryway of the small Church of St. Joseph (CJ), first built V–VI CE,[52] is 3 m higher than the foundation of its apse at the eastern end (see *Illus. 5.5*). Of course, the floor of the CJ rests on a built up foundation which masks the underlying slope of the hillside.[53] This is the spot where tradition locates the "Workshop of St. Joseph," and in Roman Catholic tradition it is the place where Jesus was reared ("House of the Nutrition"). As for the Church of the Annunciation, we see from *Illus. 5.3* that the terrain under the eastern half of the edifice slopes severely, and indeed possesses the remarkable grade of 24%. It is a most unlikely spot for ancient habitations, unless we credit the rural Jews of Roman times with modern engineering skills or suppose that Mary's home ("M" in *Illus. 5.3*) was tilted, as also Joseph's residence 100 m to the north.[54] The ancient Nazarenes did not have concrete and steel girders, nor modern construction and engineering techniques for erecting edifices on slopes. Nor is there any evidence that these folk laboriously cut into the side of the Nebi Sa'in to make flat areas on the hillside on which to build their dwellings. Finally, we are left with the obvious question: why would they not choose the valley floor on which to settle? We cannot suppose reasons of defense weighed in this, for living halfway up the hill is hardly a safer proposition in case of attack.

The hillside venue for the village is understandable when we recall that it does not proceed from practical considerations but from scripture. The evangelist Luke writes that Nazareth existed on a hill. Accordingly, the first pilgrims looked to the hillside for a possible venue for the house of Mary. They saw numerous caves and assorted hollows in the limestone, and hence arose the tradition that the humble virgin lived in a cave.

The cavities in the ground

The Franciscan area is literally honeycombed with underground chambers and tunnels. This caused problems during construction of the edifices. Kopp writes:

> "As I have been told, the foundations of the convent began to sag during construction [*in 1930*], for one hollow opened up into another. No fewer than 68 silos were counted and filled with cement.[55]

---

[52] Viaud 141.

[53] In 1754 the Franciscans took possession of the area above the putative house of St. Joseph and built a chapel there. It was destroyed by earthquake in 1838, and a second edifice constructed. The third edifice and present CJ dates to 1914.

[54] The only fairly level area is in the venerated area is the western portion of the CA, where no habitations are claimed.

[55] Kopp 1938:189.

In an anonymous 1930 report we read:

> Its construction [*i.e. of the Franciscan Convent/Monastery*] has presented exceptional technical difficulties, not only on account of the unevenness of the terrain, amounting to about 14 m from one end of the building to the other, but also on account of the great number of silos and cisterns met with in sinking the foundations.[56]

In addition, Bagatti numbers twenty-three cavities under or next to the Church of the Annunciation, and a further thirty-three adjacent and leading to the Church of St. Joseph. Another dozen or so are close by. These artificially-worked cavities were certainly not fashioned all at once, but must have accumulated over many centuries. In the course of time, succeeding generations added to the complexity of the silos, and many of the underground cavities became connected.

Some of the silos go as far back as the Iron Age.[57] It is clear that cavities from one era were reused and expanded in subsequent eras, resulting in the honeycombed state found in the modern excavations. Some of the silos are double, that is, one on top of another. There are also triple silos and one instance, quite exceptional, of a quadruple silo under the present Church of St. Joseph (*Illus. 5.4* and discussion below). Placing silos one on top of the other offered several advantages: (a) Surface area was economized. (b) Large amounts of "emergency" grain could be safely stored in lower silos, away from the possibility of theft. At the same time, such provisions were available in times of famine. (c) The location of lower silos was unknown to foreigners or attackers from outside the village. Thus a considerable amount of food could be kept safe, secret, and ready to use.

The question of habitations

The size, complexity, and sheer number of hollows in the Franciscan zone of Nazareth betray two uses: agricultural and funereal. The datable evidence shows us that use began again in Middle Roman times (Chapter 4). Nevertheless, the tradition has insisted upon interpreting the hollows in terms of habitations and, furthermore, in backdating their use to the time of Christ and even before. Bagatti writes of "habitations of an agricultural character" (*abitazione di carattere agricolo*)[58]—an interesting phrase which perfectly encapsulates his underlying posture: the archaeologist interprets the many silos, cisterns, and presses in the area as *adjuncts* to habitations. This maneuver is logically reversed, for he interprets the overwhelming agricultural evidence that he sees in terms of what he does not see—habitations. This comes from the pressing

---

[56] *Exc*:220.
[57] Chapter 1, pp. 49*ff.*
[58] Bagatti 1955:6.

need to validate a village at the venerated sites, a need which forces him to
view the agricultural installations as appendages of invisible habitations. This
was not new. "It is a city of troglodytes" wrote Kopp a generation earlier, also
suggesting that the ancient Nazarenes lived in caves.[59]

In a 1977 article, Bagatti writes:

> In the excavations in 1955, it was found that the ground below the
> surface was riddled with cavities and hollows: pear-shaped granaries, vaulted
> cells for storing wine and oil jars, pits, and small wells. Several oil presses
> were found at surface level. *In the rock-cut cavities, it was possible to detect
> traces of houses.* Some uniform depressions apparently held the foundations
> of walls. The remains of these structures vanished when the bishop's palace
> was built. In several granaries, pottery from the Israelite period was found
> – sherds of jars with two handles and a short spout – indicating that the
> granaries were no longer in use in later times. Since Roman and especially
> Byzantine sherds were found in most of the cells, it seems that these rooms
> were buried under earth during the construction of the medieval buildings.
> The cells are similar to others discovered beneath St. Joseph's Church and
> the Franciscan friary, *and it can therefore be concluded that the early town
> extended up to the present-day site of these two churches. The boundaries of
> the ancient graves also confirm this assumption.*[60] [Emphasis added.]

The area described is the wine and oil press complex a few meters north
of the Church of the Annunciation. This is where "several oil presses were
found,"[61] and the location is confirmed by his descriptive, "bishop's palace."
This refers to a part of the old Franciscan monastery in the area Viaud calls the
"Grand Divan."[62] The surrounding agricultural installations clearly show that
these "uniform depressions" must be associated with them. Only tendentious
reasoning can suggest otherwise. This was in all probably Nazareth's main
wine and oil press complex. As such, it was an important and very busy area,
not a domestic dwelling.

The scholarly Nazareth literature routinely overlooks the unsuitability
of the venerated area for habitations. The acknowledgement by Tonneau in
1931,[63] later confirmed by Kopp—that no signs of ancient habitation were
found in the venerated area—has never been rebutted by evidence. Bagatti
indeed found a short flight of steps, a wall, and a doorjamb under the Church
of the Annunciation. But these elements were associated with a communal
granary, as the archaeologist's own admission makes clear:

---

[59] Kopp 1938:187.
[60] EAEHL, "Nazareth," p. 922.
[61] *Exc.* 52-60.
[62] Viaud 35.
[63] *Revue Biblique* XL (1931), p. 556. *Cf.* Chapter 2, p. 65.

Silo No. 48... An aperture by means of a stairway led us into [*a*] subterranean place, 9.30 m. long, used as a granary, with the excavation of six silos and two corridors for ventilation.

The steps, as can be seen from fig. 34, taken from above, a little to [*the*] southwest side, are cut in the rock and are very worn. There follows the door which had a wooden frame as can be gathered from the two holes made in the rock to the right, usual for closing wooden doors with a bolt.

The rock was ruined on the west side and so the grotto was closed already of old by a rough wall, made of blocks, fairly well dressed and laid in regular courses. As we see in fig. 35, taken from inside, from the north, the walls are very irregular and sinuous, especially to the left on entering and to the right towards the end after the wall.

The ceiling is fairly level, but the floor is uneven. In this were cut the silos which are distributed in four mouths appearing on the floor, and two others on the interior of one of them. [64]

Six silos, two corridors, an uneven floor—these are obvious signs that we are not dealing with habitations. Bagatti concurs and writes on the following page:

Yet on the walls the inhabitants did not make any signs, and since trace of life is missing, as hearths, smoke, niches for holding objects, which, on the contrary are found in grottos that were inhabited, we can affirm that the place was used solely as a granary.

In fact, no hearths (with or without smoke evidence) have been found in the venerated area. As for "Niches for holding objects" (*i.e.* oil lamps), these were common in Roman agricultural workspaces as well as in tombs. They are not a criterion determining habitations! This is yet one more indication that the interpretation of evidence at the venerated sites is tendentious. In short, there is no evidence for the prominent and persistent claims of habitations in the venerated area. Those claims usually are modeled after Bagatti. They conceive of "caves" in the area which have been modified for domestic use, as J. Strange's claim of "Late Hellenistic to early Roman caves with domestic installations, some used as late as the Byzantine period."[65]

Bagatti admits that "we have found but few masonry remains [*of the ancient village*] because little was excavated in this regard." The statement is curious, since he personally excavated the area for almost a decade. The archaeologist continues:

But we believe that the village was in great part transformed in later times. Yet there is evidence of its existence in the literary texts and in the abundant pottery found in the silos, which bespeaks the presence of houses which have now disappeared.[66]

---

[64] *Exc.* 67.
[65] "Nazareth," OEANE, 1997.
[66] *Exc.* 234.

Thus, Bagatti is able to find evidence of habitations from pottery in silos. His tendentious posture is quintessentially stated in a 1960 writing:

> [S]ince it is certain that within the zone delimited by the tombs there were habitations in ancient times—of which we have remains—it is equally certain that such remains are not to be found outside [*of that area*], so that we are forced to admit that the space occupied by the ancient village was situated on the small hill which is contiguous in the northwest to the Jebel Sa'in and extends towards the valley between two ravines or wadis which border it.[67]

These pages amply demonstrate that each element in the above passage is false. (1) The remains of habitations that the archaeologist claims are pure invention, despite his certainty. (2) His claim that habitations do not exist elsewhere (*e.g.*, on the valley floor) is a false rationalization owing to a false premise. It is also pure invention. (3) We are hardly "forced" to admit that the village existed where Bagatti claims, namely, in the venerated area. That, too, is pure invention.

The home of the Blessed Virgin

Quoting a fourteenth-century pilgrim, Kopp leads the reader to suppose that the domiciles of Mary and Joseph were two outlying houses removed from the main village and cleaving to the side of the hill.[68] The houses (marked by the present Churches of the Annunciation and that of St. Joseph) are one hundred meters apart. Joseph and Mary, evidently, were neighbors from youth.

The Greek Orthodox venerate the spring at the northern end of the basin as the home of Mary (see above), and this tradition has roots going back to Byzantine times. The Latins claim that she lived in the Franciscan zone, but beyond that they are not entirely clear. "M" in *Illus. 5.3* marks the Chapel of the Angel, where Mary allegedly received the visitation from the angel. This chapel is considered a vestibule of Mary's dwelling in the adjoining cave.[69] Immediately to the west (Locus 29, which we shall discuss below) was "a little room without light where Jesus the adolescent lived."[70] In fact this was a tomb, which neither Viaud, Kopp nor Bagatti deny.

Many factors show that the venerated grotto was part of a busy agricultural area. First of all, the northern side of the cave is connected by a short tunnel to a wine press complex.[71] Secondly, on the south side of the cave, and

---

[67] Bagatti 1960:328.
[68] Kopp 1938:191.
[69] Grotto A-R at Viaud fig. 36 (p. 81).
[70] Viaud 115.
[71] *Exc.* 52–57.

immediately adjacent, are no less than three large silos (nos. 30, 30a, and 32), far too large for one family's storage and certainly intended for communal use.[72] The entrance to the cave lies between two of these silos. Thirdly, to the west of the cave are depressions, long since cut away, which indicate the original existence of three more silos or agricultural basins.[73] Fourthly, two holes are in the roof of the cave. They would have admitted rain into a dwelling. Bagatti conveniently assumes that these holes postdated the time of the Holy Family and suggests they were used for Jewish-Christian services of veneration (to let candle smoke escape).[74] More likely is that these holes were carved at an early time in order to admit sunlight into the cave, and possibly to also pass items from above to below. Fifthly, we recall M. Aviam's observation that the caves of Galilee "are wet or damp from December to May, and can only be used during the summer and autumn."[75] This, too, would mitigate against the domestic uses the Church proposes for these caves. Sixthly, the ground in this area is steep and rocky. It is inconceivable that people would have chosen to dwell there rather than on the flat plateau only a hundred meters to the east (*Illus. 5.2*). Finally, we shall learn that this locus is less than ten meters away from kokh tombs dating to the Middle Roman period. No Jewish family would have lived in such close proximity to tombs. For all the above reasons it is quite clear that the cave known as the Venerated Grotto was part of a busy agricultural area in Roman times.

In particular, the most holy sites under the CA were an elaborate winemaking installation. The main elements of the complex are noted in *Illus. 5.4.* The press [A] was located in the so-called "Virgin's Kitchen,"[76] a grotto 10 m north of the Chapel of the Angel. The remaining elements of the winemaking complex were downhill (south) of the press. A tunnel linked the press to the "Grotto of the Annunciation" [B] where the Virgin reputedly lived. This was probably a treading area. From there, the wine went to a stepped basin [C] which the tradition insists was a miqve, but which Joan Taylor has shown was a wine collecting vat. She has analyzed the various work installations, and writes:[77]

> The entire area was, during the Roman period, a hive of agricultural activity; this makes it extremely improbable that any cultic use was made of its caves or basins. Only 20 metres away from basin no 12…[C] there is a wine-pressing zone with a small sloping treading area (no. 34, in the

---

[72] *Exc.* 51, 179–80, and Fig. 137. The pear-shaped silos have diameters of 5–6 feet. The same situation exists under the Church of St. Joseph (see below).
[73] *Exc.* 182 and Fig. 137.
[74] See *Exc.* 183 and Fig. 137, top.
[75] Aviam 2004:90.
[76] Bagatti Nos. 34–38. *Cf.* Viaud Fig. 36 (p. 81).
[77] A, B, and C have been added to reflect this work.

> 'Kitchen of the Virgin' [A]), about 3 metres square and 40 centimetres deep, and an underground fermenting vat (no. 35) to which the juice ran through a hole. As was stated above, this complex was connected to the Grotto of the Annunciation (no. 31[B]) by a tunnel... so that it is safe to assume that the cave formed part of the complex.[78]

Nevertheless, the guidebooks carefully point out the exact spots where Mary sat and where the angel stood, and the adjoining loci where the Blessed Virgin and Jesus the adolescent may have lived. For Christians, this is the most venerated place in all the Holy Land outside of Jerusalem. For over fifteen centuries countless prayers have been offered here, and the thoughts of the pilgrim have fallen into the deepest meditation. For those who know the truth, it is a surreal scene, one beyond easy explanation. All of Christendom, as it were, pays heartfelt tribute here to an illusion. The moment of wonder before a humble cave, the wide eyes of the youth, the submissive gaze of the aged—these witness nevertheless to a sublime fact. It is one that even science cannot, and should not, take away. That wonder, those eyes, that gaze—they are timeless and not linked to any place. *They* are what is truly holy, not a piece of earth.

Early in the twentieth century, a cave a few meters northwest of the Chapel of the Angel suggested tantalizing possibilities to Father Viaud.[79] He conducted an exploratory excavation, which at that time was a few meters outside the north wall of the (much smaller) Church of the Annunciation. Viaud dug approximately one meter but, finding nothing, he instructed the workmen to refill the hole and left for the day. When one of the laborers asked permission to dig down to bedrock, Viaud assented. Later that evening the workman came running up to the priest and exclaimed excitedly, "Father, a statue!" When Viaud arrived on the scene several men were frantically uncovering five beautiful capitals, each ornately incised with reliefs of apostles and biblical figures.[80] The capitals date to Crusader times, and we now know that they were buried for safety in 1187 CE, in the days immediately before Saladin's forces retook Nazareth. Viaud considered the surrounding grotto more significant than the capitals themselves:

> If indeed, as I believe, [*the grotto*] was contemporary with the Holy Family, it must have had some connection with the Holy Family itself, and the examination of the internal arrangement of the one can help us understand the primitive arrangement of the other, that is, of the grotto of

---

[78] Taylor 250. Bagatti discusses the complex of the press at *Exc.* 52*ff. Cf.* EAEHL 922.

[79] No. 41 in *Illus. 5.4.*

[80] On these capitals see Folda 1986; Barash 1964. Viaud describes the discovery on pages 55-57 of his book.

the Annunciation and of the room which preceded it. For us, nothing can be of greater interest. (Viaud 57)

The priest excavated the chamber with the utmost reverence. The Catholic Church has clearly embraced the troglodyte tradition, despite our observation that humidity renders the caves of Lower Galilee uninhabitable during the wet season.[81] In his book, *Nazareth et ses deux Églises*, Viaud devotes several pages and illustrations to this grotto. He asks: "What could this room have been?" A comparison with *Illus. 5.3* ("x") above shows that it is located in a rare level portion of the venerated area.[82] In Viaud's photo it indeed appears to have a level floor.

The Frenchman does not definitively answer his own question. In one photo an unworked rock column rises in the middle of the room—it is ugly and scarcely reminds one of a habitation. A meter away a hole appears in the ground—a silo for storing grain. One would suppose these features exclude the room from having been a domicile, yet the priest asks: "Could it have been the habitation of the parents of the Holy Family?" Finding no proof, he contents himself with the possibility that "Mary and Joseph, and even the child Jesus, visited [*that rom*] some times. This alone gives it a great value."[83]

Bagatti is circumspect regarding the associations of this grotto (his locus 41) with the Holy Family.[84] He notes typical holes in the wall "for tying animals" and the presence of a feeding trough (manger) at one end. He maintains that these elements of a stable are "not original" and do not go back to Roman times. Adjoining the grotto is a large bread oven (locus 40) which the Italian insists was "strictly for family use and not a public bakery." Except in wealthy homes, however, ovens in ancient times were communal property, not private, as they still are today in poorer parts of the world. In any event, one wonders how the archaeologist knows such details of daily life long ago when larger questions remain undecided. Certainly, his observation regarding the oven is consistent with the need to find domestic evidence on the hillside.

---

[81] Chp. 2:9.

[82] The slope is also given in *Exc.* Fig. 36 (p. 77).

[83] Viaud 61.

[84] This is Bagatti's No. 40 (*Exc.* Fig. 16, p.47, discussion pp. 60–62).

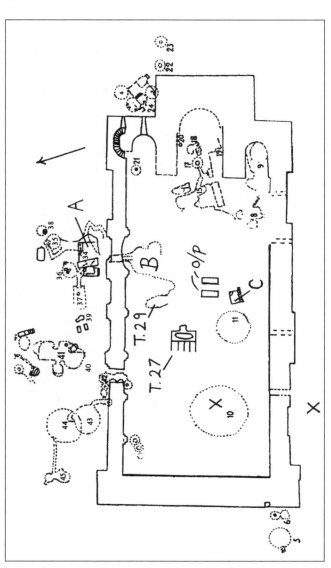

Illus. 5.4. **Tombs and winemaking installations under the CA**

A. Winepress complex ("Virgin's Kitchen") o/p Remains of two graves at lowest stratum
T. 27 Roman Period tomb with remains of 5 kokhim T. 29 Small grotto with remains of one grave ("Martyrium of Conon")
B. Treading area connected by opening to winepress ("Venerated Grotto," just north of the "Chapel of the Angel")
C. Wine collecting vat ("baptismal basin") 41 "Room of the Capitals" 10, 11, 43, 44 Cisterns X Additional possible tombs

The base of the oven was formed of a reused millstone (*Exc.* 62). This detail reveals that (like the stable) the oven postdates Roman times. Furthermore, it shows that the earlier (Roman) stratum was characterized by agricultural evidence. Millstones, silos, cisterns, and a nearby press complex all unambiguously demonstrate that this was a busy agricultural area in antiquity. Concurrently, the tombs show that the entire hillside was used for burial.

The Church of St. Joseph

Approximately 100 m north of the CA is the more modest Church of St. Joseph. The terrain and foundation under the church are given in *Illus. 5.4*, which is a computer scan from Viaud's 1910 book. The interior floor of the church is the top level of the diagram, whose foundation has been considerably built up to the east (left) to compensate for the slope of the hill.

Underneath the church is the most incredible complex of hollows yet found in the Nazareth basin. *Illus. 5.5* shows a quadruple silo together with a large grotto. Not shown in the illustration are other cisterns underneath the church, as well as four additional silos (some double) in the floor of the "Great Grotto."[85] Taylor has shown that a rock-cut basin on the premises was a collecting vat "used in wine-making." She writes that it was "associated with other agricultural installations—cisterns, silos, another basin, and a large cave—found under the Church of St. Joseph... The entire area was, during the Roman period, a hive of agricultural activity."[86] Another wine press complex exists under the Church of the Annunciation.

The quadruple silo is aligned vertically, and the second silo has been artificially extended to make the grotto, which measures 10×5 m and 2 m in height. A long corridor connects this grotto with others beyond the premises of the church. "Similar corridors," writes Viaud, "branch off to the east and west." He notes niches for lamps here and there.

"What is this grotto?" asks Viaud. "We have found no cultic traces," he adds, "but it was inhabited and is certainly very ancient." Like Bagatti after him, Viaud here focuses upon habitations that do not and could not exist. First of all, the floor of the grotto, as can be seen from the illustration, is not level. Secondly, it has no less than five silos in the floor of the grotto itself, four of which are not shown in the illustration. These silos would render habitation in the chamber inconvenient, to say the least, and probably dangerous, too. We may ask: what need did a private family have for five large silos in the ground, most of them multiple? In sum, it is palpably obvious that no one lived there. The site was clearly part of the settlement's agricultural storage area.

---

[85] Viaud Fig. 64.
[86] Taylor 249, 250.

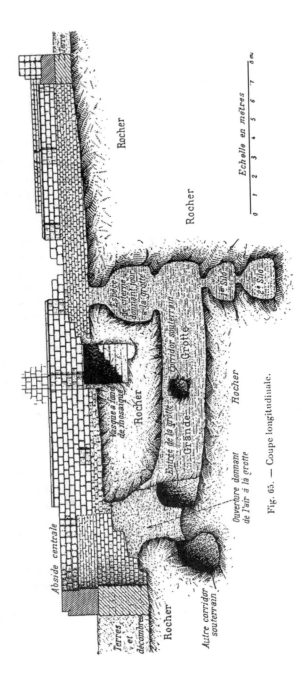

Fig. 65. — Coupe longitudinale.

Illus. **5.5. Section under the Church of St. Joseph.**
(From Viaud:1911, p. 135. *Cf.* Bagatti 1971a:16–17.)
The view is from the north (east is to the left).

Viaud attempts to link the CJ with a description furnished by Arculf, the seventh century pilgrim. The latter noted a church "in the middle of the town." Viaud writes that "This condition appears quite well fulfilled by the church with which we are here concerned." It does not occur to the priest that the ancient village had nothing to do with the hillside. Hence, "in the middle of the town" certainly meant in a different place. This is made plain by Arculf's next observation that under the church there was a spring.[87] Arculf is obviously describing the church over Mary's Spring which we have discussed above, known today as the Greek Orthodox Church of the Annunciation. Viaud should have been aware of this competing tradition, for the Greeks have been in the Nazareth basin longer than the Latins. In any case, he is not dissuaded, and looking about for ancient signs of water he indeed finds them. Two "basins" (*vasques*) persuade Viaud that "rather powerful channels led abundant waters to this spot."[88] With that interesting observation we take leave of the priest's pious digression.

The tombs under the Church of the Annunciation

Bagatti writes: "The Church of the Annunciation is situated on a small hill surrounded by ancient graves south of Saint Joseph's Church."[89] It is a revealing statement, because the tradition has identified only two Roman-era tombs in the vicinity (numbers 70 and 73). Many more tombs, however, have been suspected. Mansur noted "natural protrusions under the Church of St. Joseph" and a "bulging extension" near the CA, all which he thought were once tombs.[90] He noted similar "protrusions" and "extensions" under the 100-meter Franciscan monastery, excavated in 1930. Most of these possibilities, at least in the venerated area, must forever remain unverified, for this plot of land has long since been reshaped by the assiduous attentions of the Church.

It should be noted that several tombs of the Bronze Age, studied in Chapter 1, are located either under or immediately next to the Church of the Annunciation (tombs 1, 7, 8). Tomb 1 is located between five and ten meters south of the Byzantine structure. Tombs 7 and 8 are approximately ten meters apart from one another and are located under the Byzantine, Medieval, and modern structures. The fact that the area under the Shrine of the Annunciation was a necropolis in the Bronze and Iron Ages is not in doubt. The question

---

[87] *Inferius inter eosdem tumulos lucidissimum fontem conlocatum, quem totus civium frequentat populus de illo exhouriens aquam...* Geyer: 274, quoted at *Exc.* 24–25.

[88] *Toutefois les deux vasques qui se voient encore... montrent au moins qu'une canalisation assez forte amenait en cet endroit des eaux abondantes.* Viaud 146-47.

[89] NEAEHL (1993) "Nazareth," p. 1105.

[90] Above, p. 223.

we shall now consider is whether this hallowed ground also served as a necropolis in Roman times.

In a particularly revealing paragraph, Père Viaud raised the possibility already in 1910 that many tombs existed under the "courtyard" of the CA, that is, under the western half of the structure. Of course, he was excavating before the construction of the large modern edifices, and thus had access to many structures which have since been destroyed. Viaud writes:

> *Sépulchres.*— Devant cet escalier, à un mètre environ vers l'ouest, nous avons mis à jour plusieurs sépulcres de l'époque des croisés [*T. 27*]. Ils sont placés dans une sorte de chambre creusée dans le roc et dont l'entrée était à l'Orient. Peut-être était-ce primitivement une chambre sépulchrale de l'époque byzantine, ruinée avec la première église et réutilisée par les croisés. Ceci justifierait l'opinion du P. Meistermann, qui voit dans les deux citernes situées dans la cour, à gauche [*10+*], d'anciennes chambres sépulchrales transformées. Quant à celle du droit [*11*], nous allons voir que si elle est aussi une ancienne chambre sépulchrale transformée, cette transformation a eu lieu du temps même des croisés.[91]

The reference numbers in brackets are used below to refer to the various structures Viaud mentions. It is clear from his statement that this section of the CA alone contained no less than four pre-Crusader tombs, three of which were converted into cisterns. Meistermann suggested others. Kopp allows as many as five tombs under the CA, all dating to the Roman-era. Bagatti himself does not dispute three tombs, though he argues for their later dating. We shall consider the most significant tombs below.

A note is in order regarding the sea-change in attitude that Bagatti, in the post-War years, attempted to effectuate regarding the Nazareth tombs. As has been mentioned, he was the first to truly recognize the danger that Roman-era tombs posed for the tradition. However, in the earlier part of the century the Catholic attitude was completely different. From the preceding citation, it is evident that Meistermann sees an old tomb in virtually every cistern under the venerated area. Viaud mentions several tombs contiguous to the Chapel of the Angel, and Kopp writes that the entire venerated area was a necropolis. The modern researcher can only be thankful to the forthrightness of these

---

[91] Viaud 52. "In front of this staircase, about one meter to the west, we uncovered several tombs of the Crusader era. They are located in a sort of room cut into the rock whose entrance was to the east. Perhaps this was originally a tomb of the Byzantine era, destroyed with the first church and reused by the Crusaders. This would justify the opinion of P. Meistermann, who sees in the two cisterns located in the courtyard, to the left, ancient tombs that have been transformed. As to the one to the right, we shall see that if it is also a transformed tomb, that transformation took place even at the time of the Crusades."

early investigators. Why, we may wonder, were Fathers Viaud, Meistermann, and Kopp so enthusiastic about finding Roman-era tombs at Nazareth?

The answer lies in the texts themselves. The priests were looking for tombs of the Holy Family, and were thrilled at the search. Viaud continually asks: "What could this be?" He constantly tries to link what he is seeing to the Holy Family. This includes the tombs. What Viaud really wanted to find was the tomb of Joseph, and the tomb of Mary. He even entitles one of his sections: "*Est-il de saint Joseph?*"[92]

The alacrity of these early researchers in documenting tombs proved a headache for Bagatti. His task was to neutralize, as much as possible, all of the funerary claims made by his predecessors. The task was not easy, but he did it very well. Most of the tombs of Meistermann, Viaud, and Mansur are not even mentioned in Bagatti's *Excavations in Nazareth*. He speaks of tombs under the CA only when absolutely necessary. This is the case in regards to locus 27 (see below), where Bagatti refutes prior contentions that the tomb went back to Roman times. The Italian also allows very brief mention of Tomb 29 in his tome, yet without any comment whatsoever. Both these tombs, as it happens, adjoin the Chapel of the Angel.

Artefacts and tombs

The artefacts found also contribute to our understanding of the venerated area's history. We recall that fourteen bow-spouted oil lamps are the earliest datable evidence from Roman Nazareth.[93] All but two of them came from the venerated area, or from close by. This is not surprising, perhaps, since only there have major excavations been conducted. Five of the lamps came from kokh tombs (one tomb yielded two examples). Because the kokh-type tomb first appeared in the Galilee *c.* 50 CE,[94] we can therefore date these five oil lamps after that time. What is presently of interest is that for topological reasons, we have seen that habitations were not possible in the venerated area (above, p. 241*f.*). This means that the nine bow-spouted lamps found there[95] were either funereal or were linked to agricultural activity (placed in nitches, etc.). In this connection, Varda Sussman writes: "Most oil-lamps surviving from antiquity were discovered in tombs."[96] This is cause for pause, for *the tradition denies that even a single Roman lamp from the venerated area came from a tomb.* We may also bear in mind that for every example of pottery or of an oil lamp that has survived, either whole or in part, there are probably

---

[92] Viaud 93 (in reference to Tomb 29).
[93] Chapter 4, *Illus. 4.3.*
[94] Chapter 4, pp. 160–164. All but four of the Roman tombs found at Nazareth are of the kokhim type (*Illus. 4.2*).
[95] Chapter 4, *Illus. 4.3*, nos. 1–9.
[96] Sussman 1982:3.

a number of additional items that have not survived, or that are represented today only by mutilated and undatable shards. This renders the Church's position all the more precarious.

The exact find spot for four of the itemized bow-spouted lamps is not known (Chapter 4, *Illus. 4.3*, nos. 6–9), though they came from the venerated area:

> Even though we do not know exactly where they were found, we are certain that they come from the area excavated, that is, from the zone situated near to the Shrine of the Annunciation and that of St. Joseph.[97]

Another five bow-spouted lamps (nos. 1–5) were found in the area, but their archaeological contexts are only vaguely given. This is a general problem in Nazareth archaeology. Unfortunately, the lack of stratigraphical method in the Franciscan excavations is coupled with imprecision—and even complete uncertainty—regarding the exact find spots (and hence contexts) of many artefacts reported in Bagatti's *Excavations in Nazareth*. It is of course regrettable, and can unfortunately mask a good deal of misinformation.

Yet, if these nine bow-spouted oil lamps were *not* funerary, then only two possibilities remain: they were either domestic, or they were used in connection with agricultural work. Regarding the former possibility, we have seen that domestic habitations could not have existed on the hillside which, besides sloping steeply, is characterized by scores of cavities in the ground. As regards the latter, it is of course theoretically possible that all these lamps were used in connection with agricultural activity. But there is certainly no obvious connection—after all, agricultural activity was carried out during the day.

Though the tradition today denies the existence of Roman Period tombs in the venerated area, it has not always done so. Nor can it deny the existence of such tombs close by. Tomb 70—a kokh tomb from the Roman Period— lies a scant 30 meters south of the CA. It contained seventeen oil lamps from many eras, including three bow-spouted lamps.

In his discussion of stone vessels,[98] Bagatti does not give the precise location of the two handles, and locates their find spot generally in "the Byzantine atrium." A review of his terminology shows that this is a rectangular area, 20 by 15 meters, in the western zone of the CA (including the massive cistern, no. 10). The Italian writes that "Small pieces of 'Herodian' lamps found at the threshold and a little inside show clearly how this place was in use already in the first century" (*Exc.* 46). It is possible to link these

---

[97] *Exc.* 305. These are the lamps marked "fig. 235" in Chapter 4, *Illus. 4.3*. Two of the nine bow-spouted lamps were found directly under the Church of the Annunciation, and three were discovered 20 m to the north. All are represented by shards, but they reveal enough to allow determination of the lamp type.

[98] *Exc.* 318. See Chapter 4, pp. 181–195.

"Herodian" lamps to rumors of tombs mentioned by Viaud and Meistermann (see below).

Arguably the earliest oil lamp found at Nazareth was a unique example of Smith's Type 1,[99] an unornamented bow-spouted lamp which we called an "outlier." It's find spot is locus 51c (*Exc.* 299). In antiquity this was part of an extensive agricultural installation roughly 20 m north of the CA. That installation includes a massive plastered cistern (L. 51) over five meters deep and five meters wide, together with nearby storage pits and channels. It is evident that the cistern was not made by the very first settlers to the basin, for it is simply too impressive and clearly would require (and support) a substantial number of people The entire installation is complex, and shows that the area was worked in more than one era. Thus, Bagatti mentions a "Crusader" wall (*Exc.* 71), a ceiling "remade with the repaving from the room above," "in the modern period the complex was touched up," and so on.

Certainly, this area (presently under the Franciscan Convent) was once a busy and multi-layered site, used for various purposes over many centuries. A careful examination of Bagatti's text and diagrams[100] raises a number of questions that will probably never be answered. Especially noteworthy are several small, underground chambers for which the archaeologist gives no clear *raison d'être*. He notes "a little room (e)," attached through a corridor "to another one, which is a little irregular (f)." These are part of the locus 52, which no doubt predated the huge cistern cutting into it. Another small room (53 h) lies a few meters to the west. These underground chambers do not appear to be either for storage of grain or liquid, nor are they large enough for habitation. They are, in fact, roughly the size of kokhim tomb. One chamber has "an elbow to the west" (52 f) which in the diagram looks like a possible kokh shaft. With all the reworking this area has undergone, it is now impossible to reconstruct the exact features of the earliest installation. However, I do not believe it can be ruled out that the single bow-spouted lamp found in locus 51c may be a remnant of an early kokh tomb.[101]

As regards the area under the Church of the Annunciation itself, already at the turn of the nineteenth century Père Viaud wrote about and diagrammed a grave (T. 29) several feet north of the Chapel of the Angel—the locus where the Virgin Mary ostensibly spoke with the Archangel Gabriel.[102] Viaud wondered if St. Joseph himself might have been buried there. The priest also signaled other burials nearby. One is a scant two meters south of the Chapel

---

[99] See Chapter 4, pp. 165–167.

[100] *Exc.* 70–72; fig. 33.

[101] The possibility that there were secret underground "hiding" places for the Nazarenes, in case of attack, also cannot be discounted. These have been discovered in the Galilee dating I–II CE, and will be considered in Chapter 6.

[102] Viaud 81, 90*f.*

of the Angel (o/p in *Illus*. *5.4*). Another is ten meters away, on the western side of the Chapel (T. 27).[103]

In the 1930s Kopp examined all these burials. He noted with astonishment that the house of Mary was surrounded by graves and that the sanctuary itself was built over a "Jewish kokhim tomb."[104] We shall now consider the most important of these burials in turn.

Tomb 27

Figures:

Viaud 1910 "Sépulcres" (p. 35, Fig. 2); "Tombeau" (p. 81, Fig. 36)

Kopp 1939-40 (JPOS 19, p. 113) Pl IX, "H"

Bagatti 1955, Tavola I, no.15.

Bagatti 1969 Pl. XI no. 27; Fig. 9 no. 27 (p. 38)

Discussion:

Viaud 1910:52: "sépulcres de l'époque des croisés" or "byzantine"

Kopp 1938:197: "eine typische Kokimanlage"

Bagatti 1955:16; Bagatti 1969:49-50: "sepoltura dai Crociati"

In his 1955 article, Bagatti repudiated Kopp's notice of a kokh tomb under the CA:

> In rural areas, it is not rare to find cisterns and presses associated with tombs, but there is not the least trace of the latter *from the Roman period*, even if some cut rocks, not clearly visible, could be considered as such. One of these, called a "kokhim" chamber, was a remnant of a pit under the floor of the church, reused as a sepulcher by the crusaders.[105]   Emphasis added.)

The above passage was prompted by several unsettling observations of Kopp, themselves a response to Viaud's remarks cited above. In 1938 the German signaled "a typical kokhim tomb" at the center of the Church of the Annunciation, marked T. 27 in *Illus*. *5.4*.[106] We have seen that the kokh type of tomb arrived in Galilee in mid–I CE and was the most common form of burial in Middle and Late Roman times. Bagatti was more aware than Kopp that the presence of such a tomb under the CA is not compatible with the dwelling there of the Holy Family. In the above citation, he is correct in affirming that tombs and agricultural installations often shared the same areas

---

[103] Viaud 81 and 83 (figs. 36, 38, 39), 95.

[104] Kopp 1939–40:91. See his discussion pp. 87*f.* and Pl. IX p. 113.

[105] Bagatti 1955:16.

[106] The alleged tombs under the CA are referred to either as "tombs" (*e.g.*, "T. 27"), or as loci ("L. 27"), depending on the context. The number is invariable, and allows the reader to locate the site.

outside Jewish villages. Though Jews did not *dwell* in the vicinity of tombs, they felt at liberty to work near them. We note that *the Italian does not deny the presence of tombs in the venerated area*—it is their dating to the Roman period that he contests.

For his part, Kopp was simply echoing what Viaud had already reported (and diagrammed) before him. Despite some redundancy, I translate what the German wrote in 1938:

> Under the floor of the old church, 1–2m from the present western wall, Viaud found graves about which he writes: "They are in a sort of room cut into the rock, whose entrance was from the east. Perhaps it was originally a tomb of the Byzantine Period, destroyed in the construction of the first church and then reused by the Crusaders." But according to his diagram we are dealing with a typical kokhim tomb [*handelt es sich um eine typische Kokimanlage*]; on the western long-wall are four grave shafts, in the center is a sunken grave; that on the eastern side, which he sees as the entrance, could on closer scrutiny prove to be a damaged kokh.[107]

A glance at Viaud's diagram[108] (redrawn in *Illus.* 4) indeed suggests what Kopp describes. We see what appear to be four kokhim to the west and the remains of one kokh to the east. What Kopp calls a "sunken grave" (*Senkgrab*) in the center is probably the area dug out of the floor to permit workmen and visitors to stand. The installation looks similar to the Richmond tomb (T. 72), a kokh tomb located 350 m to the southwest of the CA.[109] The main difference between locus 27 and the Richmond tomb is that the former has only one kokh to the east, and not four. But even this may have a ready explanation. That side of L. 27 was cut by the wall of the Byzantine atrium (*Exc.* Pl. XI). It also abuts the wall of the 1877 structure, the "Église actuelle" of Père Viaud. In other words, a great deal of building activity has taken place immediately to the east of L. 27, and the original installation no doubt sustained damage and resultant attenuation.[110] It appears that one side of Viaud's sketch represents the remains of several kokhim.

Bagatti will have none of this line of reasoning. Consistent with his 1955 opinion (cited above), he maintains that this was an agricultural installation during Roman times, and then a tomb in the Crusader era:

---

[107] Kopp 1938:197.

[108] Viaud 1910:fig. 2, p. 35, labeled "Sépulcres."

[109] The plan of T. 72 is given in Chapter 3, *Illus. 3.2*.

[110] Bagatti may confirm this when he writes "We know the east wall, on the south side, for half a metre only" (*Exc.* 49). This appears to be a garbled translation from the Italian original.

Grotto No. 27 (fig. 9, upper right, in section). A little to the north of these cuttings there is the entrance to a grotto, used by the Crusaders for the construction of tombs... Below, near the pavement, we have noted Byzantine sherds, then above (b) tombs constructed by the Crusaders with the usual system of placing the bodies between small stone walls... The grotto was seen already by Fr. Viaud, who left it intact, as we also... This room, according to C. Kopp became "eine typische Kokimanlage," yet the likeness with other loci and the certain determination that the tombs belong to the Crusader period, makes us believe that this grotto had the same utilitarian scope as the others and was not funerary. Regarding kokhim there is absolutely no question. (*Exc.* 50)

Bagatti's interpretation of the evidence raises a number of questions. First of all, his description of "the usual [*Crusader*] system of placing the bodies between small stone walls" is not evident from the drawings. Even in *Excavations*, the section provided shows a traditional kokh.[111] The fact that Bagatti uncovered a Byzantine layer below the tombs does not resolve the matter, for that layer might itself have superceded a Roman layer.

The nub of Bagatti's hypothesis rests on two assertions: (a) that the pre-Crusader (Roman) layer of this tomb was agricultural and not funerary; and (b) that the Crusaders buried people at this site. Regarding the former, Bagatti simply goes beyond the evidence, for he gives no reason for that opinion. The Italian mentions the "likeness with other loci," but we have both agricultural and funereal loci from Roman times in the immediate neighborhood (kokh tomb 70 is a mere 40 m away), which robs his comparison of any force. Then again, Viaud's depiction is not similar to anything else diagrammed in the venerated area. It is unique, detailed, and (at least in Kopp's view) obviously a kokh tomb. Thus, Bagatti's comparison with nearby structures is at best a two-edged sword. In fact, he does not address the possibility of an underlying Roman stratum at all.

However, the real problem with the Italian's proposition lies in his second implication, that Crusaders buried people at this site. This is—to be charitable—untenable. If the Crusaders buried their dead at the site of the Annunciation, then we have no record of the macabre Christian custom, except for Bagatti's claim. Why, we may ask, would the Crusaders have buried their dead *under the house of the Blessed Virgin*? Is not the very idea preposterous? Then again, who did the Crusaders deem sufficiently worthy for burial in this hallowed ground? Would even a Christian monarch have been so presumptuous? The very idea is repugnant and sacrilegious, if not ludicrous. Furthermore, we are dealing with not one but several burials. Viaud's drawing indicates at least four, and a probable reconstruction suggests eight graves a few meters from the alleged spot of the Annunciation.

---

[111] *Exc.* 38, fig. 9, 27c (top right).

Since the time this area began to be venerated, that is, in the fourth century of our era, the Church would not have countenanced burying people under this holiest of all ground, neither in Byzantine nor in Crusader times. This leaves only one possible solution: the burials under the Basilica of the Annunciation preceded the Church's presence in Nazareth. That is, *they preceded the fourth century.*

Thus we have a *terminus ante quem* for the tombs under the venerated area—the time of Constantine the Great and of his mother, Helena, a devout Christian. We can be sure that these tombs precede the fourth century, when Joseph of Caesarea began building shrines in the Holy Land, and when pilgrims began coming to Nazareth. In other places we have established a *terminus a quo* of mid-I CE for these tombs—more likely, 100 CE due to the artefacts found at Nazareth.[112] These two *termini* define the digging and use of the tombs in the venerated area to the time between roughly 100 CE and 300 CE.

The "Crusader" explanation, as adopted by Bagatti, appears to be a desperate attempt to counter convincing evidence of kokh tombs at this very sacred place. The maneuver was also used, as we shall now see, in connection with the neighboring locus, Tomb 29.

Tomb 29

Figures:
Viaud 1910:81 "n" — "Tombeau"; photo Fig. 42; "Tombeau" p. 83 (fig. 38)
Baldi and Bagatti 1937:259 (fig. 7), Pl. 2
Kopp 1939–40:113; Pl IX, "E"
Bagatti 1969 Pl. XI, no. 29; Figs. 137 (section), 146
Finegan 1992 — Fig. 46, "F"

Discussion:
Viaud 1910:92–94, 115 "*Est-il de saint Joseph?*"
Kopp 1939–40:87–90 "*Recht möglich, dass Josef von Tiberias in dieser Grabkammer seine letzte Ruhestatt fand*"
Baldi and Bagatti 1937:249–50; 258–62
Bagatti 1969:185*ff.* "Martyrium of Conon"
Finegan 1992: 53 "used in relation to baptism"

Like Tomb 27, neighboring Tomb 29 must be placed at the center of the theological storm, for it is attested by all parties and is immediately adjacent to the Chapel of the Angel, between five and ten meters from the spot where Mary allegedly received the angel Gabriel.[113] It is a small grotto about four meters in length and two meters at the widest point. Over the years, a good deal has been written about this chamber. The grotto has been extensively

---

[112] See Chapter 4: *Illus. 4.3* and accompanying discussion.
[113] Kopp 1963:62.

altered and reworked, as the various surrounding edifices have been built, torn down, and rebuilt over the centuries. Though no bones were of course found at the spot, none of the archaeologists working at Nazareth has denied that this small space once contained a grave (see literature above). It is even possible that originally more graves were associated with the site, for the burial appears to be a kokh (loculus),[114] which rarely occurs singly.

The tomb has a fascinating history. On its walls are six layers of plaster profusely adorned with graffiti. Those scribbles have undergone the most minute inspection by Bagatti, who devotes no less than 38 pages to them (*Exc.* 190–218)—more than 10% of his book. He hardly even mentions that a tomb is there. We, however, shall take the opposite approach, and shall spend a good deal of time on the tomb, and hardly any on the graffiti. Those markings have been interpreted by Fathers Bagatti and Testa as evidence of very early Christian veneration at this site. That veneration, if true, would vindicate the central Roman Catholic tenet that the sites under the Church of the Annunciation are attested even back to the time of Jesus. However, a careful review by Joan Taylor has shown that the graffiti in question are clearly Byzantine and do not predate the fourth century of our era.[115] They are the markings of pilgrims, and sometimes even of children.

On the floor of the front part of the tomb is a fifth century mosaic with a Constantinian Christ monogram. A second, larger mosaic is five meters south of the entrance to T. 29.[116] It contains the words in Greek: "Gift of Conon, deacon of Jerusalem." Thus, the tomb was dubbed "The Martyrium of Conon" by Bagatti.

Burials at this most venerated place are a keen source of embarrassment for the Church, and tombs are the last thing pilgrims would expect to find at the house of the Virgin Mary. It is no surprise, then, that one does not learn of the existence of this tomb from standard reference sources on Nazareth. Jack Finegan, for example (*The Archaeology of the New Testament*), mentions no burial here. He supposes that this space was used by early Jewish Christians in an elaborate water ritual, one which also involved the nearby cisterns and wine collecting vat ten meters away—this last interpreted as a baptismal basin.[117] Finegan is evidently proceeding from an entirely different set of assumptions than those underlying this work, yet his assumptions are wholly catholic.

---

[114] Baldi-Bagatti:260; Kopp (1939–40):89. The area has been greatly reworked. Other loculi could be to the west and south of the tomb (see Viaud p. 81 = Baldi-Bagatti:248). Viaud, in fact, shows another tomb immediately to the west (not marked as such in Baldi-Bagatti).

[115] Taylor 255.

[116] *Exc.* 100.

[117] Finegan 1992:53.

The first to rediscover the small Grotto 29 in modern times was Brother Benedict Vlaminck in the late nineteenth century. He was the first to affirm that a burial originally existed there. Bagatti cites Vlaminck's description of the discovery in his *Excavations in Nazareth*:

> To the north of the mosaic work [*of Conon*] I noticed an opening, which I hastened to clear away. It admitted me to a kind of antechamber six feet long by five feet wide, covered with mosaic, which bore a Christian monogram. At the far end I found a roughly built stone bench, which led me to conclude that an ancient monument existed at that spot. I removed the bench and saw that it concealed a small basin or trough, three feet six inches in height, with circular bottom, built against some ancient stucco work, discovering afterwards, to my great regret, that in building this trough the workmen had destroyed the original form of the rock, *which in former times must have contained a tomb, judging, at least, by the remains of a recess still visible.* They had also taken away a part of the mosaic work in order to replace it by a large slab, which served as a stepping-stone into the basin or trough. Alongside this stepping-stone I remarked a small round hole made to carry off the dirty water.[118] [Emphasis added.]

It may be noted that in the 38 pages Bagatti devotes to this locus, the word "tomb" appears nowhere except in the above citation. So, it may be understandable that Finegan, too, ignores the funerary aspect of this chamber. Finegan interprets the site as baptismal, and sees support in Vlaminck's description of a "small circular basin or trough" with "a small round hole made to carry off the dirty water." However, Vlaminck clearly shows that this basin (too small to serve for immersion) postdated a grave. It is very unlikely that heterodox Jews ("Jewish-Christians") would have modified a gravesite for baptismal purposes for, in a religious context, graves were ritually unclean. Much more likely, however, is that at some subsequent period the inhabitants of Nazareth used the hillside—including some old tomb sites—in connection with agricultural work. This appears to be the case with T. 29. Clearly, the grave preceded the basin, which Vlaminck shows is intrusive. A glance at *Illus.* 21 shows that this site is very near the treading area (B) associated with the winepress (A), and we are probably dealing here with another wine-collecting vat, similar to that at (C) but smaller.

This discussion sheds some light on the history of Nazareth, in that at least some places on the hillside were first used for burial and then modified for agricultural purposes. When those modifications took place is not entirely clear. This funerary-agricultural sequence will be observed again when we consider the nearby graves o/p.

---

[118] *Exc.* 186.

A few years after Vlaminck's work, Fr. Viaud noted Tomb 29 with curiosity, described it, identified it on plans of the Church, and proposed a number of theories to explain this unexpected grave either under or immediately next to the house where the Virgin Mary grew up. The Frenchman writes:

> Tomb. – If we now go back down to the Chapel of the Angel by the same southern staircase, we find ourselves facing, in the northern side, a tomb (fig. 42). For one going down by the western staircase, it is on the left.[119]

Viaud was particularly interested in who had been buried there. Only a very holy person, his reasoning went, would have been interred in such hallowed ground. Viaud proposed that it was St. Joseph, the husband of Mary. This theory was not new. Already in 1172 CE the grave was described by Theodoric as that of St. Joseph.[120] After considering this possibility, however, Fr. Viaud demurs. He notes that this tomb cannot be from a time when the house was inhabited, nor when Jews were living in the vicinity, due to purity laws regarding contact with the dead:

> [T]his tomb, of course, cannot go back to the time when the house was still inhabited, nor even to a time when the Jewish element completely occupied the area.
> However, one fact is evident: a tomb existed next to this house, and it was taken into account in the early treatment of this part of the dwelling that we today call the Chapel of the Angel.
> The memory of some personage, considered saintly and venerable, was therefore attached to this tomb. [121]

Viaud struggles with this problem of an unidentified grave at the very heart of the Church of the Annunciation, one "which apparently was ruined and deformed at a very ancient time."[122] In order to deal with the Jewish taboo against living in the vicinity of tombs, he suggests a novel explanation towards the end of his book:

> Now we know that Jesus left Nazareth practically at the beginning of his ministry, and moved with his Holy Mother to Capernaum. If one considers that this house of the Holy Virgin was situated opposite the village—which in all probability was established in the region of the spring—can one not suppose that it was henceforth considered outside the town, and therefore no hindrance remained to placing a tomb there?

---

[119] *Tombeau.—Si maintenant nous redescendons à la chapelle de l'Ange par le même escalier méridional, nous voyons en face, dans la paroi nord, un tombeau (fig. 42). Pour celui qui descend par l'escalier occidental, il se trouve à main gauche.*

[120] See Daniel the Abbot, *Zhitie* 90 (in Russian).

[121] Viaud 94–95.

[122] Viaud 93.

So, once again the question arises: whose tomb is this? Of saint Joseph, the fiancé of Mary, say the Abbot Daniel and the monk Theodoric. We find the echo of this tradition once again in P. Martinov who, in 1360, still maintained: "On the other side of the Jordan, where the archangel announced the birth of the Son to the Virgin in Nazareth, one sees the tomb of Joseph, the husband of Mary."[123]

According to this theory, then, the Holy Family moved to Capernaum when Jesus was about thirty years of age (his home is Capernaum at Mk 2:1 and 15).[124] When Joseph died his body was then returned to his home village and buried in the old homestead, which was no longer considered part of the village and was (presumably) vacant.

Of course, we must leave aside the southern (Judean) tradition that Joseph's paternal village was not Nazareth but Bethlehem (Mt 2:22; Lk 2:3–4). We also note that the site of the tomb, being the place of the Annunciation, was not Joseph's home at all but the home of Mary before her marriage. Why his corpse would be transported thirty-five kilometers and buried inside the house not even of his wife, but of her parents, seems odd. To my knowledge Viaud's suggestion is not found again in the Nazareth literature.

In one of his first articles on Nazareth, Bagatti sought to put an end to such pious (and dangerous) speculation. He wrote in 1937 that this tomb dated to Byzantine times and, for corroboration, invoked the nearby mosaics which date to the fifth century:[125] "The mosaics are of the same era as the stonework, since the rocks have no other floor than they."

But a couple of years later Fr. Kopp objected, unwilling to jettison the cherished notion that St. Joseph was buried at this spot. In 1939 he wrote that this grotto had a particularly ancient significance:

> However, the cave had a special meaning even before the building of the wall and the laying of the mosaics. For of the fragments of the six layers of plaster on the eastern wall of the inner niche, two were between the wall and the mosaic; their greater age is thus demonstrated."[126]

According to Kopp, the mosaic was laid between the second and third layers of plaster. In turn, the first layer of plaster must have been laid after the tomb was dug, and also after the grotto ceased being used as a grave. This scenario (which is, in fact, correct) is compatible with a dating of the original grave to Roman times. In addition, Kopp rejected the possibility that the grotto was domestic:

---

[123] Viaud 116.

[124] *Cf.* Mk 3:21, 31; 4:1.

[125] Taylor dates the earliest Nazareth mosaics "to the beginning of the fifth century" (Taylor 243).

[126] Kopp 1939–40:88. He cites Baldi-Bagatti 1937:261.

THE MYTH OF NAZARETH

Was this rock cave the grave of a saintly person? Hüffer[127] would like to consider it part of the dwelling of Mary, and thus interprets it as an integral part [*Bauglied*] of the Basilica which received veneration and distinction through crosses, inscriptions, and mosaics. However, the grotto—even though it has meanwhile been enlarged—is too small and primitive to be a dwelling space [*Wohnraum*].[128]

To the end of his career Kopp cleaved to the idea that St. Joseph could have been buried here. In his 1963 book, *The Holy Places of the Gospels*, he asks:

> Was this the grave of St. Joseph, as some have supposed? Did the people of Nazareth continue for a time to use the silos, the presses, and the cisterns of the rock, although they no longer dwelt there, so that he could have been buried there according to Jewish lay? That would explain how this cave tomb came to have such a close relationship to the grotto of the Annunciation.[129]

Similar to other suggestions of Kopp, this is a curious and complicated scenario with several steps: the house (of Mary's parents, we recall) becomes vacant. The Nazarenes (inexplicably) begin using the premises for agricultural work. Joseph dies and is buried at the old (now vacant) homestead among winepresses and the like.

Bagatti was also exercised by the presence of this grave. Before the Second World War the dating of kokh tombs was still largely unknown, and in 1937 the Italian pronounced that T. 29 was of the kokhim type, unaware that in so doing he was dating it to Roman times: "*Il loculo era quindi scavato a forno*," he wrote. Translated, this reads: "The loculus [*an alternative name for kokh*] was therefore dug [*in the form of*] an oven." "Oven" is the Italian's common if quaint term for kokh, used frequently in Bagatti's writings. In the same article, the Italian proposed that the interred person might have been a fourth century noble, Count Joseph of Tiberias:

> In conclusion, it is to be understood that the date of alteration of the grotto by the construction of a wall and of the mosaic—[*as evidenced*] in the construction technique and in the mosaic iconography—points to the fifth century.
>
> The opinion, then, that the examined tomb belonged to Count Joseph of Tiberias is not contradicted by archeology, since such a tomb may very well go back to the fourth century.[130]

---

[127] G. Hüffer, *Loreto*, vol. 2. Münster, 1921.
[128] Kopp 1939–40:88–89.
[129] Kopp 1963:64.
[130] Baldi-Bagatti:262.

Kopp expanded on this theory in 1939:

> Bagatti maintains that a grave originally existed here "of the baking-oven type" [*nach Art eines Backofens*], that is, that it was a kokim... Archaeologically, it appears to him properly possible [*mit Recht möglich*] only that Joseph of Tiberias found his final resting place in this tomb. This hypothesis was much popularized by Klameth.[131] He maintains that Joseph built the first church on this site and thus his body was brought here: "Certainly, this would have represented the most handsome thanks for this benefactor of the Church." Later, obscurity intervened and people substituted St. Joseph for him because both bore the same name.[132]

In later writings Bagatti mutes references to kokhim under the Church of the Annunciation. In fact, in his 1969 book (Italian edition 1967) the archaeologist entirely ignores the fact that T. 29 was once a grave. The three decades between Kopp's 1938 article and his tome produced more exact knowledge of ancient Jewish burial customs, including the fact that the kokhim tomb was the typical form of Jewish burial in Roman times.

This explains the changing Catholic posture regarding kokh tombs between the 30s and the 60s of the last century. In 1937-39, both Bagatti and Kopp identified tomb 29 as a kokh tomb, and Kopp considered the nearby tomb complex which we have already considered (T. 27) "a typical kokhim tomb."[133] By the 1960s, however, Kopp no longer uses the word "kokhim" in relation to tombs in the venerated area, and Bagatti no longer calls tomb 29 "*a forno*" and objects vehemently to the characterization of T. 27 as kokhim, as we have seen. Of course, his subsequent objection does not remove the fact that several tombs in the immediate vicinity are known with certainty to be kokhim. They include Tomb 72 (30 meters south of the CA), Tombs 73a and b under the Sisters of Nazareth Convent (75 meters to the west) and, of course, Tombs 27 and 29 under the CA itself.

The era of kokh tombs in Palestine extended into the fourth and perhaps even the fifth century after Christ. Thus, it is theoretically possible that the fourth century Count Joseph of Tiberias *was* buried in T. 29.[134] This man was a Christian convert from Judaism, allegedly commissioned by Emperor Constantine to construct churches in Palestine, including in Nazareth. Of course, were he buried at Nazareth, we have no record of the interment. But if this were the case, it would remove some of the difficulties presented by T. 29 as far as the tradition is concerned. A case (unlikely though it is) could be

---

[131] E. Klameth, *Die neutestamentlichen Lokaltraditionen Palästinas.* Vol. 1, Münster, 1914.

[132] Kopp 1939–40:89.

[133] This tomb is marked only in the oldest literature (Viaud 81).

[134] Kopp took a less sanguine view. "As long as this hypothesis lacks any historical validation," he writes, "it were better left out of consideration" (1939–40:90).

made that Jewish purity taboos would not apply, for the Count—having built a church at Nazareth—would have been buried on Christian property, not Jewish (we recall that the town was Jewish until VII CE). Also, the problem of contemporaneity with the relatives of Christ is removed—the tomb dates much later. Finally, the fact that it is kokhim in form does not present a problem, for the type was used into Byzantine times.

We shall consider the Count's story more closely in Chapter 6, as well as the theory that he built the first church in Nazareth. The Count was, however, not the only "later" candidate proposed for T. 29. Just outside the tomb is a mosaic in the floor bearing an epigraph in Greek letters: "Gift of Conon, deacon of Jerusalem."[135] This deacon probably lived in the fifth century (the date of the mosaic).[136] In his 1969 book, Bagatti links this deacon with another Conon who allegedly lived in the third century. However, the earlier Conon was legendary.[137] He is known only from a very late source, a tenth-century manuscript.[138] It relates that this Conon was a Christian martyr killed in Asia Minor in the reign of Decius (about 250 CE). At his trial, he claimed to be a relative of Jesus. This medieval claim allows Bagatti to suppose that the martyr had lived in Nazareth, and even at the very house which once was Mary's—namely, the spot under discussion.[139] James Strange also follows this line of reasoning: "In the 3d century the Christian martyr Conon from Nazareth of the family of Jesus was killed in Asia Minor (Bagatti 1969:16)."

In the fifth century, the Deacon of Jerusalem—also with the name Conon—was inspired to commission a mosaic at the site of the Annunciation, one which gave tangible witness to his devotion. That much is true. What is *not* true is the linking of him to an earlier, legendary Conon whom the Church considers to have been a relative of Jesus. This complex of inventive detail is transparently contrived in order to establish an early presence of Jesus' family in Nazareth. That has been a pre-eminent goal of the Church for a long time, perhaps even since the Middle Ages, as the tenth-century document mentioned above shows. Only an unbroken presence in Nazareth of Jesus' relatives, from generation to generation, can authenticate the holy sites. The invention of facts and people, the writing of fictitious documents to validate those inventions, the outright defense of such inventions, and the suppression

---

[135] *Exc.* 100.

[136] The earliest mosaics at the Church of the Annunciation, including the Conon mosaic, date to V CE (Taylor 243). Strange dates the mosaics one century too early (ABD 1050).

[137] See Taylor 243.

[138] Bagatti (*Exc.* 16, n. 26) offers the following bibliography: P. Hanozin, *Le Geste des Maryrs*, Paris 1935, pp. 134–38; *Analecta Bollandiana*, XVIII, p. 180; G. Garitte, *Le calendrier palestino-géorgien du Sinaiticus 34* (10th cent.), Paris 1958, p. 173.

[139] *Exc.* 16, 198-99. *Cf.* 100–102.

of documents and people who contradict those inventions—these have been major preoccupations of monks, prelates, and inquisitors through the ages.

Graves o/p

Figures:
Viaud 1910:81 "o/p" (fig. 36); Fig. 39 ("Tombeau dans le roc")
Kopp 1939–40 (JPOS 19, p. 113) Pl IX, "g–g"
Bagatti 1969 (No figure)

Discussion:
Viaud 1910:95
Kopp 1939–40 (JPOS 19, p. 93)
Bagatti 1969 (No mention)

Two graves ("*tombeaux*") were identified by Viaud. They are marked "o" and "p" in his figure 36, and are noted in *Illus.* 4. These graves are immediately south of the Chapel of the Angel and, like kokhim shafts, are parallel to one another. They are oriented perpendicularly to Tomb 27, which is only 7m to the northwest. This proximity, together with the alignment, suggests that T. 27 and graves o/p are related. They are certainly close enough to occupy two neighboring tomb chambers connected by a passage which has long since disappeared. We have examples of such multi-chambered kokh tombs elsewhere in Nazareth. Tomb 77, located about 400 m north of the CA (see *Illus. 5.2*), has three chambers oriented in a straight line and contained at least 24 kokhim.[140] Tomb K22, across the valley, had no less than four chambers, a round blocking stone ("rolling stone"), and an undetermined number of kokhim.[141] Finally, under the Sisters of Nazareth Convent, only 100 m west of the CA, are two kokh tomb chambers which were in all likelihood connected in antiquity. It also had a rolling stone.

Viaud writes that graves o/p are "in a rock-cut funerary chamber." Much had been damaged by his time, for a stairway existed here long ago. Kopp is not sure what to make of the two graves. "Surely," he writes, "they tell us something of the existence of the oldest structure and have undergone various changes through the ages, along with the basilica."[142] The graves are "at least 2 m under the old basilica," he adds, showing that this is the oldest stratum of the site. The implication is that the tombs preceded the agricultural installations, which are sometimes intrusive. This is an important observation for dating the relative chronology. The tombs apparently were first, followed by the agricultural installations. Even these latter betray different eras, for they occasionally intrude upon one another (*cf*. cisterns 43 and 44 in *Illus. 5.4*).

---

[140] This is Kopp's tomb no. 13. He discusses it with diagram at Kopp 1938:201.
[141] This is Bagatti's T. 71. It yielded approximately two dozen artefacts (*cf*. Chapter 6).
[142] Kopp 1839-40:93.

Conclusions

It is clear from the preceding pages that the venerated sites are located in the midst of a necropolis and, furthermore, that the site of the Annunciation is situated in a Roman tomb. Tomb 29 is a scant five meters east of Tomb 27, which in turn is less than 10m from graves o/p. All these burials abut the "Chapel of the Angel." It is probable that in Roman times they all belonged to a multi-chambered tomb complex, one no more elaborate than others in the basin.

Additional Roman Period tombs may have been in the immediate vicinity, as suggested by Meistermann and Mansur early in the twentieth century. However, one looks in vain in the standard Nazareth literature for any mention of burials in the venerated area. For example, in his popular *The Archaeology of the New Testament*, Jack Finegan offers a map with the tombs of the basin.[143] Not only are none noted in the venerated area, but even tombs 70 and 73 are omitted. The former lies only 30 m south of the CA. It has thirteen kokhim, yielded numerous artefacts from the Roman period, and has been extensively documented by Bagatti and others. The latter tomb is also of the kokh type and lies under the Sisters of Nazareth Convent, 100 m west of the CA. Finegan omits all tombs within a radius of 300 m of the CA.

Again, James Strange's article "Nazareth" in the *Anchor Bible Dictionary* (arguably the most referenced scholarly source on the site) mentions caves, a "Jewish-Christian synagogue," a "Jewish ritual bath," and "Herodian" tombs on the outskirts of the village—which, according to Strange, enjoyed a renaissance in the Hellenistic Period. It is difficult to imagine a portrait of the settlement farther from the truth.

The Church has asserted that habitations have existed continuously in the venerated area since the time of Abraham.[144] Conflicting scriptural traditions have resulted in confusion on the ground, as different traditions vied for "the truth" and established competing shrines. The imagination of pilgrim and scholar alike has been allowed free rein, so long as it conformed with catholic doctrine. For example, reading in the scriptures that Jesus preached in the Nazareth synagogue (Lk 4), one writer follows Bagatti and Strange, suggesting an unattested synagogue already in Roman times: "All this was part of an early church before Constantine's time, a church built on a synagogue plan."[145] No such early structure is known. It could not have been at the Church of the Annunciation, for the tradition has insisted that Mary lived there. She certainly did not live in a synagogue! (As we have seen, the locus was among tombs.) Elsewhere (*Exc.* 25, 233–34) Bagatti writes that the synagogue was "north of St. Joseph's church." Thus, he apparently proposes *two* ancient synagogues. All this is part of the confusion mentioned above,

---

[143] Finegan 1969:27; 1992:44.

as orthodoxy tries to reconcile tradition in opposition to empirical fact, often enough simply concluding what is convenient.

In insisting that Jesus' village existed in the vicinity of the Franciscan property, catholic doctrine requires a double displacement—in space and time. In space, because the village was in fact located on the valley floor; in time, because it came into existence in the second century of our era. Furthermore, the Roman tombs conclusively show that no one lived on the hillside or in the venerated area while the settlement was Jewish, that is, until the seventh century.[144]

It would appear that the tradition has fallen victim to the ancient scriptures it reveres, which relate that Jesus' town was on a mountain. Long ago the early pilgrims embraced the idea and, finding grottos on the slope of the Nebi Sa'in, they chose a cave as the dwelling of Mary and as the site of the Annunciation. Thus, the fourth century pilgrim Egeria was shown "a big and very splendid cave in which [*Mary*] lived."[145] Such legends are understandable.

But they are not true.

---

[144] Kopp (1938): 215.
[145] Pet. Diac. *Lib*. T., quoted in Wilkinson 1981:193.

Chapter Six

Nazareth and Nazara
(70 CE–337 CE)

Between the Revolts

Chronology 60 CE–135 CE
Contested dates and/or events are italicized.

CE

60	*Martyrdom of Paul*	[Koester II:104]
62	*Martyrdom of James the Just*	[Schürer I:ii.187]
64	Nero's persecution of Christians accused of setting fire to Rome	
66	Beginning of the First Jewish War	
68	Destruction of Qumran	
70	Destruction of Jerusalem by Titus, including the Temple	
73	Roman capture of Masada; final end of hostilities	
79	Eruption of Mt. Vesuvius, destruction of Pompeii	
c. 70–130	Establishment of Nazareth	
c. 95	*Persecution under Domitian*	[Grant 79]
115–117	Jewish revolt in Cyrene, Cyprus, and Egypt	
	Ignatius writes letters en route to Rome and martyrdom	
132–135	Second Jewish War	

Chronology 135 CE–337 CE

144	Marcion expelled from Rome; Valentinus teaches
157	Montanus teaches
160	Justin, "Dialog with Trypho"
c. 177	Martyrdom of Christians in Lyons; Tatian's "Diatessaron"; Pantaenus visits India and then establishes Catechetical school at Alexandria
c. 220	Julius Africanus mentions the villages of "Nazara and Cochaba." This is probably the first reference to Nazareth not based in scripture (quoted in Eusebius, *Hist.* I.7)
231	Origen banished from Alexandria, establishes Caesarea school
250	Persecution under Decius
303	Emperor Diocletian designates Feb. 23 as date for the "termination of Christianity"; persecution follows
307	Accession of pro-Christian Constantine in the East
309	Diocletian erects a colossal statue to the sun god at Sirmium on the Danube; Constantine also worships the sun
311	Edict of Milan extends toleration to Christians
312	Under Christian banners, Constantine is victorious at battle of Milvian bridge; embraces Christianity
319	Arius champions subordinationist teaching
324	Constantine sole emperor
325	Constantine convenes the Council of Nicaea
c. 335	Joseph of Tiberias possibly builds a Christian shrine in Nazareth
337	Death of Constantine

THE MYTH OF NAZARETH

After a prolonged siege and aided by deep divisions within the defending Jewish population, the Romans under Titus took the city of Jerusalem in September, 70 CE. The temple was in flames, and the invaders systematically exterminated the survivors before razing the city to the ground—leaving only three gates and part of the wall standing.[1] Titus celebrated his victory in Caesarea before returning to Rome, but the war was by no means over as rebels controlled much of the countryside, including several fortresses. It took three more years for the Romans to reduce these obstinate pockets of resistance, culminating in the legendary mass suicide at Masada (April, 73 CE).

Following the war, the emperor Vespasian made Palestine "a private possession, and the taxes levied went into his own purse." Schürer continues:

> The inhabitants of Palestine became impoverished, and by the seven years' war their number had been terribly reduced. A Jewish magistracy, of the kind formerly possessed, no longer existed. The one gathering point which still remained for the people was the law. Around this they now gathered with anxious and scrupulous faithfulness, and with the indomitable hope that some day, under an established civil government, and even among the nations of the world, it would come again to have a recognized place and practical authority.[2]

After the First Jewish War a series of governors administered Judea (now a separate Roman province) from Caesarea. The depopulated and completely destroyed city of Jerusalem functioned as little more than headquarters of the tenth legion Fretensis. Pagan cities were established, such as Flavia Neapolis near Shechem in Samaria. A center of Jewish revival appeared at Jamnia (Jabne) near the coast, largely due to the efforts of the Pharisee Johanan ben Zakkai, an elderly merchant and judge. Jamnia had been a Jewish town since Maccabean times, and now that the Pharisees were in the ascendancy it was quickly made a center of Rabbinic studies. Johanan established an informal council there which became known as the Sanhedrin, and its president the Rabban. The council "was gradually recognized by the Romans as exercising control over the religious affairs of Judaea, and even of the Dispersion as well."[3] Jamnia maintained a preeminent position in the years between the two Jewish revolts, after which Sepphoris (Diocaesarea) and Tiberias in the Galilee assumed dominance.

The Pharisees and Rabbis received the monetary contributions formerly given to the temple of Jerusalem.[4] They assumed the former authority of

---

[1]   Schürer I:2.247.
[2]   Schürer I:255–56.
[3]   M. Grant 208.
[4]   Schürer I:2.277

266

the Sadducees and priests, and "formed now even more exclusively and unrestrictedly than before the rank of the highest authorities among the people."[5] Their hegemony came just at the time that the "Nazorean" heresy was appearing in Judaism. The Pharisees of Jamnia included an imprecation against such heretics in a prayer to be recited by all Jews thrice daily. Variously called the *Amidah, Shemoneh Esreh,* or simply *Tefillah* ("prayer"), it consisted of eighteen blessings—nineteen when we include the twelfth against the *Notsrim* or *minim* (various wordings are extant), added in the time of Rabbi Gamaliel II (*c.* 100 CE):[6]

> 12. To Notsrim let there be no hope, and let all workers of wickedness perish as in a moment; and let all of them speedily be cut off; and humble them speedily in our days. Blessed are You, O Lord, who destroys enemies and humbles tyrants.[7]

Scribal animosity towards the emerging heresy is amply reciprocated in the New Testament, reflecting a state of affairs that existed not before 70 CE but towards the end of the first century. In the Christian scriptures Jesus often interacts bitingly with haughty scribes and Pharisees in the Galilee, something hardly likely before the war. There is some evidence of early postwar pharisaic activity in the Galilee: Johanan ben Zakkai himself sojourned for some years in Arav (Arab), about 15 km north of Nazareth, where various legal questions were propounded for his decision."[8] M. Grant writes that "henceforward Galilee, rather than the ancient core of Israel, was destined to become the centre of Jewish population, and it was there in particular that synagogues and schools began to multiply."[9]

The Mishna ("Repetition" or "Instruction") was begun at Jamnia and completed in the Galilee a century later under Rabban Judah the Prince. Other pertinent non-Christian writings of the interwar decades include the *Jewish*

---

[5]   Schürer I:2.274. *Cf.* The New Testament expressions "the scribes of the Pharisees," "the scribes of the people," "scribes and Pharisees," (Mk 2:16; Mt 12:38, *etc.*). The great improbability that scribes went up to Galilee "from Jerusalem" (Mk 3:22) will be considered elsewhere. In general, the evangelists fail to reconcile prewar and postwar settings for Jesus' activity.

[6]   Schürer II:2.88 (text pp. 85–87).

[7]   The original wording may have contained the word *Notsrim* (De Boer 251). In the mid-second century Justin Martyr was already familiar with the *birkath ha-minim,* which he interprets as directed against believers in Christ (Trypho *c.* 16). Later, Epiphanius and Jerome know versions of the imprecation against "Nazoreans" and "Nazarenes" respectively. The latter word is also found in a ninth-century version of the Amidah discovered in the Cairo Geniza (Heinemann 3336).

[8]   Schürer II:1,366.

[9]   M. Grant 209.

THE MYTH OF NAZARETH

War of Josephus Flavius (completed in Rome 75–79 CE) and his *Antiquities* of *the Jews* (*c*. 93–94), written perhaps a decade before the Gospel of Luke.[10]

In 115 CE, while the emperor Trajan was occupied in the East, multitudes of Jews in Egypt and Cyrene (Libya) rose up and, "as if driven along by the wild spirit of revolution, began to make riots against the non-Jewish inhabitants of the land."[11] The protracted disturbances— which amounted to a war—were suppressed only by Hadrian upon his accession in 117 CE. This emperor "looked with contempt upon all foreign superstitions" (Schürer). In 130 CE he founded Aelia Capitolina at the site of Jerusalem, now a thoroughly pagan city (Jews had been forbidden to enter the premises of the holy city since 70 CE). Furthermore, Hadrian erected a temple to Jupiter on the site of the Jewish temple. According to Dio Cassius, this last provocation led directly to the Second Jewish Revolt.[12] Spartian adds that a Roman prohibition was enacted which forbade circumcision. This is tantamount to an attempted annihilation of the Jewish faith.[13]

Nazoreans and Pauline Christians did not participate in the Second Revolt. The former may have been pacifists, while the latter acknowledged Jesus Christ (not Simon bar-Kosiba) as the true messiah. Justin Martyr and Eusebius testify that Jesus-followers were particularly persecuted by the Jews on account of their noncooperation. The Jews managed to liberate Jerusalem before Julius Severus—a distinguished Roman general sent from Britain— quashed the rebellion. The rebels resorted to mountain fastnesses, but they were all eventually exterminated. Dio Cassius writes that fifty fortresses and 985 villages were destroyed, and that 580,000 Jews fell in battle. "All Judea was well-nigh a desert."[14]

The Bar Kochba revolt was also very costly for the Romans. So great were his losses that in his letter to the Senate Hadrian omitted the customary introductory formula, "I and the army are well." However, unlike the situation in 70 CE, Jerusalem was not totally destroyed, for the Romans had plans for the pagan city of Aelia Capitolina. A temple to Jupiter was erected on the temple mount. Several writers tell us that the Jewish population was driven out of the city,[15] and, indeed, no Jew was permitted to set foot in it under penalty of death. The forced exodus may have some significance for

---

[10]   Koester 1990:337, and H. Schreckenberg, "Flavius Josephus und die Lukanischen Schriften," in *Wort in der Zeit: Neutestamenliche Studien,* ed. W. Haubeck. Brill: 1980.

[11]   Eusebius, *Eccl. Hist.* IV.2

[12]   Dio Cassius lxix.12.

[13]   Spartian, Hadrian, 14 (discussed at Schürer I.2.291).

[14]   Dio Cassius, lxix.14

[15]   Eusebius, *Demonstratio evangel.* VI.18.10; *Eccl. Hist.* IV.6; Dio Cassius lxix.12.

the settlement of the priestly course of Hapizzez in Nazareth, which occurred sometime after the Second Jewish Revolt (see below).

Hadrian's successor, Antoninus Pius, rescinded the ban on circumcision, but even into the fourth century no Jew was allowed into Jerusalem except on one day out of the year (ninth of Ab, the day of the city's destruction) for the purpose of mourning.[16]

The Roman Evidence

In Chapter 4, those artefacts from the Nazareth basin which might date before *c.* 100 CE were reviewed. Special attention was paid to the oil lamps, which are particularly valuable for dating purposes. Together with the fact that kokh tombs appeared in the Galilee only after *c.* 50 CE, it became clear that the settlement of Nazareth did not yet exist at the turn of the era.

Further, we determined that it is not possible to envisage a named settlement of Nazareth before *c.* 100 CE (Chapter 4, p. 206). After the village came into being it grew rapidly, as is attested by the many tombs and a wealth of pottery and oil lamps datable to Middle Roman times. We shall now review the material record of Nazareth in the first centuries of our era.

The structural evidence

The post-Iron Age Nazareth tombs, as shown in Chapter 5, *Illus. 5.2,* are all of the kokh or later types. There are at least twenty kokh tombs[17] spread widely throughout the basin. Other similar tombs probably existed under the venerated area (Chapter 5, pp. 249–52) as well as on the side of the Nebi Sa'in. A comprehensive summary of the Nazareth tombs is given in *Appendix 4.* The total number of individual kokh shafts is impressive, amounting to well over one hundred. Were one to include the completely destroyed kokhim, the number of burials would probably double. Each kokh, of course, was used multiple times.[18]

Kuhnen writes: "Remarkably obvious is the persistence [*Fortleben*] of the kokh type in Galilee…"[19] Nevertheless, two other forms of burial continued

---

[16]   Schürer I.2.320. For the subsequent history of Nazareth, see the summary in Appendix 4.

[17]   T. 27 and 29 (under the CA) are counted as one tomb, as are the two kokh chambers under the Dames de Nazareth convent.

[18]   Contrary to general practice, in T. 70 several kokhim were found with multiple skeletons (Kopp 1938:196). No ossuaries survive from the basin (Kopp 1938:205), though ossuary fragments were found not far away at the "Fright" (Chapter 4, pp. 187*f*)

[19]   Kuhnen 257. He notes on the same page that kokh tombs continued in use through late antiquity.

side-by-side with this type. (a) The shelf grave (*Bankgrab*) was simply a niche carved lengthwise into a wall of the chamber, forming a shelf on which the body was placed. (b) In a further development, the shelf was dug out to form a sunken pit in which the body was placed. This is called the trough grave (*Troggrab*). In both the shelf and trough grave, the top of the niche was often rounded or bowed (hence, the German names *Bogenbankgrab* and *Bogentroggrab*) giving these forms of burial a common name: *arcosolium*.

Kuhnen writes that the trough grave became very popular and continued to be hewn as late as the fifth century. However, the kokh tomb was by far the preferred form at Nazareth. Both trough and shelf tombs are hardly represented. K 14 is a trough grave, and from Kopp's description K 20 appears to have arcosolia.[20] In the rubble of the latter two hollowed out niches were identified, one measuring only 80 cm in length. This small grave, perhaps incomplete, may have been designed for an infant or for the placement of an ossuary.

Unfortunately, Bagatti and Kopp do not offer the plan of some of the tombs at Nazareth, and in many cases the damaged state of those recovered does not permit certainty regarding the form of all their chambers. It is clear, however, that the kokh was by far the town's favored form of burial.

Other than tombs, the structural evidence from Nazareth consists of virtually undatable agricultural installations, as well as masonry remains from the ecclesiastical structures, which date to the fourth century and beyond.[21]

The many underground passageways which link the agricultural installations under the venerated area (*cf.* Chapter 5, *Illus.* 5.5) have given rise to the theory that some may have been associated with secret hideaway complexes, known from other places in Palestine.[22] This theory has in turn suggested to a few authors of the secondary literature that the Nazareth complexes are evidence of habitation in the basin during the First Jewish Revolt. However, most of the Judean underground complexes have been dated to the Second Revolt (132–135 CE), as has the first Galilean complex to be published (near H. Ruma).[23] In addition, our review of the material evidence (Chapters 4 and 5) shows that the lowest stratum under the venerated area was funerary. It was only later that the agricultural installations and associated passageways were hewn, which argues against a I CE dating for them. Finally, we note that the Nazareth settlement was only just beginning in late I CE, and

---

[20]   Kopp 1938:201–02, 204.

[21]   Chapter 4, pp. 203*ff*; and below.

[22]   See M. Aviam, "Secret Hideaway Complexes in the Galilee," Chapter 12 of Aviam 2004. These underground warrens are difficult to date, since they have long ago been robbed of remains and since material from upper levels can penetrate to the lower chambers.

[23]   Aviam 124.

it is hardly likely that enough people were present already in 70 CE to hew passageways for defense or any other purpose. Even the first kokh tombs were hardly so early, but appear to date between the two Jewish revolts. In sum, whatever use these passageways served, the weight of material evidence from the basin points to their creation in II CE and thereafter.

The movable finds from Roman-Byzantine Nazareth

These come primarily from four tombs, but there are also many artefacts whose provenance is unknown. Naturally, most of the evidence comes from the venerated area, where systematic excavations have been conducted. Bagatti devotes almost fifty pages of his *Excavations* to objects from that area belonging to "the Hellenistic Roman and Byzantine Periods" (pp. 272–318). We have seen that there are no finds from Hellenistic times (Chapter 3), and have reviewed those which *may* date before 70 CE (Chapter 4). Having determined that no material can with certainty be dated before 100 CE,[24] we shall now continue our review of the Nazareth evidence, focussing on the Middle Roman and Early Byzantine periods.

A substantial body of factual information regarding the material evidence is tabulated in appendices at the end of this book, including *Appendix 4*, "The Nazareth tombs," which lists the post-Iron Age tombs discovered in the basin, noting those which yielded artefacts, and *Appendix 5*, "Independent datings of Nazareth lamps and pottery," which offers the opinions of three lamp and pottery specialists: (a) R. Rosenthal and R. Sivan, who date a score of Nazareth oil lamps in their comprehensive catalogue, *Ancient Lamps in the Schloessinger Collection* (1978); (b) F. Fernandez, who dates an equal number of lamps as well as a score of pottery artefacts from Roman times in his monograph, *Ceramica Comun Romana de la Galilea* (1983).

A note of caution is in order regarding Fernandez' work, which offers a number of early and unsubstantiated datings contradicted sometimes by Bagatti, sometimes by Rosenthal and Sivan, and sometimes internally by Fernandez himself.[25] The Spaniard often dates material found in Nazareth kokh tombs as early as BCE times, which is not possible as the kokh did not arrive in the Galilee until *c.* 50 CE. Florentino Fernandez is a protégé of Father Stanislao Loffreda, whose work at Capernaum and elsewhere (which also backdates a good deal of evidence) has come under growing criticism. In the prologue to his book, Fernandez writes (p. 7): "We owe our initiation into the understanding of Roman pottery to professor S. Loffreda, of the Institute of the Flagellation (Jerusalem)." The work of Fernandez is presented here simply because he itemizes a goodly number of Nazareth artefacts. In

---

24 Chapter 4, p. 206.
25 *E.g.*, the material in Tombs 70 and 71. (See below.)

Appendix 5 (B), in each case where Fernandez offers an anomalous early dating, a footnote attests to the fact. It may be noted here that the Spaniard also itemizes a great deal of "unpublished" (*inedito*)[26] Nazareth material not used in these pages. This material ostensibly was available to him while he was in residence at the Franciscan monastery in Nazareth researching his book. Unfortunately, Fernandez does not offer museum number, catalogue information, or any way to locate these "new" objects, which would permit independent verification of their existence and characteristics. Thus, what he writes does not constitute publication as regards these unpublished artefacts, but what amounts to unverifiable claims in their regard. This is particularly germane to our discussion, for Fernandez claims extraordinarily early dates for some of these unpublished objects, implausibly stretching the period of their use well back into the first century BCE (in contradiction to the views of other specialists). Even were every one of Fernandez' early chronological claims honored, however, the main thesis of this book would not be in jeopardy, for his early timespans invariably extend to include part of the period of kokh tomb use, *i.e.*, post-50 CE. What this means is that one could honor all of Fernandez' improbable claims and quite adequately defend the thesis that people resettled the basin after the First Jewish War. To proceed along these lines, however, would give the Spaniard more than his due, for he is using material which cannot be admitted as evidence, and is drawing extraordinary conclusions therefrom.

Evidence from the tombs

Appendix 4 shows that four tombs yielded artefacts. They are tombs 70, 71, 72, as well as a tomb not known to Bagatti, excavated near the crest of the Nebi Sa'in (El Batris St.) and published in a short report in the *Israel Exploration Journal*.

• ***Tomb 70.*** By far the most numerous finds were found in T. 70, located only about 30 meters from the southern wall of the Church of the Annunciation.[27] This unichambered tomb has 13 kokhim. It yielded 17 oil lamps. Of those, 7 are bow-spouted, including 4 "Darom" lamps dating between the two Jewish revolts.[28] The remaining lamps (see Appendix 2) are later and include five "round lamps with decorated discus," dating to II–III CE.[29] Of interest is

---

[26]   The unpublished pieces in question are the following: [A] "Inedito, excav. 1955": 13 jars (T 1.2, 1.3, 1.8, 1.10); 3 jugs (T 9.3, 9.5); 7 cooking pots (T 10.3, 10.4, 10.5, 10.6b, 14.1, 14.2). [B] "[*Inedito*] superficie" (*i.e.*, presumably found on the surface of the ground): 1 jar (T 1.6); 1 pan (T 15.3).

[27]   Marked "K" in Chapter 5, *Illus. 5.3*. Finds of T. 70 & 71 are diagrammed at *Exc*. Fig. 192.

[28]   Chapter 4, *Illus, 4.3*.

[29]   Discussion at Rosenthal & Sivan 85. Fernandez L 9.1c.

that the discus around the filling holes had apparently been broken out in antiquity. These surfaces held pictorial representations, which would have been offensive to religious Jews. One lamp (*Exc.* Fig. 192:12) is dated to III–IV CE,[30] while an Islamic lamp (Fig. 192:16) was found outside the entrance of the tomb and does not belong to the assemblage.[31]

The remainder of material from T. 70 consists of two pots, a pan, a terracotta juglet, and a few glass bottles. This material ranges from *c.* 50 CE–150 CE (pot #18) into early Byzantine times (pan #19), which gives a good idea of the life span of this tomb.[32]

• **Tomb 71 (=K 22).** This is the largest tomb complex in the basin, located to the east of the basin floor. We have no plan or description beyond the fact that the tomb contained four chambers (one still sealed and unexplored). The complex yielded 24 artefacts, mostly small objects of glass and metal (beads, rings). A half dozen larger objects include three jugs, a pot, and two vases.[33] The objects date *c.* 70 CE–*c.* 300 CE, that is, to the Middle Roman Period. This was noted by Fernandez, who offers the following overall conclusion:

> Two other assemblages merit particular attention: those of tombs 70 and 71, now in the museum of the Franciscan Convent of Nazareth. Their homogeneity and characteristics, supported by a fine collection of lamps and glass bottles, point to [*aconsejan*] a rather precise date, very probably not inferior to [*inferior al*] the Middle Roman Period.[34]

Presumably, *inferior al* means "earlier than" (as D. Hamidovic understood the phrase),[35] but "later than" would not significantly change the meaning, for all the artefacts in these two tombs may date to Middle Roman times. This conforms perfectly with the general *terminus post quem* for the oil lamps and kokhim tombs at Nazareth, determined in Chapter Four, *i.e.*, the latter half of the first century CE.

• **Tomb 72.** This is the "Richmond" tomb, located about 375m south of the CA. It was apparently not robbed in antiquity, and at the time of discovery yielded six oil lamps (repeatedly mislabeled "Hellenistic" in the literature—see Chapter 3), as well as numerous small objects (mostly beads), and several

---

[30] Rosenthal & Sivan No. 402 and p. 99. Fernandez L 15.

[31] *Cf.* Rosenthal & Sivan pp. 129*ff.*

[32] The pot is Fernandez type T.10.6a; the juglet his type T 8.3 (75–275 CE). For the pan ("later") see *Exc.* 287, bottom.

[33] Fernandez itemizes two jugs (T. 8.4) and one pot (T. 10.5) on pp. 115 and 119.

[34] …muy probablemente no inferior al P. Romano Medio. (Fernandez 28.)

[35] Hamidovic 99, n. 32.

glass vessels. The oil lamps are shown in Chapter 3, *Illus. 3.1*, and consist of the following (listed in chronological order):

Lower left – Bow-spouted oil lamp, Smith Type 2 (*c.* 25 CE–*c.* 135 CE)
Lower right – Bow-spouted Darom lamp (*c.* 70 CE–*c.* 135 CE)[36]
Upper left & right – Round mould-made, decorated discus (50–III CE)[37]
Lower center right – Wide neck, small wick hole, handle (IV–early V CE)[38]
Lower center left – Wide nozzle end flanked by ridges (IV–V CE)[39]

The remainder of the assemblage contains some interesting objects, including a Phoenician glass pendant with lion and star (date uncertain). Several glass vessels were also in the tomb. Though Richmond does not attempt a dating of them, Bagatti's observations regarding other glass objects from his excavations (*Exc.* 310–314, Fig. 237) uniformly point to later Roman times.

• *El Batris tomb.* This tomb, excavated in 1995, yielded sparse finds which included a bow-spouted lamp, jug, juglet, store jar, and a bowl. Smaller objects included 76 glass and stone beads. In a short prose summary, the excavator (Zvi Yavor) writes:

> The sparse ceramic finds included fragments of a cooking pot, a juglet and a store jar (Fig. 59:1–3), as well as of a bowl and a Herodian lamp. Seventy-six glass and stone beads, some decorated, were recovered, as well as a bronze spatula (length 13.5 cm) and fragments of three glass candlestick bottles (Fig. 59:4–5). These finds provide a date for the burial cave in the 1st century CE." (Yavor 1998)

The bow-spouted ("Herodian") lamp, of which we have no further information, cannot predate *c.* 50 CE since it was found in a kokh tomb. It is questionable whether the recovered artefacts permit such a precise dating ("1st century CE") as Yavor alleges. In any case, this kokh tomb dates from the latter part of I CE. The archaeologist's closing statement may be more appropriate: "A rock-cut corner (13), recorded 6 m east of Cave 11, which may belong to another burial cave, contained sparse potsherds of the Roman

[36] Rosenthal & Sivan p. 85 (upper left) contains two typographical errors (herewith corrected in bold). The text should read: "Nazareth—QDAP 1 (1932), Pl. XXXIV lower row **right**; Bagatti (1969), pp. 239 and fig. 192:7–**9** on p. 238."

[37] Rosenthal & Sivan (RS) p. 85, dating after Kahane and p. 89, bottom of rt. col.

[38] Exact typology uncertain. *Cf.* RS nos. 412 and 514; Goodenough Fig. 268:2

[39] Sellers & Baramki type VIII (S& B, p. 40, no. 74). This is similar to a lamp which Rosenthal and Sivan consider of a "local tradition" and difficult to date due to the lack of sufficient dated contexts. *Cf.* their no. 512a (RS p. 124).

period." Given the limited data, the later Roman period is as far as we can press the chronology of these two neighboring chambers.

Non-funerary finds

On pages 272–318 of *Excavations*, Bagatti considers in turn: Big jars (273); Bottles, pots, pitchers, jugs (277); Cooking pots (282); Pans (285); Plates, bowls, cups (288); Large and small basins (296); Clay lamps (299); Glass ware (310); Metal objects and scarabs (314); Stone objects (315–18).

Nine passages primarily concerned with the dating of all this material can be isolated, but the datings Bagatti offers are unusually tentative and quite vague, rarely giving a century and generally restricted to eras, *e.g.*, "Roman" (unspecified), "later Roman," or "Byzantine." One of the archaeologist's favorite expressions is "the period of the kokhim tombs," which for him signifies I BCE–I CE.[41] However, we have seen that the kokh tomb came to the Galilee in mid-I CE. Thus, the many artefacts which the Italian associates with these tombs are evidence of Middle Roman to Early Byzantine times.

Because the archaeologist is so reserved as regards chronological information, it is not difficult to tabulate the datings he furnishes with regard to the several hundred objects treated. These will be found in *Appendix 6*. The oil lamps are treated separately in *Appendix 5*.

A brief review of the appendices confirms that (1) Roman Nazareth had a wealth of kokh tombs (*Appendix 4*); (2) the earliest datable evidence, the bow-spouted oil lamps, have been independently dated from *c.* 25 CE onwards (*Appendix 5*); (3) excepting the oil lamps, very little material can be dated to I CE (*Appendix 6*); (4) the material greatly increases in II CE and throughout later Roman-Byzantine times (*Appendix 6*).

The Hapizzez and the Caesarea Inscription

In 1962, in the ruins of the ancient synagogue of Caesarea Maritima, three fragments of a gray marble plaque were found dating to the third or fourth centuries of our era.[42] The fragments contain Hebrew letters and form

---

[40] *Exc.* pages 137, 276, 280, 285, 294, 298, 309, 312, and 314.

[41] *Cf.* Chapter 4, p. 164.

[42] The primary report in English is Avi-Yonah:1962. It furnishes a description of the marble slab with diagrams and a reconstruction of the full inscription, as well as earlier bibliography (his notes 4 and 5). For Hebrew bibliography see: M. Avi-Yonah, "The Caesarea Inscription of the 24 Priestly Courses," Eretz Israel (1964), pp. 24–28; J. Naveh, ed. On Stone and Mosaic: The Aramaic and Hebrew Inscriptions from Ancient Synagogues, (1978), 87–88; H. Eshel, "A Fragmentary Inscription of the Priestly Courses?" Tarbits (1991) 61:159–61. Further Hebrew bibliography on the priestly courses is found in Fine 1996:148, n. 64.

part of a much larger inscription whose nature can be identified from finds elsewhere. The inscription lists the locations to which each of the twenty-four courses (*mishmarot*) of Jewish priests[43] were sent sometime after Hadrian's banishment of all Jews from Jerusalem.

One of the fragments contains the letters *nun-tsade-resh-tav*, "Natsareth." The recovered pieces allow us to reconstruct the locations of the seventeenth to twentieth courses:

The 17th course Hezir MAMLIAH
The 18th course Hapitses NATSARETH
The 19th course Pethahiah AKHLAH Arab
The 20th course Ezekiel MIGDAL Nunaiya

This is the oldest non-Christian epigraphic evidence for the settlement of Nazareth, and the only mention so far known of the place from a synagogue inscription.[44] Nazareth has the revealing spelling nun-tsade-resh-tav.[45]

The inscription may date as early as *c.* 300 CE, when the Caesarea synagogue was built.[46] On the other hand it could have been created much later, for such inscriptions from Palestinian synagogues were made as late as the eighth century CE.[47]

After its discovery the secondary literature quickly began using the inscription as evidence of a first-century CE Nazareth, on the theory that the Hapizzez (also spelled *Hapitses*, *Hapises*) removed to the settlement after the First Jewish Revolt. More recent reports in mainline and conservative publications continue to promote this thesis, such as the following:

> Testimony to a town at Nazareth in the first century A.D. comes from fragments of an inscription containing the name Nazareth in Hebrew, found in the Hebrew University excavation in Caesarea in 1962.... This transfer of course to Galilee must have occurred after A.D. 70.[48]

---

[43] For the twenty four courses of priests, *cf.* I Chr 24:7–19; Neh 12:1-21.

[44] Avi-Yonah 1962:139 n.6.

[45] In the Greek New Testament and in the Christian tradition, the town's name is always spelled with *zeta*, which corresponds to Semitic *zain*, not *tsade* (one sibilant is voiced, the other voiceless). Regarding "Nazareth" and cognates, this linguistic non-correspondence between the Hellenistic and Semitic traditions has long been noted by scholars. (See "Nazarêne-Nazôraios" in Kittel, p. 879). We shall revisit this issue in a second volume.

[46] Fine dates it broadly IV–VII CE (Fine:1996:171).

[47] OEANE, "Synagogue Inscriptions," p. 114. This article contains an extensive bibliography of the Caesarea find in several languages. One catalogue dates the Caesarea plaque "fourth to seventh century C.E." (Fine:171).

[48] NIDBA:330. Similarly Strange in "Nazareth," ABD 1050 col. 1, and OEANE 114; Mimouni 1998:220; *etc.*

However, no northward exodus is known after the First Jewish Revolt. In fact, despite the general destruction of the war and the razing of the temple, the priests still hoped for a revival of the holy city:

> The overthrow of [*Jerusalem in the First Jewish Revolt*] led also to the suppression of the sacrificial worship, and therewith the gradual recession of the priesthood from public life. This was only carried out by degrees. It could not for a long time be believed that the disastrous circumstances in which the people were placed were to continue. It seemed to be only a question of the time when the priests should be able again to resume their services. Naturally, all dues were exacted after as well as before the catastrophe... [49]

After the Second Jewish Revolt, on the other hand, "the defeated Jews were expelled from the territory of Jerusalem, renamed Aelia Capitolina by the emperor Hadrian" (Crossan). [50] Jews were not permitted to return to the city for many generations, probably until after the Arab conquests of VII CE. Schürer remarks:

> In order to make permanent the purely heathen character of [*Jerusalem*], the Jews still residing there were driven out, and heathen colonists settled in their stead. No Jew was allowed thereafter to enter the territory of the city; if any one should be discovered there he was put to death... At the south gate of the city the figure of a swine is said to have been engraved. The chief religious worship of the city was that of the Capitoline Jupiter, to whom a temple was erected on the site of the former Jewish temple. [51]

The Hapizzez could have gone up to Nazareth several generations after the revolt:

> The priestly division of Hapizzez is listed as located at Nazareth in the Late Roman inscription found at Caesarea. As pointed out above, assuming there is historical reliability in this tradition, the date of resettlement may well be well into the second (or even the third) century. (Horsley:110)

Nevertheless, the general exodus from Jerusalem and from Judea immediately after the Bar Cochba revolt must take precedence in our estimation for the transfer of the Hapizzez to Nazareth. The Caesarea inscription offers no support for first-century CE habitation at Nazareth.

---

[49]   Schürer I.2.272.

[50]   D. Trifon, "Did the Priestly Courses (Mishmarot) Transfer from Judaea to the Galilee After the Bar-Kokhba Revolt?" Tarbits (1989–90), 59:1–2, pp. 77-93. See also Crossan, Chp.1; Horsley:110 (cited in text); Koester, I:410; Taylor 1993:225.

[51]   Schürer I.2:315–317.

THE MYTH OF NAZARETH

The inscription also reveals that in Middle Roman times Nazareth was strictly Jewish, for a priestly course would not have settled in a small mixed town of both Jews and gentiles. Similarly, is hardly likely that the Hapizzez would have settled in a place that was a center of *minim*. In other words, this inscription is powerful evidence against the Catholic doctrine that Jewish Christians had a presence in Nazareth from the time of Christ.[52] Indeed, it shows us that the settlement had nothing to do with the subsequent growth of Christianity.

Count Joseph of Tiberias

The narrative of Epiphanius

After Emperor Constantine embraced Christianity, he rewarded an influential Jew who converted to Christianity with the rank of "Count" (*comes*), and authorized him to build churches in Galilee. One of the towns in which the Count may have built a church was Nazareth.

Our information regarding the wealthy Count Joseph of Tiberias comes exclusively from an extended and rambling narrative embedded in chapter 30 (on the Ebionites) of Epiphanius' *Panarion*, written about the year 375. Epiphanius was a younger contemporary of Count Joseph, and met him about 358 CE[53] at the latter's sumptuous home in Scythopolis (Beth Shan). At that time bitter factionalism was raging in the Church between the Nicene (orthodox) and Arian factions. Arianism was on the ascendant, and at the Council of Milan in 355 it was reinstated by Emperor Constantius II as the official state religion. As a major protagonist of the Nicene faction, Epiphanius was in Scythopolis with a few others of similar persuasion in order to receive direction from Bishop Eusebius of Vercelli, a Nicene activist from Italy who was now in jail there. Bishop Eusebius was himself at the heart of the Arian controversy. While in Italy he had been asked by the bishop of Rome (the pope) to petition emperor Constantius for a decision on the Arian question. The emperor duly convened the Council of Milan but—to the chagrin of Eusebius and the pope—its verdict went against the Nicene (though ultimately victorious) faction. Bishops throughout Christendom were forthwith required to condemn Nicene doctrine. Upon his refusal, Bishop Eusebius was exiled to Scythopolis. This was a very Arian town. According to Epiphanius, only two Nicene Christians were to be found in the whole city: Bishop Eusebius

---

[52]   On this, see Taylor 1993.

[53]   Pritz 42. Goranson 336 dates the meeting to "about the year 353."

and Joseph of Tiberias. To further rub salt in the wound, Eusebius' jailer was himself an Arian bishop named Patrophilus. Bishop Eusebius refused to accept food from Arians, and (so Epiphanius tells us) he recounted with pride that he almost starved to death on more than one occasion.

The great issue at stake was the nature of Jesus Christ. Was he essentially separate from the Creator of the Universe (and thus by nature fundamentally related to the rest of us)? This was the Arian view though, unlike the Gnostics, Arius did not maintain that Jesus was thoroughly human—a perfected man. Rather, Arius considered Jesus a demigod, "neither fully God nor fully man" in the words of Paul Tillich.[54] On the other hand, Bishop Athanasius and the Nicene faction considered Christ wholly other in nature, sharing none of the mortality and imperfection of this world. Jesus was God's inimitable and unique intervention in history, *the* only-begotten Son of God, come down to save those who believe in this very proposition. Eventually, expediency recommended a fusion of the two views: Jesus Christ was mysteriously both man and God: "Jesus" reflected the human aspect, "Christ" the divine aspect. This became the new doctrine of the Great Church. Those who endorsed it were saved. All others were damned.

Count Joseph was already an old man of seventy[55] when he hosted Epiphanius and his co-religionists. Bishop Eusebius of Vercelli was also in attendance that day. Twenty years would pass before Epiphanius wrote down his memories of the meeting, and this is only one reason to suspect the particulars of the extended narrative. Anyone familiar with Epiphanius' writings knows how prone to exaggeration, suspect, or plain wrong the church father is on a multitude of points. In this case, it does not add to our confidence that Epiphanius himself admits he is not sure of details, and may well have confused certain things due to passage of time.[56] The same problem that affected the amanuensis had also affected his narrator, for in 358 CE the Count himself was retelling events that occurred decades before—"in the latter days of Constantine," that is, prior to 337 CE.[57] Faulty recollections are, however, but one consideration when evaluating whether and where Joseph built churches. In relating the Count's sometimes fantastic, lurid, and ever boastful stories, we may wonder how much creativity entered into Epiphanius' narrative due, on the one hand, to Joseph's simply impressing upon his guests what they wanted to hear and, on the other hand, to the church father's customary indulgence in an overheated imagination.

---

54   Tillich:71.

55   *Pan.* 30.5.1.

56   *Pan.* 30.4.3; 30.7.1.

57   *Pan.* 30.4.1.

THE MYTH OF NAZARETH

The main elements of the Count's story are as follows. He was raised in the Jewish religion and held the prestigious post of *shaliach*, priestly envoy of the Sanhedrin based in Tiberias. Among other official duties, Joseph was responsible "for traveling to the various communities to collect monies for the patriarchate."[58] In this capacity he traveled as far as Cilicia, 350 miles to the north. His duties also included personally waiting upon the patriarch, for Joseph was one of a few men who stood next in rank. When the patriarch was on his deathbed he arranged to be secretly baptized in the name of Jesus Christ, by a Christian who came to him in disguise. Joseph secretly witnessed the baptism through the keyhole of the door. Deeply concerned, he wondered for a long time at what he had seen, but divulged the knowledge to no one. After the patriarch died, Joseph secretly entered the *gazophylacium*, which Epiphanius describes as the patriarchate's treasury. Joseph expected to find money, but instead came upon only old scrolls and books. To his great astonishment, Christian scriptures were among these writings, including the Gospels of Matthew and John.[59] Joseph read them and was deeply affected. But he was still not entirely convinced. "My heart was hardened," Joseph explained apologetically.

As it happened, before the patriarch died he had entrusted his son to the care of Joseph and of another elder. The boy, by the name of Ellel, was to inherit the patriarchate when he came of age. However, Joseph was greatly concerned for the child, who was of an unruly nature. The Count explained to his distinguished guests that when Ellel reached the age of full vigor he fell in with the wrong sort and learned some bad habits, including black magic, "unholy sexual unions," and the art of seducing women in cemeteries.[60]

Bishops Epiphanius, Eusebius, and Count Joseph's other astonished guests learned, however, that Ellel met his match at the Gadara hot springs. There the young man's eyes fell upon a particularly beautiful girl and, as usual, Ellel wished to do unmentionable things with her body. However, he had not the least success, for—the Count solemnly explained—she was a Christian. Thereupon the boy immediately ceased going with his friends, convinced that their magic was worthless.

Joseph had several dreams in which Christ appeared to him. But he continued to resist conversion, and even became seriously ill over this. When he was thought to be dying, a revered Jewish elder came to him and whispered in his ear: "Believe in Jesus, crucified under Pontius Pilate the governor, Son

---

[58] Pritz, "Joseph of Tiberias," p. 40.

[59] *Pan.* 30.6.9. Epiphanius mentions the Hebrew version of Matthew, and Hebrew translations of John and Acts.

[60] These were capital crimes under Roman law (Matthews 218). The character of Ellel, the future patriarch, offers full scope to Epiphanius' rabid anti-Semitism.

of God first yet later born of Mary; the Christ of God and risen from the dead. And believe that he will come to judge and quick and the dead."[61]

In a dream, Jesus spoke to Joseph: "Lo, I heal you; only rise up and believe!" Miraculously, Joseph recovered from his illness. But his heart was so hardened that he still remained obstinate. At this point the Lord made known to Joseph that, in order to prove the Christian faith, he would be permitted to work one miracle. Joseph thereupon searched the streets of Tiberias and seized a naked madman, brought him to his house, sprinkled him with holy water, and sternly intoned: "In the name of Jesus of Nazareth, the crucified, begone from him, demon, and let him be made whole!"[62] The madman fell down, drooled, retched, rubbed his forehead, and came to his senses.

At this point Saint Epiphanius, writing twenty or more years after the fact, may have been overcome by emotion at the spectacle of the retching and drooling madman suddenly made well. Perhaps to calm his nerves the Church Father got up and had a glass of wine or two, for he forgot that the boy's name was Ellel and throughout the remainder of the story calls him Judas.[63] In any case, when Judas reached full maturity he was deemed fit to assume the full duties of the patriarchate.[64] To repay Joseph for raising him, Judas sent the older man to Cilicia with official authorization to collect the first fruits and tithes from the Jews of that distant province, a task the eager Joseph proceeded to carry out without delay. It appears that while in Cilicia Joseph demoted a number of rabbis, sacked others and, in Epiphanius' opinion, generally did "what would make for the establishment of good order."[65] To Joseph's surprise, animosity grew against him in Cilicia. The Count carefully explained to the assembled bishops the real reason behind the hatred of the Cilician Jews: they had seen him reading in the Christian scriptures. He explained how they bound him, dragged him into the synagogue, whipped him, and finally threw him into the river. Through an unspecified miracle, however, Joseph escaped.

---

[61] *Pan.* 30.9.3.

[62] *Pan.* 30.10.4.

[63] It is a revealing error. Epiphanius even writes, "I guess he was called that *[i.e., Judas]*." This indicates that the church father did not bother to look back a page or two to see what the boy's name was ("Ellel" is last mentioned at 30.7.1). Such unconcern is characteristic of a man writing either far too quickly, too much, or who feels that no one is even going to read what he is writing. Indeed, at times one gets the impression that Epiphanius is simply humoring himself with words.

[64] *Pan.* 30.11.1.

[65] *Pan.* 30.11.4.

THE MYTH OF NAZARETH

Ostracized from his inherited faith, Joseph finally accepted Christian baptism.[66] Without delay he hastened to Constantinople, presented himself to Emperor Constantine, and explained that he "was a Jew of the highest rank, and how divine visions kept appearing to him, since the Lord was summoning him to His holy calling and to the salvation of His faith and knowledge."[67] Greatly moved, the emperor not only rewarded Joseph with the rank of Count, but also urged him to ask a boon.

Count Joseph humbly asked for official sanction to carry forward the Christian cause in the Holy Land, by liberating "those Jewish towns and villages where no one had ever been able to found churches, since there are no Greeks, Samaritans or Christians among the population."[68] The emperor immediately had an official letter drawn up, authorized a draft on the imperial treasury, and placed Joseph on a salary.[69]

The one who had left as a *Shaliach* returned to his hometown as an Imperial Christian emissary, Count Joseph of Tiberias. He saw to it forthwith that part of a pagan temple was made available for Christian use. The Count insisted to his guests that he also completed buildings in Sepphoris and "certain other towns."[70] He finally settled in Scythopolis, a city of mixed Jewish and gentile populations, a very wealthy man.[71] And with that we come to the end of Count Joseph of Tiberias' story.

---

[66] Such changes of faith were not rare in the fourth century. Modestus, the Christian praetorian prefect who oversaw the treason trials in Scythopolis (with which Joseph of Tiberias may have been associated—see below), rose to the rank of *comes Orientis* under the Emperor Constantius, also a Christian. When the pagan Julian became emperor Modestus was dismissed. However, he converted to paganism, regained favor, and was then promoted to prefect of Constantinople. When Valens assumed power, Modestus again converted to Christianity and was made praetorian prefect of all the East. (Jones:141.)

[67] *Pan.* 30.11.7.

[68] *Pan.* 30.11.9.

[69] R. Pritz suggests that the Count enjoyed the personal friendship of Constantine for decades, and may have had something to do with two laws passed in 315 and 336. The latter reads in part: "Jews shall not be permitted to disturb any man who has been converted from Judaism to Christianity or to assail him with any outrage. Such contumely shall be punished according to the nature of the act which has been committed." Pritz:1985:41–42. The law is cited in the Theodosian Code (CT 168, 5: May 8, 336 CE).

[70] *Pan.* 30.12.9.

[71] As one of the leading citizens of Scythopolis, it is likely that Count Joseph witnessed and also participated in the notorious treason trials held in that city in mid-IV CE. Many victims were accused of consulting oracles with disloyal intent and lost their lives. (Matthews:217–225; IDB 1:401.)

The count was eventually canonized. That signal religious honor is certainly consistent with his being the first to build churches in places previously hostile to the faith, as well as with his ardent championing of Nicene Christianity. The Church celebrates the life of St. Joseph of Tiberias on July 22, a nameday he shares with Saint Mary Magdalene.

Did Count Joseph build a church in Nazareth?

It is of course difficult to place confidence in Epiphanius' narrative of Count Joseph, which does not even preserve the names of the principal characters throughout. In all, the engineering accomplishments of the Count rest on two tenuous statements: that Joseph "finished a small church" in Tiberias and "completed buildings in Diocaesarea and certain other towns."[72] The claim regarding Diocaesarea is immediately suspect, for "no external literary or archaeological evidence for any fourth century church" in Diocaesarea has yet come to light, despite many years of excavating.[73]

The single mention of Nazareth in Epiphanius' narrative (30.12.9) does not relate directly to the building activities of Joseph, but to the unmixed character of its Jewish population. The statement tells us that no gentiles were in "Tiberias, Diocaesarea, Sepphoris, Nazareth and Capernaum." This list is too long by at least one name, for Diocaesarea *was* Sepphoris. With the exception of Nazareth, all the places named were known to have mixed populations. In rabbinic times Capernaum even had a reputation as a seat of *minim*.[74] In short, Epiphanius' statements are of virtually no value for establishing the certainty of Joseph's activity in Nazareth, nor even for establishing probability. We can (charitably) speak only in terms of "possibility." Nevertheless, the possibility is real. The contemporary building program of Constantine and Helena, and the apparent involvement of the Count in that program, suggest that Joseph of Tiberias may well have been responsible for the first Christian shrine in Nazareth.

If Count Joseph was indeed active in Nazareth then, given the thoroughly Jewish nature of the village, it is entirely likely that he had to virtually force his way into the town, and could only have effected a Christian edifice there

---

[72] *Pan.* 30.11. 9; 30.12.9.

[73] MNM 17. In the 1930s L. Waterman excavated a building in Sepphoris which he termed a Christian basilica. "However, M. Avi-Yonah raised objections to this designation, which were confirmed by Strange's excavations. It is now clear that the building's plan is that of a typical Roman house..." (NEAEHL:1327.)

[74] *M. Rabbah Koheleth* I.8. On the minim of Capernaum see Taylor 1989–90:12–14. The claim is made that Joseph of Tiberias was responsible for the transformation of "Simon Peter's house" into a church early in the fourth century (DJBP 1:113–114; IDBS:140).

with official sanction.[75] This probably underlies Epiphanius' account of Joseph presenting himself to the emperor and receiving a commission. It is unlikely that the commission was purely Joseph's idea, one due entirely to his piety. Both Constantine and his mother were zealous church-builders. The emperor instigated the building of a great basilica at the site of the Holy Sepulchre at Jerusalem, built the original Hagia Sophia in Constantinople, the first Church of St. Peter in Rome, and lesser churches in other towns.[76] He was no doubt looking for those who would carry out this Christian building policy in other parts of the empire.

The empress mother Helena was similarly engaged. During her visit to the Holy Land in 326 she founded basilicas on the Mount of Olives and at Bethlehem. She was also very interested in gaining converts to the newly-sanctioned religion. Possibly meeting with Helena on her trip, the young Joseph may have been inspired to convert, and also to make himself a useful proxy of the imperial church-building program in the region.

There is tenuous archaeological confirmation in Nazareth of a simple church which may go back to Joseph of Tiberias. From her careful study of the area under the Church of the Annunciation, Joan Taylor suspects that the place of the altar mentioned by Egeria (*c.* 383 CE) is detectable in the east-facing apse of the later Byzantine church. She writes:

> It would appear that this was where the altar was placed in the earliest period of the cave's Christian use. This coheres with Egeria's remarks that an altar was placed in a cave...
>
> The site of the Shrine of the Annunciation, once part of a wine-pressing complex, was converted to Christian use, probably to encourage pilgrimage, *c.* 335...
>
> ...Joseph of Tiberias, who, though a Jew who converted to Christianity, was not a sectarian Jewish-Christian, but almost an envoy of Constantine. He wished to encourage Christian belief in the Jewish heartland, and appears to have convinced the Jews of Nazareth and Capernaum that it would be prudent to allow Christians to visit.

---

[75] Taylor (1993:228) offers a different interpretation, supposing that a "low-key approach" on the part of Count Joseph is the reason that "the Jewish population of Nazareth did not tear down the Christian shrine the moment Joseph left the town." But in the political atmosphere of the newly-Christian Roman empire, such a course would have been suicidal for the little village. We recall that Constantine's mother, Helena, was a devout Christian and personally interested in the Christian holy sites which she visited (see below). Behind Joseph's activity were the very highest powers in the empire.

[76] Trier, Aquileia, Cirta in Numidia, Nicomedia, Antioch, Gaza, Alexandria, *etc.*

In the case of Nazareth, the so-called Jewish-Christian synagogue-church seems to be the structure built by Joseph (c. 335), and nothing would suggest that the area was venerated prior to this time.[77]

Though we are far from certain, it is very possible that Count Joseph built the first Christian shrine in Nazareth.[78]

Who was buried where?

We recall that an enigmatic grave lies under the Church of the Annunciation, one known in these pages as Tomb 29. The earliest archaeologists (Vlaminck, Viaud—Chapter 5) considered the possibility that a member of the Holy Family was buried there, but noted the impossibility of this due to the Jewish prohibition against dwelling in the vicinity of tombs. Nevertheless, the grave required explanation, and its proximity to the Chapel of the Angel indicated a very special interment. Kopp suggested that "a saint was venerated here."[79] The legendary martyr Conan, of the family of the Lord, was suggested.[80] Count Joseph of Tiberias was also suggested.

Many other nearby graves also remain to be explained, for Tomb 29 is but one of six under the CA, dating to Roman times. Kopp himself notes with astonishment that the basilica is located in a Roman cemetery:

> In the closest proximity lay the Laham tomb to the south, the Shrine is now erected over a second Jewish kokim tomb (H), others may have been converted by workmen into cisterns, it is possible that even more [tombs] have disappeared in the foundations of the church and the bishop's residence. A strong and certain recollection must have drawn the basilica into this cemetery [Gräberfeld].[81]

Kopp supposes that Tomb 29 (with a single surviving grave), together with its vestibule, is from the earliest part of the basilica. After considering the possibility that St. Joseph (not of Tiberias) was buried there, he concludes that "in IV CE fledgling Christianity fell victim to an error, in that it supposed Mary herself was buried here. Even her birth was for a long time localized in Nazareth, though Jerusalem has the older and better claim to that." Elsewhere Kopp writes:

---

[77] Taylor: 255, 267, 337–38,

[78] Cf. Taylor 1993:265; Pritz 45; Goranson 339.

[79] Kopp 1939–40:90.

[80] Chapter 5, pp. 257f.

[81] Kopp (1939–40) pp. 91–92.

> The signs of love [*evident*] in the construction, embellishment, and graffiti at so early a time can only be connected with her. The basilica took on literary life as "the house of Mary"; she, not Saint Joseph, is the soul of the sanctuary. [82]

By VI CE popular Christian tradition had localized Mary's tomb in the Kidron Valley near Jerusalem. From that time forward any connection of Nazareth to the tomb of Mary was an embarrassment. "Soon the veil of forgetfulness fell over our rock grotto," writes the German.

Unable to satisfactorily explain Tomb 29, Kopp speaks of the "riddle of this small rock cave." In Chapter Five (p. 257) we considered the possibility that Count Joseph was buried in this grave, and noted that such a burial would resolve many problems for the Church. But it is hardly likely. Are we to imagine that the Christians allowed someone to be buried under the house of Mary? Besides, the Count died in Scythopolis. Are we to suppose that his body was carried to Nazareth and interred there, a hero of the *minim* in this Jewish village? Such ideas are remarkably inventive, but have nothing to do with the evidence of Nazareth. The kokhim tombs under the Church of the Annunciation were mundane burials of inhabitants of the Jewish village. Riddles accompany these tombs only when we introduce impossible Christian expectations.

The Secondary Literature

A characteristic passage

We have covered much chronological territory in this book, from the Stone Age through Roman times. In so doing, we have seen the Nazareth basin occupied, then laid waste, then left empty of human habitation, and finally reoccupied in Middle Roman times. This chronology is entirely new, for continuous habitation or a Hellenistic renaissance are what the curious inquirer will read elsewhere. Certainly, the published literature furnishes scholar and layperson alike no *entrée* into the actual facts of the matter. A representative example of the general view of Nazareth's history is given in a popular book published in 1998. Lee Strobel's *The Case for Christ* devotes a couple of pages to "Puzzle 2: Existence of Nazareth." Strictly intended for the layperson, we read there:

> In an article called "Where Jesus Never Walked," atheist Frank Zindler noted that Nazareth is not mentioned in the Old Testament, by the apostle Paul, by the Talmud (although sixty-three other Galilean towns are cited), or by Josephus (who listed forty-five other villages and cities of Galilee, including Japha, which was located just over a mile from

---

[82]   *Ibid*, p. 92.

Nazareth and Nazara

present-day Nazareth). No ancient historians or geographers mention Nazareth before the beginning of the fourth century. The name first appears in Jewish literature in a poem written about the seventh century A.D. (Strobel:102)

Zindler's 1993 article correctly deduces many conclusions we have arrived at in these pages, without the benefit of a detailed itemization and analysis of the material record. He places the town on the valley floor, notes that the venerated area was full of tombs in later Roman times and uninhabitable, points to the lack of masonry remains from the first century, the vague (mis)use of the phrase "Roman period" to backdate evidence, and concludes that the basin was settled "some time after the expulsion of the Jews from Jerusalem in 135 C.E." This is admirably close to the date arrived at in these pages, but though correct in so many ways, Zindler's article receives short shrift in Strobel's admittedly conservative tome. Strobel solicits the opinion of an American archaeologist, John McRay (who to my knowledge has not published or dug at Nazareth). McRay in turn cites secondary literature written by James Strange, voicing opinions we have already rebutted. Strange backdates the removal of the Hapizzez from Jerusalem to after 70 CE rather than after 135 CE, and notes "first-century tombs" (which we have seen postdate 50 CE). These two claims are really the only "hard" (non-) evidence furnished for a village "at the beginning of the first century." Strobel concludes his treatment as follows:

> "Such findings suggest that Nazareth may have existed in Jesus' time, but there is no doubt that it must have been a very small and insignificant place."
> So insignificant that Nathanael's musings in John 1:46 now make more sense: "Nazareth!" he said. "Can anything good come from there?"
> (Strobel 103–04)

A comment is in order regarding this statement from the fourth gospel, which is often interpreted as above. Nathaniel's question does not speak of Nazareth's size but of its *goodness*. In fact, Nazareth was viewed with hostility by the evangelists, for it did not believe in Jesus and "he could do no mighty work there" (Mk 6:5). In all four gospels we read the famous saying, "A prophet is not without honor except in his own country, and among his own kin, and in his own house" (Mt 13:57; Mk 6:4; Lk 4:24; Jn 4:44). As is well known, at Lk 4:29 the Nazarenes even attempt to kill Jesus by throwing him off a cliff. Many scholars since W. Wrede in 1901[83] have noted the so-called "Messianic secret," whereby Jesus' true nature and mission were

---

[83] W. Wrede, *Das Messiasgeheimnis in den Evangelien.* English translation *The Messianic Secret* (1971).

THE MYTH OF NAZARETH

unseen by many, including by his inner circle of disciples (Mk 8:27–33; *cf.* only those to whom the Father reveals Jesus will be saved, Jn. 6:65; 17:6, 9, *etc.*). Nazareth, being the home of those near and dear to Jesus, apparently suffered negatively in relation to this doctrine. Thus, Nathaniel's question, "Can anything good come out of Nazareth?" is consistent with a negative view of Nazareth in the canonical gospels, and with the fact that even Jesus' brothers did not believe him (Jn 7:5). We shall consider this animus against Nazareth—which also extended to "Nazarenes"—in a subsequent volume.

Strobel's treatment is fairly typical of what the average person can expect to read concerning the history of Nazareth. It does not consider the primary literature, is based upon faulty data and unfounded conclusions in the secondary literature, and ardently defends tradition.

Arguments from silence

Each person seeking a rational conclusion about Nazareth in the time of Jesus must eventually tally up the evidence. The two sides of the tally are essentially "I BCE" and "I CE." Those who advocate a village in Jesus' time must show material evidence from the first century BCE—no other century will really do. On the other hand, those who deny a village in Jesus' time must show that no material evidence has been found from that century.

In Chapter 4 we located all of the relevant evidence on one side of the tally—to CE times. All the extant post-Iron tombs postdate 50 CE, all the oil lamps postdate 25 CE, and not even a shard necessarily predates 100 CE. Furthermore, we saw that there is *no* Hellenistic evidence from the basin, nor any from I BCE going back to Assyrian times. So, the tally—very generally set forth—looks like this:

I BCE	I CE
Evidence of Nazareth at the Time of Jesus	**Evidence of the birth of Nazareth in the common era**
——— none———	After 25 CE: All oil lamps After 50 CE: All post-Iron age tombs After 50 CE: All pottery and other movable evidence

Having reviewed the evidence regarding ancient Nazareth, the claim that a settlement existed in the basin at the turn of the era is one argument from silence that can no longer be tolerated.[84] The ledger is clear: on one side is a panoply of evidence, which unambiguously shows that people began

---

[84] Not all arguments from silence are invalid or inappropriate (*cf.* Zindler 1999).

coming into the basin in the second half of I CE, and that the settlement—one that can be deemed worthy of a name—emerged in the decades between the two Jewish revolts (Chapter 4). On the other side of the ledger lies only a glaring void. Not even the two stone vessels—the sole recovered artefacts from the basin which could conceivably date to the turn of the era—are secure evidence for Jesus' village, for such vessels continued to be used and manufactured into the second century of our era. On the basis of the surrounding context it is all but certain that the use of those vessels dates to the interwar decades. The structural evidence that is datable is equally clear. It consists of approximately two dozen tombs of kokh and later types. (The agricultural installations are not independently datable.) We have seen in Chapter 4 that those tombs postdate mid-I CE in the Galilee. Together with the oil lamps and pottery, this is powerful confirmation indeed that the village came into being towards the end of the first century of our era.

Because there is no demonstrable evidence from the turn of the era, the claim of a village at that time has no substantiation at all. Those who argue for a village at the time of Jesus have nothing material on which to base their opinion, and they must argue *against* the available material evidence. This is the situation with Nazareth: material evidence on one side confronts arguments from silence on the other.

This is not new. There has long been a tendency to overlook disturbing evidence at Nazareth (*e.g.*, tombs under the venerated area) and, where possible, to exploit lacunae in the archaeological record in order to promote the tradition view. The implications of such convenient arguments are rarely taken into account and often lead to ridiculous scenarios.

One obvious lacuna in the archaeological record is that the Nazareth valley floor has never been excavated.[85] In Chapter Five it was demonstrated that the village was not on the hillside. For some, the claim that a settlement *of Jesus' time* must therefore have been located precisely on the valley floor cannot be far behind. After all, we have noted that the inhabited portion of the settlement, in the periods when people lived in the basin, was indeed on the valley floor.[86] The issue at hand is chronology, not location. The valley floor is now heavily built over and will in all likelihood never be excavated. This is convenient for those who claim a village there in the time of Christ, but it is untenable on several grounds. First of all, it is hardly likely that the village predated its tombs. The dozens of scattered tombs from Roman Nazareth that have been excavated on the hillsides all postdate 50 CE. This shows that the village did also. As was stated: "The earliest tomb at Nazareth is a significant clue regarding the existence of a village" (Chapter 4, p. 157).

---

[85]   *Cf.* Chapter 5, p. 227.
[86]   *Cf.* Chapter 2, pp. 67*f*; Chapter 5, pp. 217*ff.*

THE MYTH OF NAZARETH

In order to deny the fairly overwhelming evidence from Nazareth, the tradition must resort to increasingly farfetched arguments from silence, such as that tombs of Hellenistic and Early Roman times are somewhere on the hillside but have simply not been discovered. A glance at a map of the basin (Chapter 5, *Illus 5.2*), however, shows this line also to be futile. Is it possible to seriously maintain that not one tomb from Hellenistic or Early Roman times has been found, though a score of later Roman tombs have?

Some arguments from silence are like kicking the proverbial can down the road. One argument is dispatched only to be replaced by another of similar ilk. This situation especially obtains when one party seeks to evade evidence rather than respect it. Unfortunately, such opportunities are theoretically unlimited. They range from refusing to engage in substantive argument, to redefining terms, to intimidation and (in bygone eras) even elimination of the opposition.

It is worthwhile to consider the various counter-arguments to the evidence, because the issue of Nazareth in the time of Jesus is so explosive. In the case of the putative Hellenistic tombs mentioned above, once such tombs are shown not to be on the hillside of the Nebi Sa'in, then one might assert that they were elsewhere—perhaps on the valley floor itself. But this too makes little sense, and is a reversal of what one would expect: presumably, the ancient Jews were living on the steep and rocky hillside, and constructing their tombs on the flat valley floor!

Other problems attend the claim of a village on the valley floor in the time of Christ. It is clear that the inhabitants used the hillsides not only for burial but also for agricultural purposes. Is it credible that no artefacts from the Hellenistic Age, from I BCE, or from the turn of the era have been found in or around those installations if they were in use during those eras?

Kicking the can again, traditionalists may retreat to yet another line of defense and claim: *Ah, but Nazareth was not in the basin at all. You see, it was somewhere else!* This is perhaps the ultimate argument from silence. A moment's thought, however, will show this line to be impossible, for it implies that there was (were) not one but two Nazareths in Galilee. The village we have been studying has been a named place for many centuries, identifiable as "Nazareth" and as a pilgrim destination since the fourth century of our era. Hence, if "Nazareth" existed somewhere outside the basin, then it must have been some other, second, Nazareth. We have no record at all of that other Nazareth, and if we did, then scholars would long since have been discussing which of the two Nazareths Jesus came from.

Sooner or later the time comes when one must credit the evidence that has been produced. Despite the fact that only a small part of the basin has been excavated, the considerable evidence that has come to light is conclusive. That evidence speaks clearly, and in any other valley of Israel it would be ludicrous to contest the issue. The burden of proof regarding Jesus' village is on the person who claims its existence yet can show no evidence of same. In the case of Nazareth, arguments from silence are seductive and facile, but ultimately of no avail, simply because it is inconceivable that a putative village at the turn of the era *left no archaeological trace at all.*

Unfortunately, the facts presented in this book and elsewhere hardly weigh in the balance when dealing with a frank refusal to acknowledge scientific data. Such a refusal is not rare in matters of religion, and is fairly widespread in the West today. Some people are even capable of denying facts which are set before their very eyes. Thinking outside the parameters of reason, they are simply not to be convinced. But for those of us who value empirical data, the birth of Nazareth *after* the turn of the era is clear.

Literary Considerations

(1) "Nazareth" outside the Gospels

In pagan and Jewish sources

Only five Roman notices regarding the Christian movement have been identified dating before c. 150 CE. They are a letter by Pliny the Younger to Trajan (112 CE), the emperor's response, a passage in the writings of Tacitus (regarding the Neronian persecution), and two short notices in the works of Suetonius.[87] These pagan notices know only 'Christians' and 'Christus' ('Chrestus' once in Suetonius), but nowhere 'Jesus' or 'Nazareth.'

Jewish literature does not mention the place Nazareth.[88] Several rabbinic passages contain the name *Yeshu ha-Notsri*,[89] somewhat analogous in form to the Gospel of Mark's *Iêsou Nazarêne* (see below), a moniker which has no necessary connection with a place called Nazareth. It remains to be determined, of course, what a *Nazarêne* (Heb. *ha-Notsri*) meant.

---

[87] These are discussed individually at Wenham 1985. English translations are in Stevenson 1957. Pliny, the imperial legate to Bithynia-Pontus in Asia Minor, writes for guidance regarding those being charged in his province as Christians. The Tacitus and Suetonius passages concern the Neronian persecution in July, 64 CE. (Tacitus, *Annals*, XV 44.2–8; *Suetonius Life of Nero*, XVI.2.). Suetonius also mentions the expul -sion of Jews (under the leadership of Chrestus) from Rome by Claudius, c. 49 CE.

[88] Zindler 2003:401n.1, notes that a late version of the *Sepher Toldoth Jeshu Ha Notzri,* published by J. Huldrich in 1705, depicts Joseph Pandera as settling in Nazareth. This element ultimately derives from the Gospel of Matthew.

[89] *b. Sotah* 47a // *b. Sanh* 107b; *b. Sanh.* 107b. The following are all variants: *t. Jul.* 2:24; *b. 'Abod. Zar.* 16b; *m. Qoh. Rab.* On 1:8; *Yal. Shim.* On Mic 1 and Prov 5:8. (See Wenham 323.)

THE MYTH OF NAZARETH

The place *Beit Lehem Tseriyeh* is mentioned once in the Talmud (*Megilla* 70a). In the nineteenth century Neubauer considered this equivalent to *Bethlehem Notseriyeh*, *i.e.*, "Bethlehem in the district of Natsareth" = the Galilean Bethlehem.[90] Granted the plausibility of this interpretation, the passage dates long after the appearance of Nazareth, and thus furnishes us no information regarding the turn of the era.

The fourth century Christian sources

It is well known that Nazareth is not mentioned in the writings of Josephus, and we have now seen that it also does not appear in early rabbinic literature. The Christian literature presents a more complex picture, in which we must separate several strands: the canonical writings, the apocryphal literature (including Gnostic and Jewish Christian texts), and the writings of the church fathers. My purpose here is not to carry out a thorough survey of all the texts, but to note the occurrence of one specific element: the appearance of the toponym 'Nazareth' (and its cognates). We shall begin with the fourth century, after the legitimation of Christianity, and work back in time. This reverse procedure is adopted because our primary goal is not the later history of the town and of the name 'Nazareth' (and cognates), but the earliest history of both.

When Christianity was officially sanctioned by Constantine the Great, the Jewish settlement of Nazareth suddenly emerged from obscurity. The reason is evident: this obscure town held a particular significance for believers of the victorious faith. The reason was also practical: now Christians were free to embark on pilgrimages to the Holy Land, while they advertised their faith without fear of official retribution. Naturally, one of the destinations they sought out was the hometown of the Lord. Only from this time do we begin to have unmistakable geographical references to Nazareth in Lower Galilee. Suddenly the small settlement was thrust into the Christian and imperial limelight—a limelight which must have been most unwelcome to the town's inhabitants, who as far as we can tell were Torah-observant Jews. As such, they would have avoided mixing with gentiles, and probably harbored rank antipathy to the Christian heresy.

This opposition colored the history of Nazareth from the fourth to the seventh century (when the Jews were expelled by Heraclius in 630 CE—see *Appendix 7*). From Constantine's time forward, Christian pilgrims to the Holy Land, coming from all around the Mediterranean, were seeking (and expecting) to find validation of their faith—a special, uplifting, and even life-changing religious experience. Arriving at their destination, however, Nazareth must have been a disappointing anticlimax to their long and laborious journeys.

---

[90] See Cheyne in EB, "Nazareth," col. 3361. Pliny the Elder (23–79 CE) mentions in passing a region in Syria which he calls *Nazerinorum tetrarchia* (*Nat. Hist.* 81).

Jesus' supposed hometown was not even sympathetic to their faith, much less Christian. The Jewish settlement was most unsatisfactory also from the Church's point of view, which found it impossible to showcase Jesus' hometown. A question must have occurred to more than a few: What sort of victory could the faith claim, if Jesus' own hometown had not converted? In fact, far from being a source of pride to Christians, Nazareth must have been an embarrassment.

It was not possible to attack Nazareth in word or deed, for the hometown of Jesus required respect. The only option remaining is what we witness in the early pilgrim accounts, and in the writings of the Church fathers: a remarkable silence. St. Helena, the mother of Emperor Constantine and a devout Christian, visited the Holy Land in 326 but had nothing to say about Nazareth. She may have been singularly unimpressed (or even irritated) by the antipathy of the locals. Helena was seeking opportunities to found basilicas in the Holy Land, and indeed did so on the Mount of Olives and at Bethlehem, but not in Nazareth. The latter task, apparently, was delegated to Count Joseph of Tiberias (see above).

Eusebius in his *Onomasticon* (*c.* 325 CE?) gives the general location of the village, and thus we know that by his time the settlement was localized to the Nazareth basin.[91] He tells us nothing particular about the place.

About 335 CE the Bordeaux Pilgrim visited Palestine and strangely makes no mention of Nazareth. It is a remarkable omission. Taylor writes that this "certainly does suggest that there was nothing to be visited in the town." Kopp is in wonderment: "It might be that at that time a sort of anathema lay upon this town which had tried to stone its most illustrious son, and still rejected his teaching."[92] His explanation is weak, however, for the pilgrims surely wished to venerate Jesus' hometown, not to condemn it.

In 373 CE Melania the Elder "hastened to bring alms to Christians who had been exiled from Egypt to Sepphoris, but she did not visit Nazareth…"[93] This again is a strange omission, particularly given the fact that she was in the very vicinity of Nazareth.

Only in 383 CE do we have the first brief mention of Nazareth in the pilgrim literature. In that year Egeria (as rerecorded by Peter the Deacon in 1137 CE) attests to the existence of a simple shrine: "In Nazareth is a garden in which the Lord used to be after his return from Egypt." And elsewhere: "there is a big and very splendid cave in which she [*the Virgin Mary*] lived. An altar

---

[91] *Onom.* 138.24–140.2. Eusebius writes: "Nazareth, from which the Christ is called Nazorean [*Nazôraios*] and we, who are now called Christians, were of old called Nazarenes [*Nazaraioi*]. Today it is still located in the Galilee opposite Legio [*Legeônos*] about 15 milestones to the east near Mt. Tabor."

[92] Taylor 1993:226; Kopp 1963:58.

[93] Taylor, *ibid.*

has been placed there."[94] This shows us that the first Christian monument had by her time been erected in Nazareth, probably earlier in the fourth century. In 386 Paula visited Nazareth "where our Lord grew up." Nothing there appears to have drawn the pilgrim's attention. Jerome, writing c. 400 CE, had virtually nothing to say about Nazareth outside the fact that it was a mere "village" (viculus) in his time.[95]

Thus, it is quite clear that after pilgrims began traveling in the early fourth century, both they and the Church were reserved with regard to Nazareth. The reason, I have suggested, is that the town was an unsatisfactory destination for pilgrimage, being populated by Jews who were not at all sympathetic to the Christian religion.

"Nazareth" in Ante-Nicene literature

The above embarrassment regarding post-Constantinian Nazareth does not apply before his time, for until the legitimation of the religion there was no Christian pilgrimage, nor any pressure to recognize the village in a special way. One might think that the growth of Christianity in the Roman empire would have been accompanied by increased curiosity regarding the hometown of Jesus. But this is not so. In the second and third centuries the Christian faith was widely reviled by the Roman populace (as well as by Jews) and was not officially accepted. To advertise one's Christian status was problematic and possibly dangerous. During these centuries far weightier matters than the hometown of Jesus were occupying the thoughts of Christians, who were sometimes at risk for their very lives. The Church was preoccupied with the battle for legitimacy, and was in a life-and-death struggle for survival. Given this atmosphere, the place of Jesus' youth was of interest to hardly anyone except perhaps a few doctors of the church.

This explains why Nazareth—as a geographical place (rather than a narrative element of the Gospels)—receives no particular attention in the writings of Justin Martyr, Origen, and others. But it does not explain two other considerations: (1) an apparent confusion regarding the actual location of the settlement; and (2) the fact that the town is not mentioned even in those innocuous Christian passages where one should expect to find it. This relative silence is curious, because many of the second- and third-century church fathers were in Palestine or spent some years there, and it would have been nothing for them to visit the town or at least take note of it. In any case, we should expect to have some fairly clear indication of the correct location of

---

94   Peter Diac. Lib. P4 and Lib. T. (Cf. Taylor 1993:226 and Wilkinson 1981:193.)

95   Jerome, Onom. 139. Nazareth is also mentioned in the fanciful *Life of John the Baptist,* allegedly by Bishop Serapion of Thmuis (in the Nile delta), c. 390 CE. In a 'modified' southern tradition, the Holy Family is transported from Egypt to Nazareth (cf. Mt 2:23) on a cloud. (NTA I:468.)

Nazareth. Instead we have a strange citation from Julius Africanus (see below) The first writer to locate the settlement in Lower Galilee is Eusebius—but not before early IV CE (above)—and he himself gives no indication of having been there, even though he lived in nearby Caesarea.

Since there was as yet no Christian pilgrimage, we must look for a different reason (other than that of embarrassment *vis-à-vis* pilgrims) for the pre-Constantinian shunning of the place. Some other factor regarding Nazareth must have been operative, one which produced hesitation and uncertainty.

That factor, I would suggest, was the unresolved conflict between the northern and southern traditions. As we have seen, this overarching conflict represented two incompatible Christian traditions, and produced two streams of Christian literature.[96] Only one became orthodox: the northern (Galilean) tradition. The southern (Judean) provenance of Jesus became heterodox from the fourth century forward. It was during that century, and with the emergence of Christian pilgrimage, that *Nazara-Nazaret-Nazareth* of the gospels was unequivocally identified with the Jewish town of Natsareth (spelled with *tsade*) in Lower Galilee. Before then, there was a certain amount of confusion in the Christian tradition, for some of the texts seemed to place the hometown of Jesus in Judea. Thus, the *Protevangelium of James*:[97]

> ... And the heralds went forth and spread out through all the surrounding country of Judea; the trumpet of the Lord sounded, and all ran to it.
>
> And Joseph threw down his axe and went out to meet them. And when they were gathered together, they took the rods and went to the high priest. The priest took the rods from them and entered the Temple and prayed... (PrJa 8.3)
>
> Now there went out a decree from the king Augustus that all of Bethlehem in Judea should be enrolled. And Joseph said: "I shall enroll my sons, but what shall I do with this child *[i.e. Mary]*? How shall I enroll her? As my wife? I am ashamed to do that..." (PrJa 17.1)[98]

In these passages Joseph lives in Judea, in Bethlehem, and near the temple.

It can be no coincidence that the earliest witness outside the canonical tradition—Julius Africanus (*c.* 200 CE)—apparently sites Nazareth in Judea:

---

[96] Chapter 5, pp. 211–19.

[97] The *Protevangelium* is generally dated to II CE. NTA I:423.

[98] The fourth-century *History of Joseph the Carpenter* also places Nazareth in Judea and within walking distance of the Jerusalem temple.

THE MYTH OF NAZARETH

> …Of these were the above-mentioned persons, called *desposynoi*, on account of their affinity to the family of our Savior. These coming from Nazara and Cochaba, villages of Judea, to the other parts of the world, explained the aforesaid genealogy from the book of daily records, as faithfully as possible.[99] (Cruse translation.)

The pertinent phrase in the Greek reads: *apo te Nazarôn kai Kôchaba kômôn 'Ioudaïkôn*. The meaning could be "villages of the Jews," or "Jewish villages"—not necessarily "villages of Judea." Thus, it is conceivable that Africanus indeed has the (Galilean) village of Nazareth in mind. Four Cochabas have been located.[100] One is a village 15 km northwest of Nazareth which, outside of this citation, plays no role at all in Christian history. Interestingly, Nazara's name, for Africanus, is a plural entity (*cf.* Colorado Springs, Grand Rapids, Los Angeles). These peculiarites are enigmatic.

A fourth-century work known as the *History of Joseph the Carpenter* belongs unequivocally to the southern tradition. Like the *Protevangelium*, it locates Nazareth in Judea and within walking distance of the temple. Bagatti noted this geographical anomaly:

> An Apocryphal [sic] that follows closely the *Protevangelium* is the *History of Joseph the Carpenter*, wherein the Lord recounts the death of his foster father. The complete redaction, preserved in Arabic, but derived from a Coptic text and from an original, probably Jewish, seeks to combine the data of the *Protoevangelium* with that of St. Luke[101] and arrives at rather curious topographical positions. For example, it has Joseph come to Nazareth after the return from Egypt (IX), and then when Joseph feels that death is near (here the account seems to begin) he has him go to the temple to pray (XII) as if going from Nazareth to Jerusalem for a dying man was walking up the garden. (*Exc.* 11–12)

The *Protevangelium of James*, the *History of Joseph the Carpenter*, and possibly the citation of Africanus, show that in some Christian texts Nazareth-Nazara had nothing at all to do with the settlement in Lower Galilee. They locate the place in Judea, even close to the temple of Jerusalem.

Given an unresolved Judean–Galilean claim to the homeland of Jesus, some confusion is understandable, even though the Jewish village of Nazareth in Lower Galilee was known from *c.* 100 CE onwards. The conflict between the southern and northern traditions best explains the hesitant, equivocal, and

---

[99]   ὧν ἐτύγχανον οἱ προειρημένοι, δεσπόσυνοι καλούμενοι διὰ τὴν πρὸσ τὸ σωτήριον γένοσ συνάφειαν ἀπό τε Ναζάρων καὶ Κωχάβα κωμῶν 'Ιουδαϊκῶν. Africanus, *Epistle to Aristides* I.5, cited also in Eusebius, *Eccl. Hist.* 1.7.14.

[100]   Map at Taylor 1993:37, where she discusses various possible sites of Cochaba.

[101]   It is in the Gospel of Matthew that the Holy Family flees to Egypt.

sometimes silent approach of the pre-Constantinian Christian literature with respect to Nazareth.

Even Eusebius (*c.* 264–340) may have been hesitant to locate Nazareth in the Galilee. The settlement is missing from a frequently noted episode in his *Ecclesiastical History* (III.20, citing the second century Hegesippus). The story concerns the presentation before the emperor Domitian (81–96 CE) of the grandchildren of Jude, "called the brother of our Lord, according to the flesh." These brothers (*cf.* James "the Lord's brother," Gal 1:19) were brought before the emperor (improbable in itself, more so if the emperor was at Rome), and their answers betray the Ebionite traits of poverty, disparagement of ambition, and a repudiation of the temporal things of the world. The narrative contrasts the spiritual kingdom of Christ with temporal power, and that stark contrast is the crux of the metaphorical meeting between the descendants of Christ and the Roman emperor.[102] Hegesippus writes that these brothers then "ruled the churches" (again, evocative of the James-Symeon dynasty) and "continued to live even to the times of Trajan" (98–117 CE).

The story, however, is almost certainly legendary. It is hardly likely that the emperor would be "as much alarmed at the appearance of Christ as Herod." Nor is it likely that he would meet with these simple country folk from the East. Most germane to our concern is the fact that Nazareth is nowhere mentioned. Hegesippus tells us that the "grandchildren of Jude" were brought before the Roman emperor, but from where we cannot be sure. Bagatti assumes that Nazareth in Lower Galilee was their home, as does Taylor,[103] but that conclusion is entirely conjectural, conforming to a later harmonization with gospel tradition. Of course, there is no justification for Bagatti's further conclusions drawn from this legendary story: "It is certain that the relatives of the Lord lived there [*i.e., in Nazareth*] for over two centuries and in particular the descendants of Jude, one of the 'brothers' mentioned in the Gospel" (*Exc.* 12).

Origen (*c.* 185–*c.* 254) also lived at nearby Caesarea, yet he is capable of writing no less than three different spellings of Nazareth on the same page:

---

[102] This is supported by the fuller version of the meeting described in the writing of Philip of Sideto (*c.* 425 CE), also drawn from Hegesippus. Bagatti summarizes the conversation with the emperor: "Interrogated regarding Christ, and his kingdom, regarding the nature, time and place of his coming they *[the grandsons of Jude]* replied that the empire of Christ was not mundane and terrane, but celestial and angelic; that it would come into being at the end of time, when He will come in glory to judge the living and the dead, will render to each one according to his works. Having heard this, [*Domitian*] did not condemn them; on the contrary he despised their lowly condition, and he set them free and issued an edict halting the persecution of the church." (*Exc.* 14.)

[103] *Exc.* 12–14; Taylor 1993:225.

en Nazarois (twice), *tên Nazaret*, and *eis Nazara.*[104]We note the interesting fact that *en Nazarois* is plural (*cf.* Julius Africanus' *tôn Nazarôn*), as if a region were intended ('the land of the Nazarenes'). Origen, of course, follows scripture in locating Nazareth "in Galilee,"[105] but writes: "some say that the Savior preached the Gospel *in Judea* for only one year"[106] (emphasis added). Elsewhere, we see the southern and northern traditions reflected in a contrast between Nazareth and Capernaum. This contrast is based on Lk 4:16*ff*, where Nazareth is associated with the Jews, and Capernaum with foreign territory. Origen writes:

> Insofar as Luke's narrative is concerned, Jesus has not yet stayed in Capernaum. Nor is he said to have performed any sign in that place, because he had not been there. Before he comes to Capernaum, it is recorded that he was in his native territory, that is, in Nazareth. He says to his fellow-citizens, "Doubtless you will quote me this saying: 'Physician, cure yourself. Do here, too, in your native territory, whatever we heard was done in Capernaum.'" For this reason, I think that some mystery is hidden in this passage before us. Capernaum, a type of the Gentiles, takes precedence over Nazareth, a type of the Jews.[107]

A few paragraphs later, Origen adds: "So, 'no prophet is accepted in his native country,' that is, *among the people of the Jews.*"[108]

Justin Martyr (*c.* 100–*c.* 165 CE) appears to describe the southern tradition regarding Nazareth:

> But when Quirinus was taking his first census in Judea, Joseph traveled from Nazareth, where he lived, to Bethlehem (to which he belonged), to be enrolled, for he was by birth of the tribe of Juda which inhabited that region. Then he was ordered [*in a vision*] to go with Mary into Egypt and to remain there with the child until another revelation should advise them to return into Judea.

Everything apparently takes place in Judea. From this passage it is not impossible to construe a meaning whereby Nazareth is located in Galilee, but in that case it is curious that Justin does not mention Galilee at all. We note also that the Holy Family returns to Judea after its sojourn in Egypt.[109]

---

104   *Comment. In Joan.* Tomus X (PG 80:308–309).

105   Mk 1:9; Mt 2:22–23; 21:11; Lk 2:29, *etc.* Origen *Hom.* 6.3.

106   *Hom.* 32.5.

107   *Hom.* 33:1 (Lienhard 134).

108   *Hom.* 33:3, emphasis added.

109   *Cf.* Mt 2:22, in contrast to the northern tradition represented by Lk 2:4, 39. Other passages worthy of note include: (a) Hippolytus mentions Ναζαρετ but gives no hint as to its location (Ref. V [Marcovich 207:31]). (b) In a corrupt passage, Irenaeus (*c.*130–*c.*200 CE) writes Ιησου Ναζαρια while discussing the Marcosians.

Nazareth and Nazara

The foregoing passages are not conclusive in delineating a southern tradition. At best, they admit a possibility, one we shall now confirm as we turn our attention to the Christian scriptures themselves.

(2) *Nazareth in the early gospel tradition*

The knowledge that Nazareth in Lower Galilee did not exist until after 70 CE is a powerful tool which can now be used to examine the canonical gospels anew, beginning with their use of Nazareth and its cognates. A question immediately arises: Why did the evangelists portray Jesus as coming from a settlement not yet in existence? The answer is revealing and complex. The following sketch does not pretend to completeness, and is preliminary to a more extended investigation.

Abandoning the reverse chronology of the previous section, we shall first consider the Gospel of Mark, generally considered the earliest of the canonical gospels. Surprisingly, Nazareth is mentioned only once in that gospel, at 1:9, with the spelling *Nazaret*.[110] In four other passages we read "Jesus of Nazareth" in modern translations where, however, the Greek contains variants of *Iêsou Nazarêne*—"Jesus the Nazarene."[111] For the time being, the possibility must simply be left open that this phrase meant something other to the Marcan evangelist than "Jesus of Nazareth."

Mk 1:9 reads as follows:

> In those days Jesus came from Nazaret of Galilee [*apo Nazaret tês Galilaias*] and was baptized by John in the Jordan.

Most scholars date the composition of Mark before 70 CE, and our archaeological investigations have shown that the settlement of Nazareth did not exist before that date. The inference immediately arises, then, that the Marcan evangelist did not know, and could not have known, of Nazareth in Lower Galilee. The text and the results of archaeology can be reconciled in one of two ways: (1) either the Gospel of Mark was later than is commonly dated; or (2) the word *Nazaret* at Mk 1:9 is the interpolation of a later, post-70 CE hand.

To my knowledge this form is unattested elsewhere (Harvey 185). (c) The Gospel of Philip (II CE?—NTA I:183) discusses Nazara, Nazorean, and Nazarene, but knows no geographical referent for these terms, which are entirely abstract in meaning and somehow related to "truth" (GPh 66.14; 62:8; 62:15; 56:12). We shall explore these meanings in a subsequent volume.

[110] Nazareth (with *theta*) is represented in some witnesses.

[111] Ἰησοῦ Ναζαρηνέ at Mk 1:24; Ἰησοῦς ὁ Ναζαρηνός (Ναζωραιος/Ναζωρηνος) at 10:47; Ἰησοῦν τὸν Ναζαρηνὸν at 16:6. Various English translations of Mk 14:67 (τοῦ Ναζαρηνοῦ ἦσθα τοῦ Ἰησοῦ) exist: "with Jesus of Nazareth" (KJV); "with the Nazarene, Jesus" (RSV); "with Jesus, the man from Nazareth" (NRSV).

THE MYTH OF NAZARETH

An examination of the remainder of the gospel shows that Mark conceives of Capernaum as Jesus' home. A number of reasons lead to this conclusion: Jesus is at home in Capernaum (2:1), there he is most active, there his family resides (Mk 6:3), and Mark knows no removal of the Holy Family from Nazareth to Capernaum—a harmonizing device first supplied by Matthew. We cannot arbitrarily retroject the movement of Jesus' family at Mt 4:13 into the Marcan story, for we shall see that it is Matthew who has invented Jesus' relationship with Nazareth of Galilee.

Because the torso of Mark's gospel unequivocally locates Jesus' home in Capernaum, and because the dating of Nazareth in Lower Galilee is post-70 CE, we can be certain that the word *Nazaret* in Mk 1:9 is the interpolation of a later hand. That interpolation was obviously made after the settlement of Nazareth came into existence and became known in the region.

Nazaret can be excised from Mk 1:9 without damaging the Greek:

> In those days Jesus came from Galilee [*apo tês Galilaias*] and was baptized by John in the Jordan.

Once *Nazaret* is removed from the verse, "Nazareth" entirely disappears from the Gospel of Mark. This new view of the text allows us to see that the enigmatic term *Nazarêne* in Mark had nothing to do with Nazareth. Indeed, it preceded the appearance of Nazareth in the gospel tradition. *Nazarêne* is more authentic, *Nazareth* a subsequent addition.

Nazara and its cognates

Mindful of the anomalous and marginalized southern tradition, whereby Nazareth was located in Judea according to certain texts (see above), we turn our attention to the toponym *Nazara*, found not only in Julius Africanus but also in Q (Mt 4:13; Lk 4:16). *Nazara* is generally considered the most primitive form of the name. In the following Matthean passage, Jesus has been in Judea with John the Baptist (Mt 3:1, 13). This citation is labeled (a) in order to distinguish it from another reading we shall encounter shortly:

> (a) Now when he heard that John had been arrested, he withdrew into Galilee. And leaving Nazara he went and dwelt in Capernaum by the sea, in the territory of Zebulun and Naphtali, that what was spoken by the prophet Isaiah might be fulfilled... (Mt 4:12-14)

As conventionally understood, this passage implies two consecutive journeys of Jesus: one from Judea to Galilee, and then one from Nazareth to Capernaum. It is an awkward construction. After all: what happened in Nazareth? Was something left out (as at Mk 10:46)? More problematic is that readers automatically equate *Nazara* in the above passage with *Nazareth* in

Galilee. However, that interesting equation is impossible, for now we know that Nazareth did not exist before 70 CE, when the putative Q document was compiled.

Nazara in Q must refer to some other place.

At this juncture, we must carefully distinguish between the compiler of Q and the evangelist Matthew. It is one thing to affirm that the compiler of Q did not know of Nazareth in Lower Galilee. This, however, does not mean that the Matthean evangelist (or a redactor), *using the words of Q,* did not know Nazareth. In other words, if we consider Q in isolation, then its *Nazara* is certainly unrelated to the settlement of Nazareth in Lower Galilee. However, in the Gospel of Matthew, the word *Nazara* clearly refers to that settlement, for the gospel (at least in its final stage) demonstrates some knowledge of a village of Nazareth located in Galilee.[112] That knowledge, however, is not extensive. The place is called *Nazara, Nazaret,* and *Nazareth,* betraying the work of three hands and three stages. The first stage, we have seen, was the Q source containing the word *Nazara.*

What we have, then, is a word being taken by Matthew from Q and being assigned a new meaning—in this case, a *geographical* meaning, one referring now to a settlement in Lower Galilee.

Many scholars date the Gospel of Matthew to the generation following the First Jewish War, and a few even to II CE. Because we have seen that Nazareth came into existence between the two Jewish Revolts—the time that Matthew's text was being written—it is chronologically feasible that the evangelist (or a redactor) learned of the existence of the new settlement and chose to adopt it as Jesus' home. Possible reasons for such a maneuver will become clearer as we continue our investigation into the use of Nazareth and its cognates in the gospels.

A moment's thought shows us that phrases such as 'Nazaret of Galilee,' and 'Nazareth of Galilee,' *must* relate to the settlement in the basin whose archaeology we have been examining in this book. It would be difficult to argue otherwise, for if one or another of the evangelists had some other Nazareth of Galilee in mind, then we have no record of that site—neither in Christian, Jewish, nor pagan sources.[113] Nor is it tenable to maintain that "Nazareth" in

---

[112] Mt 2:22–23; 21:11.

[113] The closest related name would be *Gennesaret* (also *Gennasaret*), the fertile plain on the northwestern side of the Sea of Galilee, adjacent to the reputed site of Jesus' activity at Capernaum. But Mt 4:13 shows that Nazareth is not on the Sea of Galilee: "...and leaving Nazara he went and dwelt in Capernaum by the sea..." Jesus goes from Nazareth to Capernaum, showing that the two places were quite separate in the mind of the evangelist. Finally, the use of "Nazara" or "Nazaret" for Gennasaret is unknown elsewhere.

the gospels was a pure invention from beginning to end, because we indeed know of a settlement with a very similar name. Furthermore, we know of that settlement in Galilee, even as the evangelists state.

Matthew clearly locates the settlement he intends in the district of "Galilee," a region mentioned no less than seventeen times in his gospel. By assigning Jesus to that place, the evangelist has unequivocally embraced the northern tradition. This obtains even though the Matthean birth story contains vestiges of the southern tradition.

The variability of the name *Naz+* is revealing. Variants of the toponym occur not merely between different gospels, but in the same witnesses of the same gospel. Thus, *Codex Vaticanus*, which among the uncials "has a position of undisputed precedence in the Gospels" (K. Aland), possesses three variants within the Gospel of Matthew: *Nazaret, Nazara,* and *Nazareth* (at 2:23; 4:13; and 21:11 respectively).

Examination of Matthew's use of *Nazareth* and its cognates helps us to discriminate several stages in that gospel's composition, and also the sequence of stages. In that text, the spelling *Nazaret* occurs only at Mt 2:23.[114] However, in all versions the settlement is spelled with *theta* at Mt 21:11, and it is hardly likely that the same hand rendered the place differently in two passages.[115] This lends support to the view that the Gospel of Matthew is a composite work and/or an aggregate work developed in stages.

The Matthean parallel to Mk 1:9 is as follows:

> Then Jesus came from Galilee [*apo tês Galilaias*] to the Jordan to John, to be baptized by him. (Mt 3:13)

If the Marcan parallel had contained the word *Nazaret*, then Matthew surely would have included that word in the above verse. The fact that he does not do so indicates several things: (1) that Mk 1:9 originally lacked the word *Nazaret* (this we have already determined above by other arguments); (2) that the original author of the Gospel of Matthew was as ignorant of Nazareth in Lower Galilee as were both his Marcan source and the Q compiler; and (3) that it was a redactor (subsequent to the original author of the Gospel of Matthew) who added *Nazaret* to Mk 1:9.

---

114 The literature on *Nazara* and its cognates is extensive. For initial studies see H. Schaeder, "Nazarênos, Nazôraios" in Kittel 1933–73; F. C. Burkitt, "The Syriac Forms of New Testament Proper Names," (*Proceedings of the British Academy*, 1911–12, London 1912); and W. F. Albright, "The Names 'Nazareth' and 'Nazoraean'" in JBL vol. 65 no.2:397–401).

115 Ναζαρὲθ and Ναζαρὰθ occur in a number of mss. at 4:13, but not in the best witnesses nor in Origin's citation of the passage. They also appear in 2:23 in a few witnesses.

This Matthean redactor must also be the one responsible for the single appearance of the word *Nazaret* in the Gospel of Matthew, namely, in the enigmatic verse 2:23: "And he went and dwelt in a city called Nazaret, that what was spoken by the prophets might be fulfilled, 'He shall be called a Nazorean.'" As far as we can surmise thus far, the word Nazorean (*Nazôraios*) is a pure invention by the same hand.

The Matthean redactor failed to note the parallel passage Mt 3:13, where *Nazaret* was not added, and he also failed to harmonize Mt 4:13, which contains the archaic form *Nazara*.

Thus, Matthew is a multistage document. The original author of that text had — like Q and Mark before him — no knowledge of the village Nazareth in Lower Galilee. However, a subsequent redactor did have such knowledge, and this person hurriedly added the word *Nazaret* to both the Gospels of Matthew and of Mark which lay before him. The redactor changed Jesus' provenance from Capernaum to Nazareth, and in so doing he may well have also removed obvious references to Capernaum as the hometown of Jesus in the Gospel of Mark.

In the Gospel of Matthew, the variant *Nazaret* occurs in the birth story, a portion of the gospel universally considered ahistorical but generally credited to the evangelist.[116] However, we now have reason to suppose that the birth story is from a later hand, on the basis that it contains *Nazaret*, a form of the name lacking in Mt 4:13, which reads *Nazara*. Furthermore, we have learned that the Matthean redactor who wrote *Nazaret* was the first in the canonical tradition to become aware of the settlement in Lower Galilee.

In sum, we can conclude the following: (1) Q knew only an as yet unlocated *Nazara* (see below). (2) Both Q and the Gospel of Mark did not know of Nazareth in Galilee, for they were written before that town came into existence. (3) The Matthean redactor (not the original writer) learned of the new settlement of *Natsareth* (*nun-tsade-resh-tav*) in Lower Galilee. (4) That redactor associated Jesus with *Nazaret*, his Greek approximation of the Semitic name, yet one which preserves the important voiced sibilant [z]. That sibilant is an enduring trait of the entire Hellenist Christian tradition (for reasons to be seen later). In contrast, the Semitic traditions (Hebrew, Aramaic, Mandaic, Arabic, *etc.*) uniformly use the unvoiced sibilant as second radical. (5) The redactor was responsible for Mt 2:23 and also for the interpolation of *Nazaret* into Mk 1:9.

The variant *Nazareth* betrays an even later stage. It belongs to the age of the Lucan birth narrative, the only place in the canonical gospels other than Mt 21:11 where the variant occurs.[117] This name, which successfully supplanted all the other variants, fully harmonizes with the Semitic name of the settlement—except, again, for the voiced [z] (Greek *zeta* instead of

[116] Bultmann 1963:293; Koester 1990:318.
[117] Lk 1:26; 2:4, 39, 51.

sigma), to which the Hellenist tradition was already committed (*cf.* Q's *Nazara*, Mark's *Nazarêne*, the Matthean redactor's *Nazaret*).

We are now in a position to revisit the Q passage cited above, and in so doing must apply a different interpretation than the one commonly accepted:

> (b) Now when he heard that John had been arrested, he withdrew into Galilee. Leaving Nazara he went and dwelt in Capernaum by the sea, in the territory of Zebulun and Naphtali, that what was spoken by the prophet Isaiah might be fulfilled... (Mt 4:12-14)

Only the conjunction 'and' [*kai*] has been omitted from the beginning of the second sentence, as being without force. The sense of the passage is the same as in (a) previously cited, but I wish to bring out the possibility of a *parallelismus membrorum*, namely, that the beginning of the second sentence duplicates the content at the end of the first. According to this interpretation there are not two consecutive journeys of Jesus, but one—from Judea to the north. This interpretation seems strange to us, unaccustomed as we are to locating Nazara in the south, but the sense is direct and simple: Jesus leaves Nazara *in Judea*, and journeys to Capernaum in Galilee.

The presence of a southern tradition in the texts already cited, and the impossibility that *Nazara* in Q signifies Nazareth in Galilee, force us to adopt the reading in version (b). Here we have only one displacement of Jesus: from the locus of John's activity to Capernaum. This archaic reading of the Q passage certainly predates the (now universal) reading first effected by the Matthean redactor, namely, the deliberate and artificial association of Jesus' provenance with the emergent village in Lower Galilee.

We now can understand why Matthew describes Jesus' destination as "in the territory of Zebulun and Naphtali." This makes no sense if the origin of Jesus' journey were Nazareth in Lower Galilee, for Nazareth is itself in Zebulun.[118] It makes sense, however, when we understand that the compiler of Q was not describing a journey within one province but *between* provinces, namely, between Judea to the south and "the territory of Zebulun and Naphtali" to the north.

---

[118]   The borders of Zebulun are given at Josh 19:10–16.

Pre—*c.* 70–100 CE — No knowledge of Nazareth in Galilee

Nazara (Q)	Mt 4:13
	Lk 4:16
Nazarêne	Mk 1:24; 10:47; 14:67; 16:6
	(*Nazarêne* deleted from Matthean *Grundschrift*)
	Lk 4:34; 24:19

Post-*c.* 70–100 CE — Knowledge of Nazareth in Galilee

Nazôraios	Mt 2:23 (*cf.* LXX [*Alex.*] Jud 13:5 *Nazeiraion*); 26:71
	Lk 18:37; Acts 2:22; 3:6; 4:10; 6:14; 22:8; 24:5; 26:9
	Jn 18:5, 7; 19:19
Nazaret	Mt:2:23 (first redactor)
	Mk 1:9 (interpolation)
	Jn 1:45, 46
Nazareth	Mt 21:11 (second redactor)
	Lk 1:26; 2:4, 39, 51 (later birth story)
	Acts 10:38

*Illus. 6.1. **Nazareth** and its cognates in the New Testament.*

Support for a southern location of *Nazara* is found in the other Q passage in which this early form appears, namely, Lk 4:16. Interestingly, this passage is the only mention of "Nazareth" in the Gospel of Luke (outside the birth narrative of chapters 1–2, where we read the late form *Nazareth* four times). The occurrence of *Nazara* does not mean that the entire pericope Lk 4:16-30 belongs to the oldest gospel stratum, one predating the association of Jesus with the town in Lower Galilee.[119] Rather, it has been determined that the incident in the Nazareth synagogue is a thoroughly Lucan composition based on Mk 6:1–6, with typically Lucan vocabulary.[120]

---

[119] On the relation of Mt 4:16 and Lk 4:13*ff.*, see Tannehill 64–65.
[120] See Grässer 7; Tannehill 65.

After the pericope dealing with the synagogue of *Nazara* and the attempted casting down of Jesus, Luke writes: "And he went down to Capernaum, *a city of Galilee.*" The last phrase, of course, is superfluous (and even inappropriate) were Jesus already in Galilee.[121] This is yet another indication that the Q stage of the tradition located *Nazara* in Judea.

We can now consider a detail of the Lucan pericope which has bedeviled pilgrims and scholars alike for hundreds of years, namely, that Nazareth in Lower Galilee is not on "the brow of a hill" (*ophruos tou orous*, Lk 4:29). The third evangelist has evidently seized upon a topographical element and constructed a whole story around it. It is true, of course, that such topographical aspects of an obviously invented story cannot be pressed for authenticity. Luke's freedom with much more important elements amply demonstrates this. Indeed, the entire pericope Lk 4:16–30 has it's *point de départ* in Q (possibly via Mt 4:13), from which only the original name of the place, *Nazara*, survives. Redaction critical work has shown that Luke then constructed an elaborate story with an eye to Mark 6:1–6.[122] Chronologically, then, we can locate Lk 4:16–30 after Q and after the Gospel of Mark, and before composition of the Lucan birth narrative.

The attempted casting down is a dramatic scene and presupposes a nearby cliff of considerable height. Such cliffs hardly exist in Lower Galilee, but are found in profusion in the immediate vicinity of Qumran, as anyone who has seen an aerial photo of the desolate area will attest. Precipitous ravines slice through the land on all sides of the ancient settlement, carving steep and forbidding cliffs hundreds of feet high. Here, the Nazarenes could easily have led someone to the brow of the hill on which their settlement was located, to cast him to his death.

The desolate cliffs near the Wadi Qumran offer a fitting setting for a prophet wont to go into deserted and solitary places to meditate.[123] All this is but circumstantial, were it not for the inevitable conclusion of our foregoing analysis: the earliest gospel tradition, Q, located Jesus' home of *Nazara* not in Nazareth of Galilee, but in Judea.

> (b) Now when he heard that John had been arrested, he withdrew into Galilee. Leaving Nazara he went and dwelt in Capernaum by the sea, in the territory of Zebulun and Naphtali, that what was spoken by the prophet Isaiah might be fulfilled... (Mt 4:12–14)

---

[121] Sometimes considered the earliest uncial, *Codex Bezae* (D) adds at this point: "by the sea in the regions of Zebulun and Naphtali," similar to Mt 4:13 (*cf.* above).

[122] Bultmann 1963:31, who writes that Mark 6:1–6 is itself "a typical example of how an imaginary situation is built up out of an independent saying."

[123] Mk 1:12–13; 35; 45; 6:31–35; and parallels.

This Q passage supplies us with another significant insight: in the earliest gospel stratum, *Nazara* is none other than the field of activity of John the Baptist.

Epilogue

This book began by examining the archaeology of the Nazareth basin, and has ended far away among the desolate hills of Judea. We have been led inexorably, one step at a time, to the southern province, and it is there that we must find the continuation of our search into Christian origins. Galilee was a latecomer to the tradition, postdating the migration of Jesus-followers northwards to Pella before the First Jewish War. Surely, the activity of Jesus about the Sea of Galilee reflects the onwards migration of Jesus-followers to that region, and also reflects a situation contemporary with the activity of the evangelists. For reasons yet to be explored, the canonical tradition found it necessary to divorce Jesus from Judean roots. But the gospels preserve unmistakable signs of an earlier tradition, one firmly rooted in Judean soil.

The myth of Nazareth, taken together with evidence from early Christian writings, witnesses to a deliberate, systematic, and calculated obliteration of the southern tradition from the Jesus story, one already effected at the earliest stage of the canonical gospel tradition. Indeed, the southern tradition was not entirely excised—it survives in certain elements, most notably being Jesus' activities and death in Jerusalem. But already in the Gospel of Mark, the Jesus story opens and closes not with Judea, but with Galilee:

Mk. 1.9 [*pre-redaction stage*]: In those days Jesus came from Galilee and was baptized by John in the Jordan.

Mk. 16.7: "But go, tell his disciples and Peter that he is going before you to Galilee; there you will see him, as he told you."

John was associated with Judea, and Jesus with the Galilee. Thus the evangelist Mark separated the Baptist and Jesus. That separation, however, may have been purely his invention.

———————

This work has not presented new material, but has brought a radically new analysis to material long known. The archaeology of Nazareth—based on tombs and oil lamps, pottery, graffiti, and so forth—has been in the public domain for decades. One might think that the march of time and the assiduous work of thousands of scholars would long ago have corrected the gross errors regarding this evidence. Such has not been the case. The scholarly world, despite a profusion of professors, is plainly not self-correcting—unlike the stock market, for example, with its myriad counterbalancing participants, which some experts now claim is immune to the wild gyrations of the past. Rather, academe is congenitally addicted to the opium of an invented Jesus story, one now two thousand years old.

We have removed one idol from the temple—Jesus of Nazareth. He—whoever he was (or wasn't)—certainly was not Jesus "of Nazareth" in Lower Galilee. Of that we can now be quite confident. It remains to be determined why the evangelists found it necessary to invent such a Jesus.

When someone removes the idols from the temple, deep-seated resentment is likely to ensue. After all, mythology serves a purpose, and the Christian myth fabricated in late antiquity answers to basic human needs: the need to be watched over, protected, saved, loved—even the need to be immortal. The Christian faith, in its Pauline guise, has grown because ordinary people have sensed a profound affinity for its myths and have toiled untiringly, though misguidedly, on their behalf. It is to be hoped, however, that the human species is capable of taking thought, of looking squarely at the way things are, of removing myth and delusion, and of using the powers of reason that separate humanity from bestiality. In short, it is to be hoped that we are capable of living in a world which is not make-believe. That is what it really means to be human, and that is the challenge before us all.

Appendices

Appendix 1

Itemization of the Bronze-Age Artefacts
from the Nazareth Basin
(*Excavations* pp. 258–268; 74–75)

All the items for the Bronze Age given in *Excavations in Nazareth* are presented here, arranged chronologically. Bagatti does not date all finds, but when available his opinion is furnished in quotation marks. When a different dating is indicated in the literature, both opinions are given. *Re-datings* by Amiran and others appear in parentheses to the right, and are used as primary data in this book. Undatable shards are indicated in a section at the end of each division. Suggested but uncertain datings are given under the rubric "Putative," and are not included in *Illus. 1.5*. Bronze Age finds at Nazareth have been discovered in five tombs (Nos. 1, 7, 8, 80, 81) "and partly on the surface" (*Exc.* 258).

Artefacts from Tomb 1
(Numbers to the left are from *Exc.* Figs. 208, 210, & 211:1–17.
Am = Amiran)

IP:

210:15   Jar with wide, flat base. For the form see Meyerhof Pl. 12.3:25; Pl. 13.3:47; Pl. 17.23:49; Pl. 20.33:14 (all with spouts or handles).

"EB or MB"   (IP)

MB IIA:

208:2	*Cf.* Am: 31:1, 4.	(MB IIA)
208:11	Jug fragment. Form: Am: 34:9 (*cf.*Exc 211:21).	MB II
208:17	*Cf. Arch.* 6.4.6	(MB IIA)
208:18	Jug. Am: 33:10; 34:9.; *Arch.* 6.15.10.	(MB II A or B)
210:4	Double handle. Am: Phs. 106, 108.	(MB IIA)
210:5	Triple handle 'characteristic of MB IIA.' (*Arch*:164)	MB (IIA)
210:6–8	Double handles.	(MB IIA)
210:11	Carinated bowl with ring base. Parallels: Am: Ph. 97 & Pl. 27:11 (Megiddo XII). The ring base was not conceived until the Middle Bronze period (Engberg:71).	MB (IIA)
210:12	Chalice. Am: Pl. 27:21 (Megiddo XII).	MB (IIA)
210:16	Carinated bowl. Am: Pl. 27:1.	MB (IIA)
210:31–32	Bowls. Am: 26:7-8	(MB II B-C)
211:1	Lamp. *Exc*:299. Am: Pl. 59:2	(MB IIA)

THE MYTH OF NAZARETH

211:8, 9, 11 Toggle pins.   (MB)
211:10 Toggle pin with adorned handle. *Arch*:205–06.   (MB IIC)
211:14 Scarab, 15ᵗʰ–17ᵗʰ dyns (*c.* 1670–1570). *Exc:*315   MB II (B–C)

LB:

208:10 A handle of large jar with incised "X." (See also 208:14.)   LB
208:14 "Ribbon handle with incisions." (*Cf.* 208:10.)   LB
208:15 A jar with thick walls which Bagatti states "has no parallel and is entirely singular" (p. 268). The angularity of form is similar to some Tell el-Yahudiyeh Ware (Am: Pl. 36:20). There is also resemblance to later imported Mycenaean vessels and local imitations (Am: Pl. 57:7). The base and angularity have parallels with Iron I-II Palestinian jars (Am: Pl. 78:11; 79:8)   LB
208:1 A Palestinian commercial jar (Am:141). A similar jar was found in Tomb 7 (Exc:263). Bagatti notes that "many other ceramics" also date to LB, but does not itemize them (*Exc*:268).   LB (I)
208:12 "Medium vase" (*cf.* 208:13). The top half is missing and we do not know if this is a jar or a jug. Bagatti acknowledges (*Exc*:268) that both 208:12 & 13 have "points of contact" with Tell el-Yahudiyeh Ware. We note the characteristic "punctured design arranged in geometric patterns" (Am::118). A potter's kiln was excavated at nearby 'Afula (in the Jezreel Valley ten kilometers south of Nazareth) in which many fragments of Tell el-Yahudiyeh Ware were found (Am:120). Such ware dates to MB IIa (2000–1730), an era well represented at Nazareth. However, Bagatti's opinion is that these vessels are in fact Black Impressed Ware dating to LB I (p. 268). This opinion needs to be revisited, and one wonders if the inventiveness of the MB IIA potters (Am:106) may not have extended to such vessels as these.   "LB I"
208:13 Fragments of either a jug or jar with some similarities to 208:12. See immediately preceding discussion.   "LB I"
208:21 Jug with straight neck. Am: 46:8.   (LB I)
210:10 "Jug of black clay." Am: (p. 146) calls this type the "gray juglet" of N. Canaanite origin.   LB (I)
210:17 Am: 38:1   (LB I)
210:18 Am: 39:6   (LB I)
211:2 Lamp. *Exc*:299. [Like Fig. 235:1] Am: Pl. 59:11   (LB I)
208:16 Pilgrim Flask. Am: Pl. 51:3 & 8, Ph. 167.   LB II (1410–1200)
208:20 Jug or juglet. Am: 46:14.   (LB II A)
210:14 Am: 38:14.   (LB IIA)
208:19 Jug with pronounced shoulder and slightly flaring neck. Am: 46:22.   (LB II B)

LB IIA–Iron I:
210:23, 25, 26Large bowls with carinations immediately below the rim. Am: 39:14, 18. "This type of Late Bronze Age bowl has been found up to the present only in the south of the country. In the Iron I, at least as far as form is concerned, the type also appears to have spread to the north of the country" (Am:129).

(LB IIA–Iron I)

Putative MB IIA or LB:
210:1-3 Shards with button base.   (MB IIA?)

210:27   Thick-walled bowl, profiled rim. *Cf*. Am: Pl. 25:4   (MB IIA?)

210:19   Am: 42:13.   (LB IIA-B?)

210:22   (Am: 39:6 ?).   (LB I?)

210:28-30   Four thick-walled bowls, poorly fired, with pronounced ridge below the rim. *Cf*. Am: Pl. 62:25(Iron II A–B?)

Miscellaneous undated:
Shards: 208:3–9; 210:9; 210:13; 210:20–21; 210:24–26; 210:33; 211:3–4.
Lance-heads: 211:5–7. *Cf*. Kenyon p. 13; Meyerhof Pl. 34.3.108.
Metal objects: 211:12–13, 15–17.

Artefacts from Tomb 7
(*Excavations* Fig. 211:18–23)

IP:
211:18   Jar with diagonal incisions around the neck. Am: 23:11& 14; 24:12; Meyerhof 19.33:44; 22.33:21 & 43. "EB/MB"   (IP)

211:19   Jar with wide, flat base and ledge handle. Meyerhof 7.4:17; *Arch*. Fig. 5:11. "EB/MB"   (IP)

MB II:
211:22   Jug(s) with red burnished slip and double handle. Am: Ph. 108.

MB (IIA)

211:20   Rose clay jug with "almost pointed" foot. *Exc*:267. Am: 34:9. "MB and LB."   (MB II B–C, 1730–1550)

211:21   Rose clay jug with button base, poor firing. The button base is typical of MB II B-C (Am:/112). *Exc*:267. Am: 34:9 + 15, 16. "MB and LB."   (MB II B–C, 1730–1550)

Undated:
211:23   Three bowls. (Drawings and descriptions are inconclusive.)

Artefacts from Tomb 80
(*Excavations* Fig. 213)

Late IP:

213:9 Jug with incisions on handle. Am: 24:8 = MB I, Group C. *Cf.* Meyerhof Pl. 15.20.9.. "MB."   (Late IP)

MB II:

213:3 Oil lamp. Am: Pl. 59:3.   (MB IIA)

213:4 Bowl. Am: Pl. 26:5 (Megiddo XII.)   (MB IIA)

213:5 Bowl. Am: Pl. 26:8 (Megiddo XI. (MB IIB)

213:1-2 Alabaster jars, probably imported from Egypt. "The widespread distribution of alabaster vessels began at the beginning of Middle Bronze II B" (*Arch*:202), i.e., after *c.* 1730 BCE.   MB (II B–C)

213:7 Jug. Am: 34:6.   (MB II B–C)

Miscellaneous undated:

213:6 Jug. (*Cf.* Am: Pls. 33:2; 46:14).

213:8 Jug with decoration in upper part.

213:10 Shard.

213:11 Storage jar with shoulder handle(s).

Provenance unknown:

235:1 Lamp. (*Cf.* Fig. 211:2). Placed in Chart 3 with the Tomb 1 material.   (LB I)

Artefacts from Tomb 81
(Yeivin:145; *'Atiqot* IV [1965] Suppl., p. 14; RB 70 [1963] p. 563; RB 72 [1965] p. 547; *Exc*:246.)

MB IIA:

— 3+ teapots

— 2 small jars with ring handles

— 1 large jar (photo at DBS:323.)

The results of this appendix are incorporated in *Illus. 1.5.*

Appendix 2:

Itemization of the Iron Age Artefacts
from the Nazareth Basin

Sources:
Bagatti, "Ritrovamenti nella Nazaret evangelica," LA 5 (1955)
Bagatti, *Excavations in Nazareth* Figs. 211, 214–216 (1969)
Bagatti, "Scavo Presso la Chiesa di S. Guiseppe a Nazaret," LA 21 (1971)
Loffreda, "Ceramica del Ferro I Trovata a Nazaret," LA 27 (1977)
Vitto, "An Iron Age Burial Cave in Nazareth," *'Atiqot* XLII (2001)

Abbreviations: S= Silo; CA= Church of the Annunciation;
CJ= Church of St. Joseph

The Iron Age Evidence

(1) From the area around the Church of the Annunciation
(Numbers to the left are from *Exc.* Figs. 211, 214–216)

LB II-Iron I
211:26   (S. 57)   Cooking pot.   LB II or Iron (*Exc*:272)
214:3   (S. 22)   Large four-handled jar. Bagatti gives parallels with *Megiddo Tombs*, pl. 65:9 and 61:1, dated LB II and Iron I respectively. Amiran appears to date this type of jar to Iron III in the South (Am. Pl. 82:1, 3; Ph. 247).

Generally dated "Iron Period"
214:4–5   Shards.   (S. 22)
215:3   Shard.   (S. 22)
211:27–34   Shards. No. 30 with Grecian style decoration. (S. 57)
215:1-4, 6–7 Shards.   (S. 57)
214:6 & 215:5 The top and two shards of a storage jar. Am. Pl. 77–82.
              (Found between the silos, CA.)
215:2   Handle, found "inside northern Medieval apse." (CA)
215:4   Shard "found in the Byzantine atrium." (CA)
215:1, 6   Shards (provenance unspecified).

Iron I-II: 214:1 Large wide-mouthed bowl. (S. 22)

THE MYTH OF NAZARETH

Iron III:
211:24-25   Wholemouth jars. Am. Pl. 81:4-8; Ph. 246.   (Iron III) (S. 57)
214:2   Jar with three handles and spout. Am. Pl. 81:13.   (Iron III) (S. 22)
This type is pictured at Amiran Ph. 250 and dated by her to Iron III. Bagatti dated it to Iron II, along with "a small homogenous group" of artefacts. The original fragment (top portion of jar) is pictured at Bagatti 1955:18, and wholly restored at DBS:323 and *Exc.* Pl. IV:5.

(2) From the area of the Church of St. Joseph
("Scavo" 1971, pp. 5-32).

The area of this excavation was disturbed and the shards recovered were quite small. At *Scavo*:18, Bagatti offers a photo of 8 of the shards (Fig. 11). Underneath them is a diagram of the remaining 21 finds, also shards (Fig. 12). One of the items in the photo and one in the diagram are the same piece or are from the same vessel (11:8, 12:7), so that there may be 28 fragments in all. Bagatti typologically compares 13 of these fragments to examples in Amiran's *APHL*. Amiran's dating for the comparable types follows:

(Fig. 12) *Scavo*	(Plate and No.) Am.	Description	# finds	Iron Period	Date
1-4	82:5-6	Lge. vessel mouths w/collar	4	III	800-587
5-6	75:20-21	Rims of pots	2	III	800-587
7-10	75:1-16	Rims (*bocche*) with ridges	4	I—II	1200-800
17	76:13	Rim	1	IIB–III	900-587
20	87:10-11 88:18	.Fragment of juglet	1	II	1000-800
21	100:16	Oil lamp	1	III	800-587

(3) *The Vitto Tomb*

Item	Stratum	Parallel	Dating
1. Bowl.	Megiddo VI A.	Loffreda #11	1100–1000
2. Bowl	Keisan IX	Loffreda #12	1100–1000
3. Shard	—	—	—
4. Chalice	Megiddo VI	—	1100–1000
5. Jar	Megiddo VIIB–VIA	—	1100–1000
6. Shard	—	—	—
7. Jug (?)	Megiddo VI	—	1100–1000

316

8. Jug (?)	Megiddo VI	——	1100–1000
9-10+ Five additional shards		——	——
11 Scarab	Megiddo VI	——	1100–1000

12+ Pendant, various beads, cowrie shells, bracelets (common in the Iron Age).

The Vitto tomb offers one of the clearest datings in Nazareth. All the pottery is from the eleventh century, possibly including late XII **BCE** (Megiddo Stratum VIA). The various beads and other objects found in this tomb are compatible with this dating.

(4) *The Loffreda material*

The chronological labels in the middle column accord with the schema used in this book. The dates given in the right hand column are those of Loffreda (subsequently dated by Vitto more precisely to XI **BCE**).

1. Amphora	Iron I	1200–1000
2. Pitcher	Iron IA	1200–1100
3. Flask	Iron I–IIA	1200–900
4. Jug	Iron IIA	1000–900
5. Flask	Iron IB	1100–1000
6. Jug	Iron IIA	1000–900
7. Amphora	Iron I	1200–1000
8. Small flask	Iron IIB	900–800
9. Pyxis	Iron I–IIA	1200–900
10. Bowl	Iron IB–IIA	1100–900
11. Bowl	Iron I–II (Vitto #1)	1100–1000
12. Bowl	Iron IB	1100–1000
13. Oil lamp	Iron I–IIA	1200–900
14. Two juglets	Iron I–IIA	1200–900
15. Small cup	Iron IIA	1000–900
16. Bone dagger handle	——	——
17. Three metal bracelets	——	——

The above information yields the following chronological schema according to Loffreda:

Dates	Period	# items	Lof. #
1200–1100	Iron IA	1	2
1200–1000	Iron I.	2	1,7
1200–900	Iron I–IIA	5	3,9,13,14a/b
1100–1000	Iron IB	3	5, 11, 12
1100–900	Iron IB–IIA	1	10
1000–900	Iron IIA	3	4,6,15
900–800	Iron IIB	1	8

F. Vitto dated twelve Iron I objects to Iron I B–XI BCE (Vitto 2001:161–65), and also concluded that all the Loffreda material "should be pinpointed to the eleventh century BCE" (Vitto:167).

The results of this appendix are incorporated in *Illus. 1.5*.

Appendix 3:
The Stratigraphy of Megiddo

Megiddo, twenty kilometers from the Nazareth basin, was arguably the most powerful city in Northern Palestine during the Bronze and Iron Ages. Knowledge derived from its 25+ strata has helped with relative datings as far away as Egypt and Syria. However, the stratigraphy of the site is one of the hotly contested issues of Palestine archaeology and is presently in flux. This brief resume does not presume to make any contribution to that discussion, nor to be definitive or complete. It follows the so-called Low Chronology and is presented as a general reference subject to future adjustment.

Period	Dates	Stratum	Egypt
Pre-Pottery Neolithic	6000—*c*.3300	XX	Predynastic

Various stages of the Chalcolithic period. First dwellings of unfortified settlement with lime floors on bedrock, mud brick walls, pits, and ovens.

EB I	*c*. 3300–2900	XIX	Narmer ("Menes") Early 1st dyn

Megiddo is the largest urban site in the country, covering c.130 acres (55 hec.). Cylinder seal impressions show connections with Syria, Mesopotamia, and Egypt. The huge temple has several walls 4 m thick. Finds include scratched drawings; gray-burnished "Esdraelon ware" and "grain-wash" pottery.

EB II	2900–2650	XVIII	End of 1st–2nd dynasties

A massive city wall, c. 5 m thick, is built. Megiddo becomes a fortified but smaller settlement.

EB III A	2650–2550	XVII-XVI	3rd–early 4th dynasties

[Exact stratification uncertain.] City wall further widened to 8 meters thickness; well-preserved buildings; huge 'megaron' temples on site of earlier compound, with enormous round altar. A great quantity of animal bones attest to animal sacrifice. Megiddo is a major urban center during this period.

EB III B	2550–2350	XVII–XVI	Late 4th–5th dynasties

Decline of settlement at Megiddo; abandonment of some urban sites in Israel.

EB IV	2350-2200	XV	Late 5th–6th dynasties

The city of Stratum XVI suffers total destruction. Some continuity of settlement in central cult area. Eventual abandonment of Megiddo and remaining urban sites in Israel.

THE MYTH OF NAZARETH

Period	Dates	Stratum	Egypt
Int. Period **(EB IV, MB I)**	2200–2000	XIV	7th–11th dynasties, 1st Int. Period

Shaft tombs; wheel-made, gray pottery (Grp. C, Amiran:83). Small, poorly-constructed dwellings.

MB IIa (MB I) 2000–1800   XIII–XII   12th dynasty

Stratum XIII B: *The first wave of re-settlement. The town is unfortified (Arch:166). The great altar continues to be used, but is now associated with multiple shrines or temples. Graves exist below and between houses.*

Stratum XIII A: *Continuation and improvement of the previous construction; five-foot thick city wall is erected of mud-brick, with an exceptionally strong L-shaped gateway.*

Stratum XII: *City wall is broadened and the town becomes a planned, organized site. A buttressing wall is added to the outer face of the city wall. Large houses (palaces) built over the remains of the old city wall, as well as stone-built tombs with multiple burials inside the city. The first Hyksos scarabs presage Hyksos ascendancy in Palestine.*

MB IIb(–III) 1800–1550   XI–X   13th–17th dyns., 2nd Int. Period

Stratum XI: *A new city wall built with sloping glacis, a characteristic feature of the Hyksos period. Renovation of a temple; appearance of carved ivories and bronze figurines, axes, and adzes.*

Stratum X: (Late 17th–early 16th cents.): *Repairs and additions to earlier structures. Close of the Middle Bronze Period.*

LB I   1550–1400   IX–VIII   18th dynasty

Thutmose III of Egypt besieges and conquers Megiddo (c. 1470 BCE). The city revives and experiences its greatest material wealth.

LB II   1400–1300   VIII   El-Amarna Period

Impressive palace built with 2 m. thick walls, a large courtyard, a bathroom with floor of seashells set in lime, and a hoard of ivory and gold objects. Destroyed by fire.

LB III   1300–1200   VII B   19th dynasty

A wealthy but declining city destroyed by Merneptah in 1208.

Iron I   1200-1000   VII A–VI B   20th–early 21st dynasties

Stratum VIIA (1200–1130) *A prosperous city. Destruction of most of VII A town (after 1130, probably by the Philistines) marks the end of Egyptian rule in Canaan and of the Bronze Age.*

Stratum VI B (11th cent.) *A poor settlement. Philistine bichromeware appears. Clear signs of continuity in ceramic tradition and house layout (Finkelstein).*

Period	Dates	Stratum	Egypt

Iron II A–B 1000–800 VI A–IVB Late 21^s–early 23rd dyns.

Stratum VI A (10th cent.) *Era of David and Solomon, influx of Israelites. Bichromeware disappears. Partial rebuilding includes new, extensive and densely-built residences. Most of the buildings are baked brick on stone foundations. Temple, palace, and city gate not rebuilt. 'Orpheus' jug and hand-burnished pottery. Strong metalworking tradition. Town is destroyed by Shishak I of Egypt c. 922 (Finkelstein), leaving a burnt stratum more than 1 m deep. Another view (Alt, Mazar, Yadin) considers this fourth destruction layer to be Kg. David's conquest c. 1000 BCE.*

Stratum V B (early 9th cent.). *Modest and poor settlement without fortifications or town planning.*

Stratum V A–IV B (9th cent.) *Megiddo fortified and rebuilt, including three palaces of ashlar construction, with courtyards and monumental entrances. Appearance of red slipped, irregularly burnished vessels. A prosperous city. City destroyed (foe unknown).*

Iron III 800–587 III–II Late 22nd/23rd–26th dyns.

Stratum IV A (8th cent.) *Palaces dismantled, building of complex city gate (mislabeled "Solomonic Gate"), new wall, massive water system with vertical shaft 120 ft. deep. Megiddo is a garrison city with stables, center for Israelite cavalry units. No residences uncovered.*

Stratum III (Late 8th cent.) *Megiddo conquered by Tiglath-Pileser III (732 BCE). Capital of the Assyrian province of Magiddu. Massive palaces in new style, new gatehouse and northern "stables" built. Town has central courtyard, residential blocks, evenly-spaced and parallel streets. Israelite chariot units headquartered at Megiddo probably were incorporated directly into the Assyrian army.*

Stratum II (7th cent.) *Residential quarters uncovered and a fortress with walls 2.5m thick. King Josiah executed at Megiddo by Pharoah Neco (609 BCE). Clear signs of decline.*

Babylonian–Persian 586–332 I Late 26th–30th dynasties

Small houses, some storerooms and cist tombs. Conquest by Alexander (332 BCE) and final abandonment of settlement at Megiddo.

Hellenistic–Hasmonean 332–63 (*No settlement.*)

Roman 63 BCE–324 CE

South of the Megiddo mound the Jewish village of Kefer 'Otnay existed from c. 100 CE. The second and sixth Roman legions were stationed there in II–III CE and the place became an administrative center called Legio (later the Arab Lejjun). Associated aqueducts, tombs, and a theater have been discovered.

Appendix 4

The Nazareth Tombs

(Does not include the Bronze-Iron Age tombs of Japhia;
[!] indicates a tomb of particular embarrassment to the tradition.)

Bagatti #	Kopp #	Description data / location	# kokhim	Movable Finds?
—	1	Discovered 1935.	6	—
—	2	Large tomb. Had <u>rolling stone</u>.	13	—
72	3	"Richmond" tomb	9	√
		Another kokh tomb could have abutted this one (Kopp 1938:194)		
—	4	Once connected to nos. 3 & 5?	6	—
—	5	Has stone ledge.	16	—
70	6	"Laham" tomb (*Exc.* Fig. 192) Had <u>rolling stone</u>.	13	√
73	7	Sisters of Nazareth (2 chambers) <u>Rolling stone</u>.	7+	—
—(!)	8	Unfinished.	1+	—
74	9	"A classic kokhim tomb" (Kopp)	10	—
—	10	Destroyed.	?	—
76	12	Greatly damaged.	6	—
77	13	Large kokh complex.	24+	—
—	14	Trough tomb.	2	—
79	15	With graffiti (Bagatti:1967b).	12	—
—	16	Made into cistern (filled in)	14	—
—	17	(No plan available.)	8	—
78	18	One chamber destroyed.	6+	—
—	19	Destroyed. (Contiguous tombs?)	4+	—
—	20	Sunken graves ("*Senkgräber*")	2+	—
—	21	Unspecified no. of sunken graves.	?	—
		("Many similar [*unexcavated*] tombs" nearby [Kopp 1938:204])		
71	22	4 chambers (largest tomb in basin). Many		√

Bagatti: "A description is wanting" (*Exc.*240). When Kopp visited the site, he wrote that a <u>rolling stone</u> sealed the still unexplored 4th chamber.

—	23	Largely destroyed.	8	—
27(!)	—	Under CA. (Kopp 1938:196–97)	5+	—
29(!)	—	Under CA.	?	—
o/p(!)	—	Under CA.	2+	—
—	—	El Batris St. (ESI 18[1998]:32). (3–4 chambers. Sparse finds.)	5+	√

Appendix 5

Independent Datings of Nazareth Lamps and Pottery

A. Rosenthal and Sivan 1978 (RS)
An asterisk signifies that the lamp is also dated by Fernandez 1982.

• RS 81 "Herodian lamp": 4 bow-spouted oil lamps (*Exc*: 239 & fig. 192:6*; *Exc.* Fig. 233:1, 2, 3* on pp. 300, 305, 307, and fig. 235:3–4[1] on p. 304).

$\rightarrow$ *c.* 25 BCE–*c.* 150 CE[2]

• RS 85 "Mould-made lamp": 4 "Darom" lamps (QDAP 1 [1932], pl. 34:2 lower right[3]; *Exc.* pp. 239 and fig. 192:7*, 8*, 9*on p. 238).[4]

$\rightarrow$ *c.* 70 CE–*c.* 135 CE.

• RS 89 "Round lamps with decorated discus": 4 Middle Roman lamps (QDAP 1 [1932], pl. 34:2 upper row left and right; *Exc.* pp. 239 nos. 13–14[5] and fig. 192 on p. 238).

$\rightarrow$ *c.* 50 CE–III CE

• RS 100 "Lamps of the third and fourth centuries": 1 Roman lamp (*Exc.* pp. 239:12 and fig. 192:12 on p. 238).

$\rightarrow$ III–IV CE

• RS 111 "Ovoid lamps with low relief decoration on the rim and discus": 3 Roman lamps (*Exc.* fig. 235:17, 18, 20*).

$\rightarrow$ III–IV CE

• RS 112 "Bi-lanceolate lamps": 2 Roman lamps (*Exc.* fig. 81*, left; fig. 235:21).

$\rightarrow$ III–IV CE

• RS 120 "Large lamps: Radiated decoration": 1 lamp (*Exc.* fig. 234:17).

$\rightarrow$ VI CE "at the earliest"

• RS 138 "Lamps with linear pattern": 1 lamp (*Exc.* fig. 234:27).

$\rightarrow$ VI CE+

• RS 137 "Mameluke lamp": 1 lamp (*Exc.* fig. 234:14).

$\rightarrow$ XIII–XIV CE

---

[1]   RS 81 corrected from "fig. 235:7–8."

[2]   These lamps were found in kokh tombs and thus date after *c.* 50 CE. The beginning of the bow-spouted lamps was finalized by V. Sussman in the 1980s, after RS and Fernandez published their works, which date the lamp's appearance too early. On this point, see discussion at Chapter 4, pp. 167-172.

[3]   Corrected ("left" in RS).

[4]   Corrected ("fig. 192:7–10" in RS).

[5]   Corrected ("Nos. 10–11" in RS).

THE MYTH OF NAZARETH

B. Fernandez 1982
(An asterisk signifies that the lamp is also dated by
Rosenthal and Sivan 1978.)[6]

Oil lamps

Page		Type	Date
32, 63	The "Hellenistic nozzle" (*Exc.* fig. 192:15)	L 1	Uncertain.[7]
33	Bow-spouted lamp (*Exc.* fig. 192:6*)	L 3.2	15 BCE–60 CE[8]
34	Bow-spouted lamp (*Exc.* fig. 233:3*)	L 3.4b	40 CE–80 CE[9]
36	Bow-spouted lamp (*Exc.* fig. 192:10)	L 7	70–115 CE
36	Bow-spouted lamp (Berytus 14/2 [1963], n. 516)	L 8.1	80–140 CE
37	3 lamps "Darom" (*Exc.* fig. 192:7*, 8*, 9*)	L 8.2	80–140 CE
37	Roman lamp (*Exc.* fig. 235:9b)	L 9.1a	50–130 CE
38	2 Roman lamps (*Exc.* fig. 192:13, 14)	L 9.1c	100–260 CE
39	3 Roman lamps (*Exc.* fig. 235:10. 11. 13)	L 10.2	130–340 CE
40	2 Roman lamps (*Exc.* figs. 81* and 235:21)	L 12	275–360 CE

---

6   Fernandez' problematic datings (some of which conflict with Bagatti and others, and are unsustainably early—see Chapter 4, n. 52; above pp. 271–272) are included here for completeness, as he has dated a considerable quantity of Nazareth material.

7   Fernandez is unaware of the local Galilean tradition to which this nozzle belongs (Pt. 3:16*ff.*). He writes: *Desgraciadamente no contamos con ningún punto de apoyo directo para fijar una datación a este tipo* ("Unfortunately, we cannot count on any direct point of support in order to fix a date for this type." Fernandez 63). Perhaps swayed by the "Hellenistic" characterizations of the shard in the literature, he ventures an early date for it: *c.* 80 BCE–40 BCE (Fernandez 105; *cf.* Pt 3:25).

8   Fernandez is unaware of the appearance of this lamp type only after Herod the Great's reign (d. 4 BCE), and of its later appearance in the Galilee. Also, the Spaniard's very early *terminus ante quem* (60 CE) is not followed by Sussman, Rosenthal, or others. This Nazareth lamp was found in a kokh tomb (post-50 CE).

9   As with the preceding note, the *terminus ante quem* is far too early. These lamps continued to be made through the Bar Cochba revolt (see Chp. 4:169). In kokh tomb.

326

41	Roman lamp		L 14	260–350 CE
	(*Exc.* fig. 235:20*)			
41	Roman lamp		L 15	230–330 CE
	(*Exc.* fig. 192:12)*Pottery*			

C. Bagatti *Excavations*

<u>Page</u>	<u>Artefact</u>	<u>figure #</u>	<u>Type</u>		<u>Date</u>	
108	Jar	(217:4)	T 1.5	60	BCE–70	CE[10]
112	Flask	(220:6)	T 5.1	80	CE–290	CE[11]
115	Jug	(192:20)	T 8.3	70	CE–300	CE
	Jug	(192:22)	T 8.4	40	BCE–210	CE[12]
119	Cooking pot	(192:26)	T 10.5	70	BCE–70	CE[12]
120	2 cooking pots	(192:18; 224:7)	T 10.6a	50	CE–180 CE	
	Cooking pot	(224:8)	T 10.6b	150	CE–300 CE	
121	Cooking pot	(224:9)	T 10.6c	260	CE–360 CE	
	Cooking pot	(224:3)	T 10.6d	250	CE–360 CE	
124	Kettle	(224:10)	T 12.2	120	CE–300 CE	
126	Pan	(226:1)	T 15.1c	200	CE–360 CE	
127	Pan	(226:4)	T 15.2a	50	CE–170 CE	
	Pan	(226:2)	T 15.2b	150	CE–250 CE	
	Pan	(226:14)	T 15.2c	200	CE–290 CE	
128	Pan	(192:19)	T 15.3	225	CE–375 CE	
	Pan	(226:13)	T 15.4	250	CE–360 CE	
131	Bowl	(231:11)	T 21.1	10	BCE–125 CE[13]	
	2 bowls	(231:9, 10)	T 21.3	180	CE–315 a[13]	

[10] This "ovoid jar" (*Exc.* fig. 217:4) is dated by Bagatti to Late Roman times, "III–IV CE" (see Appendix 6).

[11] Bagatti dates this artefact IV–V CE (with remaining contents of cistern 51b-c).

[12] Fernandez compares the cooking pot (T. 10.5) to a type (T. 1.5) studied by Loffreda at Capernaum and also dated egregiously early. Even Bagatti knows nothing of these early dates. The Italian assigns the jug (192:22) to later Roman times (after "the period of the kokhim tombs"), by comparison with a similar jug "seen in the Laham collection" (192:20, *cf. Exc.* 240). In any case, both the jug and cooking pot were found in kokh tombs, as were also the bow-spouted oil lamps (L.3.2; L.3.4b), all of which Fernandez dates to BCE times. This is quite impossible, if only because the kokh tomb did not arrive in the Galilee until *c.* 50 CE

[13] Another anomalously early dating, which Fernandez admits is wholly hypothetical (he represents the entire dating range on his chart [p. 231] with a dotted rather than a solid line). In all of Palestine, the Spaniard offers only two extant examples of this type of bowl: one from Nazareth and one from Beth Shan. However, the Beth Shan artefact (no. 549 p. 131) is itself problematic, for cataloguing information is not given and thus it is unverifiable (see discussion of this issue in text above, pp. 271–2),

Appendix 6

Pottery and Movable Artefacts from Nazareth
(As dated in the primary literature. Post-Iron Age material only).

• **"Roman" and "Period of the kokhim tombs" (=Middle Roman–Early Byz.)**
— Bagatti 1971a (St. Joseph material) p. 23: Fig. 13:6, 14:3, and 16:1–2.
(Small vessel for oil, parts of three jugs.)
— *Exc*. Fig. 231:23, mortar (p. 298, bottom)
— *Exc*. Fig. 79:2, 14, 21, 22, 23 (pots—see p. 137)
— *Exc*. Fig. 224:2, 4–7 (p. 285) Cooking pots
— *Exc*. Fig. 237:1 (glass bottle)[14]

• **I–II CE**
— 1 small bowl of yellow ware painted red. The three fragments "recall to mind the Roman products of the first period" (*Exc*. 290).
— "The sparse ceramic finds" of the El Batris tomb, claimed by the archaeologist (Z. Yavor) to date to the "1st century CE" (see p. 11).
— Mouth of jug (*Exc*. 236:26. Incorrectly: "First Roman period," *Exc*. 290)

• **II–III CE**
— 12 plates (*Exc*. Fig. 227:1–4, 6–8, 14–18)
— Several Roman oil lamps "with a cavity" [= "concavity"]. See *App. 2.*
— *Exc*. Fig. 81, several oil lamp shards (p. 138)
— Rims of vessels (Bagatti 1971a, Fig. 14:3; 16:1–2)
— 2 pans (*Exc*. Fig. 224:11–12)
— 1 cooking pot (*Exc*. 224:1)
— 1 small vessel for oil (Bagatti 1971a, Fig. 13:6)
— [An inscription on a granite column probably from Caesarea, Beth Shan, or Sepphoris, and transported to Nazareth (*Exc*. 317).]

• **III CE**
— 9 basins (*Exc*. Fig. 231:12–20 & p. 298)
— 4 "soup plates" (*Exc*. Fig. :7–10 & p. 298)
— 3 jugs (*Exc*. Fig. 219:1; 220:1: 221)
— "Glazed cup of celestial color" (*Exc*. 296)
— Fragment of terra sigillata ware (*Exc*. Fig. 79:28 & p. 138)

• **III–IV CE (Also: "Late Roman")**
— 5 pots (*Exc*. Fig. 223:8–9; Fig. 224:3, 8, 9)
— 4 "ovoid jars" (*Exc*. Fig. 217:3–6)

though Bagatti signals that it is in the Nazareth museum (*Exc*. 296). In contrast to the Spaniard, the Italian dates the other artefacts in his diagram (*Exc*. fig. 231:7–10, 12–20) to "around the 3rd century [CE]" (*Exc*. 298).

[14] Bagatti arbitrarily associates the two stone vessels (Exc. 318) with kokh tombs, but they were not found in tombs and there is no evident correlation of the one with the other (*cf.* Chapter 4, pp. 181–5).

— 4 pans. (Bagatti 1971a, Fig. 13:6; 16:5–6; *Exc.* Fig. 192:19)
— 2 large jars and a vase (*Exc.* Fig. 217:8, 9, 11)
— 2 glass bottles and 1 cup (*Exc.* Fig. 237:2–4)
— 1 metal buckle (Constantinian, *Exc.* 315)
— 1 incense burner (Bagatti 1971a, Fig. 15:4)
— 1 handle with pronounced ridges (Bagatti 1971a, Fig. 13:7)
— *Exc.* Figs. 222 and 223 (about two dozen pottery fragments)

• **IV–V** CE (Also: "Late Roman or Byzantine")
— 12 bottles, jugs, and pitchers (*Exc.* Fig. 220:2–11, 13)
— 9 pans (*Exc.* Fig. 226:4–12)
— 8 handmade basins (*Exc.* Fig. 232:1–8)
— 5 plates (terra sigillata, *Exc.* Fig. 227:1–4, 12)
— 4 vases (*Exc.* Fig. 223:10–13)
— 2 large jars (*Exc.* Fig. 217:1–2; cf. Hayes Pl. 8 and p. 33)
— 2 pots (*Exc.* Fig. 224:11–12)
— 1 glass fragment (*Exc.* Fig. 79:17)
— Pottery fragments (*Exc.* Fig. 229:1–15)

• **"Byzantine"**
— 18 pans with rouletting (*Exc.* Fig. 228:1–18)
— 10 terra sigillata shards, including one with Christian cross
    (*Exc.* Fig. 230 = Bagatti 1955 Fig. 12)
— In Tomb 1: "Many sherds of the Byzantine period" (unspecified, *Exc.* 32)
— In Grotto 5: "Byzantine sherds" (unspecified, *Exc.* 35)
— In Tomb 7: "some Byzantine sherds" (unspecified, *Exc.* 37)
— In Tomb 8: "Many [sherds] of the Byzantine period" (unspecified, *Exc.* 37)
— 3 bowls (*Exc.* Fig. 226:13–15)
— 3 oil lamps. (Bagatti 1971a, Fig. 11:4, 11; *Exc.* 70, with Christian cross)
— 2 cooking pots (*Exc.* Fig. 224:11–12)

• **VI** CE
— 5 jars, jugs, and vessels (*Exc.* Fig. 220:10–13, *cf.* Hayes color Pl. 1, "after
    400 CE")

• **Arab**
— 10 lips and rims of bowls (Bagatti 1971a, Fig. 23:1–10)
— 9 shards (Bagatti 1971a, Fig. 22:1–9)

• **Medieval**
— 22 shards of jars and jugs (Bagatti 1971a, Fig. 21:1–22)
— 16 shards (Bagatti 1971a, Fig. 20:1–16)
— 14 pans and vessels (Bagatti 1971a, Fig. 18:1–14)
— 5 shards (Bagatti 1955, Fig. 13)

Besides the above, numerous artefacts described in *Excavations* are undated.

Appendix 7

Nazareth Timeline From *c.* 135 CE

After 135 CE   The priestly course of **Hapizzez** go to Nazareth sometime after the the Second Jewish Revolt, when the Emperor Hadrian (117–138 CE) expelled Jews from the whole of Judea.

II CE   **Hegesippus** writes five books of memoirs against the Gnostics (included in passages preserved in the writings of other Church Fathers). He does not mention Nazareth.

Late II CE   The **synagogue** at nearby Japhia is rebuilt.[15]

***c.* 160–*c.*240**   **Julius Africanus**, a native of Jerusalem, is the first to mention Nazareth apart from the Pauline Gospel tradition. The citation is preserved by Eusebius (*Eccl. Hist.* I.7.14).

***c.* 185–254**   **Origen**, who lived for quite a long time at Caesarea Maritima, never visits Nazareth (50 km away).

III–IV CE   **The Caesarea Inscription**
Three fragments of an inscription were discovered in 1962 in the ruins of the Jewish synagogue of Caesarea. This inscription is the first reference to the town of Nazareth outside of Christian sources. The spelling of the name is not with *zayin* but with *tsade*. It confirms the view (known from other sources) that Nazareth was a thoroughly Jewish settlement at the time.

***c.* 260–*c.* 340**   **Eusebius of Caesarea**
[See above entry under 'Julius Africanus" and 'Hegesippus.']
Eusebius mentions Nazareth in his *Onomasticon* 138.24–140.2. He seems to know where it is, for he locates it "opposite Legio, about 15 miles to the east near Mt. Tabor."

312   **Battle of the Milvian Bridge**, which Constantine fights under the Christian banner.

---

[15]   RB 30 [1921], pp. 434–438.

313   **Edict of Milan** whereby Constantine establishes the toleration of Christianity.

324   **Constantine** becomes sole Roman emperor of East and West.

326   **St. Helena**, the mother of Emperor Constantine and a devout Christian, visits the Holy Land but has nothing to say about Nazareth, where she may have been singularly unimpressed (or even irritated) by the antipathy of the locals. Helena founds basilicas on the Mount of Olives and at Bethlehem, but none at Nazareth. The latter task, apparently, was soon delegated to Count Joseph of Tiberias (see below).

c. **335**   **The Bordeaux Pilgrim** visits Palestine but does not mention Nazareth.

c. **335**   Under imperial edict, **Joseph of Tiberias** probably constructs "a small and unconventional church [in Nazareth] which encompassed a cave complex." (Taylor 1993:265).

373   **Melania the Elder** hastens to bring alms to Christians who had been exiled from Egypt to Sepphoris. She bypasses Nazareth (as did the Christian refugees) which is in the vicinity (Molinier 69 *f.*)

c. 315-403 **Epiphanius, Bishop of Salamis** gives an extensive report in his *Panarion* (30.4.1–30.12.9) regarding the activities of Count Joseph of Tiberias (see above). He writes that "Until the reign of Constantine Nazareth had only Jewish inhabitants" (*Adv. Haer.* 1.136).

c. **383**   **Egeria** visits Nazareth and notes the presence there of a simple Christian shrine. This is our first indication that the tradition had by this time settled upon the place as the hometown of Jesus, and also that someone (presumably Joseph of Tiberias) had erected a Christian monument there.

386   **Paula** visits Nazareth "where our Lord grew up," but nothing there appears to have drawn the pilgrim's attention.

390   **Jerome** (*c.* 342–420) notes that Paula visited Nazareth. He has no comment concerning a modest ecclesiastical structure there. Jerome writes that Nazareth is a mere village (*viculus, Onom* 139).

460   The *Descriptio Parochiae Jerusalem* offers **indirect evidence of a church in Nazareth** (Tobler-Molinier 325).

Early V CE   A **Byzantine basilica** is erected at the site of the present Church of the Annunciation. This is the first verifiable Christian structure in Nazareth, which continues to be thoroughly Jewish.

V CE   **The Conon Mosaic**
    A floor mosaic was created in the Byzantine Church of the Annunciation which includes the words, "From Conon, deacon of Jerusalem." 10th century tradition linked this mosaic with a legendaryChristian martyr Conon, said to have died in the persecution under the Roman emperor Decius (249-251). In her book *Chistians and the Holy Places* (p. 223) Joan Taylor shows this martyr to have been legendary.

V–VI CE   A **church** is built over the **"house of St. Joseph"** (Viaud:141, 146).

530   **Theodosius** records the name **"Nazareth"** with no ancillary information (*De Situ* iv).

570   **The Piacenza Pilgrim** ("Anonymous of Piacenza"). This Christian pilgrim noted a Christian structure in Nazareth: "The house of St. Mary is a basilica."[16] He also noted the beauty of the Hebrew women of the town and the general fertility of the area. He is shown the Virgin's garments, and remarks on their healing powers. This is the first of a number of stories suggesting the gullibility of Christian pilgrims visiting Nazareth. The pilgrim writes: "Though there is no love lost between Jews and Christians, these women are full of kindness" (*CCSL* 175 [1965], *Itin.* v).

614   The **Persians** under their king Chosroes II **invade the country** from the north. "When he was heading for Jerusalem, the Jews, all there were in Tiberias, the hills of Galilee, Nazareth and the adjoining country-side, joined him, made for Jerusalem, and helped the Persians to destroy churches and murder the Christians."[17] Kopp writes: "In all the history of the land, this was the worst campaign of annihilation ever directed against everything Christian" (Kopp 1938:215).

622–630   The **Emperor Heraclius** vanquished the Persians and entered Jerusalem in triumph. He reluctantly singled out Nazareth for special punishment. "At all events, 629–30 saw the **end of Jewish**

---

[16] P. Geyer, *Itinera Hierosolymitana Saeculi iiii–viii* (1898), p. 161.
[17] Eutychius, *Annales* 212: PG CXI 1083.

Nazareth. Its people died by the sword or were scattered abroad in flight." (Kopp 1963:55–56). Thus ended the first (Jewish) period of Nazareth history.

638   The **Arabs conquer Palestine** and occupy Nazareth.

670   **Arculf**, bishop of Gaul, visited the Holy Land during nine months in 670 CE. According to his amanuensis, Nazareth was situated on a hill with two quite large churches. The one, in the middle of the town, rests on two arched supports over a limpid spring *(i.e.*, the present Church of St. Gabriel).[18]

723–26   **St. Willibald** traveled in the Holy Land between 723 and 726. He relates that the church marking the site where Mary received the annunciation had to be repeatedly purchased from the Saracens who threatened its destruction (Tobler 1974:25).

IX–X CE   An anonymous author of the lives of St. Helena and Constantine ascribes the building of the **Church of the Annunciation** to the empress.

808   The *Commemoratorium de casis Dei* of **Charlemagne** mentions "12 monks" in Nazareth.

943   The Arab **Al Mas'udi** visits Nazareth and sees the same church as Willibald.

c. **1100**   **Tancred** refurbishes the Church of the Annunciation and transfers the bishopric to Nazareth from Scythopolis. "Under the rule of the Crusaders, Nazareth was a purely Christian settlement with a bishop, later an archbishop" (RPTK 678).

1102   The English visitor **Saewolf** writes that "Nazareth is completely razed to the ground except for the place of the Annunciation, where there is a nice monastery."

1107   **Daniel the Prior** (Fr. *l'Higoumène Daniele*) visits the Holy Land and writes that "A large and high church with three altars rises up in the middle of the town.... Entering by the western door, on the

---

[18]   The passage was copied word-for-word by the Venerable Bede in his *Liber de Locis Sanctis* of 720 CE. I am indebted for the information in this and many of the following notes to Baldi-Bagatti 1937:230 *ff*.

right is a cell whose entryway is very narrow (*exiguë*) and in which the Holy Virgin lived with the Christ. He was raised in this little holy cell which contains the bed on which Jesus lay. It is so low as to appear practically on the same level as the floor. On entering the same grotto by the western door, on the left one has the tomb of St. Joseph [*i.e.*, T. 29], the fiancé of Mary, who was buried by the most pure hands of Christ. From the nearby wall of his tomb oozes – like some holy oil – a while water collected to heal the sick…" (Baldi-Bagatti 246).

1137   **Peter the Deacon** writes: "The grotto in which (Christ) lived is large and full of light, where also an altar has been placed; and there in the same grotto is the place from where water was raised up." This evidently refers to the church above Mary's Spring.

1172   **Theodoric** visits Nazareth and comments on the grotto under the Church of the Annunciation. Like Daniel the Prior (see above), he notes the tomb there of Joseph, husband of Mary. (Baldi-Bagatti 249 n.1.)

1177   **Phocas**, a Greek pilgrim writes: "The house of St. Joseph has been transformed into a very beautiful church." This apparently identifies the domicile of Joseph with the Church of the Annunciation, an identification consistent with that of Daniel the Prior (above) which makes Joseph and Mary already man and wife at the moment of the annunciation.[19] It also conforms to the very popular story in the *Protevangelium of James* (II CE).

1108   **Saladin** conquers many sites in the Holy Land, including Nazareth.

1197, July 4.   At the **Battle of Hattin,** Nazareth is conquered, "its population killed or imprisoned," and the sanctuary "renowned in all the world" is profaned, according to the medieval writer **Raul of Coggeshall.**

1251, March 24. King **Louis IX of France** celebrates mass at the CA.

1263   **Baybars** retakes Nazareth and orders the complete destruction of the town, including the **Church of the Annunciation** (annals of Abu el-Feda). The Church remains in ruins for 400 years.

---

[19]   Baldi-Bagatti 233. The Roman Catholic tradition emphasizes that in Judaism betrothal is tantamount to marriage (*cf.* Deut 22:23).

THE MYTH OF NAZARETH

1283   **Burchardt of Mount Sion** writes of Nazareth.

1294   **Ricoldo di Monte Croce** writes of no Christian presence in Nazareth, except for permission given the Franciscans to pilgrimage there. A small chapel is over the grotto of the annunciation.

1517   The **Turks** conquer Nazareth.

1551–64   The **Franciscan Custodian** of the Holy Land, **Boniface of Ragusa**, writes *Liber de perenni cultu Terrae Sanctae*. He reports the tranferral of the House of St. Joseph by angels to Loreto (in Italy), in order to prevent its falling into the hands of infidels.

1559   The pilgrim **G. Cootowick** writes that the ruins of the house of St. Joseph (**Church of the Nutrition**) "are at a stone's throw north of the Church of the Annunciation."

1620   Present area of venerated sites acquired by the **Franciscans** through the favor of the Druse emir **Fakr ed-Din** (1620–1634), and the initiative of the Custodian of the Holy Land, Fr. Tommaso Obicini.

1626   **Quaresmius** writes of Nazareth, including the Church of the Forty Martyrs. (Viaud 14–15; Kopp 1938:113; Finegan:33.)

1637, Nov. 19   According to the *Franciscan Chronicle,* all the friars are imprisoned by Fakr ed-Din's successor, and then freed after payment of a large sum of money.

1644   **Père Eugène Roger** writes *La Terre-Sainte* and complains that a "Moor" still lives on the putative site of the house of St. Joseph and place of the Nutrition (Baldi-Bagatti 1937:240 n.1).

1674   The Jesuit priest **P. Nau** writes *Voyage nouveau de la Terre-Sainte*.

1697–1770   In return for the payment of an annual sum to the Pasha of Sidon, the **Franciscans** acquire juridical **authority over Nazareth**.

1730   The **third Church of the Annunciation,** a modest edifice, is quickly built in seven months over the Venerated Grotto.

1741   Construction of the **Church of the United Greeks.**

1754 Franciscans take possession of the area above the putative **house of St. Joseph**, build a chapel there. Many Christians settle in Nazareth.

1767 Construction of the present **Church of St. Gabriel** over old ruins.

1775–1814 Rule of **Pasha Ahmed ed-Djezzar** (based in Acco) causes difficulties for the Christians of Nazareth.

1838–39 **Earthquake** destroys the **Chapel of St. Joseph**, which is rebuilt. In the ensuing decades the entire area between and around the venerated sites is acquired by the Franciscans.

1877 The **Fourth Church of the Annunciation** is built. It is an enlargement of the 1730 church.

1884–89 G. Schumacher excavates the tombs under the present convent of the Sisters of Nazareth. (*Cf.* Baldi-Bagatti 1937:253.)

1892 The (medieval) **Church of St. Joseph** is excavated. (Finegan 1992:57.)

1892, 1895 Brother B. Vlaminck excavates the Byzantine stratum around the sacred grotto, as well as the plan of the Crusader basilica that lay under the present Church of the Annunciation.

1889, 1907–09 Père P. Viaud excavates within the precincts of the Churches of St. Joseph and of the Annunciation. Publication of *Nazareth et ses Deux Églises* (Paris, 1910).

1911 **Fifth Church of the Annunciation** constructed on older plan. (Baldi-Bagatti 1937:240.)

1914 Construction of the **Church of St. Joseph**.

1925–28 **Excavation** of cisterns and caves on Franciscan property under **J. Schoppen OFM** (*LTK* [1935] col. 465).

1930 Other **excavations** during construction of the **Franciscan convent.**

1954   **Demolition** of the 1730/1877 church begins.

1955, *17 January*: Permission received from Dr. Yeivin of the **Israel Antiquities Dept.** to conduct excavations on the site of the Church of the Annunciation. *March*: demolition of older structure complete. *April-August*: **Fr. Bagatti's** principal **excavations** employ over 100 laborers.

1956   Beginning of construction of a large **Church of the Annunciation**, the **sixth structure** at the site. Secondary excavations continue.

1959   Removal of the **mosaic floor** of the **Byzantine Church of the Annunciation**. Excavation down to bedrock.

1960   Removal of the **Byzantine "convent."** Discovery of two **Bronze Period tombs**.

1966   The **Church of the Annunciation completed**.

1967/69   Publication of *Excavations in Nazareth* (Italian/English). Termination of excavations in the venerated area.

1969   Formal dedication of the modern **Church of the Annunciation**

Bibliography

Bibliography

Abbreviations and multi-volume reference works

ABD 1992. Freedman, D., editor in chief. *The Anchor Bible Dictionary* New York: Doubleday.

AEHL 2001. *The Archaeological Encyclopedia of the Holy Land*. A. Negev and S. Gibson, eds. New York: Continuum.

AJA *American Journal of Archaeology.*

APHL Amiran, R. *Ancient Pottery of the Holy Land: From its Beginnings in the Neolithic Period to the End of the Iron Age*. Rutgers Univ. Press, 1970.

Arch. 1992. Ben-Tor, A., ed. *The Archaeology of Ancient Israel.* New Haven: Yale University Press.

BASOR *Bulletin of the American Schools of Oriental Research.*

BDB 1906/2003. Brown, F., S. Driver, and C. Briggs. *The Brown-Driver-Briggs Hebrew and English Lexicon*. Peabody: Hendrickson.

CAH 1970–. *The Cambridge Ancient History*. Cambridge; New York: Cambridge University Press.

CCSL 1953–. *Corpus Christianorum Series Latina*. Ed. P. Geyer. Turnhout-Leipzig: G. Freytag.

CE 1911. Herberman, C., ed. *The Catholic Encyclopedia*. New York: Rbt. Appleton. (1967 edition. Washington D.C. The 2003 article "Nazareth" is a reprint of the 1967 edition).

CHJ 1984. Davies, W. and L. Finkelstein, eds. *The Cambridge History of Judaism*. 3 vols. Cambridge: University Press.

DACL 1935. Cabrol, F. and H. Leclercq, eds. *Dictionnaire D'Archaeologie Chretienne et de Liturgie*. Paris: Letouzey et Ané. Pt. CXXX, cols. 1021–1054.

DB 1960. Bagatti, B. *Dictionnaire de la Bible. Supplément VI.* "Nazareth," cols. 318–329.

DJBP 1996. *Dictionary of Judaism in the Biblical Period: 450 B.C.E. to 600 C.E.* 2 vols. J. Neusner, ed. in chief. New York: Macmillan Library Reference.

EAEHL 1977. Avi-Yonah, M. and E. Stern, editors, English edition. *Encyclopedia of Archaeological Excavations in the Holy Land*. Jerusalem and Englewood Cliffs, NJ: Oxford University Press.

EB   1899–1903. Cheyne, T. and J. Black, eds. *Encyclopaedia Biblica: a critical dictionary of the literary political and religious history, the archaeology, geography, and natural history of the Bible.* London: Adam and Charles Black.

EJ   1972. *Encyclopaedia Judaica.* Jerusalem, New York: Macmillan.

ESI   *Excavations and Surveys in Israel.* (Hadashot archeologiyot.) Jerusalem: Israel Dept. of Antiquities and Museums, 1984–

Exc.   1969. Bagatti, B. *Excavations in Nazareth,* vol. 1. See below, "Primary Reports."

IAA   *Israel Antiquities Authority.*

IDB, IDBS 1962/1973. Buttrick, G. *et al.* (eds.) *The Interpreter's Dictionary of the Bible: An Illustrated Encyclopedia.* 4 vols. + Supplement. Nashville: Abingdon Press.

IEJ   *Israel Exploration Journal.*

LA   *Liber Annuus.* Jerusalem: Franciscan Printing Press.

LTK   1998. *Lexikon für Theologie und Kirche, Band 7,* "Nazaret." Herder: Freiburg.

NEAEHL 1993. Stern, E., ed. *The New Encyclopedia of Archaeological Excavations in the Holy Land.* New York: Simon and Schuster.

NGP   1985. *New Gospel Parallels.* R. Funk, ed. 2 vols. Philadelphia: Fortress Press.

NHL   1977. *The Nag Hammadi Library in English.* New York: Harper & Row, 1977.

NIDBA 1983. *The New International Dictionary of Biblical Archaeology.* E. Blaiklock *et al* (eds.). Grand Rapids: Zondervan Publishing House.

NSH   1910. *The New Schaff-Herzog Encyclopedia of Religious Knowledge.* New York: Funk and Wagnalls.

NTA   1991. *New Testament Apocrypha.* W.Schneemelcher, ed. 2 vols. Louisville: John Knox Press.

OEANE 1997. Meyers, E., ed. in chief. *The Oxford Encyclopedia of Archaeology in the Near East.* New York: Oxford Univ. Pr.

OTP   1985. Charlesworth, J. (ed.) *The Old Testament Pseudepigrapha.* 2 vols. New York: Doubleday.

PEFQS *Palestine Exploration Fund Quarterly Statement.*

PEQ   *Palestine Exploration Quarterly.*

QDAP   *The Quarterly of the Department of Antiquities in Palestine.* Jerusalem and London: Oxford Univ. Press.

Bibliography

RB   1915–. *Revue Biblique*. Paris : Librairie V. Lecoffre.
RPTK   1903. Hauck, D., ed. *Realencyklopädie für protestantische Theologie und Kirche*. Leipzig: J. C. Hinrichs.
TDNT   1964. Kittel, G. and G. Friedrich. *Theological Dictionary of the New Testament*. Tr. by G. Bromiley. 9 vols. Grand Rapids: Eerdmans Publ. Co.

Primary reports on Nazareth archaeology

Bagatti, B.
   1955. "Ritrovamenti nella Nazaret evangelica." *Liber Annuus* 5:5–44.
   1969. *Excavations in Nazareth. Vol I: From the Beginning till the XII Century*. (Publications of the Studium Biblicum Franciscanum 17). Jerusalem: Franciscan Printing House, xi + 320 pp., 240 figures, 11 plates, index. Translation from Italian of the 1967 work.
   1971a. "Scavo Presso la Chiesa di S. Giuseppe a Nazaret (Agosto 1970)." *Liber Annuus* 21:5–32.
   1971b. "Communication du P. B. Bagatti: Nazareth: Église S. Joseph." *Revue Biblique* 78:587 (resumé of 1971a).
Baldi, D. and B. Bagatti. 1937. "Il Santuario della Nutrizione a Nazaret." *Studi Francescani*, IX, No. 4:225–264.
Fernandez, F. 1983. *Ceramica Comun Romana de la Galilea*. Madrid: Ed. Biblia Y Fe, Escuela Biblica.
Köppel, R. 1935. "Das Alter der neuentdeckten Schädel von Nazareth." *Biblica* 16:58–73.
Loffreda, S. 1977. "Ceramica del Ferro I trovata a Nazaret." *Liber Annuus* 27:135–144, figs. 13–18.
Mansur, A. 1924. *Tarikh al-Nasirah min aqdam azmaniha ilá ayyamina al-hadirah* ("History of Nazareth: From its Remotest Times to the Present Days "). Cairo: Al Hillal, 1924 (Arabic).
Richmond, E.T. 1931. "A Rock-cut Tomb at Nazareth." *The Quarterly of the Department of Antiquities in Palestine* [*QDAP*]. Vol 1 N. 2, page 53 and plates xxxiii-xxxiv. Jerusalem: Published for the Government of Palestine by Humphrey Milford. Oxford University Press, London, E.C.4.
Rosenthal, R. and R. Sivan. 1978. *Ancient Lamps in the Schloessinger Collection. Qedem 8. Monographs of the Institute of Archaeology*. Jerusalem: The Hebrew University of Jerusalem.
Viaud, P. 1910. *Nazareth et ses deux églises de L'Annonciation et de Saint-Joseph d'après les fouilles récentes*. Paris: Librarie Alphonse Picard et Fils.

Vitto, F. 2001. "An Iron Age Burial Cave in Nazareth." '*Atiqot* XLII:159–167.

Vlaminck, B. 1900. *A Report of the Recent Excavations and Explorations conducted at the Sanctuary of Nazareth*. [No publisher information.] Washington, D.C. 5 pages text + 3 pages diagrams. [As cited and quoted in other works.]

Primary brief reports

Alexandre, Y. 2000. "Nazerat (Nazareth)." *Hadashot Arkheologiyot: Excavations and Surveys in Israel* 112:118. Jerusalem: Israel Antiquities Authority. [Unsigned.]

[Anonymous.] 1963. "Nazareth." *Revue Biblique* 70:563. [Virtually identical to *Revue Biblique* 72:547 (1965).]

Avi-Yonah, M. 1962. "A List of Priestly Courses from Caesarea." *Israel Exploration Journal* 12:137-39.

Frey, J.B. **1952**. *Corpus Inscriptionum Iudicarum*. Vol II. Rome (Citta del Vaticano): Pontificio Istituto di Archeologia Christiana 988:173. [*CII*]

Haiman, M. 1999. "Nazerat (Nazareth) Area, Survey." *Hadashot Arkheologiyot: Excavations and Surveys in Israel* 110:90. Jerusalem: Israel Antiquities Authority.

Mansur, A.
 1913. "The Virgin Fountain, Nazareth." PEFQS 46:149–153;
 1923. "An interesting discovery in Nazareth." PEFQS pp. 89–91.

Raban, A. 1993–94. "Nazareth and 'Afula Maps, Survey" in *Excavations and Surveys in Israel. English Edition of Hadashot Arkheologiyot: Archaeological Newsletter of the Israel Antiquities Authority* 12:19. Jerusalem.

Schumacher, G. 1889. "Recent discoveries in Galilee." *Palestine Exploration Fund Quarterly Statement*, pp. 68–74 with plates.

Yavor, Zvi. 1998. "Nazareth." *Hadashot Arkheologiyot: Excavations and Surveys in Israel* 18:32. Jerusalem: Israel Antiquities Authority.

Yeivin, Z. 1963. "Notes and News: Nazareth." *Israel Exploration Journal* 13:145.

Secondary literature and related sources

Alexandre, Y.
 2000. "Nazerat (Nazareth)." *Hadashot Arkheologiyot: Excavations and Surveys in Israel* 112:118. Jerusalem: Israel Antiquities Authority. [Unsigned];

Bibliography

2003. "An Iron Age IB/IIA Burial Cave at Har Yona, Upper Nazareth." *'Atiqot* 44:183-89;

2005. "Elut" (report date 11/4/2005). *Hadashot Arkheologiyot: Excavations and Surveys in Israel* 117. Jerusalem: Israel Antiquities Authority.

Alexandre, Y., Covello-Paran K. and Gal Z. 2003. "Excavations at Tel Gat Hefer in the Lower Galilee, Areas A and B." *'Atiqot* 44.

Alt, A. 1959. *Kleine Schriften zur Geschichte des Volkes Israel.* Vol. 2. Munich: C.H. Beck.

Amiran, R. 1970. *Ancient Pottery of the Holy Land: From its Beginnings in the Neolithic Period to the End of the Iron Age.* Rutgers Univ. Press. [*APHL*]

Arav, R. 1989. *Hellenistic Palestine: Settlement Patterns and City Planning, 337–31 B.C.E.* BAR International Series 485.

Aviam, M. 2004. *Jews, Pagans and Christians in the Galilee: 25 Years of Archaeological Excavations and Surveys – Hellenistic to Byzantine Periods.* First part of the series, "Land of Galilee." Institute for Galilean Archaeology. Rochester: University Press.

Avigad, N. 1976. *Beth She'arim III. Catacombs 12–23.* Jerusalem.

Bagatti, B. (See also "Primary Reports" above);

1960. "Nazareth," *Dictionnaire de la Bible* [DB], *Supplement VI.* Paris: Letouzey et Ané, 1960;

1967. "I Vetri del Museo Francescano di Nazaret." *Liber Annuus* 17:222–240, figs. 1-7;

1971a. *The Church from the Circumcision: History and Archaeology of the Judaeo-Christians.* Jerusalem: Franciscan Printing Press (esp. pp. 122–128);

1971b. *The Church from the Circumcision: History and Archaeology of the Judaeo-Christians.* Jerusalem: Franciscan Printing Press (esp. pp. 122–128).

Bagatti, B. and J. Milik. 1958. *Gli Scavi del "Dominus Flevit."* Vol. 1: *La Necropoli del Periodo Romano.* Pubblicazioni dello Studium Biblicum Franciscanum, No 13. Jerusalem: Tipografia dei PP. Francescani.

Bailey, D. M.

1972. *Greek and Roman Pottery Lamps.* The Trustees of the British Museum;

1975. *A Catalogue of the Lamps in the British Museum: I. Greek, Hellenistic, and Early Roman Pottery Lamps.* The Trustees of the British Museum.

Barnavi, E. (ed.). 1992. *A Historical Atlas of the Jewish People: From the Time of the Patriarchs to the Present.* New York: Schoken Books.

Bartlett, J. 1997. *Archaeology and Biblical Interpretation.* New York: Routledge.

345

THE MYTH OF NAZARETH

Batey, R.
1992. "Sepphoris: An Urban Portrait of Jesus," in *Biblical Archaeology Review*, May-June 1992:52–62.
2001. "Sepphoris and the Jesus Movement." *New Testament Studies* 46:402–409.

Ben-Tor, A., ed. 1992. *The Archaeology of Ancient Israel*. New Haven: Yale University Press.

Ben-Tor A. and Y. Portugali. 1987. "Tell Qiri: A Village in the Jezreel Valley." Jerusalem: *Qedem* 24.

Benzinger, I. 1908–1914. "Burial" in *The New Schaff-Herzog Encyclopedia of Religious Knowledge*. New York & London: Funk and Wagnalls.

Berman, A. 1988–89. "Kafr Kanna," in *Excavations and Surveys in Israel. English Edition of* Hadashot Arkheologiyot*: Archaeological Newsletter of the Israel Antiquities Authority*. A. Sussman, *et al.*, editors. Jerusalem. Volume 7-8:107–08.

Black, M. 1961. *The Scrolls and Christian Origins*. New York: Charles Scribner's Sons.

Bultmann, R. 1963. *The History of the Synoptic Tradition*. New York: Harper & Row.

Burrage, C. 2001. *Nazareth and the Beginnings of Christianity*. (Reprint of 1914 edition.) Santa Clara: Church History Publishing.

Chancey, M. 2002. *The Myth of a Gentile Galilee*. Cambridge: University Press.

Covello-Paran K. 1999. "Migdal Ha-'Emeq." *Explorations and Surveys in Israel* 19:19–20.

Crossan, D. 1991. *The Historical Jesus: The Life of a Mediterranean Jewish Peasant*. New York: HarperCollins.

Crossan, J., and J. Reed. 2002. *Excavating Jesus: Beneath the Stones, Behind the Texts*. San Francisco: HarperCollins.

Dalman, G. 1935. *Sacred Sites and Ways: Studies in the Topography of the Gospels*. New York: The Macmillan Co.

Daniel the Abbot. *Zhitie I knozhenie Danila rus'kyya zemli igumena 1106–1108*. Ed. M. Venevitinov. St. Petersburg: Palestinskiy Prvoslavnyy Sbornik 3, 9. 1883–5.

De Boer, M. 1998. "The Nazoreans: living at the boundary of Judaism and Christianity." In *Tolerance and Intolerance in Early Judaism and Christianity*. G. Stanton & G. Strounsa, eds. Cambridge Univ. Press.

Deines, R. 1993. *Jüdische Steingefässe und pharisäische Frömmigkeit*. Wissenschaftliche Untersuchungen zum Neuen Testament, 2 Reihe 52. Tübingen: J.B. Mohr.

Dessel, J. 1999. "Tell 'Ein Zippori and the Lower Galilee in the Late Bronze and Iron Ages: A Village Perspective," in E. Meyers (ed.), *Galilee Through the Centuries: Confluence of Cultures.* Winona Lake: Eisenbrauns, pp. 1–37.

Dothan M. 1956. "Excavations at 'Afula." *'Atiqot* 1:18-63.

Edwards, I. *et al.* 1973. *The Cambridge Ancient History. Vol. II part 1: History of the Middle East and the Aegean Region c. 1800–1380 B.C.* Cambridge: University Press. [*CAH*]

Ehrman, B. 2000. *The New Testament.* Third Edition. New York: Oxford University Press.

Ellegård, A. 1999. *Jesus: One Hundred Years Before Christ.* Woodstock: The Overlook Press.

Engberg, R., and G. Shipton. 1934. *Notes on the Chalcolithic and Early Bronze Age Pottery of Megiddo.* Chicago: University Press.

Eshel, H. 2000. "CD 12:15–17 and the Stone Vessels Found at Qumran." *The Damascus Document: A Centennial of Discovery.* J. Baumgarten, *et al.* (eds.) Leiden: Brill.

Evans, C. 2004. "Archaeology and the Historical Jesus: Recent Developments." *SBL Forum* #335 (online).

Feig, N.
1983. "Nazareth 'Ilit'." Communication by the archeologist. *Israel Exploration Journal* 33, no. 1–2:116–117;
1990. "Burial Caves in Nazareth." *Atiqot* 10:67–79 (Hebrew).

Fine, S. (ed.) 1996. *Sacred realm: The Emergence of the Synagogue in the Ancient World.* New York: Oxford University Press : Yeshiva University Museum.

Finegan, J. 1969, 1992. *The Archaeology of the New Testament.* Princeton: University Press.

Finkelstein, I. 1995. "Two notes on Early Bronze Age urbanization and urbanism." *Tel Aviv*, vol. 22, No. 1:47–69.

Finkelstein, I., and N. Na'aman, eds. 1994. *From Nomadism to Monarchy: Archaeological and Historical Aspects of Early Israel.* Jerusalem: Israel Exploration Society.

FitzGerald, G.
1930. *The Four Canaanite Temples of Beth-Shan. Part 2: The Pottery.* Philadelphia: Univ. of Pennsylvania Museum;
1931. *Beth-shan Excavations, 1921–1923; the Arab and Byzantine Levels.* Philadelphia: Univ. of Pennsylvania Museum.

Folda, J. 1986. *The Nazareth capitals and the Crusader Shrine of the Annunciation.* University Park [Pa.]: Pennsylvania State University Press.

Frescobaldi, Gucci, and Sigoli. 1948. *Visit to the Holy Places of Egypt, Sinai, Palestine, and Syria in 1384.* Jerusalem: Franciscan Press.

Freyne, S.

1980. *Galilee, from Alexander the Great to Hadrian, 323 B.C.E. to 135 C.E.: a study of second Temple Judaism.* Wilmington: University of Notre Dame Press;

1988. *Galilee, Jesus, and the Gospels : literary approaches and historical investigations.* Philadelphia: Fortress Press;

1997 "Archaeology and the Historical Jesus," in J. Bartlett (*op. cit.*), pp. 117–138;

2002 *Galilee and Gospel: Collected Essays.* Leiden: Brill;

2004. *Jesus, a Jewish Galilean: a new reading of the Jesus story.* London: T & T Clark.

Gal, Zvi.

1988. "The Late Bronze Age in Galilee: A Reassessment," in *Bulletin of the American Schools of Oriental Research* 272:79–84;

1991. "A stone vessel manufacturing site in the Lower Galilee." *'Atiqot* 20:25–26 (Hebrew), English summary, pp. 179–80;

1992. *Lower Galilee during the Iron Age.* Eisenbrauns: Winona Lake, Ind;

1994a. "Iron I in Lower Galilee and the Margins of the Jezreel Valley," in *From Nomadism to Monarchy*, ed. I. Finkelstein & N. Na'aman. Washington: Biblical Archaeology Society, 1994;

1994b. "Tel Gat Hefer," in *Excavations and Surveys in Israel. English Edition of* Hadashot Arkheologiyot: *Archaeological Newsletter of the Israel Antiquities Authority.* A. Sussman, *et al.*, editors. Jerusalem. Volume 14:54;

1998. "Israel in Exile." *Biblical Archaeology Review* 24:3.

Galling, K. 1936. "Die Nekropole von Jerusalem," *Palästina Jahrbuch* 32:73–101.

Geyer, P. 1898. *Itinera Hierosolymitana saeculi IIII–VIII.* In *Corpus Christianorum Series Latina*, vol. 39. Leipzig: G. Freytag.

Gibson, S. 1983. "The Stone Vessel Industry at Hizma." *Israel Exploration Journal* 33, Nos. 3-4:176–188.

Goodenough, E. 1953. *Jewish Symbols in the Greco-Roman Period.* 13 vols. New York: Pantheon Books.

Goodenough, E.R. 1953. "Jewish Tombs of Palestine," in *Jewish Symbols in the Greco-Roman Period.* Vol 1 of 13. New York: Pantheon Books, pp. 61–102.

Gophna, R. 1984. "The Settlement Landscape of Palestine in the Early Bronze Age II–III and Middle Bronze Age II." *Israel Exploration Journal*, vol. 34, No. 1:24–31.

Bibliography

Goranson, S. 1999. "Joseph of Tiberias Revisited: Orthodoxies and Heresies in Fourth-Century Galilee," in E. Meyers, ed. *Galilee Through the Centuries: Confluence of Cultures*. Winona Lake: Eisenbrauns, pp. 335–343.

Grant, M. 1973. *The Jews in the Roman World*. Phoenix.

Grant, R. 1970. *Augustus to Constantine*. New York: Harper & Row.

Grässer, E. 1961. "Jesus in Nazareth (Mark VI.1–6a)," in *NTS* 16:1–23.

Guy, H. 1955. *The Origin of the Gospel of Mark*. New York: Harper & Brothers.

Guy, P. and R. Engberg. 1938. *Megiddo Tombs*. Chicago.

Hachlili, R., and A. Killebrew. 1983. "Jewish Funerary Customs During the Second Temple Period, in the Light of the Excavations at the Jericho Necropolis." *Palestine Exploration Quarterly*, 7–12:109–132.

Hachlili, R. 1992. "Burials." *The Anchor Bible Dictionary*, vol 1:785–94. D. N. Freedman, editor-in-chief. New York: Doubleday.

Hamidovic, David. 2004. "Nazareth avant Jésus: Un nouvel examen historique." *Ancient Near Eastern Studies* 41:95–197.

Harvey, W. (ed.) 1857. *Sancti Irenaei: Libros quinque adversus Haereses*. Vol. 1. Cambridge: University Press.

Hays, J.W.
>1980. *Ancient Lamps in the Royal Ontario Museum: A Catalogue*. Royal Ontario Museum;
>1997. *Handbook of Mediterranean Roman Pottery*. Norman: Univ. of Oklahoma Press.

Heineman, 1975. *Literature of the Synagogue*. New York: Behrman House.

Herford, R. 1903. *Christianity in Talmud and Midrash*. London, Williams & Norgate (repr. 1966).

Holum, K. and R. Hohlfelder, *et al.* 1988. *King Herod's Dream: Caesarea on the Sea*. New York: W.W. Norton & Co.

Horsley, R.
>1995 *Galilee: History, Politics, People*. Valley Forge, Pa: Trinity Press International, 1995;
>1996. *Archaeology, History and Society in Galilee: the social context of Jesus and the rabbis*. Valley Forge, Pa: Trinity Press International.

Jones, A. 1964. *The Later Roman Empire, 284–602*. Vol. 1. Oxford: Basil Blackwell.

Kahane, P. 1961. "Rock-cut Tombs at Huqoq. Note on the Finds." *'Atiqot* III, pp. 126–47 (English Series).

Kenyon, K. 1966. *Amorites and Canaanites*. London: Oxford University Press.

Klijn, A. 1992. *Jewish-Christian Gospel Tradition*. Leiden: Brill.

Klijn, A., and G. Reinink. 1973. *Patristic Evidence for Jewish-Christian Sects*. Leiden: Brill.

THE MYTH OF NAZARETH

Kloner, A.
1980. *The Necropolis of Jerusalem in the Second Temple Period.* Ph.D. diss. Hebrew University. Jerusalem (Hebrew; English summary, pp. I–XIX);
1999. "Did a Rolling Stone Close Jesus' Tomb?" *Biblical Archaeology Review,* Sept–Oct. 1999:23–29, 76.

Kloppenborg Verbin, J. 2000. *Excavating Q: The History and Setting of the Sayings Gospel.* Minneapolis, MN: Fortress Press.

Koester, H.
1980. *History and Literature of Early Christianity.* 2 vols. Philadelphia: Fortress Press;
1983. "History and Development of Mark's Gospel (From Mark to Secret Mark and 'Canonical' Mark)." In B. Corley, *Colloquy on New Testament Studies.* Macon: Mercer University Press,1983. Pg. 35–57;
1990. *Ancient Christian Gospels.* Philadelphia: Trinity Press International.

Kopp, Clemens.
1938. "Beiträge zur Geschichte Nazareths." *Journal of the Palestine Oriental Society,* Jerusalem, vol. 18:187–228;
1939. "Beiträge zur Geschichte Nazareths." *Journal of the Palestine Oriental Society,* Jerusalem, vol. 19:82–119, 253–285;
1940. "Beiträge zur Geschichte Nazareths." *Journal of the Palestine Oriental Society,* Jerusalem, vol. 20:29–42;
1948. "Beiträge zur Geschichte Nazareths." *Journal of the Palestine Oriental Society,* Jerusalem, vol. 21:148–164;
1963. *The Holy Places of the Gospels.* "Nazareth," pp. 49–86. Herder and Herder.

Kuhnen, H. P. 1990. *Palästina in Griechisch-Römischer Zeit.* München: C. H. Beck.

Lagarde, Paul de. 1966. *Onomastica sacra* [Eusebius Pamphilus] Hildesheim: G. Olms.

Lance, H. 1981. *The Old Testament and the Archaeologist.* Philadelphia: Fortress Press.

Lapp, N. 1964. "Pottery from some Hellenistic loci at Balatah (Shechem)," in *Bulletin of the American Schools of Oriental Research,* Number 75 (October 1964), pp. 14–26.

Lapp, P. 1961. *Palestinian Ceramic Chronology: 200 B.C–A.D. 70.* New Haven: American Schools of Oriental Research.

Levine, L. (ed.). 1992. *The Galilee in Late Antiquity.* New York and Jerusalem: The Jewish Theological Seminary of America.

Bibliography

Lienhard, J. 1996. *Origen: Homilies on Luke, Fragments on Luke.* Vol. 94 of *The Fathers of the Church.* Washington: Cath. Univ. of America Press.

Marcovich, M. (ed.) 1986. *Hippolytus: Refutation Omnium Haeresium.* Berlin: De Gruyter.

Matthews, J. 1989. *The Roman Empire of Ammianus.* London: Duckworth.

Mazar, B. 1973-76. *Beth She'arim.* 3 vols. New Brunswick, N.J.: Rutgers University Press on behalf of the Israel Exploration Society and the Institute of Archaeology, Hebrew University.

Meistermann, B. 1923. *Guide to the Holy Land.* London.

Metzger, B., and R. Murphy (eds.). 1991. *The New Oxford Annotated Bible with the Apocryphal/Deuterocanonical Books.* (NRSV) New York: Oxford University Press.

Meyerhof, E. 1989. *The Bronze Age Necropolis at Kibbutz Hazorea, Israel.* BAR International Series 534. Oxford: BAR.

Meyers, E.
1992. "Roman Sepphoris in Light of New Archeological Evidence and Recent Research." In Levine, *op. cit.*, pp. 321 *ff*; (ed.).
1999. *Galilee Through the Centuries: Confluence of Cultures.* Winona Lake: Eisenbrauns.

Meyers, E., E. Netzer, and C. Meyers. 1992. *Sepphoris.* Winona Lake: Eisenbrauns.

Meyers, E., and J. Strange. 1981. *Archaeology, the Rabbis, & Early Christianity.* Nashville: Abingdon.

Miller, R. ed. 1992. *The Complete Gospels: Annotated Scholars Version* Sonoma, CA: Polebridge Press.

Mimouni, S. 1998. "Les nazoréens. Recherche étymologique et historique." *Revue Biblique*, vol. 105 no. 2:208–262.

Molinier, A., and C. Kohler. 1879. *Itinerum Hierosolymitanorum et descriptionum Terrae Sanctae series chronologica.* Geneva.

Najjar, A., and N. Najjar. 1997. "Nazareth." *Excavations and Surveys in Israel.* Jerusalem: Israel Antiquities Authority. Volume 16:49.

Neidinger, W. 1982. "A typology of oil lamps from the mercantile quarter of Antipatris." *Tel Aviv*, vol. 9, pp. 157–169.

Orni, E., and E. Efrat. 1964. *Geography of Israel.* Jerusalem: Israel Program for Scientific Translations.

Painter, J. 1999. "When is a house not home? Disciples and family in Mark 3.13–35." *New Testament Studies* 45:498–513.

Porat, L. 2005. "En Zippori" (report date 8/5/2005). *Hadashot Arkheologiyot: Excavations and Surveys in Israel* 117. Jerusalem: Israel Antiquities Authority.

Pritz, R.
  1985a. "Joseph of Tiberias: The Legend of a 4th Century Jewish Christian," in *Mishkan* No. 2:38–43;
  1985b. "Messianic Jewish Theology," in *Mishkan* vol. 2, 43–45;
  1988. *Nazarene Jewish Christianity*. Leiden: Brill.

Rahmani, L. 1994. *A Catalogue of Jewish Ossuaries in the Collections of the State of Israel*. Jerusalem.

Rast W. 1978. "Ta'anach I: Studies in the Iron Age Pottery." Cambridge, MA.

Reed, J.
  1999. "Galileans and the Sayings Gospel Q," in Meyers (ed.), *Galilee Through the Centuries*. Winona Lake: Eisenbrauns;
  2002. *Archaeology and the Galilean Jesus: A Re-examination of the Evidence*. Harrisburg: Trinity Press International.

Robinson, E., and E. Smith. 1841. *Biblical Researches in Palestine, Mount Sinai and Arabia Petraea*. Vol. III. Boston: Crocker & Brewster.

Sanders, E. P. 1993. "Jesus in Historical Context." *Theology Today*, vol. 50 (Oct 1993), pp. 429-448.

Sanders, E,. and M. Davies. 1989. *Studying the Synoptic Gospels*. Philadelphia: Trinity Press International.

Schalit, A. (ed.) 1972. *The Hellenistic Age: Political History of Jewish Palestine from 332 B.C.E. to 67 B.C.E.* Vol. 6 of *The World History of the Jewish People: First Series—Ancient Times*. New Brunswick: Rutgers Univ. Press.

Schiffman, L.
  1991. *From Text to Tradition: A History of Second Temple and Rabbinic Judaism*. New Jersey: Ktav Publishing House;
  1998. *Texts and Traditions: A Source Reader for the Study of Second Temple and Rabbinic Judaism*. New Jersey: Ktav Publ. House.

Schürer, E. 1890. *A History of the Jewish People in the Time of Jesus Christ*. Three vols. in five. Edinburgh: T. Clark. Repr. Hendrickson 1998.

Schütz, D. 1931. "Die Ossuarien in Palästina." *Monatsschrift für Geschichte und Wissenschaft des Judentums*, 75:286–463.

Sellers, O., and D. Baramki. 1953. "A Roman-Byzantine Burial Cave in Northern Palestine." *Bulletin of the American Schools of Oriental Research*, Supplementary Studies Nos. 15–16. Yale Station, New Haven.

Simon, M. 1981. "La migration à Pella: Légende ou réalité?" In *Le Christianisme Antique et Son Contexte Religieux: Scripta Varia*. 2 vols. Tübingen: Mohr.

Singer, I. 1994. "Egyptians, Canaanites, and Philistines in the Period of the Emergence of Israel," in Finkelstein, I., and N. Na'aman, eds. *From Nomadism to Monarchy: Archaeological and Historical Aspects of Early Israel*. Jerusalem: Israel Exploration Society.

Smith, R.
1961. "The 'Herodian' Lamp of Palestine: Types and Dates." *Berytus*, vol. 14:53–65;
1964a. "The Household Lamps of Palestine in Old Testament Times." *The Biblical Archaeologist* XXVII:1, 2–31;
1964b. "The Household Lamps of Palestine in Intertestamental Times." *The Biblical Archaeologist* XXVII:1, 101–124;
1966. "The Household Lamps of Palestine in New Testament Times." *The Biblical Archaeologist* XXIX:1, 2–27.

Smith, W. 1906. *Der Vorchristliche Jesus*. Gieszen: Alfred Töpelmann. [Translation of *The Pre-Christian Jesus*.]

Steen, E.J. 2005. "The Sanctuaries of Early Bronze IB Megiddo: Evidence of a Tribal Polity?" *American Journal of Archaeology*, Volume 109, No. 1:1–20.

Stern, E. 1982. Material Culture of the Land of the Bible in the Persian Period, 538-332 B.C. Jerusalem: Israel Exploration Society.

Strange, J.
1975. "Late Hellenistic and Herodian Ossuary Tombs at French Hill, Jerusalem." *BASOR* 219 (Oct. 1975), 39–68;
1983. "Diversity in Early Palestinian Christianity: Some Archaeological Evidences," *Anglican Theological Review*, vol. LXV, pp. 14–24;
1992. "Some implications of archaeology for New Testament studies," in *What has Archaeology to do with Faith?* pp 23–59. Harrisburg: Trinity Press Int'l;
1993. "Archaeology and the New Testament," *Biblical Archaeologist*, vol. 56 (Sept. 1993), pp. 153–157;
1997. "First century Galilee from archaeology and from the texts," in *Archaeology and the Galilee*, pp. 39–48. Atlanta: Scholars Press;
1997. "The sayings of Jesus and archaeology," in *Hillel and Jesus*, pp. 291–305. Minneapolis: Fortress Press;
1999. "Ancient texts, archaeology as text, and the problem of the first-century synagogue," in *Evolution of the Synagogue*, pp. 27–45. Harrisburg: Trinity Press Int'l.

[See also articles by Strange entitled "Nazareth" in the *Enc. of Archaeology in the Biblical World* (1991), *ABD* (1992), the *Macmillan Dict. of Judaism in the Biblical Period* (1996), and the *Oxford Enc. of Near Eastern Excavations* (1997).]

Stevenson, J. 1957. *Early Witnesses of the Church*. London: Macmillan.

Strobel, L. 1998. *The Case for Christ*. Zondervan: Grand Rapids.

Sukenik, E. 1947. "The Earliest Records of Christianity," *AJA*, LI, pp. 351–365.

Suriano, Fra Francesco. 1385. *Treatise on the Holy Land*. Printed by the Franciscan Press, Jerusalem 1949.

Sussman, V.
 1982. *Ornamented Jewish Oil-Lamps*. Israel Exploration Society: Aris & Phillips; 1985. "The Changing Shape of Ancient Oil Lamps: A Chronological Guide." *Biblical Archaeology Review*, Mar–Apr 1985:44–56;
 1990. "The Lamp," in S. Wachsmann, *The Excavations of an Ancient Boat in the Sea of Galilee (Lake Kinneret)*. *'Atiqot* 19. Jerusalem: The Israel Antiquities Authority.

Szentleleky, T. 1969. *Ancient Lamps*. Amsterdam: Adolf M. Hakkert

Tal, O. 1995. "Roman-Byzantine Cemeteries and Tombs Around Apollonia." *Tel Aviv*, vol. 22 No. 1:107–120.

Tannehill, R. 1972. "The Mission of Jesus," in *Jesus in Nazareth*. New York: W. de Gruyter.

Taylor, J.
 1989–90. "Capernaum and its 'Jewish-Christians': A Re-examination of the Franciscan Excavations." *Bulletin of the Anglo-Israel Archaeological Society*. 9:7–28;
 1993. *Christians and the Holy Places: The Myth of Jewish-Christian Origins*. Oxford: Clarendon Press.

Testa, E. 1967. "Due frammenti di Targum sull'Incarnazione scoperti a Nazaret." *La Terra Santa*, 99–104.

Tcherikover, V. 1961. *Hellenistic Civilization and the Jews*. Philadelphia: The Jewish Publication Society of America.

Tillich, P. 1967. *A History of Christian Thought: From its Judaic and Hellenistic Origins to Existentialism*. New York: Simon and Schuster.

Tischendorf, C. 1869. *Novum Testamentum Graece*. Leipzig: Gieseke & Devrient.

Tobler, T. 1974. *Descriptiones Terrae Sanctae ex saeculo VIII.IX.XII. et XV.* Hildesheim: Georg Olms.

Vitto, F. 2000. "Burial caves from the Second Temple Period in Jerusalem." *'Atiqot* XL. Jerusalem: IAA.

Wachsmann, S. 1990. *The Excavations of an Ancient Boat in the Sea of Galilee (Lake Kinneret)*. *'Atiqot* 19. Jerusalem: The Israel Antiquities Authority.

Walker, W. 1987. "'Nazareth': A clue to synoptic relationships?" In *Jesus, the Gospels, and the Church*. Ed. E. P. Sanders, Mercer Univ. Press, pp. 105–118.

Watzinger, C. 1935. *Denkmäler Palästinas*. Vol. II. Leipzig.

Wenham, D. 1985. *Gospel Perspectives: The Jesus Tradition Outside the Gospels*, vol. 5. JSOT Press.

Wexler, L. and G. Gilboa. 1996. "Oil lamps of the Roman Period from Apollonia-Arsuf." *Tel Aviv*, vol. 23, pp. 115–131.

Wilkinson, J. 1981. *Egeria's Travels*. Warminster.

Williams, F., translator. 1987. *The Panarion of Epiphanius of Salamis*. 2. vols. Leiden: Brill.

Wood, B. 1990. *The Sociology of Pottery in Ancient Palestine. Journal for the Study of the Old Testament: Supplementary Series*, 103. Sheffield: JSOT Press.

Yadin, Y. 1976. *Jerusalem Revealed: Archaeology in the Holy City 1968–1974*. New Haven and London: Yale Univ. Press and the Israel Exploration Society.

Zindler, F.

1997. "Where Jesus Never Walked," *American Atheist*, vol 36, Winter 1996–97:33–42;

1999. "Loud Arguments From Silence," *American Atheist*, vol 38, Autumn 1999:22–29;

2003. *The Jesus the Jews Never Knew: Sepher Toldoth Yeshu and the Quest of the Historical Jesus in Jewish Sources*. New Jersey: American Atheist Press.

GENERAL INDEX

General Index

THE MYTH OF NAZARETH

Kopp —107
Ben-Tor, Amnon: on Beth Yerah ware —29; his description of seminary-trained archaeologists; Bagatti as example of —xiv; on amateurism in Biblical archaeology —xi
Bet Ha-Kerem Valley: —19
Bet Netofa Valley: —19
Beth Shan: —29, 101: trade routes in relation to —19; Count Joseph and Epiphanius at —278
Beth Shan Valley: —100
Beth Shean: *See also* Scythopolis; abandonment of —32
Beth Yerah: —29; abandonment of —32
Beth Yerah ware: — 9; Ben-Tor on —29
Bethlehem: —211, 212, 213, 214, 215, 255; as Messianic city —213; events transposed to Nazareth from —215
Bethlehem Notseriyeh: Nazareth in relation to —292
Beth-Shan/Beth Shearim: —189; catacombs at —161; sarcophagi in relation to —189
Boat: Galilee discovery —119
Bordeaux Pilgrim: —293
Boule: —100
Bow-spouted oil lamps: *See also* Oil lamps. —245, 246, 247
Bronze Age: —80, 82, 83, 87, 89, 90, 141, 221, 243; Bagatti on —36; chronology of (chart) —27; Early Bronze Age — 27-29; finds at Nazareth —36; settlement near Nazareth beginning —25; Nazareth basin artefacts of; itemization of— 311
Bronze Age, Early: Nazareth basin settlement in relation to —28
Bronze Age, MB IIA: —39
Bronze Age, Middle & Late: discussion of —35
Brow of a hill: Lk 4:29 —306
Bultmann, R.: —203

Burial customs: Jewish, rules concerning —109
Burial practices: Kathleen Kenyon on —32
Byblos: destruction of —31
Byzantine Period: —114; shards datable to —127; Nazareth movable finds of —271; no habitations found predating at Nazareth —36
Byzantine wall: near CA —49

C

CA: *See* Church of the Annunciation;
Caesarea (Maritima): —154, 156; Herod's creation of —154; Eusebius living at —295; Titus celebrates at —266; synagogue inscription from, the Hapizzez in relation to —275
Caesarea Inscription: no support for 1st-century habitation at Nazareth —277; the Hapizzes in relation to —275
Caligula: —155
Cambyses: —62
Cambyses II: —62
Canaan: reassertion of Egyptian control of —41
Canaanites: —45, 46; enter Nazareth basin —45; Hyksos as, Egypt controlled by —41
Capernaum: —254, 255; Loffreda in relation to —271; Nazareth *vs.* —298
Capitals: of Crusader period, Viaud discovery of —238
Carpenter; St. Joseph as —81
Case for Christ, The: of Lee Strobel; critique of Zindler's "Where Jesus Never Walked" —286
"Casting down": site of, problems in discovery of —202
Casuistry: in writings on archaeology of Nazareth —89
Catacombs: at Beth Shearim —161
Catholic Church: attempts

to reconcile archaeology with doctrines of —65; doctrine of continuous habitation of —61; doctrine of, Kopp's logic dependent upon —68
Catholic literature: —86
Cave: —211, 215, 216, 219, 232, 255, 256, 261; as home of Virgin Mary— 211; Egeria says Virgin Mary lived in —293
Cave complex: wine-making in relation to —195
Cave dwelling: —66
Cave of the Leap: —25; prehistoric skulls discovered at —23
Caves: —28, 30, 38; of Galilee; dampness of; troglodyte theory in relation to 66; with alleged domestic installations 147
Cavities: in ground beneath Franciscan property —232
Cement: —63, 66
Cemetery: Greek (Melchite) —37
Census: —212, 213; Roman, not historical —213
Ceramica Comun Romana de la Galilea: of F. Fernandez —116, 271
Cestius Gallus: —156; enters Palestine with 12th legion —156
Chalcolithic Age: —27, 28; Bronze Age in relation to chronology of (chart) —27
Chancey, Mark: on abandonment of Galilee —60; 100; on circulation of Hasmonean coins —146; on lack of settlement in Galilee interior —100
Chapel of the Angel: —212, 238, 244, 245, 247, 251, 254, 259, 260; kokh tomb near —76
Chrestus: in Suetonius —291
Christ: Nazareth settled after time of —173; time of —151; chronology of (chart) —153
Christendom: vulnerability of to findings of archaeology —xii
Christian Archaeology: —72, 73

(*Illus.* 1.4) —34; found only in tombs —36; manufacture of poor-quality —32; of Middle Bronze Age —35; Megiddo in relation to —40; of Nazareth, Bagatti on —30; workshops —40; Nazareth —64; earliest, Finegan in relation to —87; earliest, Nancy Lapp on —115; earliest (Appendix 5) —325; alleged 1st-century —175; no objective study of from Nazareth —177;

Pre-Paleolithic: chronology of —23

Presses: —195-197, 234, 238; olive —104; wine —88, 195, 221, 233, 234, 248, 256

Priestly Courses: in Caesarea Inscription —276

Procurator (*epitropos*): Hyrcanus II as Judean —154

Protestants: —86, 97

***Protevangelium of James*:** —76, 212, 214, 215, 228; Greek Orthodox following of in locating Mary's home —228; places Jesus' hometown in Judea —295

Proto-Cro-Magnon: at Qafza cave —25

Ptolemaic Period: in Palestine —98

Ptolemais: *See* Acco

Purity taboos: Jewish —184, 258

Q

Q Document: Nazara in —301

Qafza Cave: excavations at —25

Qafza, Jebel: hominid skulls discovered at —23

Quarries: —185

Queen Helen of Adiabene: tomb of, rolling stone of —186

Qumran: —306

R

Rabbi Judah the Prince: at Sepphoris —148

Rabbinic studies: at Jamnia —266

Rabbis: receive temple contributions —266

Rahmani: ossuaries in relation to —187

***Raisins*:** Finegan's mistranslation of French word —88

Redactor: of Matthew, *Nazorean* as invention of —303

Reed, Jonathan: —141, 190, 196, 198, 199, 200, 207; misdating of stone vessels by —199

Reina: —184, 200

***Revue Biblique* (journal):** Bagatti's omission of 'Hellenistic age' in communication to —123

Richmond, Ernest Tatham: —105, 179, 180, 184, 201, 202; Bagatti's false attribution of term 'Herodian' to him —180

***Richmond Report, The*:** —105

Richmond Tomb: —109; *See also* Tomb 72; oil lamps from —130

Ridge Route: through Galilee —19

Ring of tombs: —220, 221, 225, 228

***Ritrovamenti nella Nazaret Evangelica*:** of Bagatti —74; quotation from —175

Robinson, E.: 203

Rolling stones: —143, 160, 186, 187, 197; discussion of —186; of some Nazareth tombs —187

Roman-Byzantine Period: Nazareth movable finds of —271

Roman Catholic Church: traditions of —211

Roman Period: Bagatti's dating to —112; cooking pots of —123; Bagatti's vague use of term —176; burial customs in Palestine —158; Nazareth basin tombs dating to —164

Roman Period, Middle: Great Hiatus lasting from Late Iron Age until —36; Richmond lamps dated to —106

Romans: take Jerusalem —266

Rosenthal, Renate: —106, 167, 169, 171, 172, 177, 181, 185, 186; *Ancient Lamps in the Schloessinger Collection* of —106, 271; on chronology of Herodian lamps —171;

Rosenthal and Sivan: independent datings of Nazareth lamps and pottery by —325

Russia —29

S

Sadducees: —154, 267

Saknin Valley: —19

Samaria: —47-49, 100, 266; given to Herod's son Archelaus —155; given to Herod's son Philip —155; foreigners settle in — 47

Samaritans: —63, 99

Samaritan Temple: —59

Sanballats: —63

Sanhedrin: —266; at Sepphoris —148

Sarcophagi: —188; discussion of —188

Sargon, King: destruction caused by —31

Sargon II: —59, 61

Saul: —46

Scarabs: —41, 51

***Scavo Presso la Chiesa di S. Giuseppe a Nazaret*:** of Bagatti —121

Schiffman, Lawrence: on Jewish temple at Elephantine —63; on Hasmoneans —103

School: of Franciscan Monastery —229

Schumacher: alludes to coins under Dames de Nazareth convent —196

Schürer: —155

Scribes: in New Testament —267

Scripture: instead of evidence as guide for Christian archaeologists —205

Scripture, Jewish: Nazareth unknown to —x; Nazareth not mentioned in —64

Scythopolis: —100; Count Joseph and Epiphanius at —278

Sea Peoples: —43